Ecological Economics

Ecological Economics
Concepts and Methods

Malte Faber
Alfred Weber Institute, University of Heidelberg, Germany

Reiner Manstetten
Alfred Weber Institute, University of Heidelberg, Germany

John Proops
Environmental Policy Unit, Keele University, UK

Edward Elgar
Cheltenham, UK • Brookfield, US

Published by
Edward Elgar Publishing Limited
8 Lansdown Place
Cheltenham
Glos GL50 2HU
UK

Edward Elgar Publishing Company
Old Post Road
Brookfield
Vermont 05036
US

British Library Cataloguing in Publication Data
Faber, Malte
    Ecological economics: concepts and methods
    1. Environmental economics
    I. Title II. Manstetten, Reiner III. Proops, J.L.R. (John L.
    R.)
    333.7

Library of Congress Cataloguing in Publication Data
Faber, Malte Michael.
    Ecological economics: concepts and methods / Malte Faber, Reiner
    Manstetten, John Proops.
    Includes bibliographical references and index.
    1. Environmental economics. I. Manstetten, Reiner, 1953–   .
    II. Proops, John L.R. 1947–   . III. Title.
    HC79.E5F228 1996
    333.7—dc20   96–6435
                                                             CIP

ISBN 1 85898 283 9

Printed and bound in Great Britain by
Hartnolls Limited, Bodmin, Cornwall

Contents

Figures

Tables

Contributors

Malte Faber was born in 1938 in Düsseldorf, Germany. He studied Economics and Mathematics at the Free University of Berlin. He then took his MA in Mathematical Economics at the University of Minnesota, USA. His PhD was on Stochastic Programming, from the Technical University of Berlin, where he also became Privatdozent in Economics. Since 1973 he has been Professor in Economic Theory at the University of Heidelberg, Germany. He has published widely in capital theory, public choice, the role of the entropy concept in environmental economics, input-output analysis applications to the management of water, waste and carbon dioxide emissions, and the conceptual foundations of ecological economics. He has served as an adviser on environmental matters to the Federal and State governments of the Federal Republic of Germany.

Reiner Manstetten was born in 1953 in Würselen, Germany. He studied Philosophy, German Philology and Music at the Universities of Cologne, Freiburg and Heidelberg. He took his Diploma and PhD in Medieval Philosophy at the Department of Philosophy at the University of Heidelberg. Since 1985 he has been an Assistant at the Department of Economics in Heidelberg. He has published on the philosophical foundations of ecology and economics, and the philosophy of mysticism.

John Proops was born in 1947 in Bristol, United Kingdom. He studied Physics and Mathematics at Keele University, UK, and Engineering Physics at McMaster University, Canada. During a period as a Lecturer in Mathematics in Northern Nigeria he became interested in economics and development. He returned to the University of Keele to take his PhD on the application of concepts from modern thermodynamics to the structural evolution of economic systems. Since 1977 he has progressed from Lecturer in Economics to Professor of Ecological Economics at Keele University. He has published on energy modelling, input-output analysis of environmental issues, the application of concepts of thermodynamics in economic analysis, and the conceptual foundations of ecological economics.

Stefan Baumgärtner received his Diploma in Physics from Heidelberg University, and is an Assistant at the Department of Economics in Heidelberg.

Hans-Christoph Binswanger is Professor Emeritus in Economics at St. Galen University, Switzerland.

Frank Jöst has a Diploma and PhD in Economics from Heidelberg University, where he is an Assistant in the Economics Department.

Georg Müller-Fürstenberger received his Vordiplom in Chemistry and his Diploma and PhD in Economics from Heidelberg University. He is an Assistant in Economics at Berne University, Switzerland.

Stefan Speck received his Diploma in Economics from Heidelberg University and his PhD from Keele University. He is a consultant at the Wuppertal Institute for Climate and the Environment, Germany.

Gerhard Wagenhals received his PhD and Habilitation in Economics from Heidelberg University, and is Professor of Economics and Econometrics at the University of Hohenheim, Germany.

Preface

This book lies at the interface of economics, natural science and philosophy. In the development of the discipline of ecological economics we can identify three main strands: conceptualisation, modelling and policy analysis. Elsewhere we have pursued modelling extensively (Faber and Proops, 1993a), as well as policy analysis (Proops, Faber and Wagenhals, 1993). In this book we concentrate almost exclusively on conceptualisation, although the final part also has two policy applications.

This book derives from an extremely close collaboration between the three authors over the past twelve years. Ecological economics is intrinsically interdisciplinary and although we all three now contribute in all three areas, our initial training was in respectively economics, philosophy and physics. We also know that none of us individually could have written, or even attempted to write, a book of this nature. As in any jointly authored book, each chapter has a different weight of contribution by the authors. However, so close is our working relationship, and so shared are our contributions, that even when the original version of a chapter was only singly or doubly authored, the influence of all three of us is present in every chapter. Further, we have been very fortunate to have had the collaboration of a number of colleagues on various aspects of ecological economics. Their contributions are noted in the relevant chapters.

The material in this book has been developed over the past twelve years, and of the fourteen chapters, eight have been previously published as research articles, while six are newly written.

The chapters in this book are largely self-contained, so apart from Chapters 6 and 7, on entropy, they can be read in any order. For use in teaching in particular, we hope the independence of these chapters will prove useful.

Over the years, we have received comments on the various chapters from a large number of colleagues, and we gratefully acknowledge the assistance of the following:

John Benson, Friedrich Breyer, Clóvis Cavalcanti, Paul Christensen, Mick Common, Ralph d'Arge, Jens Faber, Philip Gay, Alexander Gerybadze, Michael Hammond, Bruce Hannon, Stephan Hartmann, Bob Herendeen, Alan Holland, Jörg Hüfner, Klaus Jacobi, Frank Jöst, Bernd Klauer, Reiner Kümmel, Helmut Lang, Ramon Margalef, Juan Martinez-Alier, Peter Michaelis, Dick Norgaard, Bryan Norton, Frank Oldfield, Hans Opschoor, David Pearce, Thomas Petersen, Jerry Ravetz, Leslie Rosenthal, Matthias Ruth, Armin Schmutzler, Stefan Schuster, Gunter Stephan, Anthea Trodd, Robert Ulanowicz, Wolfram Unold and Gerhard Wagenhals.

We thank the following for permission to reprint material.

Elsevier Publishing for the use of the following in Chapters 2, 4 and 9, respectively.

Proops, J.L.R. (1989) Ecological economics: rationale and problem areas. *Ecological Economics* 1:59-76.

Binswanger, H.-C., Faber, M. and Manstetten, R. (1990) The dilemma of modern man and nature: an exploration of the Faustian imperative. *Ecological Economics* 2:197-223.

Faber, M., Manstetten, R. and Proops, J.L.R. (1995) On the foundations of ecological economics: a teleological approach. *Ecological Economics* 12:41-54.

Island Press for the use of the following in Chapter 3.

Faber, M., Manstetten, R. and Proops, J.L.R. (1992b) Toward an open future: ignorance, novelty and evolution. In: R. Costanza, B. Norton and B. Haskell (eds.), *Ecosystem Health: New Goals for Environmental Management.* Island Press, Washington, D.C.

I.S.M.E.A. Paris and Les Presses Universitaires de Grenoble for the use of the following in Chapter 5.

Faber, M., Jöst, F. and Manstetten, R. (1995) Limits and perspectives on the concept of sustainable development. *Economie Appliqée* 48:233-251.

Harwood Academic Publishers for the use of the following in Chapter 8.

Faber, M. and Proops, J.L.R. (1991a) Evolution in biology, physics and economics: a conceptual analysis. In: S. Metcalfe and P. Saviotti (eds.), *Evolutionary Theories of Economic and Technological Change.* Harwood, London.

Kyklos for the use of the following in Chapter 10.

Faber, M. and Proops, J.L.R. (1985) Interdisciplinary research between economists and physical scientists: retrospect and prospect. *Kyklos* 38:599-616.

White Horse Press for the use of the following in Chapter 11.

Faber, M., Manstetten, R. and Proops, J.L.R. (1992a) Humankind and the environment: an anatomy of surprise and ignorance. *Environmental Values* 1:217-241.

Malte Faber   Alfred Weber Institute, Heidelberg, Germany

Reiner Manstetten   Alfred Weber Institute, Heidelberg, Germany

John Proops   Environmental Policy Unit, Keele, UK.

1. Introduction

1.1 WHAT SHOULD ECOLOGICAL ECONOMICS BE?

Why do we need Ecological Economics? The need for such a discipline was not recognised until recently. During the last two decades, however, more and more lay-people as well as scientists have demanded research in areas at the boundaries of, or even outside, traditional sciences. Examples of these include the depletion of resources, the pollution and destruction of the environment, the extinctions of species, the appearance of such problems as deforestation, ozone layer depletion, and the anthropogenic greenhouse effect. These have posed new problems for humankind, which have demanded new responses. It is evident that all these problems stem from economic activity, in particular of the Western type, so these problems have been a challenge for economists. However, since the negative repercussions of economic activity have become manifest in the natural environment, they have also been a challenge for natural scientists.

It seems to us that all these issues, although very important, reflect only the *external* aspects of the environmental crisis. Behind these are hidden social and philosophical questions. Though many societies in the past had environmental problems, of a regional and temporary kind, modern Western society is alone in having created environmental problems of a global and non-temporary nature, such that global ecosystem health is endangered. It is been tempting to assume that science and technology, together with political liberalism, the main pillars of the Western world, are also the keys to overcoming the environmental crisis. But this view overlooks the fact that science and technology have been employed by Western humankind to dominate nature in such a way that, on the one hand, human wants could be fulfilled to an ever increasing extent and, that on the other hand, environmental problems were created by the use of the technology. The approach of solely using science and technology to solve environmental problems reminds us of someone who tries to fight a fire with an extinguisher in one hand while pouring gasoline on to the fire with the other.

To overcome this self-defeating attitude, it is necessary to understand

1

the dynamics of modern society. One therefore has to seek the roots of these dynamics. Only thereafter will it be possible truly to find an answer to environmental problems, which is not infected itself by the dynamics which produces such problems.

On the basis of such considerations, it is evident that Ecological Economics should not be a science in the traditional sense; there has to be more to it. However, this should not imply that it is unscientific or arbitrary. Therefore the question arises: what should Ecological Economics be?

Before we attempt to develop concepts, categories, methods and aims for Ecological Economics, we have to ask what position this discipline should have in society? Such a position cannot be determined in an abstract way, for we have first to recognise that we depend heavily on historical developments, especially in the Western world, and also social circumstances. This does not mean that Ecological Economics is only a function of the conditions of the present society. Rather, we consider it to be a response to the dynamics of society. To find such a response, however, requires first that one pose the right questions. From our discussion so far it is apparent that we believe these questions have historical, social and philosophical aspects, all of which have to be encompassed by Ecological Economics.

Of course, such an approach is only one perspective of research in Ecological Economics. A further important one is a stock-taking of what we already know about how to deal with the environmental crisis. In spite of all the criticism of science and technology, such a stock-taking makes us immediately aware how essential science and technology are to this end. Natural sciences show us where the problems emerge in the environment; economics shows how they are generated, in the extraction of resources, in production and consumption. Research in the natural sciences is a prerequisite for technical solutions, which have to be realised by the engineering sciences. Research in economics is the basis for the introduction of economic schemes, such as charges, licences, etc., which have to be enforced by the political process. The understanding of this political process requires, in addition, political economy, sociology, psychology and, in particular, political philosophy.

For this reason the natural and engineering sciences, as well as resource and environmental economics, and the humanities mentioned above, are all necessary parts of Ecological Economics. It is not sufficient to add these different disciplines together to make a 'multi-discipline'. Interdisciplinary research has to emerge so that scientists of different disciplines can really be in the 'same boat', such that they are able to contribute to a truly sustainable development of the economies of the earth.

In our stock-taking we may realise that many tools and procedures are available for such interdisciplinary approaches. However, they are not sufficient for the creation of Ecological Economics. In our opinion, one has to go further. It is necessary to conceive of new concepts and methods which enable one to integrate insights of several sciences and humanities into a coherent framework. As we shall try to show, such an integration seems to be possible. However, such an attempt inevitably raises fundamental questions of an epistemological and ethical nature. These concern the limits of the scientific approach, the interaction of science and society, as well as ethical aspects of economic behaviour. Also, non-scientific approaches have to be included, as the attentiveness to, and the discovery of, environmental problems are due to laymen in many cases.

If one sees such issues as an essential part of Ecological Economics, it is apparent that this discipline has many scientific traits, but that it cannot be circumscribed completely by them. The Ecological Economist has to be trained in scientific methods, but this will not be sufficient. He or she needs an ethical attitude of respect for humankind, as well as for animals and plants; also required is wisdom in practical matters, which can only derive from experience. From this it follows that a solely scientific education cannot form an Ecological Economist.

Only when all these requirements are in the process of being fulfilled can we expect that Ecological Economics can really contribute to a new relationship between humans and non-human nature.

1.2   CONTENTS OF THE BOOK

This book contains four parts. Parts I, II and III deal mainly with methodological and conceptual issues of the evolving discipline of Ecological Economics, while in Part IV environmental and resource issues are discussed.

In Part I, *An Introduction to Ecological Economics*, Chapter 2 attempts to set the scene, by discussing the reasons we need Ecological Economics, and some of the problems that the new discipline might address and the modes of discourse it might use. In particular the concept of entropy is introduced (discussed in detail in Chapters 6 and 7), and there is discussion of the roots of human attitudes towards nature, through the holding of 'Paradigmatic Images of the World'.

Chapter 3 addresses the issue of ecosystem health, using the notion of the 'openness of the future', relating it to concepts such as evolution, novelty, chaos, surprise, ignorance, Faustian dynamics, welfare and hubris. It also stresses the need for an interdisciplinary approach to these issues to allow the formulation of policy recommendations. These various issues are taken up in detail in the later chapters, but in particular in Chapters 4, 5, 8, 9, 11, and 12.

Chapter 4 analyses the dilemma of modern humans in terms of a dialogue between an economist and an ecologist, which results in an impasse. For this reason a writer is asked to resolve their problems from his point of view. To this end he gives them an interpretation of the second part of Goethe's *Faust*. From this it becomes clear that modern humans are driven by what we call a Faustian dynamics, which leads to permanent economic growth and consequent destruction of the environment.

Chapter 5 deals with the limits and perspectives of sustainable development. Two approaches are explored: first, a natural science, technical and economic route; second, an ethical-philosophical path. It is argued that both approaches are necessary to formulate policies for sustainable development.

In Part II, *Conceptual Foundations of Ecological Economics*, Chapter 6 argues that entropy is a unifying notion for activities in the economy and the natural world. The evolution of the notion of entropy is outlined historically, and is employed to discuss the two 'arrows of time', namely dissipation (often associated with the name of Georgescu-Roegen) and self-organisation (associated with Prigogine).

In Chapter 7 it is shown how the entropy concept has been used to analyse environmental problems and the limits of its applications are outlined. Various problems encountered in applying entropy in Ecological Economics are discussed, and it is shown that these can almost always be attributed to a misunderstanding of the concept, particularly with respect to the issue of system boundaries. On a positive note, it is suggested that the notion of entropy is useful to give economics a bio-physical underpinning.

Chapter 8 addresses a key concept of Ecological Economics, namely evolution. In contrast to other approaches in the literature, a broad perspective is taken of evolution, so that phenomena in such diverse disciplines as physics, biology and economics can be dealt with coherently. In particular, the biological concepts of genotype (potentialities) and phenotype (realisation of potentialities) are generalised, to allow an understanding of which processes give rise to predictable outcomes.

In Chapter 9, nature is characterised as the emergence of far-from-equilibrium, self-organising dissipative structures (FFESODS), which are called organisms if they contain their genotype within their phenotype. The behaviour of organisms is described teleologically (i.e. in terms of 'ends'), where the sustainability of an ecosystem requires a balance and harmony between mutually supporting tele. This teleological approach is then extended to an analysis of environmental problems in the developed and less developed regions.

Chapter 10 deals with problems of interdisciplinary research between economists and physical scientists. In particular, it focuses on the need for interdisciplinary researchers to master and internalise the concepts from their cooperating disciplines, rather than simply rely on the expertise of their collaborators. As Ecological Economics is necessarily interdisciplinary, the need for trans-disciplinary breadth of understanding by its practitioners is evident.

In Part III, *Epistemological Perspectives on Ecological Economics*, Chapter 11 offers an anatomy of surprise and ignorance. In order truly to understand ignorance one cannot confine oneself to the field of environmental questions, and a general taxonomy of ignorance and surprise is developed. This leads to a high level of abstraction, well beyond any particular environmental problems. Hence these considerations are broadly philosophical. However, they are necessary for a deepened understanding of ignorance, which in turn is essential in gaining a new attitude towards environmental problems; an attitude of openness and flexibility, instead of one of closure, control and inflexibility.

Chapter 12 deals with two approaches to knowledge; the modern one, for which Kant is paradigmatic, is opposed to the ancient Greek approach, with which Aristotle is associated. It is suggested that the modern approach to knowledge, with its direct transformation into technical progress and economic growth, has contributed to a considerable extent to the present environmental crisis. In contrast to the two notions of the modern approach, i.e. science and technique, the Aristotelian perspective distinguishes five categories of knowledge, three of which are associated with wisdom, reflection and caution in human affairs. Finally, it is pointed out that knowledge of whatever sort only becomes effective in altering the world if it is reinforced by the will, and it is concluded that for confronting environmental problems, the will must be informed by knowledge that recognises the unity of nature.

In Part IV, *Environmental and Resource Issues*, problems of the environment and production are addressed. Chapter 13 argues that joint production is a key concept for Ecological Economics, as it allows the linkage of the economic production process with its impact on the environment, through the production of pollution. Joint production is particularly evident in the chemical industry, and we draw upon material from a larger study of the German experience of environmental protection legislation and technical change in this sector.

Chapter 14 gives a non-mathematical summary of a study concerning the reduction of CO_2 emissions, which took an intertemporal input-output approach. In particular, it gives a comparison between the emissions in Germany and the UK from the late 1960s to the late 1980s, and shows that the achievement of the 'Toronto Target' of a 20% emission reduction over 20 years is achievable through the exploitation of technical progress and the resulting economic structural change.

PART I

An Introduction to Ecological Economics

2. Ecological Economics: Rationale and Problem Areas

2.1 INTRODUCTORY REMARKS

In this new interdisciplinary area of Ecological Economics it may be helpful if practitioners engage themselves in analysis and debate around a generally accepted range of problem areas, both practical and conceptual. As part of that engagement it might also be useful if the stimuli for and aims of, ecological economics were assessed. This chapter attempts to offer a range of problem areas derived from an assessment of the stimuli and aims of ecological economics. The chapter is in seven sections.

Section 2.2 enumerates some of the perceived aims of ecological economics, as expressed by its practitioners. Section 2.3 is a discussion of the social and psychological sources of stimulus of ecological economics. Section 2.4 assesses the relationship between theories of history, models of possible futures ('Utopias'), and scientific endeavour, and the implications of these relationships for ecological economics. Section 2.5 explores some of the 'Paradigmatic Images of the World' that seem to underlie and impel modes of reasoning in ecological economics. In the light of Sections 2.2 to 2.5, Section 2.6 presents a series of problem areas to which those interested in ecological economics might wish to give their attention. In Section 2.7 we offer some concluding comments.

2.2 THE PERCEIVED AIMS OF ECOLOGICAL ECONOMICS

A useful preliminary would be to define clearly what is meant by 'ecological economics'. Now different authors in the field, with different intellectual backgrounds (ecology, physics, chemistry, engineering, mathematics, economics, political science, sociology), quite naturally have different emphases. However, for the purposes of this paper we shall offer the following brief definition:

9

> *Ecological economics studies how ecosystems and economic activity interrelate.[1]*

From this definition it is clear that the subject matter of ecological economics embraces some of the most serious problems faced today. The use of fossil fuels and carbon dioxide concentrations; the disposal of nuclear waste; the consequences of genetic engineering; deforestation and species loss; all of these problems call for an ecological economics approach, and all are pressing problems of global dimensions.

We divide the aims of ecological economics into two groups. The first relates to Scientific Aims and Problems, the second to Political and Ethical Issues.

2.2.1   Scientific Aims and Problems[2]

Establishing an Historical Perspective on Social-Natural Interactions

The carbon dioxide problem has been relatively recently recognised, but its roots run deep in history. As industrialisation has spread from Britain, first to continental Europe, then to North America, and now to nearly all parts of the globe, there has been a corresponding growth in the use of fossil fuels, and hence the level of atmospheric carbon dioxide. Human social activities have profoundly influenced the global ecosystem, and the long-run interaction by no means began with industrialisation. The very extensive moorlands, heathlands and downlands of Western Europe, unlike the North American prairies, are not 'natural' features. They were established from neolithic times onwards by agricultural activity and are largely maintained through the effects of human activities, such as animal grazing; the 'natural' state of these areas is woodland (Hoskins, 1973). In much of the industrialised world humans live in a fabricated landscape, inhabited by species that often have been introduced by humans. Ecological economics offers one forum for analysis and debate of the long-term dynamics of human-natural interactions.

Finding a Common Language and Set of Concepts for the Analysis of Economies and Ecosystems

There is a surprising degree of overlap between some of the concepts and tools of economic and ecosystem analysis. Economists are familiar with the analogy drawn by Mandeville (1714) between the behaviour of social insects and human social behaviour, in his 'Fable of the Bees'. Conversely, the notion of economic activity has been extended to the social insects (Heinrich, 1979). Game theory models have found application in models of natural evolution as well as in social science (Maynard-Smith, 1984). The mapping of energy 'flows' for use both in economic and ecosystem analysis has been suggested by Odum (1971) and continues to be a source of debate and analysis (Odum and Odum, 1981; Odum, 1984). The flow of goods or 'value' in economic systems is often modelled using 'input-output' analysis (Leontief, 1966), and such analysis of flows has been adapted to modelling the flow of energy and matter in ecosystems (Costanza, 1984; Hannon, 1973). Recently there has also been discussion regarding the use of 'prices' and 'interest rates' in ecosystem work (Hannon, 1985a). On the other hand, ideas about evolution and co-evolution are being generalised from biological science to economics (Norgaard, 1984).

The Area of Intersection Between Natural Science and Social Science

In recent years there has been growing disquiet about the divorce of economic analysis from its 'biophysical foundations'. The economic activities of production and consumption are not independent of, or neutral with respect to, the global ecosystem. Human artefacts need matter for their expression; a unit of fuel once burned cannot be burned again. In other words the laws of thermodynamics are binding upon economic activity in its broadest sense. (For discussions of the role of thermodynamics in economic analysis see Proops (1985; 1987). For a fuller discussion see Chapters 6 and 7.) This issue has received great prominence since the publication of Georgescu-Roegen's (1971) *The Entropy Law and the Economic Process*. But humans are not simply users of materials; they are also inventors and constructors. In particular human societies are 'open systems' in the sense of Prigogine (1980). Such open systems are characterised by acting as 'conduits' for the flow of energy, which they 'tap' to allow the normal tendency to disorder, that would characterise a closed system, to be countered. Further, open systems may exhibit steadily increasing degrees of structure and organisation over time. The physical theory of open systems is relatively new and still being formulated and generalised, but already it offers insights into the behaviour of systems which are far from thermodynamic equilibrium. In particular the open systems approach offers an alternative and complementary viewpoint on the biophysical nature of human activity (Jantsch, 1980; Prigogine and Stengers, 1984; Proops, 1983. Also see Chapters 6 and 7).

2.2.2   Political and Ethical Issues

As a Forum and Structuring for Policy Analysis

It is generally recognised that the world is a complicated place, and single causes can have many outcomes, and single outcomes many causes. The interaction between the ecosystem and human social activities is particularly rich in such relationships. For example, the impact on climate, ecosystem development and economic activity of increasing levels of carbon dioxide is a widely recognised area for study and concern (Edmonds and Reilly, 1985). It is not yet, however, an area where a simple and generally accepted prognostication is available, unlike the fluorocarbon debate. Ecological economics offers a forum for the consistent and coherent analysis of such areas of interaction.

A Framework for the Ethical Analysis of Intertemporal and Interspecies Choice

Much of the literature on resource use hinges upon the way present generations view their human successors. It is apparent that future generations cannot share in current market activities. Future generations can offer nothing to the present generation to 'exchange' for the right to use resources in the future. How can the putative rights of future generations be established and accounted for? Similarly, human life is only one of the forms of life in the ecosystem, yet in conventional analysis only the desires and needs of humans are considered. Can and should the 'rights' of non-human species be considered? Both of these issues can be sensibly discussed only in a wide social-natural framework, such as is offered by ecological economics (Daly, 1980).

The Influencing of Decision Makers

Often expressed is the concern that ecological economics gives high priority to influencing those who take decisions which have substantial consequences for the ecosystem. For example, the banning of the production and sale of fluorocarbons is a current issue. The use of civil nuclear power is another. In both cases practitioners have sought to put the arguments, usually against, in a way likely to achieve the policy changes they desire.

2.3   THE SOURCES OF STIMULUS OF ECOLOGICAL ECONOMICS

That ecological economics has a subject matter has, we hope, been established by the preceding section. The antecedent question is: 'What are the social and psychological roots of such enquiry?'. This is, we believe, an important issue which should be confronted if ecological economics is to make good and well-founded progress. In this section we shall briefly discuss four areas of motivation which are, we believe, important in giving impetus to the formulation and study of ecological economics.

2.3.1 The Perception of 'Things Getting Worse'

The majority of people in the Western economies are well-fed, well-clothed, and employed in comparatively interesting and untaxing labour, at least by the standards of the preceding periods of arduous peasant agriculture and sweated industrialisation. For the great majority in the industrialised West the quest for material comfort can be regarded as over, although improvements in technology and levels of consumption continue at rates which are historically unprecedented. But industriali-sation has its penalties in the form of historically high population den-sities, industrialised agriculture, and the rapid depletion of natural resources. Have the costs outweighed the benefits? Are we now facing a future where standards of comfort can be expected to drop as natural resources become scarcer, food and water supplies become ever more polluted, and humans, especially poor humans in the developing countries, become ever more numerous and clamorous for consumption goods. This view was particularly strongly voiced during the early seventies, at the time of the Limits to Growth debate (Meadows et al., 1972), by, inter alia, Commoner (1971) and Ehrlich and Ehrlich (1972).

2.3.2 The Ecological Categorical Imperative

Kant saw morality as being an objective requirement, independent of what anyone may want. He termed the guidance to action given by morality a 'categorical imperative'. For many environmentally minded persons this moral imperative extends to the natural world also. They see humans as having squandered nature's riches and abused the implicit contract with past and future generations to act as steward over the natural world. Humans no longer live in harmony with nature. Are Western bloc industrial capitalism and Eastern bloc state capitalism short-lived aberrations, resulting from humans breaking faith with their nature? (See Pearce (1987) for a discussion of the problem of the intrinsic value of the natural world for economics.)

2.3.3   Ecological Economics as a 'Revolutionary' Activity

During the nineteenth and early twentieth centuries the key social ills were seen to be the poverty and economic and political oppression that were the common lot of the great bulk of the industrial population. The source of this suffering was held to be the inequitable distribution of wealth and income then prevalent, which meant that low average income per capita for all was reflected by abject poverty for many and considerable affluence for a very few. The political force which arose to confront and to right these wrongs was socialism, particularly Marxism; this drew together the energies of, predominantly, the young and the intellectuals (Lichtheim, 1970). The sacrifice of earlier generations of working people has resulted in generally much improved material conditions for the majority of the industrial population. It may be argued that in the Western world the problem has now moved from the issue of social justice to that of the sustainability of social institutions, as resources are depleted and the environment poisoned. Again, the young and the intellectuals have drawn together, this time under the banner of environmentalism.

2.3.4   The Opening Up of World Views

Social analysis and the perception of the natural world are inseparable (Cotgrove, 1982). However, economic analysis as currently practised is divorced from, and even does not recognise, its biophysical foundations. On the other hand, ecosystem analysis makes no sense if human activity is excluded; human activity is pervasive, fast-acting and often irreversible, but it too is 'natural'. The growth of interest in the entropic foundations of economic and natural activities (Georgescu-Roegen, 1971; Faber, Niemes and Stephan, 1987) has encouraged the opening up of world views, and there is a growing recognition of the value of multi-disciplinary work in establishing the inter-relations between social behaviour and the natural world (Faber and Proops, 1985).

Having suggested some of the motivations behind ecological economics, we now turn to an examination of how the above concerns can be placed within the framework of our understanding of the historical process, and our visualisation of possible futures.

2.4   THEORIES OF HISTORY AND 'UTOPIAS'

To make sense of the world, and to inform our actions, we must both look backwards, to our history, and look forwards, to our potential futures. Both historical analysis and assessing the future are difficult and demanding activities. Both to a greater rather than a lesser extent are socially conditioned activities. In particular, our notions of the past, and how to undertake historical analysis will influence our notions of the future.

2.4.1   The 'Open' and 'Closed' Models of History and the Future

How does the world evolve? Are there general historical laws that lay out the direction, even details, of historical events (Carr, 1961)? That is, is history a necessary process? Or is history a contingent process? Contingent, that is, upon the minutiae of the world; the failed coup, the drunken general, the inspired inventor. If the former is held to be the case we have a 'closed' model of history. The past flows into the future like a well-channelled river, and the place of humankind on the stream of history can be charted and predicted. In such a world view, knowledge of the past allows us to know a substantial amount about the future. An analogy would be that, in a well-channelled stream a boat can be navigated by looking only to the stern, as the local shape of the stream just past gives sufficient information for the local shape of the stream ahead to be judged.

But what if the minutiae of history do matter? The passage of time ceases to be an unrolling of a largely preordained future, as in the Newtonian model of planetary motion. Instead the future becomes rich with radical uncertainty. We have an 'open' model of history. The stream is no longer well contained, but ever branching like a river delta (Passet, 1987; Faber and Proops, 1986, 1989). Looking backwards is no longer sufficient to allow us to steer the boat along a steady and uninterrupted course.

2.4.2   Ecological Economics as a Dialectical Science

Ecological economics deals with the interactions between humans and the natural world, interactions which themselves are ever evolving as the very interactions impact upon the ecosystem and alter it, and as perceptions of the environment also change (Common, 1988). One could say that ecological economics seeks to understand the human position in the world, where that world is being simultaneously created and destroyed by humans. That is, it is not sufficient to consider the world as in 'being', as the nature of the world is continually transforming the world; the world is always 'becoming'. (For an excellent discussion of the roles of 'being' and 'becoming' in the natural world see Prigogine (1980); for a dialectical analysis of biological evolution see Levins and Lewontin (1985).) Ecological economics is therefore, from its subject matter, a very dialectical subject. Its object of study is the process of social creation and ecological transformation and destruction.

2.4.3 The Future and 'Utopias'

Any assessment of the future requires that we have a standard of reference, against which we can judge likely or possible outcomes. Many of us carry within us a largely ill-formed but still important image of the world as it might be. *The Republic* of Plato (c400BC) is often cited as the earliest such vision fully enunciated and internally consistent. The *Utopia* of More (1516) is perhaps the most famous and most copied. Indeed, with no disrespect to More, nor in any derogatory sense, we shall refer to such world views as 'Utopias' henceforward. Published modern versions of Utopias include *A Modern Utopia* by Wells (1905), *The Dispossessed* by Le Guin (1974), and much modern science fiction writing. Also within the term 'Utopia' we shall encompass anti-Utopias, or Dystopias, such as those in *Gulliver's Travels* by Swift (1726), *The Time Machine* by Wells (1895), *Brave New World* by Huxley (1932), and *Nineteen Eighty Four* by Orwell (1949). (For excellent discussions on various aspects of Utopias see Manuel (1965) and Kumar (1987).)

A Utopia is not a description of a real world, either past or future; instead it is an enunciation of what the world could be like. It seems to me that the predominant neoclassical paradigm of economics has much in common with such a Utopia: if only humans were rational, self-interested beings, and all production processes were 'well-behaved', then the neoclassical paradigm describes what the world would be like.

We do not wish to imply that Utopias are in any sense a bad thing. Indeed, from their ubiquity they may even be necessary for humankind to confront and make sense of historical experience. However, there are dangers to Utopias. Utopias are not real and, in principle, can never exist. In most cases, perhaps even all, they are not images towards which we should strive; rather they are imaginings against which we can judge likely outcomes. If policies seem to be leading us towards a state of the world we can characterise as '1984', most of us would urge a reassessment of those policies. We feel that dangers lie in taking a Utopia and making it a concrete objective. For example, we believe the notion of the 'Steady-State Economy', as enunciated by Daly (1973, 1977) is such a Utopia. It gives a description of a world as it might be, under certain strong assumptions. This is clearly recognised by Chapman (1975), in his parable of the 'Island of Erg'. If only men were sensible, if only social institutions were just and forward looking, if only politicians were less short-sighted and avaricious; if only! Our expectation is that we are unlikely to achieve a Steady-State Economy by rational and beneficial policies. However, as a Utopia it does offer a very useful yardstick for the policies that can be recommended, and for those that should be resisted.

2.4.4　History, Utopia and Scientific Activity

We suggested above that two approaches to history as a process may be taken: history as 'closed' and history as 'open'. We also indicated we felt that the model of history used would be likely to be influential in the establishment of Utopias; anticipation of the future springs from understanding of the past. Is it possible to indicate how different Utopias might derive from these two models of history? Consider first history as 'closed', with the world unfolding in an ordered way. This unfolding may be necessary but this does not imply that it is good. If the world is a 'Newtonian' mechanism, and if man is outside this mechanism and can influence it, then man may be able determine the future in terms of a preferred Utopia. Alternatively, it may be that the world is running down by necessity without any possibility for man to influence its development. On the basis of either concept of closedness, regularities occur both between past and present, and between social and natural relations at any one time. Relations can be identified, and a 'good' and 'natural' state of the world suggests itself. It is clear that Utopias will offer themselves where regularity and order prevail.

On the other hand, an 'open' notion of history suggests new possibilities, altering relationships between nature and humankind. Such an approach to history makes the formulation of a Utopia much more difficult. By its nature, a Utopia is an image of the World as it might be, but an 'open' model of history demands the recognition that there are an infinity of ways the World might be. In these circumstances a Utopia becomes evanescent, no longer serving as a Platonic ideal, but rather as a sketch of an imagining, a transient speculation.

How, then, can the concept of history and its attendant Utopias impact upon scientific discourse and social policies by humans towards nature? To use a term of Koestler (1967), we believe this to be a Janus-like[3] operation. One face of Janus is towards the past, with its established knowledge and received wisdom. The other face is towards the future, towards Utopias and potentials for action. Within Janus itself there is the need for scientific investigation and policy formulation, the bridge between inherited knowledge and concepts, and imaginings of the future and how they might be achieved.

2.5   PARADIGMATIC IMAGES OF THE WORLD

Where do Utopias come from? Why do individuals have differing Utopias? Why do social groups often share Utopias? We think some sense can be made of this by going one step further back in this chain of relationships. We believe that underlying any Utopia there must be a notion of what constitutes 'The World'. With regard to Utopias relevant to ecological economics, particularly important is the notion of 'Nature and the Natural'. We shall call such a notion a 'Paradigmatic Image of the World' (PIW). We suggest there are four predominant PIWs at present; these are:

1. Undisturbed Nature: The Hunter-Gatherer World

2. Humankind in Nature: The Agricultural World

3. The Human as Creator: The Industrial World

4. Gaia: the Creative and Self-Sustaining World.

As the PIWs that constitute belief structures are usually implicit deep below the surface activities of science, the enunciation of a PIW is often most clearly achieved by reference to the cultural behaviour that takes the expression of belief structures as its central aim; that is, creative literature. Unusually, therefore, in a scientific paper, we shall draw freely on literary sources in the remainder of this section.

2.5.1   Undisturbed Nature: The Hunter-Gatherer World

An evocative statement of the Undisturbed Nature PIW is to be found in the 'Canadian Railroad Trilogy' of the Canadian singer-songwriter Gordon Lightfoot (1981:side 2, track 2):

There was a time in this fair land
When the railroads did not run,
When the wild majestic mountains
Stood alone against the sun,

Long before the white man
And long before the wheel,
When the green, dark forest
Was too silent to be real.

This is, we feel, a powerful expression of the image of North America, in this case Canada, in its 'natural' state; it suggests the natural world to be a strong, elemental force; it is virgin, uncorrupted, untainted by humans who seek to control nature. Here humans are present only as actors within nature, hunting and gathering much as non-human animals do. The ecological equilibrium that exists is not perceived to be significantly different from that which would prevail if humans had not evolved. This PIW seems, to this European, to be particularly strong among North American ecological economists. It views humans, at least agricultural/industrial European humans, as intrusive upon a world of nature. The human is the intruder, the despoiler. This PIW has been excellently documented in the literature of North America by Marx (1964). For a recent comment on this PIW, from a European perspective, see Reed (1988).

2.5.2   Humankind in Nature: The Agricultural World

With a history of several thousand years of established agriculture in Europe, it is not surprising that this seems to be the predominant PIW among Western European ecological economists. Humankind is part of nature through harmonious agriculture and husbandry. An ecological equilibrium has been achieved, but this is very different from that which would result without human activities. The landscape is accepted as embodying humans and their works, but these are seen as humankind and nature in synergy rather than conflict. As Wordsworth (1798) put it in 'Tintern Abbey':

.... *Once again I see*
These hedge-rows, hardly hedge-rows, little lines
Of sportive wood run wild; these pastoral farms,
Green to the very door; and wreaths of smoke
Sent up, in silence, from among the trees!

A harsher judgement upon this PIW has been given by a Marxist social critic, in this case in the context of political analysis (Nairn, 1977:262):

... this ... English world where the Saxon ploughs his field and the
sun sets to strains by Vaughan Williams.

2.5.3   The Human as Creator: The Industrial World

Nature is the background and inspiration for human achievements. Human resourcefulness and inventiveness rejoice in the challenge of nature. There is unlikely to be an ecological equilibrium achieved, as human activities are continually altering the relationships between species. Nature is a tabula rasa upon which humankind can write its destiny. For example, Wells (1895:79) expressed it thus:

> *It is a law of nature we overlook, that intellectual versatility is the compensation for change, danger, and trouble. An animal perfectly in harmony with its environment is a perfect mechanism. Nature never appeals to intelligence until habit and instinct are useless. There is no intelligence where there is no change and no need of change. Only those animals partake of intelligence that have to meet a huge variety of needs and dangers.*

This paradigmatic image of the world is, we believe, close to that of some of the less mainstream branches of economic thought, such as the Austrian School (Rizzo, 1979), and the evolutionary economists (Nelson and Winter, 1982).

2.5.4   Gaia: The Creative and Self-Sustaining

Gaia is the world, all it contains, all it has been, all it might become. It created itself, and all the elements within it work in harmonious ways to sustain it as it changes over the eons. The role of humanity is not privileged, nor very significant to Gaia. The destiny of individual species, or even whole groups of species, is unimportant. As Shelley (1816) expressed it in 'Mont Blanc':

> *The fields, the lakes, the forests, and the streams,*
> *Ocean, and all the living things that dwell*
> *Within the daedal earth; ...*
> *All things that move and breathe with toil and sound*
> *Are born and die; revolve, subside, and swell.*
> *Power dwells apart in its tranquillity,*
> *Remote, serene and inaccessible:*

This PIW has been clearly expressed in its scientific rather than literary aspects by Lovelock (1979). Gaia stands opposed to the other three PIWs, for in Gaia humans are not central nor even significant. Unlike the others, the Gaia PIW is not anthropocentric, in as far as a human world view can avoid anthropocentricity. As Lovelock (1987) recently noted:

Friends of the Earth are really friends of the people of Earth. No-one speaks for the planet.

2.6   PROBLEM AREAS FOR ECOLOGICAL ECONOMICS

To summarise the discussion so far, ecological economics is already being practised by individuals with a wide range of backgrounds. Interest in ecological economics has a number of practical, conceptual and ethical sources and, in our view, the aims of ecological economists need to be understood in terms of their concepts of history, and their formulation of Utopias. These Utopias, we believe, are themselves largely dependent on the underlying Paradigmatic Image of the World held by that individual/group/society.

This range of backgrounds, concerns, understandings of history, Utopias and PIWs means that ecological economics presents many challenges, both in terms of problems and methodologies. We now offer a list of what we perceive to be the major problem areas for this new interdisciplinary approach. We order these areas under three headings: Measurement and Policy; Ethical Values; and Concepts and Methods. However, it will be apparent that this subdivision is not absolute, and that some of the problem areas overlap two or even three headings. The listing of problem areas is not meant to be exhaustive, but is intended to stimulate discussion.

2.6.1   Measurement and Policy

How Can We Tell if Things are Getting Worse?

A fundamental tenet of ecological economics is that there are problems to confront in the relationship between humankind and nature. Are these problems fundamentally different and more intractable than those faced by previous generations? Is human ingenuity coping with the problems as they arise? Or are the problems growing in magnitude and becoming of a qualitatively different type? Are things getting worse? If so, by what standards?

How Can We Judge the Effectiveness of Policies?

When a problem is identified and policies are established to ameliorate it, how are we to judge the effectiveness of these policies? Is a relatively narrow judgement appropriate, or should a wider assessment be taken, involving all the possible consequences of the policy itself? That is, under what circumstances is a 'partial equilibrium' approach suitable, as opposed to a 'general equilibrium' approach, remembering that a partial equilibrium approach will be less expensive and can be much more easily interpreted?

How Can We Assess and Cope with Global Phenomena?

Some issues in ecological economics are of a local nature, but many are global issues. What are the analytic tools available to deal with such issues as 'public goods'? How appropriate are they to problems involving many nations, with differing political ideologies and vastly disparate levels of wealth and income? What social institutions are appropriate to decision making on such issues?

How Important is Resource Use vis à vis Pollution?

Two distinct strands appear in ecological economics: the use of resources, and the generation of pollution. How far are these linked, and to what extent can they be conceptually separated? Which of these is likely to have the greatest impact in the long-run? Which is most threatening to the survival of humankind?

The Growth Debate: What Does it Mean?

What do we mean by 'economic growth'? What are the social roots of growth, and how are these dependent on relations with the ecosystem? What are the consequences of reduced growth rates? If a long-run aim were to be economic activity in harmony with the global ecosystem, does this necessarily imply a zero economic growth rate? What policies might lead to socially equitable harmony with the global ecosystem?

Are Some Utopias 'Better' than Others?

What are our underlying notions of 'what the world might be like'? How important are current Utopias in determining our policy stances? How well founded are our Utopias in our understanding of history and science? How dangerous might be Utopias in our formulation of social policy?

Environmentalism: Science or Social Movement?

How far is environmentalism a reasoned response to threats to the ecosystem, and how far a focus for more general social discontent? How far should ecological economists maintain scientific objectivity ('aloofness')? What is the place of normative analysis in ecological economics?

2.6.2   Ethical Values

Population as Pollution: The Ethical Dilemma

On a global scale, are humans a renewable resource or a particularly virulent form of pollution? If the aim of social policy is to generate the 'greatest good for the greatest number', what is that 'greatest number'? How can considerations of ecological economics be integrated with demographic analysis and notions of social justice?

The Present Status of Future Generations

How far is the welfare of far distant (potential) generations important today? Does the present generation have a view that past generations 'could have done better by us'? What is the social trade-off between the poor today and the maybe-poor-maybe-rich of future generations?

The Ethical Hazards of Myopic Decision Making

What sort of time horizon is appropriate in decision making? How far should future generations be included in present decision making? Does myopic decision making accept the openness of the future, or simply ignore the rights of future generations? Does the use of full intertemporal models of choice lead us to a form of intertemporal authoritarianism?

Can We Reconcile Ecological Economics with Anthropocentricity?

Is ecological economics the study of the relations of humans with nature, or of humans in nature? Is the status of humans privileged only because of a 'faulty telescopic faculty'? Do other animal species have 'rights'? Do plants have 'rights'? Do depletable resources have 'rights'?

2.6.3   Concepts and Methods

Establishing Concepts and Analytical Tools for Ecological Economics

What are the common tools and methods available for examining natural and social systems? Can we devise a common language and set of concepts for dealing with the wide range of interests and backgrounds of workers in the field of ecological economics? What is the role of energy analysis and energetic modelling in ecological economics? Does the notion of an 'energy theory of value' offer useful insights? Does 'co-evolution' offer a coherent conceptual framework for ecological economics?

Entropy and Open System Analysis

Does the notion of entropy and the Second Law of Thermodynamics provide a common basis of discussion for economic and ecosystem analysis in the long-run? Does it help to establish the biophysical roots of economics? Does open-system analysis offer a contrasting perspective on economies and ecosystems? How far are these approaches contradictory, and how far are they complementary?

Risk and Uncertainty in Decision Making

How do we assess the risk associated with the impact of economic activity on the ecosystem? How do we formulate policy in the face of risk? When we face radical uncertainty about the future effect of present policies, how do we cope? What stance can we take to options being kept open for future generations?

History as Open or Closed

Does history offer us useful insights into the future? Can we reduce uncertainty about present actions by studying the past? How far does human ingenuity and inventiveness force a view of history as 'open' and contingent? What are the implications for how we study human-natural interactions of these two different approaches to history?

2.7   CONCLUDING COMMENTS

We shall close on a cautiously optimistic note. Human activity is, for the foreseeable future, likely to be Earth based. Economists are increasingly coming to recognise that the study of human activities on a finite planet, in the long-run, requires a different set of concepts to those useful for the economic analysis of households, firms and nation states in the short- and medium-run. In a complementary way, ecologists, and other natural scientists, are increasingly recognising that economic activity is 'here to stay'; human activities are coming to dominate the global ecosystem, and ecosystem analysis which does not explicitly include economic activities makes less and less sense. The stage seems to be set for a coming together of these two disciplines so that problems of resource use and pollution in the global ecosystem can be discussed and assessed in a conceptual framework worthy of these problems.

However, this coming together needs to be firmly based; a short-term coalition between economists and natural scientists will be insufficient. Economists and natural scientists will need to do more than talk together occasionally. Economists will need to familiarise themselves with the tools and concepts of natural science, and the natural scientists with those of economic analysis. Only when these tools and concepts have been digested and internalised will there come into being a shared language and set of concepts. Only then will there be the opportunity for long-term fruitful dialogue.

NOTES

1. Here the term 'interrelate' is intended to be very wide. Although this means the definition of the term 'Ecological Economics' runs the risk of being so general that it includes almost all scientific and social scientific disciplines, we feel that it would be inappropriate to arbitrarily limit the meaning of the term before the limits of the discipline become apparent to its practitioners. In particular, the recognised discipline of environmental economics, with its usually neo-classical paradigm, is, in my view, a rather limited subset of ecological economics.
2. The discussions at the Conference on Ecological Economics in Barcelona, September 1987, were particularly helpful in indicating the breadth of concerns of practitioners in this field.
3. Janus was a Roman god, who acted as the doorkeeper to heaven. To aid him in this task he had two faces, one on the front of his head and one on the back.

3. Towards an Open Future: Ignorance, Novelty and Evolution

3.1 INTRODUCTION

Economic activities in the industrialised world place more and more pressure on ecological systems; there is a tendency by modern economies to cause stress, illness and destruction to the ecological systems within which they are embedded. This situation confronts us with problems which are very pervasive and extremely difficult to solve. To come to grips with these problems we will use *'openness'* as the key concept. While the notion of *'open systems'* is already well known in the literature, we shall introduce the notion of the *'openness of the future'* to this debate. The purpose of this chapter is to develop an evolutionary conceptual framework, relating the openness of the future to our response to the ecological impact of human activity, using such related concepts as surprise, novelty, chaos and ignorance. We apply this conceptualisation to problems in environmental policy. (The concept of evolution in Ecological Economics is developed more fully in Chapter 8; surprise and ignorance are discussed in Chapter 11.)

In order to explore the consequences of this important generalisation for the interaction of human economic systems and natural ecological systems, we begin by asking: what attitude has led humankind to the continued endangering of nature and thus of its livelihood? In Part I, we characterise the driving force of this attitude (the attempt to create a human world which is closed against the influence of uncontrollable nature) in general terms. Our endeavour in Part II is to offer a conceptualisation of closure and openness within an evolutionary framework, in order to develop a scientific basis for the analysis of the notions of novelty and ignorance, and to explain their relevance for what we can know, what we can control, and what we can do. In Part II, we outline some of the policy consequences of a new attitude towards closure and openness. In particular, we show that, because of the different types of novelty they generate, the problems of resource use will tend to be less difficult to address than are problems of pollution. Finally, we will explain some of the implications of our analysis for concerns about ecosystem health and integrity.

3.2   THE TWO HOUSES OF HUMANKIND

Within the name 'Ecological Economics' we find the Greek word 'oikos' twice. The meaning of 'oikos' is house. Since Aristotle (1984:38ff-1253b1ff) economics is the science of the 'oikonomia', i.e. the science of all problems concerning the allocation and distribution of labour, goods and services within the 'oikos'. Here 'oikos' can mean the house of the family as well as a town or even a state. The 'oikos' in the words economy and economics is clearly a house whose founder and master is humankind.

The word 'ecological', however, draws our attention to the circumstance that we, as human beings, live together with animals and plants in a common house, oikos, which comprises the whole living space. This oikos has a certain internal order, which is responsible for the development and evolution of life within it; this order is indicated by the suffix '-logical', which is derived from the Greek word 'logos'. The literal meaning of logos is 'word', but it may also be translated as 'concept' or 'structure'. In the philosophy of Heraclitus (6th century B.C.), logos is the principle of all beings and thus of the whole universe.

The concept of logos is useful in formulating a broad definition of 'ecology': ecology is the science of the principles of the self-organisation of nature. According to these principles new orders, ecosystems, species, plants, materials, etc., evolve, and old ones are overcome or destroyed. The embodiment of these principles we will call the logos. For Plato and Aristotle, as well as philosophers of many religions, the assumption of a logos[1] or similar concepts (be they derived from a divine creator, or be they a principle of nature itself) was a prerequisite for the true understanding of nature.[2] We believe that any adequate theory of the management of economic systems, which simultaneously protect ecological health, must rest on a clear recognition that the structure of ecological systems is a function of their ability to organise themselves. (This idea is extended, using teleology, in Chapter 9.)

It is evident that the house of nature and its principles were not founded by humankind; we are guests in this house, as are all other living beings. In modern industrial times, however, it appears that humankind has claimed the common house as its property. In many respects, humankind behaves as if the common house, with all its inhabitants, were founded only for *its* use. It appears, therefore, that modern humankind has conceived the common house of nature as a part of the human house. In contrast to this view, in an ecological perspective the human house (the economy) is part of the house of nature. This perspective is still rather new in the attitude of modern societies, and we have to admit that Western humankind up to now has not made enough effort to understand the logos of nature's house.[3]

In the view of many modern scientists the assumption of such a logos is not necessary, and may even be an obstacle to the understanding of nature. In modern natural science, as well as in Kant's *Critique of Pure Reason*, we find concepts of nature which try to do without the assumption of such a logos. This is so because the application of the concept of logos has inherent difficulties for the following reasons:

(i) the significance of this concept cannot be fully explored, and

(ii) the conditions for the application of the concept cannot be specified exactly.

During the last two decades, however, humankind has increasingly become aware that it has considerably influenced and changed the order of its common house. Therefore, it seems to us to be appropriate to take a fresh look at the concept of nature's logos. Humankind will be unable to live in accordance with nature without acknowledging its logos, and hence without knowing how it influences and changes its common house, and what consequences its actions have.

The main question ecological economists are confronted with is:

> *Can we live in our human house, in a modern economy with its intrinsic dynamics, and at the same time respect nature's own logos? And if we can, how can we achieve that?*

These tasks are also formulated by Ehrlich (1989:14):

> *Somehow a new ecological-economic paradigm must be constructed that unites (as the common origin of the words ecology and economics imply) nature's housekeeping (i.e. the logos of nature, the authors) and society's housekeeping, and make clear that the first priority must be given to keeping nature's house in order.*

In the following we shall discuss some prerequisites to deal with this encompassing task.

3.3   PART I: CLOSURE AND OPENNESS IN THE PRESENT WORLD

Our first approach to describing the attitude of modern humankind is not guided by science but by poetry, namely by the last act of Goethe's drama *Faust*. (We expand upon this approach in Chapter 4.)

3.3.1 Faustian Activity: The Exclusion of Nature from the House of Humankind

Let us imagine a rather infertile stretch of land near the sea. A few people earn their living by fishing, raising livestock and a little agriculture. Their economy is self-sustaining and stationary. After coming into being the economy does not affect the ecosystem anymore. The life of the people is hard: fishermen sometimes die at sea, famines and epidemics come and go.

Let us further imagine that in this archetype of a pre-modern life-style, there arrive entrepreneurs and engineers. They see that this stretch of land is utilised in an 'inefficient' way. They propose to restrain the sea by constructing a system of dykes, and to drain and to cultivate the land. This will enable them to erect towns and industries: a living space for millions of people can be secured. Of course, this is only possible if the former inhabitants give up their way of life and take over the new life-styles of the entrepreneurs and engineers. The latters' view is also that of Faust, the hero of Goethe's drama.

The dykes may be conceived of as a symbol for the Faustian intention to separate the house of humankind (economy) from the house of nature (ecosystem). The dykes are the walls of the house of humankind, into which nature is allowed to enter only if it is necessary or useful for human purposes. In all other cases the house of humankind has to be kept closed against the uncontrolled forces of nature, which in the drama of Faust are symbolised by the wild sea. But this uncontrolled nature, seemingly kept outside, presses against the dykes day and night. Since even one hole may have disastrous consequences, the dykes have always to be completely supervised. Hence there exists an enduring danger: 'But Care through the key-hole slips stealthily in' (Goethe, 1908:Part 2, Act 5). However, as long as the human house can be kept closed, in the way described above, humans can suppress their cares and anxieties and lead their lives according to their desires. Thus humans gain safety, sanity and welfare; they are able to pursue their own happiness. All developments in the house of humankind seem to depend only on humans themselves and on nature in a narrow sense, because it is viewed only as a stock of resources for the fulfilment of human wishes. The only 'logos' of this kind of nature is derived from human will, and consists in its utility for human intentions.[4]

It is important, however, to recognise that the house of humankind is built without considering nature's own logos. Now nature outside the house of humankind is experienced as having no sense in itself and as being potentially dangerous. Thus much intellectual and psychic effort, as well as many resources and much energy, are needed to keep the human house closed against those aspects of nature not corresponding to human intentions.

Having described how nature's logos is excluded from the house of Faustian humankind, we now turn to the perception of time.

3.3.2   The Future in the Faustian World

The dominating force in this Faustian world is the will of humankind. It is the will to be, as far as possible, the master of everything that can happen. This will also deeply affect the treatment of time.

When the approach to the world is guided by the Faustian will, the perception of time does not take regard of the past. The past seems to be nothing but a presently accessible stock of information and material of all kinds (resources, capital goods, consumption goods, etc.). These can be utilised to bring and to keep under control whatever is encountered. It is in this sense that: '... time is reduced to only one function, namely to the future as the space where economic growth takes place' (cf. Chapter 4 for a more detailed explanation).

There are three kinds of future events with which Faustian humankind has to deal.

(a)   Events that seem to be dangerous; their effects have to be neutralised.

(b)   Events that are advantageous; their effects have to be utilised.

(c)   Events that are neither dangerous nor advantageous; their effects can be neglected.

In this Faustian world, humankind is convinced that if human control of events can be achieved and maintained, then the future will be characterised by progress and increasing welfare. This implies the expectation that humankind will be able increasingly to solve all problems in the future. This opinion is expressed by Keynes, who believed that humankind can solve its problems by its own efforts, although he admitted that this may be difficult:

> *The pace at which we can reach our destination of economic bliss will be governed by four things: our power to control population, our determination to avoid wars and civil dissensions, our willingness to entrust science to the direction of those matters which are properly the concern of science, and the rate of accumulation as fixed by the margin between our production and our consumption; of which the last looks easily after itself, given the first three.* (Keynes, 1963:373; see also in a similar vein Solow, 1973:42.)

The creative mind of humankind in the Faustian world allows an inventiveness which seems to guarantee infinite progress. The future, and thus time, is open, but *only* to progress.

However, to understand the consequences of the attitude which has lead to the above categorisation of future events, we shall look for its implicit premises. This attitude can only be sustained:

(i)   if all future events which concern the interest of humankind are either predictable or, if not, immediately controllable,

(ii) if the prediction can be made sufficiently in advance of the event, and

(iii) if there are techniques available to control these events in accordance with the interests of humankind.

If these premises are fulfilled, humankind is able to control everything which concerns it. In this respect, humankind may regard itself as godlike, being at least omniscient and omnipotent. (The power and pervasiveness of modern telecommunications may even give the illusion of omnipresence; i.e. the abolition of space.) The Faustian illusion of omnipotence itself requires the illusion of omniscience, for if everything is to be controlled, then everything must be known.

We therefore see that the Faustian will to control excludes the possibility of ignorance, either in the present or in the future. The assumption of perfect knowledge about the future itself presupposes that there can be no emergence of novelty in the future.

3.3.3   The Handling of the Future in Traditional Science

The Faustian illusion of omniscience and omnipotence implies a view of nature that it is, in essence, predictable. Modern scientific method, deriving as it does from a society dominated by the Faustian imperative to control, quite naturally takes the predictability of the world as its cornerstone. Scientific method therefore includes among its intellectual and social functions the following:

(i)   the enlargement of the scope of predictability,

(ii) the enlargement of the period of time over which predictions may be made, and

(iii) the development of technologies to deal with the predicted events.

In the following we shall concentrate on the first aspect, which is of fundamental importance for the second and the third aspects.

When scientists analyse any natural or social process, they attempt to understand it in such a way that the whole structure of the corresponding process and all its interdependencies can be explained by scientific laws. In the ideal scientific case this structure is a causal one, i.e. any state of the process can uniquely be conceived as the effect of earlier states, and the cause of future states, of the process. This implies that at any given point in time, one can reconstruct all past states and predict exactly all future states. This reconstruction is only possible if there exists no unwanted novelty, and if there is no ignorance.

If, in this way, one could successfully examine all processes in the world, and all their interdependencies, and would know the complete state of the world at any time, then it would, in principle, be possible to compute all the states of the world at any moment in the future or the past. This situation corresponds to that of Laplace's demon (Prigogine and Stengers, 1984; Faber, Niemes and Stephan, 1987:91).

While in the 19th century Laplace's demon was an ideal for natural scientists, and became one of the driving forces for society at large, we know now that this ideal cannot, even in principle, be reached. This implies that we have to accept that the future is, in principle, open; i.e. we cannot know everything that will happen (cf. Chapter 11).

Nevertheless, we are interested to know about as many natural and social processes as possible. For if one could predict the future development of such processes, and if one knew their initial conditions, then one would be able, by influencing the initial conditions, to determine the outcome of these processes, and therefore to control the future.

Hence science, and its application in the form of technology, promises the increasing realisation of human wishes and intentions, and is therefore a prerequisite for the closure of the house of humankind. Thus, for example, one can influence the yield of the crop of a field by employing specially bred seeds, artificial irrigation, chemical fertilisers and pesticides. Such an example shows that science enables one, under certain circumstances, to become secure against certain unwanted future developments, e.g. famine and drought. Positively expressed: science and technology enlarge the set of feasible possibilities, and therefore the scope of freedom of action. They are the basis of the Faustian world which was described above.

3.3.4   Welfare and Security: Hubris and Anxiety

What are the consequences of this attitude to controlling the future? In those parts of the world where humankind has achieved control over many natural (and to some extent also social) processes, it has enlarged its possibilities of action to a tremendous degree. The dynamics of this development are amazing even in retrospect. This has resulted, at least in some parts of the world, in a vast increase in security and welfare in three respects: protection against disasters and disease; the provision of plenty of food; and the delegation of much human labour to machines. This has allowed many humans to do increasingly what they want to do, rather than what they must do.

The experience that many important processes can be controlled has led to the belief that, in principle, all processes can be submitted to human management by means of science and technology. This attitude of 'overweening pride' is the 'hubris' of the Greek myths; for hubris means that humankind loses perspective and feels itself to be godlike.

Although this belief in progress does not exist in this extreme form anymore, there are still many traits and relics of it at work. For example, in the 1960s the Kissimmee River in Florida was canalised by a huge Army Corps of Engineers project. The loss of wetlands habitat was disastrous, as were the downstream effects on Lake Okeechobee. The state of Florida is now exploring the possibility of restoring the meandering river, but restoration costs threaten to be one hundred times the original cost of the canalisation.

A further example is that during the sixties and seventies in the Federal Republic of Germany it was supposed in industry, government and by great parts of the public, that nuclear power could be governed, and that the wastes from nuclear power plants could be safely disposed of, or treated in processing plants.

Hubris easily gives rise to anxiety, because humankind feels that there always exists the possibility, even if the probability is very small, that for one or other reason one might lose control. The example of nuclear power illustrates also that hubris and anxiety may be met in different groups of society, regarding the same area of concern. In contrast to the nuclear industry, in the seventies there already existed an articulate minority which expressed great anxiety because of the uncontrollability of nuclear power.[5]

Here we can recognise the following temporal pattern. First, when the nuclear programme was decided upon, hubris predominated. This also held true for the first decade of its realisation. The more nuclear power plants were brought into operation, the more people became aware of possible dangers of nuclear technology, and the more anxieties arose.

While hubris arises from an overestimation of one's abilities to control technology and the subsequently triggered natural processes, in a state of anxiety one is no longer aware of one's possibilities to react and eventually to avoid the dangers.

Of course, hubris and anxiety are exhibited, as a rule, together within one human being, though they show up in different manifestations. Thus presidents of firms may give the impression that everything is under control during the day, while in the evening they tell their spouses about their anxieties.

3.3.5 Greek Philosophy Versus Modern Science

Here it may help to contrast the attitude of modern humankind with holistic ways of understanding the world. Such ways were developed in ancient India, China, Greece, etc. For example, Plato, in his philosophy of nature, offers a view of the world which does not seek to influence natural processes, but simply to contemplate them in their eternal 'idea', and in this way to experience their essence. Thus the Greek word 'theoria' means, literally translated: contemplation (cf. Faber and Manstetten, 1988:100). Plato (1953:716ff-28aff), like many other Greek philosophers, conceived the whole world as one sentient being, with the 'finest body' and the 'most noble soul'.

All processes, be they mental, organic or inorganic, express the life of this sentient being, the 'cosmos'. The latter, in turn, is an image of the divine life itself (cf. also the Gaia concept in Lovelock (1979), discussed in Chapter 2). According to this view of the world, it is the task of all 'theoria' to recognise the right place of all things and beings in the great life of the world. This holds also for human beings. Having found one's place, a conscious being has to act according to its insight into this great life of the world. In this view, life may unfold itself newly in each moment. The future is open for fortune as well as for misfortune. The true happiness of human beings consists in this openness concerning the unfolding of the cosmos. From this it follows that the notion of predictability was not important for Greek philosophy.[6] (For a discussion of Kantian and Aristotelian approaches to knowledge, see Chapter 12.)

In contrast to Greek science, the measuring rod of modern science is not the great life of the cosmos. Such an idea has no meaning, e.g. in classical mechanics. Instead, science is orientated to improving the conditions of human life, which implies that natural processes are influenced and controlled as much as possible (cf. Faber and Manstetten, 1988:102ff). Thus the modern, Newtonian, paradigm postulates a deterministic world.

3.3.6 First Summary

The ecological crisis has led to different reactions by different groups of people. A prominent reaction is the claim for increasing one's efforts to control the economy by technological and political means, in order to protect the environment. Sometimes there is even a demand for an 'eco-dictatorship'. In our eyes, actions in this direction remain Faustian in their attitude.

It is obvious that we cannot avoid employing Faustian measures to a certain extent. However, we are dubious if it will be sufficient to rely solely on this kind of measure, because in this case one remains in a similar attitude of closedness and Faustian spirit to that which has led to the present situation (cf. Chapter 4). Faustian will and science will not solve our problems.

Therefore, we consider it essential that the spirit in which necessary measures are taken broadens towards openness.

In the following part we will try to develop a concept of openness by conceptualising the notions of surprise, ignorance, novelty and evolution. For we believe that the environmental crisis consists not only of dangers, but also opens new ways of living and thinking. It offers us the chance to transcend those concepts and attitudes which block us from access to more openness, and thus to the true fullness of life, with all its joys and sufferings. Nature is sufficiently resilient to incorporate human impacts, provided we do not destroy its logos, its capacity for self-organisation and creative reaction to novel events. Therefore we believe that the embodiment of the principles of evolution, the logos of the house of nature (in Ehrlich's (1989) terminology: nature's housekeeping) will remain intact despite destructive human activities. Clearly, this confidence is not based on science, but it is a faith, a faith in the logos of nature. This faith implies that humankind cannot essentially interfere, despite all its actions, with the very logos of nature (cf. the Gaia concept in Chapter 2).

Of course, such a faith does not correspond to any truth which can be proved or demonstrated scientifically. This very principle of the evolution of the universe shows itself in the emergence of novel solutions in a dynamic system; however, the latter cannot be known ex ante (cf. the next section, and Chapters 8 and 11). Thus the logos is beyond our knowledge, and corresponds rather to our ignorance. Hence we cannot know if and how evolution develops, but we may hope that, in spite of human-made ecological damage, the principle of evolution may generate new forms of life and perhaps of intelligence. While our knowledge could suggest that humankind is going to destroy the ecological basis for its survival, the acceptance of our ignorance makes us open to new, up to now unknown, possibilities which may allow humankind to survive. Therefore, the faith in the logos of nature does not require any theological and philosophical dogmatism, but it has, as a consequence, an attitude of openness.

Even if one accepts that the logos of nature is not a direct object of science, one will, of course, try to learn as much as possible about nature's principles. This endeavour will be furthered by an attitude of openness and an experimental attitude towards living within natural systems, even as we partially control them. This in turn will help us to accept that all our knowledge is related to a fundamental ignorance.

While the Faustian attitude causes one to fasten one's grip on the economy and the control of nature, be it for exploitation or for environmental protection, the attitude of openness (i.e. the acknowledgement of ignorance as well as the readiness to discover and learn whatever is necessary) allows humankind to let loose and to hold fast at the same time.

3.4   PART II: CONCEPTUALISATION OF OPENNESS

Here we draw upon ideas more fully explored in Chapters 8 and 11.

3.4.1   Surprise, Ignorance and Openness

A key characteristic of the fullness of life is surprise. Our everyday life is full of surprises: we experience pleasant or unpleasant situations and events which we would never have expected. On the one hand, in a Faustian society people try to insure themselves against unwanted surprise, e.g. against suffering and unpleasantness. On the other hand, if there is not enough surprise experienced in everyday life, then people tend to create it in various ways, be it that they practise risky kinds of sports or get involved in love affairs. In contrast to our everyday life, the way science has conceived and handled its tasks up to now depends heavily on the attempt to exclude surprise.

What does surprise mean? We conceive surprise to be related to human consciousness, knowledge, and in particular to ignorance. Each occurrence of a surprising event may change the state of ignorance. The relationship between the state of ignorance and surprise may be compared to the relationship between a stock and its flows. While the flows in terms of the emergence of surprising events can be observed, the stock in terms of ignorance is itself unknown. From this it follows that ignorance and surprise cannot be understood independently of each other.

In a formal mathematical framework, this relationship between surprise and ignorance has been recognised in information theory. There one may talk of the 'surprisal' associated with new information, in a closely defined sense (Shannon and Weaver, 1949; Proops, 1987).[7]

In the following we first turn to ignorance and then to surprise. We now offer a brief taxonomy of ignorance. (For a fuller taxonomy and extensive discussion of ignorance, see Chapter 11.) Before discussing this taxonomy, we represent it in Figure 3.1.

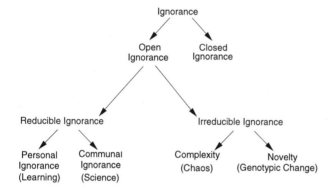

Figure 3.1. A brief taxonomy of ignorance.

(i)   We are often not aware of our ignorance, and therefore we feel no need for learning or research. We call this kind of ignorance 'closed ignorance'. Closed ignorance may either spring from the unawareness of unexpected events, or from false knowledge or false judgements.

As long as individuals remain in a state of closed ignorance they are unable to recognise their state; only if some event forces the experience of surprise can the individuals experience, ex post, the previous state of closed ignorance. However, very often individuals (e.g. politicians, scientists, social groups etc.) suppress as far as possible the possibility of surprise, and therefore remain unaware of their state of closed ignorance. Closed ignorance, particularly in the form of pretended knowledge, is a great barrier to human cognition and insight, as well as to the solution of ecological and economic problems.

(ii)   If individuals (groups, societies) become aware of their closed ignorance (forced by drastic events or guided by a changed attitude), they reach a state of 'open ignorance'. In this state one will become attentive, e.g. to events which one had neglected earlier. Only in a state of open ignorance is one able to experience surprise to its full extent. Of course, one will try to understand surprising events by learning and research. However, one is not only aware that one may generate new surprises by research and learning, but knows that one remains, in spite of one's knowledge, essentially in a state of ignorance.

We next distinguish between ignorance which is in principle 'reducible', and ignorance which is in principle 'irreducible'. By reducible ignorance we mean that which is amenable to study, learning and the application of scientific method. Irreducible ignorance is not amenable to these tools. We further subdivide reducible ignorance into 'personal' and 'social' ignorance. We also divide irreducible ignorance into 'ignorance from complexity' and 'ignorance from novelty'. We first turn to the two categories of reducible ignorance.

(1)   Surprise because of personal ignorance means that an event is unexpected only because of the state of knowledge of an individual. Knowledge which would eliminate this surprise is available within the society. Thus by learning, personal ignorance may be overcome.

(2)   Surprise because of communal ignorance means that an event is unexpected, because there is no information available to a society concerning this event. However, by research it would be possible to obtain this information.

We now turn to irreducible ignorance.

(3)   Surprise because of ignorance through novelty occurs if the 'potentialities' of a system alter. That is, the structure of the system underlying the event is changed without there being knowledge of a law governing this change. An example is the mutation of a gene or the invention of a new technique of production.

(4)   Surprise because of ignorance through complexity means that an event is unexpected because, owing to the complexity of the underlying process, the information available is not, and will never be, sufficient to predict this event. This may be so e.g. because of insurmountable limits of computability. For example, systems which exhibit 'chaos' (Gleick, 1988) have deterministic dynamics, but are so infinitely sensitive to their initial conditions that they are impossible to predict in detail with finite computational techniques.

Ignorance through complexity can be attributed to systems which are computable, and thus predictable, in principle, but not in practice. Ignorance through novelty can be attributed to changes in the structure of an objective system, where these changes are not predictable. (Other categories of irreducible ignorance are discussed in Chapter 11.)

From this it follows that in a state of open ignorance, i.e. without the barriers of closure, one is able to experience surprise. This enables an individual or society to reduce, by learning or research, the state of personal or communal ignorance. Of course, learning and research may also lead to the discovery of new areas of ignorance.

A case in point is the interaction between economic activity and the processes in the natural environment. It lays bare our ignorance and exhibits surprise to a great extent, because ex ante only few people would have expected our technological and economic measures to improve our welfare and security would lead to such environmental degradation. A concrete illustration is the use of fertilisers and pesticides, which endanger the soil, groundwater and via food chains also consumers, future generations, animals and plants.

We conclude that we need not only awareness of our ignorance and openness to surprise in our everyday life, but also in science and environmental policy, Under this perspective we now turn to some important implications for science.

3.4.2   The Concept of Evolution

When one is interested in obtaining a notion of an 'open future', which is of scientific relevance, it is expedient to take recourse to the notion of evolution, for this emphasises the openness of a process, i.e. it admits explicitly the possibility of surprise. Here we use the concept of evolution in a broad sense (as discussed in detail in Chapter 8).

The notion of evolution is used in various contexts; thus different sciences have different concepts of evolution; e.g. one speaks of geological, biological, social, political and economic evolution, as well as of the evolution of consciousness. Each science uses different concepts of evolution, according to its different aims of study. Thus in biology, the key concepts for evolution are mutation, heredity and selection, while in system theory one employs the concepts of self-evolution, self-sustained development, and self-reference.

Evolution may be understood in a narrow and in a broad sense.

(a) The narrow sense presupposes experience and knowledge about the whole time sequence of certain processes in the past, e.g. the growing up of a young person into an adult, or a seed into a tree. These evolutionary processes may safely be supposed to occur again and again in the future.

(b) Evolution in a broad sense is a process of change which starts either in the past, in the present, or in the future. Its characteristic is that it is open-ended in so far as:

   (i) one does not know if it will end,

   (ii) in the case that it does end, how it will end, and

   (iii) if it does not end, what kind of changes will occur.

We recognise evolution to include explicitly processes of open-ended change. In our view, the key characteristics of evolution are (1) process, (2) change, and (3) time. We define:

Evolution is the process of the changing of something over time (cf. Chapter 8).

The dichotomy between evolution in (a) a narrow and (b) a broad sense is an artificial one. For in reality there exists a continuous range of evolutionary processes between these two extremes; i.e. while processes of kind (a) are in principle predictable, and those of kind (b) are unpredictable, in reality we, as partly ignorant human beings, are confronted with processes whose traits are partly predictable and partly unpredictable.

3.4.3   Types of Evolutionary Processes: Phenotype and Genotype

Evolutionary processes cannot be conceived of without an observer. Human observers live in time, i.e. in past, present and future. Hence they can only experience processes in these subjective time categories.[8] However, there exist many processes where the explicit recognition of subjective time is not of much importance. Therefore, processes can be classified into those whose description is independent of, and those whose description is dependent on, the past, present and future. To the first class belongs the fall of a stone. To the second class belongs the history of Europe, or the development of modern art. It is obvious that a description of this history or this development will be different according to the period of time in which it is made. An essential distinction between the two types of processes is that the former can be sufficiently explained as realisations of a certain law, while the latter cannot be explained by any known law.

A law, be it a natural or an economic law, is usually considered as time independent. Therefore, once the law is known, the processes governed by it are always predictable. They are identical ex ante and ex post. As processes like the historical ones, however, cannot be explained completely by any law, they are not predictable. Only their past parts can be described or narrated with some certainty. Their future course can neither be explained nor narrated: they are intrinsically open to surprise.

How can predictable and unpredictable processes operationally be distinguished? We suggest that processes are predictable when their structure is time invariant and known. This invariant structure is the basis for predictability.

Predictable processes can be conceived of as a realisation of an invariant and known structure. For instance, the fall of a stone is a realisation of the Law of Gravitation. The growth of a tree is the realisation of its seed, i.e. of its genotypic structure. The formation of the price of potatoes in a free market is the realisation of the Law of Demand and Supply. The innovation of a technique is the realisation of its invention.

But if the structure of certain processes changes, and one does not know an invariant meta-structure which governs the change, there no longer exists a basis for predictability. Such processes are intrinsically time dependent, and thus change in an unknown way. Hence processes which do not have an invariant and known structure are unpredictable. For example, the seed of a tree can be changed by mutation. The mutation and the corresponding process of its realisation have the characteristic of novelty; therefore the occurrence of a mutation is unpredictable. From this it follows that the evolution of a new species of tree is, in principle, unpredictable. Similarly, the breakthrough invention of a new technique is the structural change of the technology of an economy and, again, is unpredictable. For instance, all the consequences of the invention of the steam engine were unpredictable, at least up to the time it was invented.

In accordance with the terminology of biology, we distinguish two aspects of each process (cf. Chapter 8). The underlying structure of a process is called its genotype, and the realisation of this structure is called its phenotype.

Although the phenotype is the realisation of its genotype, it is not causally determined solely by it, since there exist additional influences, e.g. the environment for the growth of a tree. From this it follows that, even with given genotypes, the phenotype can often only be predicted in broad terms.

The meaning of genotype and phenotype changes according to the area of science in which they are applied. Obviously, a genotype in biology, such as the genetic potential of a seed, is conceptually very different from a genotype in an economy, such as that expressed in a technique, an institution, or in a preference ordering of a consumer. The interplay of genotypes and phenotypes of different areas is of much importance for economic and ecological development.

Although all processes with genotypic changes are in principle unpredictable, it does not follow that processes with no genotypic changes, i.e. with invariant structures, can be predicted. For instance, the weather cannot be predicted for more than a very short time period, although the genotype in terms of natural laws is known and constant, i.e. time independent. This is so because we are not only ignorant of genotypic changes but there exist many processes which are so complex that human beings are and will not be able to predict them, as we know from chaos theory (Lorenz, 1963).

3.5   PART III: SOME APPLICATIONS TO ECOLOGICAL ECONOMICS

3.5.1   Resource Depletion vs. Pollution

The two main areas of concern in economy-environment interactions are:

(a)   the depletion of natural resources, and

(b)   the production of pollution.

In the following we wish to examine how our evolutionary framework, and in particular our concepts of novelty and ignorance, can be used to analyse these two areas.

(a) Let us consider a particular non-renewable resource. If we know the total quantity which appears presently to be extractable (i.e. the stock) and how much of it is exploited each year (i.e. the flow), we can predict the time when this resource will be exhausted. We note that the magnitude of the flow depends also on the states of individual and of social ignorance. Thus, for example, oil had almost the character of a free good before the first oil crisis in 1973, because its price was so low. The more individuals and societies at large became aware of the finite nature of oil, the less oil was used per capita. The main means to increase this awareness was the sharp rise in the price of oil.

On the basis of the knowledge of the stock, the flow, and the influence of the price, it is possible, at least in principle, to conceive political and economic measures to manage the extraction of a certain resource such that it is reasonable.

In our considerations so far we have regarded only individual and social ignorance which leads to a waste of resources. We saw already that the price mechanism is an effective means to reduce this kind of ignorance.

While these kinds of ignorance are detrimental, there are other kinds of ignorance which can be related to beneficial novelty. New deposits of a resource may be discovered, new recycling methods may be invented, new production methods using less of the resource may be found, and completely new technologies may be invented using material which up to now has not been considered to be a resource at all. The emergence of such kinds of beneficial novelty will be furthered by the means of the price mechanism, for as the resource is used up, its price will rise. This will generate a search for further reserves of the resource (prospecting), a search for techniques using less of the resource (resource-saving invention), and a search for techniques using other, cheaper resources (which may eventually lead to resource-substituting invention).

Besides these price induced inventions, there will also be considerable non-price induced research, which will tend to move the economy further away from its natural constraints.

While in the short-run many of these developments may be predictable, it is known how difficult it is to predict them in the long-run. This is well illustrated by the historical experience of industrialisation.

Looking only at the use of resources, we may conclude the problems arising from ignorance have at least a chance of being solved by the activities of humankind.

(b) Let us now consider pollution. In this area ignorance is of much greater importance than for the problem of resource depletion. Looking at water, air, soil and waste we can observe a similar pattern of occurrence. At the beginning of a certain economic activity one often is unaware that pollution is produced. When the pollution is first recognised, one does not consider it to be really harmful. If it is recognised to be detrimental, one often does not know why it is happening, as in the case of forest death. From this again it follows that one does not know what one can do. Finally if one really knows what one can do, it may be too late.

Here, the surprise that emerges is in terms of new relationships between economic activity and the natural environment. This surprise is potentially, and usually, deleterious. Examples include the hole in the ozone layer, algal bloom from fertiliser run-off, acid rain and its effects on lakes, etc. All of these are relatively new phenomena, and they were all unexpected and unwelcome.

Countering the effects of pollution by 'internalising' them via the price mechanism (e.g. by levying charges) within the market system would certainly help. However, unlike market-led resource depletion, while the scarcity of the environmental resource, such as clean water or air, would appear in its planning valuation ex ante, the effect of a new pollutant is initially unknown, because of ignorance. Therefore, the 'price' of the pollutant, and thus the corresponding cost of using it, would only be knowable ex post.

Thus resource use can be said to generate scarcity, which is reflected in a market price, which in turn is likely to generate beneficial novelty. On the other hand, new pollutants are themselves a source of deleterious novelty, and generate only slowly, and often not at all, a search for a system of market pricing to encourage the reduction of their emission.

In summary, there exists an inherent asymmetry in the recognition of problems of natural resource depletion and the degradation of the environment; this is so because of different forms of ignorance. Hence, an attitude which is appropriate for the treatment of resource problems may be completely inappropriate for pollution problems.

3.5.2 Relevance for Ecological Development

Pollution problems require an attitude of openness. One prerequisite for a new attitude of openness is that we have to see clearly the prevailing conditions of our present situation and to accept them.

(a) We have to recognise the Faustian traits of modern societies. This holds also to a great extent for ecologists. They, too, have tended to cope with environmental dangers within the area of reducible ignorance. For example, water treatment plants have been built and cars have been supplemented with catalysts. In our terminology these measures spring from a Faustian attitude. It is important for all of us to recognise how far we are involved in the Faustian world and ourselves act out of a Faustian attitude.

However, although we consider certain Faustian measures absolutely necessary, we do not believe that they are sufficient. For we cannot expect that we will be able to solve our environmental problems if we try to tackle it in the same Faustian spirit of pretended omniscience and omnipotence as humankind has used during industrialisation. A Faustian attitude cannot cope with irreducible ignorance. The complexity created in society and nature by industrialised economies is so encompassing that we cannot hope that science and technology will help us to offer more than partial solutions. We have to accept that humankind has not only been unable, up to now, to control many essential natural and social processes according to its needs, but will never be able to control all essential processes.

(b) From this it follows that we have to recognise and to accept our ignorance. This is difficult, because we are often so deeply involved in Faustian projects and Faustian measures that we are too closed to recognise our true ignorance. It is also difficult, because it is almost impossible to conceive one's true ignorance in an adequate manner. For even if we are aware of it and are open for the corresponding surprises, it is not conceivable to talk about them as they really are. For as soon as we try to speak about our ignorance and to explain it, we must have a conception of it in terms of knowledge, however slight it may be, and thus our openness is, so to speak, overcast by a shadow. Hence there is an intrinsic difficulty in drawing any concrete conclusions, in particular environmental and economic policy ones, from the awareness of ignorance. But this crucial awareness of ignorance and the consequent attitude of openness contain in themselves already the main policy conclusion of our chapter.

As a consequence, the emergence of novelty and the admission of ignorance should not be an 'add-on' to policy making, but its cornerstone and central tenet. In particular, we feel the case for such a stance is overwhelming in considerations of economy-environment interactions in the long-run. This approach leads us to the following conclusions.

(1) A simple belief in technical, economic, and social progress is in opposition to an attitude of openness. Although progress is possible, we cannot rely on progress to solve our environmental problems. Hence our plans should be open for progress, but not depend solely upon it.

(2) Any plan formulation should be open to revision as and when novelty occurs. Planning should be a continuing process, taking into account ignorance and emerging novelty. This should not only be the case in practice, but it should also be embodied in models of planning and decision making.

(3) One should value, and plan for, flexibility in response to currently unforeseen possibilities. For example, planning for systems to operate near the limits of their capabilities may be optimal in the short-run, but it severely limits flexibility of response for the long-run (cf. the seminal paper by Koopmans, 1964; see also Weizsäcker and Weizsäcker, 1984).

3.6 CONCLUSION

We are suggesting a new approach to environmental policy in which economic activities are conceived as embedded within open ecological systems, and in which these ecological systems develop and maintain their own self-organisation. Therefore economic activities are acceptable only to the extent that they do not destroy the health (the capacity for self-organising activity) of the larger ecological system within which the economy operates.

We have argued that pollution problems may prove more recalcitrant than resource availability problems, because of the different types of novelty and ignorance they present to us. Resource availability problems can be foreseen and incentives can be arranged to encourage appropriate, ameliorating, economic responses. On the other hand, pollution problems may attack the health of the system itself, and limit human opportunities for innovative responses to change. What is called for in this new approach is not more and more futile attempts to control natural systems, but more and more wisdom in terms of accepting our radical ignorance. This would allow us to become more able to discriminate against human impacts that will limit opportunities for present and future generations. A reorientation of environmental policy, away from attempts to bring more and more of nature within the human, economic sphere, where it can be controlled, towards an open view of the future through the acceptance of our ignorance, is a first step in creating a more rational approach to environmental policy.

NOTES

1. Thus the sinologist Wilhelm (1984:24-26) stated that the Chinese idea of 'way' (Tao, i.e the ultimate principle of the universe in Taoism) has many aspects in common with the idea of logos.
2. However, in the view of many scientists the assumption of such a logos is not necessary, and may be even an obstacle to the understanding of nature. In modern natural scene, as well as in Kant's *Critique of Pure Reason* we find concepts which do without the assumption of such a logos. This is so because the application of the concept of logos has inherent difficulties for the following reasons: the significance of this concept cannot be exhausted, and the conditions for the application of the concept cannot be specified exactly.
3. Of course, one may ask: are there really two houses, a house of humankind and a house of nature, or is there only one house? And further: If there is only one house, is it the house of humankind (economy) or the house of nature (ecology)? Or is it a third one (cf. Chapter 2)? However, we shall not deal further with this metaphysical question.
4. It is noteworthy that Faust, trying to translate the first verse of St John's gospel, 'In the beginning was the Logos', translates it in the following way, 'In the beginning was the Deed' (Goethe, 1908, Part I, Study). The course of the drama leaves no doubt that Faust sees his creation of the Faustian world as the true 'beginning', so that the 'Deed' is nothing but the Faustian deed.
5. That this anxiety has spread over many parts of society demonstrates the fact that in the eighties this far reaching agreement has been increasingly lost. For example, this has been shown by the demonstrations at Gorleben and Wackersdorf, and the subsequent partial retreat of the nuclear industry in the Federal Republic of Germany.
6. In Greek philosophy, the notion of prediction was reserved for eternal matters (e.g. the celestial bodies). The prediction of future events on earth was not a task for philosophers, but for oracles.
7. There is a close, but often contentious, relationship between information theory and the thermodynamic entropy concept. One might view entropy as reflecting our state of ignorance about the world (Jaynes, 1957; Kubat and Zeman, 1975).
8. One has to distinguish between 'subjective' and 'objective' time categories. The latter consist of all time categories which describe a time sequence, i.e. for instance, 'earlier' or 'later', as well as all relations between durations. In contrast, the former consist of the categories past, present and future. While the meaning of objective time categories remains always constant, the meaning of subjective time categories changes with the moment of time in which the observer is living.

4. The Dilemma of Modern Humans and Nature: An Exploration of the Faustian Imperative

with Hans-Christoph Binswanger

4.1 INTRODUCTION

One often experiences economists and ecologists talking at cross purposes. In this chapter we try to represent both viewpoints by a debate between archetypes of an economist and an ecologist, which may appear, in some respects, characterised rather one-sidedly. Both protagonists may be present within one person, even within each of the authors. For this reason, no economist or ecologist should identify themselves with the respective typification. In addition, we will introduce as 'personae dramatis' a commentator, and later a writer.

4.2 ECONOMICS

Commentator: An economist's and an ecologist's view differ very much in essential aspects. This will become apparent when comparing their answers to the question: how do they perceive economic activity?

Let us first hear the *Economist* about the subject of his science.

4.2.1 The Economist's Perspective

Economist: I will begin my statement with an often used definition of economics:

> *The economist studies the disposal of scarce means. He is interested in the way different degrees of scarcity of different goods give rise to different ratios of valuation between them, and he is interested in the way in which changes in conditions of scarcity, whether coming from changes in ends or changes in means - from the demand side*

or the supply side - affect these ratios. Economics is the science which studies human behaviour between ends and scarce means which have alternative uses. (Robbins, 1932:15)

We see that by focusing one's attention on 'different ratios of valuation' between scarce goods dependent on 'different degrees of scarcity', Robbins emphasises the choice aspect, and thus determines human behaviour as a main cornerstone of economics. Human behaviour expresses itself as a relationship between two sides: ends and scarce means. The first side of this relationship refers to interests and wishes of individuals, which are expressed in their preferences. The second side refers to material aspects of economics: primary factors of production such as land, natural resources, and energy expressed in the form of labour. The transformation of these primary factors into secondary factors of production yields buildings, capital goods, etc. Information concerning technology, stocks of primary and capital goods, and preferences as well as institutions is contained in the so-called boundary conditions of an economic problem. These boundary conditions contain also all natural data, in particular on all stocks of resources and all necessary environmental parameters. In general, we assume that all the information on the boundary conditions is given. I shall comment on three characteristics of my approach.

(i) We economists mainly consider the relationship between human ends and scarce means but take these as given.

If the boundary conditions are given we can prove with mathematical methods, i.e. with the approach of general equilibrium theory, that solutions to the allocation problem of scarce resources exist and that under certain assumptions these are even Pareto-optimal[1] (Debreu, 1959). In simple words, we can offer a good, and in some sense even optimal, solution for the fulfilment of the wishes of individuals.

(ii) If the boundary conditions change, a new solution with the same characteristic as above can be found relatively easily. By using methods of comparative statics, our main method of analysis, this new solution can be compared with the old one. However, comparative statics does not ask why and in which way these changes occur. As soon as the process of change is no longer ignored, but is also taken into the analysis, the tractability of such dynamic solutions of the allocation problem becomes intrinsically much more complicated; even with advanced methods of mathematics, often it cannot be found. Furthermore, even if such a solution exists, the characteristics of being a good solution, such as exhibiting Pareto-optimality and stability, cannot be expected in many cases. These results show that we have good reasons to leave analysis of changes of the boundary conditions outside the realm of our analysis.

(iii) Although we mainly try to explain what is and not what should be, our analysis is based on value judgements. Important values are (cf. e.g. Bernholz and Breyer, 1984:21-25): (1) freedom, (2) justice, (3) security, and (4) efficiency in production and consumption (Pareto-optimality). I believe that these values can best be achieved in a market-oriented system.

4.2.2   The Ecologist's Perspective

Commentator: How does our *Ecologist* perceive the question 'What is an economic activity'?

Ecologist: The *Economist's* language is rather foreign to me. Since I am a layman you cannot expect me to deliver a professional answer. Instead I state certain criteria which a definition has to fulfil.

In contrast to the *Economist* my point of departure is not the intentions and wishes of the individuals, but my interest in life in all its forms, of which human life is just one kind. I am interested in the whole of nature; that means, e.g., conservation of natural resources and the biosphere, development of species and plants, as well as quality of soil, water and air. All these aspects of nature should be given due regard when economic activities are carried through. This implies that I am mainly concerned with the consequences of economic activities for the environment at large. Hence, while the *Economist* takes the natural conditions, which he calls boundary conditions, as given, my main concern is the way in which these conditions are changed by economic activity. These neglected changes are often of irreversible nature, as an analysis based on an entropy approach (Georgescu-Roegen, 1971; Faber, Niemes and Stephan, 1987) clearly shows.

4.2.3   The State of the World Economy

Commentator: Having heard how the *Economist* and the *Ecologist* view the economy, we now want to find out how each of them evaluates the states of both the national and the world-wide economies today.

Economist: Though I see certain deficiencies in the realisation of the values I mentioned above at a world-wide level, I generally believe that the industrialised countries have made considerable progress in the realisation of these aims and should, in principle, just continue the presently chosen path. In this way, one of the most important values, freedom, can best be secured and even widened; the very existence of freedom even contributes essentially to the other values. I see freedom as a prerequisite for the solution of environmental and resource problems, because it leaves space for individual creativity and the realisation of new ideas.

Ecologist: The *Economist* does not seem to be concerned with the continuing extinction of species and plants and the destruction of habitats. Hence his emphasis on security concerns only human beings in a very narrow sense. In my eyes, security exists only if there is space, not only for human beings, but for all species, to live and develop. The way economies are run at present does not protect this kind of security.

Over and above that, present economic activities endanger the living conditions of future generations because of the extremely rapid extraction of resources and the accompanying pollution of air, water and soil; thus, in the long run, they jeopardise the very foundations of human life itself. But if this is the case, then the other values of the *Economist*, such as freedom, justice, and efficiency ultimately become meaningless.

I may even go one step further and reproach the *Economist* that his most esteemed value, freedom, has already led to the present deplorable state of the environment. This has happened because the freedom which allows individuals to pursue their own interests, in an unrestricted manner, take insufficient care of the living conditions of other species, and only give very limited recognition to the needs of future generations of humankind. Therefore I question a system which has individual freedom as its fundamental basis, since present economic activities cause the environmental degradation and the possible subsequent catastrophe to all life. That means I question the whole market system. In addition I maintain that all people, including the economists, who contribute to the functioning of modern market economies, are co-responsible for these consequences. This co-responsibility is stated in a vivid manner by Mayer (1988), for example:

> *By our entire (money-oriented) way of life we give our consent to the contamination of the subsoil, to the destruction of the ozone layer, to the deforestation of the tropical rainforests and the pollution of the North Sea, day after day and by small degrees ... We use up the forests, which should belong to our children, too. We bequeath them a ground which will be so sour and rich with heavy metals that it will bear, if at all, only toxic fruits. Our ruin, our death sentence, is the*

breathtaking velocity with which we change the world. In this way there is no chance left for the slowly grinding mills of evolution to raise objections at any time.

Many of us even go so far as to conclude that there has to be a radical reduction in the level of consumption and perhaps even of population, and perhaps also a drastic reduction in individual freedom. This attitude is expressed by Hannon (1985b:330):

I would rather live under a Shogun than be a part of centuries of conflict. I would rather be subjected to extensive regulation than experience or expect my descendants to experience a nuclear holocaust ... We will accept as given the importance of world unity over the individual's desire for freedom ... I am saying that the World Shogun will not arise unless the people allow it - even desire it, and their desire will be borne of natural resource scarcity.

However, there are also other ecologists who believe that it may be possible to develop new kinds of decentralised and self-sustaining communities, which are in harmony with nature. This would enable us to determine and to form our own manner of living, in such a way that we would achieve a new kind of freedom. This freedom, however, is different from the freedom of the market system, which is only too often reduced to choosing between material goods (Seymour, 1980).

I, for my part, believe we should seek solutions at two levels: (a) ideologies and values have to be changed such that the ideals of progress and economic growth are denounced; and (b) social institutions have to be changed in order to restrain economic processes.

4.3   THE CONTRASTING VIEWS

Commentator: There exists a fundamental difference between the points of views of the *Economist* and the *Ecologist*. While the *Economist* has narrowed down his object to the economy as described above, the *Ecologist* takes nature as a whole into account, of which the economy is only one part. This difference in outlook implies two consequences: (a) the former takes a partial view, while the latter has a holistic one; (b) the former is anthropocentric, while the latter tends to a so-called 'physiocentric' view (Meyer-Abich, 1986); (c) the former is mechanistic, but the latter takes an organic or process oriented approach. Therefore the *Economist* is only interested in the natural boundary conditions as far as they refer to individual human ends. The *Ecologist*, however, sees nature either as an end in itself, or as a sine qua non for the existence of human beings.

Let me highlight the asymmetry between the two views in the terminology of the *Economist*. While the ends of the individuals are at the centre of the optimisation process for an economist, and nature is included in the boundary conditions, the salvation of nature is at the centre of the intentions and actions of an ecologist, and natural needs of the individuals (food, clothing, housing) and basic needs (such as health, sanitary installations, education) are included in the boundary conditions.[2]

(i) The difference in values between our two protagonists is also revealed in the different perspectives of time which they employ. Since the boundary conditions often change, the *Economist's* method only allows for a rather short time horizon.[3] This contrasts with the length of time horizon employed by ecologists, which comprises the time span of generations.

Hence the *Economist* is concerned with short-run restrictions while the *Ecologist* is interested in long-run considerations. Irreversibilities are therefore little recognised by economists, a lacuna which was also noted by Samuelson (1983:36):

> *In theoretical economics there is no 'irreversibility' concept which is one reason why Georgescu-Roegen (1971) is critical of conventional economics.[4]*

The occurrence of an irreversibility is a qualitative change in the boundary conditions (Faber, Niemes and Stephan, 1987). In addition, the full impact of this alteration can, in general, be comprehended only within a long time horizon. This explains why the *Ecologist* is so much concerned with irreversibilities.

(ii) Our protagonists use different conceptualisations and have different kinds of knowledge.

The *Economist*, as a representative of one discipline, has seemingly precise concepts and elaborate methods. This enables him to develop a convincing solution with his box of tools, once a problem is clearly formulated within his range of study. However, this approach has two major difficulties. (a) It happens that problems within the range of economics, but which are difficult to incorporate into economic analysis, such as the long-run effects of economic activities on the environment, fall completely out of his sight or are regarded as too difficult to analyse. As a prisoner of his own conceptualisation he may not understand at all where the problem has to be located. (b) Difficulties occur also with those problems for which his tools only partly suffice. This is so because the economist is unable to formulate, within the concepts of his own discipline, the difference between those questions he is capable of analysing and those he is not; to this end he would need a meta-language. Hence he may tend to ignore important aspects of certain problems and offer only one-sided solutions. Environmental issues often belong to this kind of problem.

The *Ecologist* cannot be associated uniquely with one particular discipline, but he may be found eventually in all disciplines; often he mixes colloquial language with scientific language and argues simultaneously on several different levels. Thus, for example, a true scientific statement may be followed by a mere ethical postulate and a wrong economic conclusion, without its author realising that he has changed his level of abstraction three times. In general, such an approach does not enable him to develop clear solutions. Nevertheless, his questions and his answers offer helpful intuitive insights. His strength is to make others aware of important problems which do not occur within the range of one particular discipline.

We see that our protagonists have two different kinds of objects of study and speak two different languages. We have not yet seen how a translation may be achieved and how these two different objects of study might be integrated. We cannot expect that we can achieve this great task in our discussion. But it will be helpful to hear what each of them proposes as a means to solve the most urgent environmental problems.

4.4   POSSIBLE SOLUTIONS

4.4.1   The Economist's Approach

Economist: Let me start my answer by quoting Solow (1973:49-50):

> *Excessive pollution happens because of an important flaw in the price system. Factories, power plants, municipal sewers, drivers of cars, strip-miners of coal and deep-miners of coal and all sorts of generators of waste are allowed to dump the waste into the environment, into the atmosphere and into running water and the oceans, without paying the full cost of what they do. No wonder they do too much. So would you, and so would I. In fact, we actually do - directly as drivers of cars, indirectly as we buy some products at a price which is lower than it ought to be because the producer is not required to pay for*

using the environment to carry away his wastes, and even more indirectly as we buy things that are made with things that pollute the environment.

We see that the environmental problems occur because of a combination of external effects and the intrinsic problem associated with the supply of public goods. However, in the meantime such market failures are well known. They can be repaired by the introduction of market prices for environmental goods, such as water, air and landscape. If these prices can be determined appropriately by a state agency, the market system will deliver a good solution.

This implies that as a new value, the 'conservation of nature' has to be additionally considered. For this purpose the boundary conditions of the market economy have to be newly defined.

I insist, however, that freedom is the most important prerequisite for the solution of environmental problems. I can demonstrate this in the following way. Environmental pollution and the extremely rapid exhaustion of resources can be avoided by introducing so-called clean technologies and resource saving techniques. However, to this end, they have first to be invented and second innovated. As history has shown, both invention and innovation can best be realised in a market economy (see Schumpeter, 1942; Kornai, 1971:288; Bernholz and Breyer, 1984:Chapter 6). This is so because, given the new boundary conditions, freedom will give space for both individual creativity and competition. The market will select the best inventions and in turn innovate them. The coordination of these various activities will be carried out by the market mechanism (see e.g. Bernholz and Faber, 1988:241-243).

In general my basic attitude is an optimistic one concerning resource and environmental problems:

> *If history offers any guide, then, in the developed part of the world at least, the accumulation of technological knowledge will probably make our great-grandchildren better off than we are, even if we make no great effort in that direction.* (Solow, 1973:42)

4.4.2 The Ecologist's Approach

Ecologist: (1) To give nature, e.g. a dying species, a price is as cynical as to give a price to human beings. (2) Why did it take such a long time for the economists to become aware of market failure concerning the environment and the corresponding 'important flaws' in the price system? Why has it taken so much time to react to it? (3) A price for water, air and soil implies that it is possible to pollute water etc. to a certain extent. Since these prices are determined by the interests and wishes of the present generation and the present insufficient knowledge about environmental dangers, there is no guarantee that the resulting pollution level is not too high. Hence discharges should be avoided altogether.

History has provided ample evidence that the individualistic dynamics, which are given so much space by the market system, lead inherently to ecological damage. Therefore measures proposed by economists, and only eventually carried through by politicians, take care only of presently recognised and publicly admitted environmental dangers. The likelihood that neglected dangers lead to catastrophic consequences for the survival of the human species is at least not negligible, as the greenhouse effect in particular shows.

Therefore I conclude that, even under optimal circumstances, all the alterations proposed by the *Economist* can only lead to a partial repair of the ecological system; changes of these kinds do not guarantee that no fatal, irreversible damage occurs. The price system is therefore in no way suitable for the solution of the environmental problem.

4.4.3   Commentary and Debate

Commentator: An economically trained ecologist would additionally point out that in general equilibrium theory, which is dominant in economics, it is assumed concerning all goods (a) that the number of all goods is finite and (b) that they are known. The first step of the *Economist's* approach to solving environmental problems consists of increasing the list of goods by the correspondingly added new goods, namely those environmental goods or bads which have caused the flaw in the price system,[5] and to try to account for uncertainty. Obviously there exist a very great, if not an infinite, number of environmental goods, and this number changes absolutely not only by production and consumption but also by biological evolution (cf. Chapter 8). In addition, the known number also changes in response to the expansion of knowledge.

The time span needed to recognise a part of nature as an environmental good, and to take corresponding precautions, is often very long. (1) The biological, physical and chemical parameters have to be rediscovered. (2) The harmfulness of corresponding emissions has to be estimated. (3) The technological possibilities of reducing emissions, and of end-of-the-pipe treatments, have to be examined. Often, such technologies have first to be developed and installed. (4) On the basis of the data and interdependencies noted in the first three stages, the political bodies have to formulate environmental aims. (5) Economists have to propose how these can be achieved efficiently, for instance by standards or charges. (6) Jurists have to formulate corresponding rules, decrees or bills. (7) Political bodies have to discuss them in three readings. (8) Administrations have to carry them out and to enforce them. For these purposes it is often necessary to establish new offices or even administrations.

This chain of actions is not only complex but has, for example in the case of the water acts, such a great impact on the production structure of the economy and the income distribution that it can be successfully carried through only if there is a consensus in society (Brown and Johnson, 1982:931-932). To attain such a consensus, however, the danger of pollution, or a mode of behaviour, has to be evident not only to the ecologists and specialists, but also to the public at large. Hence, even if this process of setting a correct price, or finding an adequate market solution, is carried through in a comparatively short time, it may take too much time to avoid irreversible damage.

Economist: Let me take up the criticism of the *Ecologist*. Although I am not able to answer all of his arguments, I maintain that his kind of criticism leads to no solution at all, or to idealised solutions which are completely inefficient, both economically and ecologically.

Let me describe the consequences of such an idealised solution by giving an example which is taken from reality. In 1972 the American Congress enacted a very ambitious water law, the Clean Water Act (in the following abbreviated as CWA) of 1972. Roberts (1974:18-21) (cf. also Brown and Johnson, 1982:949 footnote 72) showed in detail that the environmental lobby had a decisive influence on its drafting. The intention of the CWA was to prohibit every discharge of pollution into the water by 1985 (Roberts, 1974:20). Brown and Johnson (1982:952) characterise the Act as follows:

> *The existing U.S. system of water pollution control is dominated by a legalistic approach in two ways. First, it emphasizes as its goal the total ban of discharges of wastes into public waters instead of applying cost-benefit principles which would proscribe only those dischargers of waste which are not cost-justified for a particular body of water, considering the alternative uses for those waters and their assimilative capacity. Second, the U.S. system relies heavily on the threat of punishment, i.e., fines and/or imprisonment, rather than on economic incentives to induce industries, municipalities, and other waste discharges to reduce the pollutants they discharge into public waters.*

The latter argument was also emphasised by Roberts (1974:12):

> *One of the striking features of the law is its starkly anti-economic viewpoint. There is to be no case by case balancing of cost and benefits, no attempt at 'fine tuning', the process of resource allocation ... Technology alone will be the constraint.*

Roberts (1974:21) summarises the basic attitude of the Act: 'A technical optimism was combined with an institutional pessimism.' At the first glance this statement may be a surprising characterisation of the ecologists' position, because they are well known for having argued so often that modern technology is the very thing which has destroyed and polluted so much of the environment. Nevertheless, as long as one does not insist on the total abandonment of everything on which modern economies are based, the only hope for a satisfactory solution of environmental problems seems to be the application of technological knowledge and technical means.

An unexpected and, perhaps for the ecologist undesired, consequence of the latter attitude is a curious coincidence of the interests of the ecologists with those of engineers and the heavy construction industry:

> *In addition, the Army Corps of Engineers played a significant role in advancing the argument that 'zero discharge' was technically feasible.* (Roberts, 1974:20)

For the Army Corps of Engineers the Act:

> *... offered a whole new range of potential projects, which were in short supply in many areas where all the relevant rivers had long since been dammed.* (Ibid.)

To understand the acclamation of the heavy construction industry for the law it is important to understand that:

> *The highway program was beginning to run down and the pressure for finding new things for that industry to build was obvious, especially in an election year.* (Ibid.)

Before the passing of the CWA of 1972 there was a lot of criticism:

> *... the ban-the-discharge approach, which was explicitly incorporated in the Federal Water Pollution Control Act Amendments (FWPCA) of 1972 ... was subjected to heavy criticism by the National Water Commission, the National Commission on Water Quality, and independent economists, who considered the concept to be too costly.* (Brown and Johnson, 1982:952)

Thus Roberts (1974:13) pointed out:

Thus there is no guarantee under the 1972 Act that economies of scale would be exhausted, that methods which act directly on the environment will be employed, that variations in the ecosystem will be responded to, that costs will be minimized or benefits maximized. Instead enforcement loopholes are to be tightened and all variety and flexibility squeezed out of the system.

To these comments I add that an actual realisation of the idealised solution intended by the ecologists, i.e. the ban-the-discharge approach, would have had tremendous impacts on the American economy, which the legislators in the Senate in their 80-0 vote (Brown and Johnson, 1982:949 fn 72) had not been aware of. The enforcement would have led to the abolition of all those many techniques for which it would have been impossible, or too costly, to fulfil the no-discharge condition. This in turn would have implied a far-reaching restructuring of the American economy with all its consequences, but to a much greater extent than was experienced after the oil-price-shock in 1973; i.e. high unemployment rates in certain industries and regions, the bankruptcy of many sectors of the economy, in particular of the chemical industry, a great redistribution of wealth and income. Such high social costs would have been accepted at best by some of the ecologists, but certainly not by the majority of the population.

For all these reasons it turned out that it was impossible to enforce the no-discharge approach:

It was not surprising that the 1977 Amendments of the FWPCA altered the emphasis of the federal program in the direction of the receiving water standards approach and away from the no-waste-discharge principle. (Ibid.)

The water legislation in the U.S. during the seventies was a failure, measured by the goals formulated in the CWA of 1972 (OECD, 1987:54).

Although the CWA was passed in the Senate unanimously, there did not exist a corresponding consensus among the parties, associations, unions, administrators and representatives of various industries. As I showed above, the consequences of the actual enforcement of the CWA of 1972 would have been very severe. In such a case, however, the resistance of even one influential group can be sufficient to prevent it, as many examples from history show (Dahl, 1956). Thus it turned out that the complete success of the ecologist lobby was a Pyrrhic victory concerning its ultimate aim of no water pollution.

These have been the consequences of an idealised solution. I shall now turn to a solution which is based on market incentives. An important example is the water legislation in the Federal Republic of Germany in the middle of the seventies, where the establishment of a consensus was decisive for its relative success.

Political support in the F.R.G. increased for a market approach to environmental management during the early 1970s. Initial proposals for water pollution control legislation looked very much like the 'ideal' systems urged by economists. Charges would be levied on waste dischargers in direct waters. Some Länder, however, especially Bavaria and Baden-Württemberg in the south, opposed these radical innovations and recommended a more moderate charge system which would operate in tandem with the traditional standards/regulatory system. By 1976, the idea of a combined system of regulations plus charges had become dominant. This system would levy charges high enough to create market-like incentives to abate pollution but, at the same time, would continue an administrative management regime for pollution control.

Industry initially opposed the idea of any effluent charge system. As political support for the system gained momentum, however, opposition shifted to implementation issues, such as the criteria for setting charges, the level of charges, and the dates when the system would go into effect. (Brown and Johnson, 1982:931-932)

This kind of law was not only successful relative to the United States but also absolutely, since the F.R.G. has the highest percentage of waste-water treatment plants on a biological or chemical basis of all countries (cf. OECD, 1987:53-54), except for Denmark (90% in 1985) and Sweden (100% in 1985). This shows definitely the superiority of economic incentives over attempts to regulate by standards.

4.5   CONSENSUS AND THE STATUS QUO

Commentator: I see a growing displeasure in the face of our *Ecologist.* He certainly is eager to contradict the *Economist,* but let me first emphasise one aspect of the *Economist's* presentation. It concerns the close inter-dependencies between economics and politics, which is of the utmost importance for the effectiveness of environmental measures. The relative success of the German water law legislation, compared with the American, was the result of a consensus. The latter was reached after years of controversy and discussion between many groups of society, for example science, industry, trade unions, associations, administration, and representatives of politics and parliaments. Such debates are necessary in order to recognise problems, neglected aspects and disadvantages, so that after such a clarifying process, a common basis for action can be reached. Only after a consensus has been found between such groupings can one hope that most of the population will generally support such important legislation.

Economist: I should like to substantiate your argument. The 1986 Nobel Laureate in Economics, James Buchanan (Buchanan and Tullock, 1962) expounded that constitutions, and likewise changes of them, should, from the viewpoint of political economy, be passed (almost) unanimously, i.e. by consensus. To explain intuitively the rationale of their approach, consider children who want to play soccer. They will only be able to begin the game after having reached unanimous agreement concerning the rules of the game.

Environmental laws are essential changes of the legal structure of a society because they have important consequences for the allocation of resources and the distribution of wealth and income. They, therefore, are similar to constitutional changes. It is no wonder that it often takes many years to pass them.

Ecologist: I have learned from the discussion that the all-or-nothing attitude may even be counter-productive for the solution of environmental problems. But I still remain sceptical towards the modified optimism of the *Economist's* position. If at night a house is burning, is it then reasonable to wake people up in order to discuss with them how the fire should be fought? Before a consensus is reached it is too late to save it. To state it less polemically, I maintain we do not have enough time to wait for a consensus.

Further, isn't it so that we, the ecologists, were the first to give up the consensus that modern human's treatment of the environment raises no problems? Just by leaving this consensus, by demonstrative actions which were often at the legal borderline, and sometimes even beyond it (think of Greenpeace) we laid the very foundations for a search for a new consensus. As a matter of fact, the demand to change important things only by consensus favours the status quo, and this in turn prevents the necessary environmental measures from being taken.

Commentator: I may add that a strong tendency to maintain the status quo holds not only for economics, but also for politics and, to a considerable extent, for science. It is certainly a merit of the environmental movement that it has made humankind aware of the neglected inherent dangers of our way of life and initiated a major shift in politics. Moreover, the ecologists have been so convincing in arguing this, that a number of economists now consider environmental quality to be a 'merit good' (e.g.

James et al., 1978; Siebert, 1987:62-63). That means, environmental quality cannot be decided by reference to individual valuations alone.

And may I add further that, despite the differences in opinion, we can presumably agree on one issue: even though nature cannot truly be priced, prices do regulate our economies. If this is so, then this price mechanism should be used as far as possible for the conservation of nature. But somehow I feel that this will only be a first step.

Beyond that, I am afraid we have come to a dead-end in our dialogue between the *Economist* and the *Ecologist*. It seems therefore appropriate to ask the *Writer*, who has listened silently up to now, if he can mediate between the two parties.

4.6   GOETHE'S FAUST

Writer: Hearing your differing viewpoints I see us all playing a *drama*. One might call it 'the drama of modern humans and nature'. We, the actors in this drama, may have some influence on how the play will end. But apparently, we do not know the roles we play in this drama, and although we all attempt to contribute to a happy outcome, it might be that we end in tragedy.

It is just for this reason that we should try to understand which roles we play in this drama of modern humans and nature, before we decide how to behave and which actions to pursue. In this situation it seems to me helpful to turn to a completely different forum. To this end, I ask a person who is not involved in this discussion. It may be surprising that I consider a poet to be an apt adviser. This is so since a poet's task, at least as I see it, is not to criticise, not to accuse, not to judge, but simply to observe and contemplate what he sees in the world, and to express this. He, therefore, does not teach us what should be, as do the *Economist* and the *Ecologist*, but simply attempts to show how reality is. As we are normally used to seeing reality filtered by our imagination and conceptualisation, the language of a poet often seems to be dark, obscure and difficult to understand. But if we pay careful attention to his words, we may learn quite often that it is not our view which is clear and the poet's view that is dark, but that the opposite is true. Frequently our conceptualisations, even if they are 'scientific', may obscure aspects of reality, and the poet may help us to see more clearly what the world is really like and how our attitudes and actions impinge on it.

As I perceive it, Goethe was such a poet who dealt with our fundamental problems in a truly visionary way. His vision is also based on thorough knowledge of political economy. Goethe was born shortly before the beginning of the industrial revolution. During his long life he always observed with keen interest its development and its dynamics (see e.g. Eckermann, 1948:599-600). Already in his youth he was interested in economics and had contacts with leading German economists. This remained so all his life, during which he studied English economists, in particular Adam Smith. He had not only theoretical but also practical knowledge, because of his activity as a high-level administrator *(Geheimer Rat)* for economic policy, taxes and finance at the court of the Duke of Weimar (for a detailed account see Binswanger 1985:147-171). For us who live in this dynamically evolving time, and are so much confronted with its environmental consequences, his insights are perhaps of more relevance than ever before.

The poetic fruit of his occupation with economic questions is most clearly expressed in his drama Faust (Goethe, 1879, 1908), in particular in the Second Part. Faust is the prototype of the modern human, for whom, in the sense of Faust, God is dead (cf. Nietzsche); the hereafter is only an imaginary product of human fantasies, wishes and hopes (cf. Feuerbach); the Earth and its life is not a divine creation, nor is there any longer a harmony in itself, but only as an accidental result of natural laws which have been, or will be, discovered by science (Faber and Manstetten, 1988:101-104). This kind of attitude has led Faust, the prototype of the modern human, to take the place of the creator (cf. Chapter 3). This in turn has implied that life in this world has to take the place of eternity, and the present Earth the place of the Kingdom of God. However, humans can only be creator if, through action, driven by the longing to realise eternity in their own lives, they can shape and form the equivalent of the Kingdom of God on earth by their own will.

Since for modern humans there exists no transcendental life, all promises of religion for the hereafter have to be fulfilled in the present life. So the Faustian human employs the forces and potentialities of nature to pursue the aim to find, using a phrase of Keynes (1963:373), 'economic bliss'. Let me first point out some important traits of Faust, and then explain their relevance to your arguments concerning the economy and the environment.

Not believing in God and eternal life, fed up with philosophy and theology, Faust suffers from a present that never offers real satisfaction; he longs to experience a moment in which he could say: 'Verweile doch! du bist so schön' ('Tarry! So fair you art!') (Part I, study). Finding this moment would mean for Faust boundless fulfilment of all his longings, and therefore complete happiness, and thus he would feel like a god. This would enable him to abandon the course of time and to experience a moment in which he feels neither hope nor fear, neither desire nor remorse, such that future and past are done away with; in this state nothing could disturb his enjoyment of the present. To reach it he is willing to give up everything, even his further life in this world, as well as salvation after death:

> *Der Erdenkreis ist mir genug bekannt,*
> *Nach drüben ist die Aussicht uns verrannt ...*

> *(The round of earth enough I know, and barred,*
> *Is unto man the prospect yonderward.)*
> (Part 2, Act 5)

In his striving, not only does Faust utilise all his own powers, but also he utilises the forces of hell, as represented by Mephisto, by employing alchemical knowledge and magic. Mephisto tries to show Faust that very moment for which he yearns, by leading him through various stages: first love, second science and third beauty and art. But neither love nor the scientific dream of making an artificial human, nor the timeless beauty of art, grant him this moment. Finally, however, it seems that Faust finds this moment with Mephisto's help in economic activity, which takes science into its service and replaces beauty by utility. Faust expresses this in a *vision which is based on economic and technical activity*.

4.6.1   Faust and Modern Economics

Since this vision is of central importance for understanding the dynamics of modern economies, I shall describe it briefly. Faust, being half a prince and half an entrepreneur, has drained and cultivated an infertile stretch of coast, and protected it against the sea by a complicated system of dykes. Only one marsh is left which threatens the new land. While calling for labourers to drain this marsh, Faust has the vision that he opens 'room for millions there' who will follow his way of life: fighting against an 'aimless' nature (symbolised by the sea with its tides) day by day, they will progressively enlarge their living space, in which the natural environment is increasingly made usable for human life and human wishes. Thus they will try to change the earth into a paradise and live in liberty:

> *Nur der verdient sich Freiheit wie das Leben,*
> *Der täglich sie erobern muß.*

> *(For liberty, as life alone deserveth,*
> *He daily that must conquer it.)*
> (Part 2, Act 5)

This vision of unstoppable technical progress and infinite economic growth implies that humankind, following the Faustian way, can be the creator of his living space, in which the natural environment and the forces of nature are made increasingly usable for human purposes. Also this vision seems to enable humankind to free itself from the course of time.

However, in order to implement such an overwhelming economic vision, several economic measures have first to be carried through. This in turn implies that many old social and economic institutions have to be partly abolished and partly changed, and also new institutions have to be invented and innovated.

A summary of this development, which Goethe describes in detail in Acts 1, 4 and 5 of Part 2 of Faust, comprises the following stages: (1) the replacement of the old natural economy, which was self-sustaining or based on exchange, by the modern money economy; (2) this made it possible to replace alchemistic attempts at making gold by the intro-duction of paper money invented by Mephisto (Binswanger, 1985:24); (3) the creation of paper money enables Faust to employ the following approach. Although the land he received from the emperor is valueless in its present form, he is able to employ workers by paying them their wages with paper money. This money is covered by the promise of the future returns from the drainage of the respective coastal strip, i.e. by the work of the workers. It is important to note, however, that Faust's kind of growing economy can only be sustained if this promise is kept; i.e. the projects of the past to utilise the resources of the environment have really to be carried through in the present, in order to pay back the credits of the past, which were used to pay the wages of the past for these projects. With new land, and in particular with technical progress available, this kind of procedure can conceptually be repeated indefi-nitely.

It is precisely this last aspect of Faust's vision, i.e. its infinite perspective of economic activity, which gives him the 'highest moment'; it is in this sense that time has been vanquished for modern humans. In a never-ending process, humankind is able to convert resources of nature into capital goods, which are utilised for the satisfaction of individuals.

To explain how these considerations relate to present today economic reality, it is helpful to ask the following two questions: (1) what is the significance of Faust's 'highest moment'? (2) What are the implications of Faust's vision for the understanding of modern economies and their long-run, often unintended, consequences for humankind and the envi-ronment?

To answer question (1): in Faust's view of the 'highest moment', economic activity offers to humankind the possibility to be the creator of its own world. In this 'creation' the vision of a completely 'humanised nature' will be increasingly realised. Faust's vision is shared by economists like Marx and Keynes. Thus the young Marx (1968:57-58) states that, particularly by human economic activity 'erscheint die Natur als sein Werk und seine Wirklichkei' ('nature appears as his work and his reality'; our translation), if he 'sich selbst in einer von ihm geschaffenen Welt anschaut' ('contemplates himself in a world created by himself'). Humans as creators of a world which is humanised by economic activity may be inclined to feel like God, of whom it is written in the Bible: 'God saw all his deeds and saw that it was very good' (Genesis 1, Chapter 1).

This perspective is fascinating: unlike all other periods, modern humans seem to have the possibility of being the creator of their own world, of their own freedom and happiness, independent from the will and the plans of a transcendent god. The economy as a creation of humankind:

> *exercises a tremendous fascination. It is the fascination of infinite growth, of eternal progress. The economy thus gains the transcendental, i.e. across the border character, which the human beings sought in religion in earlier times. Not the belief, but economic activity opens for man the outlook to infinity.* (Binswanger, 1985:61)

A great part of modern thought is pervaded by this kind of fascination; for example Keynes (1963:373) wrote:

> *The pace at which we can reach our destination of economic bliss will be governed by four things - our power to control population, our determination to avoid wars and civil dissensions, and our willingness to entrust science to the direction of those matters which are properly the concern of science, and the rate of accumulation as fixed by the margin between our production and our consumption; of which the last will look easily after itself, given the first three.*

I believe that it is just the dynamics of the Faustian kind of economic activity which determines the pace of the present development of the world economy. Science and its application, in the form of technical progress, allow for tremendous economic growth. In this view, nature in general, and the environment in particular, is reduced to factors of production to achieve this growth. The restriction which time holds over human life seems to be erased; thus time is reduced to only one function, namely to the future as the space where economic growth takes place. If this attitude is rigorously applied, there remains no room for religion, for a transcendental life, as well as for the awareness of nature as a creation of God, or an end in itself.

We should, however, be aware that all of us who use electric light, who watch TV, work with a PC, drive cars, and believe in progress, take part in this Faustian dynamic economy, which offers so many new useful things day by day. This dynamic promises us to make our lives easier and more comfortable, and come a little bit closer to the realisation of paradise.

To move to question (2): but Goethe points clearly and emphatically to the problems which arise from the Faustian vision of a human-made world, creating its own economy in terms of money and technology. We will treat them now in turn.

a) Modern humans lose their sense of the beauty of nature, which is a beauty for its own sake. Nature in its original form may be regarded as beautiful in the way Angelus Silesius describes the rose:

> *Die Ros' blüht ohn Warum. Sie blühet, weil sie blühet.*
> *Sie acht' nicht ihrer selbst, fragt nicht, ob man sie siehet.*

> *(The rose blooms without reason. It blooms, because it blooms.*
> *It doesn't care for itself, doesn't ask if it is viewed.)*
> (Our translation)

Faust behaves very much in contrast to this attitude. Seeing the wide and beautiful sea and the everlasting alternation of the tides, Faust exclaims:

> *Da herrschet Well' auf Welle kraftbegeistet,*
> *Zieht sich zurück, und es ist nichts geleistet,*
> *Was zur Verzweiflung mich beängstigen könnte!*
> *Zwecklose Kraft unbändiger Elemente!*

> *(Pregnant with might, wave upon waves there reigneth,*
> *Yet each retires, nor any end attaineth.*
> *Me to despair it doth disquiet truly,*
> *This aimless might of elements unruly.)*
> (Part 2, Act 4)

Nature in itself is considered as aimless, without any end; this view makes modern humans despair, except if they act like Faust: 'Hier möcht ich kämpfen ...' ('Here would I battle ...'). In a Faustian economy, where always the question 'wherefore?' is asked, there is no place for beauty for its own sake.

b) In the same vein Faust does not have a sense of the beauty of humankind living in harmony with nature. This is clearly revealed by his behaviour towards Philemon and Baucis, who are the representatives of the old social and economic system, which is self-sustaining and stationary.

The hut of the old couple, Philemon and Baucis, is located in the neighbourhood of Faust's palace. They believe in god and practise the traditional religion in their small chapel beside their hut. They live in unity with themselves and their world; though they are poor, they lack nothing and even have enough to be hospitable to strangers.

Although they are not willing to be labourers in Faust's project, they are keen observers of it. While they see that the new land may appear to be a paradise, Baucis emphasises that its development is paid for dearly by the sacrifice of human life. She realises that Faust is godless and that he wants to take away their living space. The beauty of the latter is described by the wanderer, who comes to the old couple in order to thank them for their former hospitality:

> *Ja! sie sinds, die dunkeln Linden,*
> *Dort, in ihres Alters Kraft.*
> *Und ich soll sie wieder finden*
> *Nach so langer Wanderschaft!*
> *Ist es doch die alte Stelle,*
> *Jene Hütte, die mich barg,*
> *Als die sturmerregte Welle*
> *Mich an jene Dünen warf!*
>
> *(Aye, 'tis they, the lindens gloomy,*
> *Yonder in their lusty age*
> *That again appear unto me*
> *After lengthy pilgrimage.*
> *'Tis the place where lay my pillow,*
> *'Tis the hut that harboured me,*
> *When on yonder dunes the billow*
> *Hurled me from the storm-tossed sea.)*
> (Part 2, Act 5)

However, Faust does not like this beauty, because he did not create it and does not own it. For this reason he cannot transform it in accordance with his wishes. He wants to build a look-out tower from where he would be able:

Zu überschaun mit einem Blick
Des Menschengeistes Meisterstück,
Betätigend mit klugem Sinn
Der Völker breiten Wohngewinn

(To gaze on all that I have done,
And in one glance to compass it,
This masterpiece of human-wit,
Confirming with sagacious plan
The dwelling place we claim for man.)
(Part 2, Act 5)

The place where Faust wants 'to gaze into infinity' is just the place which is occupied by the chapel of the old couple. The ringing of its bell particularly annoys Faust, as Mephisto remarks:

Und das verfluchte Bim-Baum-Bimmel,
Umnebelnd heitern Abendhimmel,
Mischt sich in jegliches Begebniß
Vom ersten Bad bis zum Begräbnis,
Als wäre zwischen Bim und Baum
Das Leben ein verschollner Traum.

(And the accursed ding-dong-belling,
Evening's sky with vapour veiling,
In each event, or sad or merry all,
Mingles from the first bath to burial,
As life twixt ding and dong did seem
A shadowy, forgotten dream.)
(Ibid.)

Since the old couple is not willing to accept Faust's offer to exchange their property for 'a pleasant homestead' in the newly created land, he asks Mephisto to use his power to realise this barter. In carrying out this demand Mephisto burns down the hut, the chapel and the trees. Philemon and Baucis die from fright and the wanderer is killed. Hearing of this Faust remarks: 'Tausch wollt' ich, wollte keinen Raub' ('Exchange I wished, not robbery') (ibid.).

Obviously there did not exist an equivalent for this very world, not only in the eyes of Philemon and Baucis but also in Goethe's eyes. This world is not created by men, but humankind is only part of it and his/her activity merely sustains it and cares for it. In this respect it is directly opposed to the Faustian economy. While the essential trait of the latter is that the values of all things are determined by their utility for the fulfilment of human wishes, in the former the order of all elements of nature has its own sense and meaning, and humankind acts in harmony with this order.

The narrative about Philemon and Baucis should not be interpreted as a transfiguration of past times. Instead, we may look at it as a utopia of a world which cannot coexist with the Faustian economy, which tries to destroy such worlds and also to hinder its coming into being in the future. It is of this utopia that Lynceus, Faust's tower-warder, exclaims: 'Es war doch so schön!' ('So fair hath it been') (ibid.).

c) The vision of unstoppable progress lets modern humans forget their mortality. While Faust, dreadfully blinded, believes that he is hearing the noise of the labourers working on a new ditch, a noise which initiates his great vision and therefore makes him feel completely satisfied, Mephisto comments plainly:

> *Man spricht, wie man mir Nachricht gab,*
> *Von keinem Graben, doch vom - Grab.*

> *(They talk - such news to me they gave -*
> *Not of a groove, but of a grave.)*
> (Part 2, Act 5)

d) The freedom which Faust strives for lies always in the future, never in the present. While Faust has the vision of the 'free people', the spectator recognises at the same time the presence of 'Lemures', which Mephisto characterises as: 'Aus Bändern, Sehnen und Gebein/Geflickte Halbnaturen!' ('Patched up of sinew, bone and skin / Natures but half appointed'). With this allusion Goethe hints at the one-sidedness of labour in modern economies. But the entrepreneur cannot enjoy his freedom either. To put it into the context of the Faust drama, we see that the construction of the dyke system promises economic riches and the prospect of seemingly permanent growth, but it is also associated with sorrows and anxiety. These arise from the danger that the basis for these very riches, and even the life of humankind, may be destroyed by the forces of nature; even if Faust suppresses this danger, it is nevertheless always present. Thus the devil may say:

> *In jeder Art seid ihr verloren; -*
> *Die Elemente sind mit uns verschworen,*
> *Und auf Vernichtung läuft's hinaus.*

> *(Lost are ye, lost in every manner!*
> *The elements are leagued beneath our banner,*
> *And all in nothing still must end.)*
> (Part 2, Act 5)

The present, therefore, is always endangered by the uncertainty of the future. This future is the dark shadow of that other future which promised infinite progress and growth. To illustrate this, Goethe introduces the figure of 'Care'. The Faustian economy has made humankind suppress 'Want', 'Guilt' and 'Need', so that Goethe (Part 2, Act 5) can let 'Care' say to her three sisters: 'Ihr Schwestern, ihr könnt nicht und dürft nicht hinein' ('Ye Sisters, ye cannot, ye may not fare in'). But modern humans cannot escape 'Care', who continues her statement: 'Die Sorge, sie schleicht sich durchs Schlüsselloch ein'. ('But Care through the key-hole slips stealthily in'). Behind the veil of optimism of infinite progress, modern men cannot overhear 'Care's' message:

> *Wen ich einmal mir besitze,*
> *Dem ist alle Welt nichts nütze,*
>
> ...
>
> *Ist der Zukunft nur gewärtig,*
> *Und so wird er niemals fertig.*
>
> *(Whom I make my own, with loathing*
> *Counts the whole wide world as nothing.*
>
> ...
>
> *On the Future ever waiteth,*
> *So that naught he consumateth.)*
> (Part 2, Act 5)

The present is always endangered by the uncertainty of the future, not only because of unpredictable market forces and the forces of nature, but also because of the sorrows deep in the hearts of men.

From where do the five problems I have mentioned arise? Goethe's answer may cause surprise. Life of modern humankind depends on a certain kind of magic, from which it is unable to free himself:

> *Könnt ich Magie von meinem Pfad entfernen,*
> *Die Zaubersprüche ganz und gar verlernen,*
> *Stünd ich, Natur! vor dir ein Mann allein,*
> *Da wärs der Mühe wert, ein Mensch zu sein.*
>
> *(Could I but from my path all magic banish,*
> *Bid every spell into oblivion vanish,*
> *And stand mere man before thee, Nature! Then*
> *'Twere worth the while to be a man with men.)*
> (Part 2, Act 5).

4.6.2 Commentary and Debate

Economist: I don't understand you. What does magic mean for modern humans? Hasn't magic been substituted by science and technology in modern times? Modern science and technology have enabled people to transform elements of the earth into such things as aeroplanes and televisions, which were inconceivable in earlier times. In my opinion the old magic dream has been far surpassed by modern humans. This has enabled humankind to gain security and welfare in four respects: (i) Protection against natural disasters, (ii) provision of plenty of food, (iii) protection against diseases and (iv) delegation of human labour to machines.

Writer: You are right. Obviously modern humanhind acts like a very successful magician, who is able to change completely the face of the earth and the human way of life, by technology and economics. But in my eyes modern humans are bewitched by their own power. They do not know from where this power comes, nor in which way it could be employed to support the development of life as a whole. As Goethe believed, the essence of all things, as well as the essence of humankind's power and creativity, is derived from the eternal creative principle of Nature. When Faust acts like a creator, he owes all his creativity only to the creative principle of Nature. But this aspect is completely neglected by Faust, in the same way as questions about the essence and the significance of human power are neglected in the mainstream of modern thinking. Thus modern humans acts as the 'Zauberlehrling' (magician's apprentice) of Goethe's ballad. The apprentice knows how the things function, but does not know why. Thus the Zauberlehrling is able to make the broom carry the water into the bath, but he is unable to stop it again, and therefore must confess: 'I called the ghosts but can't get rid of them!'. I think that many environmental problems, such as forest death, the ozone problem and the CO_2 problem, occur because modern humans have the same attitude as the 'Zauberlehrling'.

To summarise my interpretation of Faust: the example of Faust demonstrates that the religious striving to reach the Kingdom of God has been transferred into the restless dynamics of economic life. And it is this dynamics which lies behind many problems concerning the environment. I believe that almost all of humankind is more or less seized by these dynamics.

Ecologist: I object. This does not hold true for the ecologists. We are the ones who oppose this attitude.

Writer: I am afraid that just like most of the economists, most of you do not have a real understanding of the Faustian dynamics. Even those of you who have a certain hunch about it always believe it is the dynamics of the others. They overlook that it is their *own* dynamics, too. Therefore, ecologists who criticise Faustian activities often do not realise that their own approach has Faustian traits. Some of them reject participation in the common search for solutions, because they maintain that first it is necessary to abolish the market system. But how will they proceed if this aim is realised? Will they not try to *create* thereafter a new world in the *same spirit* as Faust *created* his world? Those economists who make active contributions do not easily escape this Faustian dynamics. For their proposals depend heavily on an implicit hope in technological solutions for environmental problems. Many of them have in common that they over-value human possibilities and believe that humans alone can determine the fate of the world, for better or worse.

Economist, Ecologist (Chorus): *Writer*, do you have a solution?

Writer: No. But above all, an essential prerequisite for a solution of our many problems is, to recognise, just as a poet does, what we do and what we really are, and how deeply we are involved in the growth dynamics of the Faustian economy. As long as the human soul is torn in a Faustian way, there will exist a rift between humankind and nature. This rift expresses itself in our present environmental problems.

Nevertheless, I believe that all of us, in particular both of you, *Economist* and *Ecologist*, have to continue in your efforts and to proceed further in your searches for new solutions. An important part of this process will be to listen to each other.

NOTES

1. A solution is Pareto-optimal, if it is impossible to make one person better off without making any other worse off.
2. How differently boundary conditions are treated by different economic approaches such as the neoclassical, Austrian subjectivist, evolutionary or neo-Keynsian one, is examined in Faber and Proops (1989).
3. This statement can be illustrated by an observation of Roberts (1974:28) who noted in his description of the political economy of the American water law legislation in the seventies: 'There was a wide-spread failure of communication as to assumption and perspective. Economists habitually talked about worlds in which all resources were mobile ... Practical men knew of course that real facilities took years to construct and could not generally be transformed to other uses. Economists tended to argue in terms of comparative-static models with a given technology and certain waste loads.'

4. See, however, the seminal paper by Arrow (1968). For recent discussion of the consideration of irreversibility in economic analysis see Freeman (1984), Ayres and Sandilya (1987) and Faber and Proops (1986, 1989, 1993a).
5. An economist might at first sight object that these environmental goods had already been recognised as free goods and have no price only because of their public good character. However, an ecologist might then point out that in many cases the environmental problem is caused by the circumstance that one has not been aware of the fact that there has existed a corresponding environmental good at all, as in the case of dioxins.

5. Sustainable Development: The Roles of Science and Ethics

with Frank Jöst

5.1   INTRODUCTION

Continuing environmental pollution and destruction have led to a debate on the re-orientation of economic activity. The key concepts in this discussion are 'sustainable development' and 'sustainability'. Instead of contributing to clear understanding and new aims, this debate has more often than not lead to a confusion of the issue. The following quotation seems to us succinctly to characterise the present state of the debate on 'sustainability':

For what is sustainable development? Who can readily and briefly explain this? But what in discourse do we mention more familiarly and knowingly, than sustainable development. And, we understand, when we speak of it; we understand also, when we hear it spoken by another. What then is sustainable development? I know well enough what it is, provided that nobody asks me; but if I am asked what it is and try to explain it, I am baffled.

These sentences were written by Augustine (1961:264), on the difficulties of understanding 'time'. However, in this often quoted statement, we have written 'sustainable development' wherever Augustine used the word 'time'. We believe that in this modified quotation the causes for the difficulties of the present debate on sustainability become evident. Many of us have a clear intuition concerning the problem which is described by 'sustainability'. Formulations such as 'we cannot go on with our economic activities as up to now, because we would endanger the basis of our living' express such an appreciation of the difficulties. However, they do not give us any hint as to how to find a way towards sustainable development, because we still do not know how to define sustainability in a really encompassing manner.

In the following we shall ask the question: 'Why, within the framework of the present debate, is it so difficult, if not impossible, to develop operational proposals for a 'sustainable economy'?' We shall further attempt to clarify the scientific, political and ethical dimensions which are behind the concept of sustainability. In this way we shall try to offer a structure which enables one to analyse problems in the field of sustainability in a more appropriate manner.

5.2   ON THE HISTORY OF THE CONCEPT OF SUSTAINABILITY

In Autumn 1983, at its 38th meeting, the General Assembly of the United Nations decided on the foundation of a Commission for Environment and Development. In Autumn 1987, at the 42nd meeting of the UN General Assembly, the final report of this commission was presented, with the title *Our Common Future* (popularly known as the 'Brundtland Report', after its chair-person). It was in this report that the need for 'sustainable development' was formulated for the current and future generations. By 'sustainable development' was meant the satisfaction of the wants of the present generation, in such a way that the satisfaction of the wants of future generations would not be impaired (WCED, 1987b:43).

This demand contained a new concept of economic development. This becomes evident when one examines the notion of 'sustainable development' more closely. For instance, in the beginning this concept was translated literally into German (WCED, 1987a:46). However, this expression was soon replaced within the German speaking area by 'lasting development' ('nachhaltige Entwicklung') or 'lastingness' (Nachhaltigkeit). The latter two concepts are taken from forestry science. There one speaks of a 'lasting development' if no more trees are taken from a forest during a period than grow in that period. It is no conceptual problem to apply this notion from forestry science to other renewable resources. Thus, one may use it for a 'lasting fishery', as well as for a 'lasting agriculture'. However, much greater, perhaps insurmountable, difficulties arise when one tries to apply the concept of sustainability to all resources which are presently used. In a first approximation one might say that resources may be employed only up to their regeneration capacities. But here, of course, immediately the question occurs, how shall one deal with non-renewable resources?

When today one talks of sustainable development in reference to the Brundtland Report, one applies it not only to the problems of natural resource use, but also to environmental issues. In this case, however, one has to examine what it means when one speaks of a sustainable management of the environment. In this connection one may say: within the framework of sustainable development one may only discharge emissions of any kind into the environment up to the extent of nature's capacity to deal with such pollutants.

5.3   THE CONCEPTUAL BASIS FOR SUSTAINABLE DEVELOPMENT

When one speaks of sustainability, one is not concerned with the conservation of an existing and unfolding nature, but with the long-run preservation of an economy, which is essentially dependent on the use of natural resources and the environment as a receiver of its discharges of productive and consumptive activities. It is in this sense that the Brundtland Report (WCED, 1987b:43-44) notes:

> *The satisfaction of human needs and aspirations is the major objective of development ... Sustainable development requires meeting the basic needs of all and extending to all the opportunity to satisfy their aspirations for better life.*

The idea of a sustainable development therefore has in common with the traditional economic theory that its reference point is the satisfaction of human wants. In contrast to many other theories of economic activity, it requires explicitly that the long-run preservation of a material basis for the satisfaction of human wants is taken into account. Hence, sustainable development exists only if the fulfilment of necessities and wants of humans is also possible, in a future whose nature is unknown. All action in the present which impairs this possibility, or even destroys it, is not sustainable. In this vein, Solow (1992:7) says:

> *If 'sustainability' is anything more than a slogan or expression of emotion, it must amount to an injunction to preserve productive capacity for the infinite future.*

In this connection it is important to note that, in present debates on sustainable development, one often encounters the idea of a far-reaching preservation of nature in general. This idea, however, does not correspond directly to the content of the concept of sustainability as it is derived from the Brundtland Report, and also from our considerations above. For within the latter framework, nature is only considered insofar as it is required for the fulfilment of present, and future, human wants.

These reflections lead us to conclude that the idea of sustainability is not primarily ecological, but rather economic. This result is certainly not satisfying from a radically ecological point of view. For if it is true, then it is not possible to establish rights for nature from the idea of sustainability.[1] The advantage of an idea of sustainability which is restricted in this way, however, is that it opens at least the prospect of developing concepts of sustainable development which are *operational*. This is so because the restriction to a purely economic perspective enables one to formulate that part of the problem which all concepts of sustainability try to solve within a simple question:

> *To what extent is the use of natural resources and the environment possible, if our economy is to exist in the very long-run?*

This question can give orientation as to how one can formulate models of a sustainable economy. But here one has to ask, what conceptual foundations exist for such models? We see two ways to answer this question. The first is based on science, and the second on human will.

The first way employs scientific results and insights concerning the carrying capacity of the Earth. Employing scientific results, and insights on ecological and economic systems, one formulates technical and political indications on how to act. These instructions in turn could form the framework for the sustainable development of the economy.

The second way has its starting point in ethical considerations. It presupposes that human norms and forms of behaviour must fundamentally change in the long-run in our present Western economies, in order for humans to live and to be able to act in an economic manner on the earth over a long period. A prerequisite for such a change is a decisive will, which is also able to articulate itself.

The two ways are not contradictory; however, from a methodological point of view it is useful first to consider them separately. We therefore deal first with the scientific-technical-economic way and then with the ethical way.

5.3.1 Sustainability as a Scientific-Technical-Economic Concept: Substitution or Preservation

Models of sustainable developments which are available in the literature so far can be differentiated according to the extent to which there are substitution possibilities between natural resources and human manufactured productive capabilities. We can distinguish two polar forms of models; strongly simplifying, we shall call them the 'optimistic' and the 'pessimistic' perspectives on sustainability. The optimists assume that for all, or at least for all economically relevant, indispensable functions of nature (as supplier of natural resources or receiver of emissions) there exist suitable possibilities of substitution. This assumption implies that the optimists can presuppose an indefinite time horizon for the economy.

Without this minimal degree of optimism, the conclusion might be that this economy is like a watch that can be wound only once: it has only a finite number of ticks, after which it stops (Solow, 1992:9).

It is just this hypothesis on non-substitution, that economic activity by humans is so dependent on nature as its basis that it has only a finitely limited horizon, which is rejected by Solow. This is supposed by the pessimists, for they do question the possibilities of substitution for essential resources and environmental discharge capacities. From their point of view it follows immediately that, if one is interested in sustainable development, one will use nature as little as possible, in order to exist as long as possible. We note that both extreme versions, the optimist as well as the pessimist, may contain accurate insights. Hence, one has to examine from case to case, whether the optimist or pessimist position is applicable.

Each of the two positions may be assigned to an area within which it appears to be plausible. The optimists could be right concerning natural resources, while the pessimists could be right concerning environmental discharge capacities, where substitution may not even be conceivable. An example of the latter is thermal pollution, which is a necessary by-product not only of production and consumption but also of environmental protection activities, because of the First and Second Law of thermodynamics (cf. Faber, Niemes and Stephan, 1987:103; Kümmel, 1980:110-111).

Concerning natural resources, the optimists can refer to historical experience. At least Western societies have coped successfully with the resource problem in the past. For example, the scarcity of wood in England in the 18th century was an incentive to substitute the scarce resource wood by the plentifully available coal. This led to many other inventions and innovations, such as the steam engine, which, in turn, made possible many other inventions and innovations. Resource scarcity thus led to the discovery of new resources and technical progress (cf. Faber and Proops, 1993a:Chapters 3, 6, 8, 12).

The opponents of the hypothesis of substitution can refer to the fact that there do not yet exist any kinds of solutions concerning many environmental problems. Most of the technical solutions during the last two decades often imply that the pollutants are transferred from one environmental medium to another. For example, the paper industry solved its sewage problems by building water treatment plants, where large quantities of toxic sludge arose. This had to be either disposed of in special deposits, or burnt in special incineration plants. Thus the water pollution problem was transformed into a solid waste or air quality problem.

However, in many, perhaps even the decisive, cases, one will not be able to decide in advance whether the optimists or the pessimists will be right (cf. Chapter 11). Therefore, on the basis of our present knowledge, it is often a question of belief, whether one sides with the optimists or pessimists.

5.4   THE ECONOMISTS' APPROACH

If we want to derive concepts of sustainable developments for the whole economy, we must be able to decide whether the optimists or the pessimists will be right. To this end, it would be necessary to have at one's disposal the knowledge on all essential factors concerning nature and society which are relevant for the economy, for the present and the future. Only if this is the case, would one be able to derive exact statements concerning a sustainable economy.

Let us assume that this is possible. How could these statements be found and implemented? As a concrete example we take the use of fossil fuel and its consequences for the environment, in particular for the climate (cf. Chapter 14, and Proops, Faber and Wagenhals, 1993). Assuming that all relevant data and relationships are known, one can imagine the following progression.

The geologists ascertain in what amounts oil, coal and gas are available on the earth. Ecologists and climate researchers determine to what extent fossil fuel may be burnt, such that only minor climate changes occur and that the global ecosystem is able to adjust gradually. The engineers indicate which techniques are available for burning fossil fuels at present, and which technologies for saving energy and using it will be possible in the future. This will enable scientists and economists to ascertain when it is necessary to substitute non-renewable resources by renewable ones. On the basis of this information, the politicians and administrators can determine, through a discourse with the scientists and economists, the limits for the emissions of trace gases. Then they will decide from case to case whether regulatory laws (emission limits or emission targets) or economic instruments (emission taxes, emission charges or tradeable emission permits) should be employed. Within these limits, and the corresponding regulatory framework, the economic agents can decide about their own plans. By doing this they can be sure that their individual behaviour will not imply harmful effects on the availability of resources or the environment. Behaving in this manner they even take responsibility for future generations.

We have illustrated how natural scientists, engineers and economists could attempt to formulate sustainable developments for the case of the use of fossil energy. Before we proceed to discuss the limits of this procedure in the next section, we wish to describe to what extent, and how, during the last two decades, environmental and resource economists have been able to derive methods to generalise this approach such that it can be applied to the whole economy. Their main indicator for sustainability is a correspondingly revised version of gross domestic product (GDP). For this revision they use the theories of external effects and of public goods. Both concern the existence of so-called market failures in market economies. These failures can be repaired by adjusting the price system, e.g. by introducing prices for environmental goods such as water, air and landscape (e.g. Mäler, 1974; Dasgupta, 1982). Employing the economic theory of exhaustible resources (Hartwick and Olewiler, 1986; Faber, Niemes and Stephan, 1987), resource prices can also be increased in such a way that they reflect, under certain crucial assumptions, approximately their intertemporal scarcity, including that of future generations.

Using these two building blocks and, in addition, the theory of capital (which is the economist's instrument to deal with time, and in particular with the future) one can supplement the framework of national accounting, such that the appropriate valuations of the flows of extracted resources and of environmental degradation of nature because of pollution can be taken care of in the gross domestic product (Peskin, 1976; Costanza, 1991; Solow, 1992; Pearce and Atkinson, 1993). To this end it is necessary to adjust the intertemporal price system considerably, because one needs to include in its computation all present and future supplies of resources, the environmental capacity for discharging emissions and degradation of pollutants, as well as labour and capital goods (the latter implies that assumptions on technical progress have to be made), and the demand of present and future generations (Dasgupta and Heal, 1969; El Serafy, 1991; Faber and Proops, 1991b, 1991c, 1993b).

However, employing a highly aggregated measure such as gross domestic product implies that the economists' approach depends heavily on the assumption of substitution between the factors of production in the form of labour, capital goods, natural non-renewable and renewable resources, environmental capacity to degrade pollution, the existence of various species, as well as the amenities of landscapes. This, in turn, implies that the economists, almost by profession, belong to the group of optimists. In defence of the economists' view Solow (1992:22) pointed out:

> ... *there is a lot to be gained by transforming questions of yes-or-no into questions of more-or-less. Yes-or-no lends itself to stalemate and confrontation, more-or-less lends itself to trade-offs. The trick is to understand more of what and less of what.*

A further advantage of the economists' approach of using the adjusted gross national product (and its components, as well as differences between different years) as a measuring rod, is that it can easily be used to inform the public in general, and politicians and administrators in particular. This, in turn, may help:

> ... *the clarity brought to the idea of sustainability by this approach could lift the policy debate to a more pragmatic, less emotional level* (Solow, 1992:19).

In the following we shall cite Solow's (1992) paper often, because we consider it to be one of the best contributions by an economist to the debate on sustainability. In addition, Solow's contribution is rather representative of the main paradigm of economics, i.e. neoclassical economics. This is not only because he is a Nobel laureate, but also because he has made major contributions to the theory of capital and technical progress, as well as environmental and resource economics, three areas which are central for our theme.

5.4.1 Limits of the Scientific-Technical-Economic Concept of Sustainable Development

The reader should be aware that all models of sustainable development rest on strong assumptions; this holds particularly for those based on the neoclassical paradigm. We shall deal with three of these assumptions. The first concerns general aspects of time; the second relates to problems of complexity, uncertainty and ignorance; the third concerns difficulties of political implementation.

1. All such models presuppose that two essential questions concerning time have been answered. (i) One has to decide how many generations of resource use, and of degrading and discharge capacities of the environment, will be considered: i.e. the length of the time horizon has to be determined. (ii) Connected with this question is the problem of how much will the present generation sacrifice for future generations. This concerns the time preference of the society,

i.e. the social rate of discount. Both questions are, however, not scientific, but ethical ones. How difficult they are to answer, and how wide is the spectrum of their values, became evident when well known experts in this field gave their estimates for the social rate of discount concerning the evaluation of national energy options; they varied from 2 to 20 per cent (Lind, 1982:9)! Everyone familiar with long-run planning knows that this variation would imply completely different policy prescriptions. But only after these two decisions, concerning the length of the time horizon and the social rate of discount, have been made, is it possible to develop models of sustainable development.

2. As noted above, in our illustration on the sustainable use of fossil fuel, natural scientists, engineers and economists have to combine their knowledge to compute an optimal intertemporal price system which can serve as a guide for a sustainable development. This is a problem of tremendous inherent complexity.

This second problem becomes even more complex if we seek to take account of time-lags and intertemporal repercussions. Many types of damage to the environment become evident much later than their causes, as with the greenhouse effect. In particular, there exists much uncertainty and ignorance in respect of the magnitude, and even the nature, of such damage. From this it follows that we are unable to ascertain the limits to our behaviour which guarantee sustainability.

The case of the greenhouse effect demonstrates that, in contrast to resource problems, it will be very difficult, if not impossible, to find a scientific-technical-economic solution to pollution problems. This is because we are not yet, and perhaps never will be, able to limit the consequences of our production and consumption behaviour in space and time (Förstner, 1990:Chapter 12). Solutions to resource problems appear to be comparatively simpler than those concerning pollution, since one can then restrict oneself to relatively few parameters. In contrast, concerning environmental impacts one is confronted with many connected areas (cf. Chapter 10 and Faber and Proops, 1993a:Chapter 12). There is hardly any sector of the economy which has no direct or indirect effects on the environment, and often these are even of very special kinds. Therefore, to find sustainable solutions would imply either that there is no uncertainty and ignorance, or that one is omniscient (cf. Chapters 4 and 11).[2]

3. A further assumption for the application of scientific-technical-economic solutions is that the corresponding limits, contingencies, and behaviour of the individuals are taken account of in the political process, and these solutions are legally established. Of course, this is by no means an easy task, for it is not only conceivable but very likely that there would be noticeable constraints on the freedoms we are used to in Western societies, resulting from policies towards sustainable development. In addition, we know that such encompassing changes in the political, legal and economic frame-work lead to drastic alterations of the income and wealth distribution. We know from the theory of public choice that this would probably lead to social unrest, and could not be carried through politically in a democratic state. How difficult this is, even in a rather simple case, became evident in the recent negotiations on whaling. To this end, therefore, an 'omnipotent' state, in the sense of a world state, would be required.

These three comments on the nature of policies for sustainability may appear, at first sight, rather pessimistic. But we believe they *only* show that the *exclusive* perspective on science, technology and economics is too restricted. This perspective is neither appropriate, nor sufficient, for establishing sustainable developments. The urge to solve this problem solely by scientific, technical and economic means, is on the one hand presumptuous, while on the other hand it builds up a tremendous burden for all those who are charged with finding solutions. It is presumptuous because it supposes that scientists know everything, and technicians, economists, entrepreneurs, administrators and politicians can implement anything. It is burdening because it puts strain on all decision makers which they cannot possibly meet. The aspect of presumption reminds us of the ancient Greek notion of 'hubris'; it is possibly this attitude which has led Western economies into their present environmental and resource problems. As noted in Chapter 4, the experience that many important processes can be controlled has led to the belief that, in principle, all processes can be submitted to human management by means of science and technology. This attitude of overweening pride is the hubris of the Greek myths; for hubris means that humanity loses perspective and feels itself to be godlike.

Having dealt with the scientific-technical-economic concept of sustainability, and its limits, we turn now to the second way to tackle this problem. Here we will be mainly concerned with ethical considerations. We will call this the way of the will.

5.5 RULES FOR SUSTAINABLE ECONOMIES: LAWS OF NATURE OR DUTIES?

Solow (1992:15) emphasises that the insight into the necessity of sustainability of the economy imposes duties on us. The question concerning duties as the main connecting thread for human action belongs to the field of ethics. Duties thus have sense and meaning only if (i) they are *recognised* as such, and (ii) the *will* exists to satisfy them. This holds equally for those duties which follow from sustainability; they appeal to the will of each individual, as well as to the will of society, which is established through the political process.

Duties have a different status from laws of nature, because they (iii) presuppose *freedom* of action. Since this condition is very important, we shall illustrate it with an example. The law of falling bodies is a law of nature. It can be used to calculate with what amount of kinetic energy a human, who is standing on a precipice, would strike on the ground if s/he were to take one further step. But this law of nature does not say anything as to whether the human will take this step or not. Neither can it speak of whether s/he is or is not permitted to take this action. There exists no law of nature which will tell us, with any certainty, just what a human will do. What the person *is allowed to do*, can only be determined by a *norm*. Such a norm may say, for example, that humans are not allowed to kill themselves. But even if this norm is generally accepted as a duty, it is not excluded that, under certain circumstances, human kill themselves. We see that a law of nature can establish an if-then-relationship, and the duty can tell whether the 'if' *may* occur. Nevertheless, the human is free to decide to infringe the duty. As noted above under (iii), freedom belongs *always* to the essence of a duty. From this it immediately follows that there always exists the possibility that one can decide against the duty.

The relevance of this example becomes evident when we transfer it to the implementation of certain threshold values concerning the environment. Let the latter be determined by scientists, and let them be such that infringing them implies that sustainability is no longer possible in the long-run. Assume, further, that violating them is forbidden by law. This implies certain duties for every individual. The observance of the law depends, to a great extent, on the willingness of the individuals to be so constrained. Though individual breaking of this duty can be accepted, this is not possible if a great number of people are not willing to keep to the law. In such a case its obedience cannot be maintained, even by order of the police. From this it follows that the fulfilment of the duties derived from laws concerning threshold values is always fundamentally based on the will of the great majority of the people of a society.

Up to now we have dealt with the hypothetical case that scientists are able to determine the threshold values exactly. As shown above, however, in general this is not the case. Hence, there exists a very great range for political and individual decision-making. This is the case insofar as the decision concerning sustainable development always has an open, and therefore not scientifically safeguarded, aspect.

5.5.1 The Will Towards Sustainability: Fairness Between Present and Future Generations

It is evident that the will to achieve sustainability has to be a decisive one. It has to be the will to do right concerning the preservation of the foundations of life for future generations, and to avoid doing wrong. The will, to do the just thing and to avoid unjust actions, is called, in the philosophical tradition, the 'good will'. The one who acts according to a 'good will' and, in addition, with the right insight, acts justly. It is in this sense that the demand for a sustainable economy is a demand for justice, in a special sense. The content of the justice concerning sustainability is according to Toman (1992:4) 'fairness' between the present and future generations: '... intergenerational fairness is a key component of sustainability.' Redclift (1993:8) speaks similarly of 'intergenerational equity'.

This demand for 'fairness' or 'equity' seems to be reasonable. However, one immediately asks: what is 'fair' between succeeding generations? How can 'equity' between them be established? One answer to this question is provided by Solow (1992:15), who formulates the content of the 'duty' concerning sustainability:

> *The duty imposed by sustainability is to bequeath to posterity not any particular thing ... but rather to endow them with whatever it takes to achieve a standard of living at least as good as our own and to look after the next generation similarly.*

Almost all adherents of the idea of a sustainable development formulate similar criteria. The background for this is a conception of justice which goes back to Aristotle. Justice of exchange has to be orientated to equality: one may not give less than one has received (cf. Nicomachean Ethic V 7 1332 b 12-20). Although there is no direct exchange between present and future generations in a strict sense, one may say, in analogy to Aristotle: an economy is only sustainable if it lets the next generation have not less than it received from the former generation.

5.6   SUSTAINABILITY AND NON-SATIATION

We have explained the duty to sustainability. We will now give reasons why the content of this duty to sustainability is not sufficiently clear to derive an operational formulation. To this end, let us remember Solow's (1992:15) demand: future generations have to be provided with a standard of living that is as good as ours. Before we are able to fulfil this requirement we must, among other things, answer the following questions: how good is our present standard of living, and under what circumstances can a standard of living in the future be called as good as ours? Here we encounter all the difficulties mentioned above, when dealing with the economists' approach to using gross domestic product as a measuring rod. In addition, however, do we not also mean the *quality* of our way of life? And does it not belong to our standard of living that we strive always for more welfare, in the well-founded expectation that our standard of living will rise in the future? Would we not evaluate our standard of living much lower without such a prospect? Here a dynamic aspect enters the discussion, which is difficult to analyse, as we know from theories of intertemporal allocation and of uncertainty. As a response to this crucial question one may ask, however: is our standard of living really so good that we want to keep it, and to extend it, in the way we have done up to now? Are not the increasing problems of social disorder, violence, drugs, etc., consequences of the level of our present standard of living?

All of these questions do not immediately deal with the life of future generations, but rather with our present lives. In particular, the question of whether the expectation of steadily rising welfare belongs to the standard of living of our society mirrors a central problem. The latter is a central anthropological principle, which is mentioned in almost all introductory textbooks of economics. A central assumption of neo-classical economics is that of 'non-satiation'. Often it is formulated implicitly by presupposing that 'for each person some goods are scarce' as Alchian and Allen (1974:21) wrote in their widely used introductory textbook.[3] These two authors elaborate this assumption:

Despite work, we are unable to produce enough to satisfy all the wants of all people all the time. Desires for more goods exceed known bounds. People prefer more. Even affluent America is a society of scarcity. Choices among opportunities are still required: better hi-fi equipment, wall-to-wall carpeting, walnut panelling, longer vacations. There are conflicting demands for more missiles, airplanes, hospitals, schools, highways, and houses - and for more foreign aid to buy peace and influence and foster foreign economic growth. Nature simply has not provided enough to satiate desires of every living being - not merely people, but animals and plants, for they, too, are busily claiming all the earth.

In the following we will deal with this assumption, since it leads us into the arena of economic and ethical problems, which are directly related to sustainable development.

Ever since ancient times, philosophers who were interested in economic affairs have maintained that economic issues are always connected with the problem of satisfying wants. Pre-modern economic theories saw the aim of the economy to be to find the *right measure* for the satisfaction of wants, and to determine how the necessary means can be provided. A too great abundance of material goods was considered to be just as bad as too little. In proceeding in this way they assumed that there exists a certain natural and interior measure for human wants. It was considered to be an ethical task of humans to find this natural measure, since from this followed, in a natural way, a limit to the wants of goods.

Thinkers, such as Aristotle, who taught these kinds of ideas, viewed economics as acting always within the context of an all encompassing human striving towards bliss (cf. Aristotle, Politics:I 2, 1252 b 28-1253 a 6). Although a certain provision of goods is necessary for a 'good life', this is, by no means, a sufficient requirement. Aristotle saw, however, that there were humans who did not strive towards a 'good life' within the community, but whose total endeavour was directed to obtaining more and more goods. Aristotle called such an attitude 'pleonexia' (literally: 'to have and to want to have always more': Aristotle, Politics:I 9 1257 b 40-1258 a 8). He considered it to be unnatural, and to constitute real injustice (Aristotle, The Nicomachean Ethics:V 4 1130 a 15-27). He saw in 'pleonexia' the potential to destroy the beneficial social life of man. Aristotle believed that a society would necessarily decline if its individuals are not able to limit their wants to such a measure as is necessary for a 'good life'.

In contrast to this view, modern economics conceives the striving to obtain always more to be an essential trait of humans. Voluntary self-restraint by humans is considered to be the exception rather than the rule. Therefore, modern economists take this trait to be self-evident, and formulate it as the assumption of non-satiation, as noted above. Again in contrast to the pre-modern evaluation of an attitude of non-satiation, modern economics views the unceasing striving for more goods to be ethically neutral, as long as the individual acts within the legally given framework. From a national economic point of view this striving[4] is even desirable, according to modern economics, because it leads, via the discovery of new resources, and investment and increased international trade, to a permanently improving provision of goods. Indeed, non-satiation in Western economies may be considered to be a continual stimulus to economic growth during recent centuries. At the same time, it leads to scientific and technical progress, and to the extension of education. All these circumstances provided increasing ability to satisfy increasing wants. The assumption of non-satiation has, however, a significance which one does not necessarily see at first sight. For it leads to the assumption that one does not need to pose the problem of the will and that of right action within modern economics. Within the framework of general equilibrium theory (see e.g. Debreu, 1959; Hildenbrand and Kirman, 1976), which is the core of neoclassical economics, the aims of the producers and of the consumers are neither just nor unjust. These aims express solely the maximisation of profit for the former and reflect the preferences of the latter. The only responsibility of the economic agent consists in not transgressing the given legal framework.

Our standard of living today doubtless results from past generations not being satisfied with their standard of living, and looking for means to increase it. An important prerequisite in this process was that nature provided the necessary resources. This prerequisite, however, has rarely been dealt with by economists in an appropriate way in the past.[5] Considering that the assumption of non-satiation implies limitlessly increasing wants, there is a tendency to use more resources, as well as more of the waste disposal and waste degrading capacities of the environment.

It has been a considerable achievement of modern economics to prove that an economy with unsatiated individuals can lead to a socially desirably economic state, i.e. to an equilibrium which is, at the same time, Pareto optimal (see e.g. Debreu, 1959:74-97). As soon as resource and environmental constraints are introduced in an essential (i.e. long-run) way into the analysis, we know that, because of intertemporal external effects, the problem of sustainability has to examined. It is in this context that the limits to the use of resources, and the thresholds for the disposal and degrading capacities of the environment, have to be explicitly taken into account, with all their intertemporal implications. Even if one supposes, as do the optimists, that over the course of time, all non-renewable resources can be substituted for by renewable ones, one has to set limits for the latter, because one cannot use them at a faster rate than they grow, at least not in the long-run. To do otherwise implies non-sustainable development.

Of course, one could try to make use of the circumstance that economically active individuals have the duty to stay within the given legal framework. For in this case one can, as mentioned above, scientifically determine the limits which are necessary for the establishment of sustainable development, and then enforce them legally. However, there exists a major and easily overlooked difficulty here. For individuals who behave according to the assumption of non-satiation, the existence of limits will always pose a potential problem in a democratic society, since they always tend to attempt to extend the limits of their consumption as far as possible. From this it follows, if we suppose non-satiation, and if non-satiation leads to an ever increasing use of resources and the environment, that a real limitation to the exploitation of nature leads to an abolition of the type of behaviour characterised by non-satiation. This, in turn, would be in opposition to an essential behavioural assumption of our economy. Hence, it is conceivable that non-satiation and sustainability are incompatible.

If this consideration is valid, then far-reaching consequences would follow. There is either (i) the possibility that we proceed 'economically', in the same non-sustainable way as we have done before. Alternatively, (ii) non-satiation has to be rigorously suppressed, for instance by an environmental dictatorship. The latter may imply, however, that the foundations of modern society have to be fundamentally changed or even destroyed. This is because the development of modern Western societies is essentially dependent on individual freedom, be it for better or worse. Hence if one attempts to suppress non-satiation against the consent of the members of a society, then one has to suppress individual freedom also. As the history of socialist societies has shown in this century, this would destroy all possibility of development for modern economies. For the latter depends crucially on individual creativity and responsibility, in short on individual freedom.

A dictatorial suppression of non-satiation, therefore, seems to us neither desirable nor, in the long-run, possible. By this we do not wish to state that it is unreasonable to set thresholds for the use of resources, etc. However, we suggest that this endeavour may have great consequences for the working of our economy and therefore for the whole of society. It might change its very foundations. As the theory of public choice has demonstrated, such fundamental changes of economic order can, in a democratic society, only be carried through at a constitutional level (Wicksell, 1886:110-113; Buchanan and Tullock, 1962; Bernholz and Faber, 1988). Hence the introduction of sustainable development can only be achieved if a great majority of the members of a society really do have the corresponding will, including the readiness to bear all the foreseeable consequences, such as social friction and economic hardship.

5.7   CONCLUDING REMARKS: HOW DO WE WANT TO LIVE?

In our opinion there exist two decisive questions which have to be answered before formulating concrete thresholds for a sustainable economy.

(i)   What is so essential in our way of life that we have to require that all future generations enjoy the same essentials? Of course, this question refers principally to the material dimensions of life, but it cannot be appropriately answered if one does not consider other dimensions in addition. We, therefore, have to be willing to enable future generations to live in a world where principles such as freedom, human dignity, justice, peace and respect towards nature are valid.

(ii) As a background to these considerations, we may pose a second question. What are the consequences of our insight into these essentials for our own and present lives, individually as well as socially? Both questions are beyond science. The answers to these two questions are, however, prerequisites for a scientific discourse on sustainable development, because within their field the corresponding goals have to be formulated. Only thereafter is it possible that science, technology and economics develop operational concepts and material means to achieve these goals. Here it becomes immediately evident what status and what importance the scientific-technical-economic approach has for the realisation of sustainability.

If society has clarified its goals at the level of its will, if it further has expressed its readiness to keep within the boundaries necessary for sustainability by formulating corresponding laws, and if the great majority of the members of the society are willing to accept them, only then can scientists, technicians and economists develop their proposals on how the limits have to be set and shaped in single cases.

Of course, there are many ways in which society may formulate its goals, and many means towards sustainable development. Nevertheless, given the willingness to achieve the goals it holds that, for any these ways, we must be prepared to set certain limits concerning our non-satiation. We believe that it is not so important *where* these limits are set. For if a great majority of the members of society decides voluntarily to restrict itself concerning its wants, this alone would be a tremendous change.

NOTES

1.   The question of whether nature may be attributed its own rights, plays an important role in arguments in the field of ecological economics (see Chapter 2, and Sagoff, 1992:57-60; Manstetten, 1993a).
2.   The limits of human knowledge are analysed in Chapter 11.
3.   For explicit statements see e.g. Debreu (1959:55) and Hildenbrand and Kirman (1976:44).
4.   In our economic-ecological interpretation of Goethe's Faust, we have called this striving the Faustian imperative (cf. Chapter 4).
5.   To what a great and decisive extent resources have played a role in raising the standard of living has been analysed recently by Wright (1990:665), who argued that 'the importance of mineral resources in American industrial history (has) been underappreciated'. The result of his study on the origins of the industrial success of the United States between 1879 and 1940 and its emergence 'to a position of world economic pre-eminence' at the turn of the century, are surprising. 'They suggest that the single most robust characteristic of manufacturing exports was intensity in non-producible natural sources' (ibid. 657). See also Faber and Proops (1993b) for the impact of natural resources on the structure and dynamics of an economy.

PART II

Conceptual Foundations of Ecological Economics

6. Entropy: A Unifying Concept for Ecological Economics

with Stefan Baumgärtner

6.1 INTRODUCTION

Every process of change, be it in nature or economies, can only be achieved by using energy. If we want to understand the changing of the world we must know something about energy. It was one of the great achievements of nineteenth century physics to have understood that whatever the energetic process, one specific form of energy, namely heat, necessarily occurs, and the decisive variable to measure the *quality* of heat is *entropy*. Entropy is involved in all processes, be it in nature or in economies, and is a quantitative measure for the irreversibility involved in any transformation processes of energy. The physicist Arthur Eddington (1882-1944) even considered the empirical fact of time irreversibility through entropy increase as more fundamental than any other law of nature:

> *The law that entropy always increases holds, I think, the supreme position among the laws of Nature. If someone points out to you that your pet theory of the universe is in disagreement with Maxwell's equations, then so much the worse for Maxwell's equations. ... But if your theory is found to be against the second law of thermodynamics I can give you no hope; there is nothing for it but the collapse in deepest humiliation* (Eddington, 1928; quoted after Zeh, 1984:3).

Because of its ubiquitous nature, entropy is a very useful variable to describe all kinds of processes in the world, in particular human economic activity. It is of special importance for resource extraction, the use of these resources by economies, and the impact of their diffusion into the environment by production and consumption activities. All of these are transformation processes of energy or matter; hence, entropy is appropriate to be considered a basic variable for ecological economics. It offers a unifying approach for this discipline, which links economics and ecology. It can be employed for four tasks. One has been already

95

mentioned above, namely, describing the world. The second one is that it helps one to become aware of problems, and third, to pose important questions concerning the interaction between economic activity and the natural environment. Finally, it can contribute to general insights into the solution of these questions.

We first present the historical framework of the First and Second Laws of Thermodynamics. To this end we describe the development of Phenomenological Thermodynamics and Statistical Mechanics (Section 6.2). The notion of entropy is at the centre of both of these fields. Then we turn to a discussion of how entropy relates to time irreversibility. Here we deal with the First and Second Arrows of Time, Georgescu-Roegen's contribution, and self-organisation in the economy (Section 6.3). At the same time this chapter may serve as a basic introduction to the notion of entropy for readers who have not yet had any exposure to this physical concept. Chapter 7 extends the discussion, by critically surveying the applications of the entropy concept in ecological economics.

6.2 HISTORICAL FRAMEWORK OF THE FIRST AND SECOND LAWS OF THERMODYNAMICS

We first want to sketch historically how the concept of entropy and related questions have developed during the last century and a half. They developed thanks to a fruitful interplay of different disciplines, namely, thermodynamics, analytical mechanics, statistical physics, and communication theory.[1]

6.2.1 Phenomenological Thermodynamics

The science of thermodynamics was initiated by engineers who wanted to understand heat engines, machines built to transform heat into mechanical work, such as the steam engine developed by James Watt in 1765. During the eighteenth century scientists had recognised heat as being 'quantitative'. They had distinguished it from temperature which rather reflects the 'intensity' of the heat. It was Sadi Carnot (1796-1832), a French engineer, who in his *Réflexions sur la puissance motrice de feu* (1824) first analysed how heat could be transformed into mechanical work by the means of a so-called heat engine. Carnot compared this heat engine to a water wheel of a mill: as water is capable of producing work when it flows from high to low elevation, so can heat produce work when it 'flows' from high to low temperature in a heat engine. He also realised that the amount of potential work heat could produce is independent of the material which serves to transport heat; it depends only on the respective temperatures of the bodies between which the heat transport takes place. Carnot's statement about the maximum yield, the efficiency, of thermal engines functioning between two heat reservoirs at different temperatures has many important technical applications. It can be viewed as the first explicit formulation of what we call today the 'Entropy Law', although the notion of entropy was coined only 30 years later.

It took so long fully to understand the meaning of this fundamental law because it was first necessary to recognise the equivalence between mechanical work and heat, which are both different forms of energy. Carnot himself understood between 1825 and 1832 that the quantity which was conserved in the transformation process was not heat, as he had still thought in 1824, but energy. Unfortunately, his idea was not published until after 1878, more than 30 years after other scientists had published their experimental and theoretical results,[2] which showed a quantitative equivalence of work and heat. These results established the principle of conservation of energy, the 'First Law of Thermodynamics': energy can be neither created nor destroyed, but can appear in different forms, such as heat, chemical energy, electrical energy, potential energy, kinetic energy, work, etc. In a closed system, the sum of the energies in their particular forms does not change with time.

According to this insight into transformation processes, only the form in which energy appears changes, while its total amount is conserved. Consider, for example, a freshly filled fireplace in a hermetically sealed room. After the wood has been burnt, the energy available in the form of chemically bound energy has been transformed into a higher room temperature. The energy content of the fireplace has thus been reduced by the same quantity by which the energy of the air has increased. The total energy of the room, however, has remained constant. The energy has changed its form from chemical to heat energy.

In view of the First Law, Carnot's ideas about heat engines appeared in a new light. In 1848, William Thomson, the later Lord Kelvin (1824-1907), introduced the notion of absolute temperature. This made it possible to give a simple expression for the efficiency of reversible engines. Kelvin (1852) also noted that it is impossible to construct a perpetual motion machine of the second kind,[3] which would produce work in a closed cycle, taking heat from a single source at uniform temperature. This means that there is a fundamental asymmetry between work and heat: work (and all other forms of energy except heat) can always be completely transformed into heat, whereas a transformation of heat into work is only possible under very specific conditions and, in addition, *always* results in the wasting of a certain amount of heat which cannot be transformed into mechanical work. Work, therefore, can be considered more useful than heat, since it can directly be exploited to drive mechanical machines. In contrast, energy in the form of heat has first to be transformed into work, inevitably giving rise to the wasting of a certain amount of heat, as mentioned above. More generally speaking, in any energy transforming process the quality of energy is somehow downgraded, from 'more useful' to 'less useful'. It was this insight which established what was called the Second Law of Thermodynamics. Hence, the numbering of the laws of thermodynamics is in logical and not in temporal order, because it neglects the fact that Carnot's formulation of the very same fact was actually made before the formulation of the principle of conservation of energy, i.e. the 'First Law'.

Up to the middle of the nineteenth century, the Second Law was still a rather intuitive and therefore vague formulation of empirical facts about energy transformation processes. In 1854, Rudolph Clausius (1822-1888) made a decisive step to come to represent it analytically: he formally defined what he termed 'equivalence value', later to become the 'entropy'. The inspiration for this idea came from a formal representation of the First Law given by J. Willard Gibbs. He knew that energy can neither be created nor destroyed. Yet, the energy of a particular sub-system can change. Gibbs realised that infinitely small changes of energy (dU) can formally be represented by a product of some 'intensive' variable of the system and an infinitely small change of the corresponding 'extensive' variable:

$$dU = \text{(intensive variable)} \cdot d\text{(extensive variable)}.$$

Intensive variables of the system are quantities which do not change when two identical systems are coupled. In contrast, extensive variables are quantities whose value for the total system is simply the sum of the values of this quantity in both systems. For example, temperature and pressure are intensive variables, volume and particle number are extensive variables. Using p to denote pressure and V for volume, a change in the system's energy could thus be represented by:

$$dU = p \cdot dV.$$

Gibbs' claim was that the change of the system's energy could generally be represented as a sum over all possible variations of extensive variables multiplied by their corresponding intensive variables:

$$dU = \sum_i X_i.dY_i \qquad \text{with} \qquad X_i = \frac{\partial u}{\partial Y_i}.$$

Here X_i represents the intensive variables and Y_i represents the extensive variables. For all intensive variables being used at the time, the corresponding extensive variables were well known, with one exception. There was no known extensive variable corresponding to the intensive quantity temperature, T. Clausius' response was to define the variable S through the relationship $dQ = T.dS$.[4] Here Q is the heat and S is the extensive variable corresponding to the absolute temperature T. He further showed that the variable S is a function of the state of a system; it remains constant in any reversible cyclic process, and increases otherwise. He gave it the name 'entropy' (Clausius, 1865); this name was based on the Greek τροπη (transformation) by analogy with the name 'energy'. Now Clausius' formulation of the Second Law is that in an isolated system entropy always increases or, in reversible processes, remains constant. This implies, given the definition of the entropy variable, that spontaneous exchanges of heat between two bodies can only take place in one direction, from hot to cold, in line with experience.

At this point, two terms in Clausius' statement need further explanation. These are the terms 'system' and 'isolated'. A thermodynamic system is defined by specifying a spatial boundary around some objects (which may be involved in interactions or 'processes') with respect to the potential exchange of energy and matter between the inside and the outside. Physicists distinguish between *isolated*, *closed* and *open* systems.

Isolated systems exchange neither energy nor matter with their surrounding environment.

Closed systems exchange energy, but not matter, with their surrounding environment.

Open systems can exchange both energy and matter with their surrounding environment.

Whenever we use the word 'system', we refer to such a thermodynamic definition.[5] Whether truly isolated natural systems exist at all is an open question. Real systems on the Earth always exchange at least energy with their environment, albeit only in small amounts. The universe as a whole could be an isolated system, but that conjecture is beyond testing in physical experiments. However, let us suppose, for the sake of this discussion, that the universe is an isolated system.

6.2.2   Statistical Mechanics

The various formulations of the Second Law given by Carnot, Kelvin and Clausius all stated, in a fully equivalent way, the irreversibility of the evolution of macroscopic systems, an empirical observation in phenomenological thermodynamics and in everyday experience, e.g. when burning a piece of coal. Yet the notion of entropy and the Second Law of Thermodynamics still remained rather mysterious. This is owing to the fact that Clausius' definition of entropy is rather abstract and left entropy as a variable which, at first sight, has nothing to do with irreversibility. Further, equilibrium thermodynamics does not explicitly deal with time. For that reason, temporal irreversibility is hard to grasp in the framework of equilibrium thermodynamics. The relationship between entropy and irreversibility became somewhat clearer, at least as far as the physics of gases was concerned, thanks to Ludwig Boltzmann (1844-1906). He gave a mechanical interpretation for entropy which enabled him to explain why it always increases with time.

Statistical mechanics, which had been developed starting in 1860 by James Clerk Maxwell (1831-1879), views gases as assemblies of molecules, described by distribution functions depending on position and velocity. This view allowed the establishment of connections between the thermodynamic variables, that is the macroscopic properties such as temperature or pressure, and the microscopic behaviour of the individual molecules of the system, which was described by statistical means. In 1877, Boltzmann made the decisive step by introducing the concept of microstates and macrostates of a system. The microstate is an exact specification of the positions and velocities of all individual particles; the macrostate is a specification of the thermodynamic variables of the whole system.[6]

Figure 6.1 explains the concept of macrostates and microstates. We consider a container which we conceive as being split into two halves, containing four balls which are indistinguishable. For the sake of the theoretical treatment let us nevertheless number them. We observe a certain number of balls in one half of the system. These different observable states are the macrostates of the container. The container can be in one of five macrostates (Figure 6.1a). The microstate of the system is the specification of the exact configuration in which half of the container each individual ball is found. In general, one given macrostate can be realised by different microstates. The macrostate (4-0) can be realised by exactly one microstate (Figure 6.1b), the macrostate (3-1) can be realised by four different microstates (Figure 6.1c), and the macrostate (2-2) can be realised by six different microstates (Figure 6.1d).

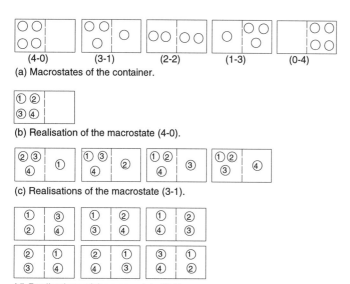

(a) Macrostates of the container.

(b) Realisation of the macrostate (4-0).

(c) Realisations of the macrostate (3-1).

(d) Realisations of the macrostate (2-2).

Figure 6.1. Microstates and macrostates.

Boltzmann assumed that all microstates have equal a priori probability, provided that there is no physical condition which would favour one configuration over the other. By counting the number of different microstates realising the same macrostate, he posited that the macroscopic thermal equilibrium state is the most probable state, in the sense that it is the macrostate which can be realised by the largest number of different microstates. The larger the number of particles a system contains, the more likely it is to find the system in its most probable state. In the example of the container with four balls, it would thus be most likely to find the container to be in the macrostate (2-2), with an equal number of balls in each half.[7]

Boltzmann related the quantity W, counting the number of possible microstates realising one macrostate, to the thermodynamic entropy S of that macrostate, by $S = k \log W$, where k is Boltzmann's constant. Entropy has thus become a measure of likelihood: highly probable macrostates, that is macrostates that can be realised by a large number of microstates, also have high entropy. The irreversibility stated by the Second Law in Clausius' formulation (in any isolated system entropy always increases or remains constant) now appears as the almost intuitive insight that any given system always evolves from a less probable to a more probable state, where W and S are larger.

6.2.3 Phenomenological Thermodynamics vs. Statistical Mechanics

It should be stressed, however, that Boltzmann's statistical mechanical notion of entropy (even for ideal gases) is not truly equivalent to the notions of thermodynamic entropy in the sense of Carnot, Kelvin and Clausius, although such an equivalence is often maintained even in many physics textbooks. In the latters' formulation the Second Law of Thermodynamics is an absolute law of nature: in any isolated system entropy always increases or remains constant, it never decreases. For Boltzmann, however, this is only a question of probability: it is highly probable that the entropy of an isolated system increases; it could, however, with very low probability also decrease. As mentioned above, the larger the number of particles a system contains, the higher the probability of finding the system in the macrostate of maximum entropy. Hence, strictly speaking, statistical mechanics supports the Second Law of Thermodynamics only in the limit of large numbers.

This point has been noted from the very beginning of Boltzmann's formulation of statistical mechanics and has been subject to wide criticism and many controversies. Physicists today agree (see e.g. Gal-Or, 1974) that statistical mechanics itself does not produce irreversibility. In order to obtain irreversible evolution from reversible mechanical laws for the individual particles one needs to employ further assumptions, be it about correlations among the particles prior to and after collisions, or about very special initial conditions (Prigogine and Stengers, 1984). Others (e.g. Prigogine, 1980) have tried to give a different microscopic definition of entropy which should result in true irreversibility, but so far there is no convincing microscopic foundation for the Second Law.

In phenomenological thermodynamics, the entropy concept was always intimately connected with that of heat. It is the merit of statistical mechanics, despite its shortcomings mentioned above, to de-couple these two concepts and to show the more general nature of entropy, namely as a measure of likelihood or, equivalently, as a measure of disorder. For instance, the mixing of two distinguishable gases at the same temperature and with the same density is not accompanied by any thermal effect, but nevertheless it leads to an increase in entropy. The concept of mixture/disorder later on replaced the idea of heat transfer in understanding the meaning of entropy, and served as a guide in generalising the entropy concept and transferring it to other disciplines, such as information theory (Shannon and Weaver, 1949) and economics.

6.3   TIME IRREVERSIBILITY

In physics there has been a tremendous change over the past two hundred years in the way scientists look at time. Now economists have a long tradition of employing concepts from the physical sciences.[8] As we have stated elsewhere 'it is our conviction that economics now needs conceptual re-orientation with respect to time irreversibility, not unlike that which has already occurred in natural science' (Faber and Proops, 1993a:82).

6.3.1   Reversible Time

Before 1850, the paradigm governing physics was Newtonian mechanics. The law of gravitation and Newton's three laws of motion allowed the description of the motion of bodies and their interactions in the form of equations which are, in the absence of energy dissipation, symmetrical with respect to replacing the time variable t by $-t$. Such motion is said to be reversible in time. That means, if some motion of a body is in accordance with Newton's laws, then the same motion running backward in time is also perfectly consistent with Newton's laws and could not be ruled out on physical grounds. For instance, the planets rotating around the sun would, if someone suddenly 'switched' time from running forward to running backward, just rotate the other way around the sun. This is a result which, in the framework of Newtonian mechanics, does not contradict any physical law. Indeed, in frictionless mechanical systems time plays the role of a fourth spatial variable (Prigogine, 1980; Prigogine and Stengers, 1984), in the sense that past and future are essentially equivalent.[9] This interpretation of time which views the future merely as a continuation of the present, without any occurrence of novelty or evolution, is captured in the idea of 'Laplace's Demon' (Prigogine and Stengers, 1984). This idea states that, given the present positions and velocities of all particles in the universe and its boundary conditions, one can infer their past and predict their future with equal facility.

It has been suggested (Mirowski, 1984) that the explicit acceptance of Newtonian mechanics as a guide for modelling economic systems by Jevons and Walras has caused general equilibrium analysis also to exhibit time reversibility (Proops, 1985). In fact, general equilibrium analysis treats static allocation problems in formally the very same way as intertemporal allocation problems.

> *After general equilibrium theorists gave their description of a general*
> *equilibrium with dated goods and state-contingent goods, the*
> *apparent distinction between statics and dynamics disappeared from*
> *equilibrium analysis... The choice could be between apples and*
> *oranges today. Or it could be between apples today and apples*
> *tomorrow* (Romer, 1994:11).

In this neoclassical world time only plays the role of some parameter.
Although all quantities carry a time-label, there is no truly dynamic
evolution, in the sense of change and occurrence of novelty. Rather, the
evolution is 'pseudo-dynamic' in that the time label serves to project
future states out of a present static equilibrium state. In the most trivial
case this results in steady-state evolution. This procedure is perfectly in
line with the idea of Laplace's Demon. There is more and more concern
in economics about how neoclassical theory deals with time (see e.g.
Faber and Proops, 1985, 1986, 1989). For instance, Romer gives an
illuminating explanation of why:

> *any analysis that treats a dynamic economy as being formally*
> *equivalent to a static economy characterized by plentitude - fullness*
> *in the set of goods - cannot ... capture the essential aspects of growth*
> *and change* (Romer, 1994:20).[10]

6.3.2   Isolated Systems: The First Arrow of Time

The everyday experience that time matters, in the sense that in
macroscopic systems there are processes which are irreversible in time,
gave rise in the middle of the nineteenth century to the various formulations of the Second Law of Thermodynamics. Its statement that, in
Clausius' terms, the entropy of an isolated system always increases or
remains constant, but certainly never decreases, allows one to define a
time direction, the so-called First Arrow of Time (Layzer, 1976). For
example, an ice cube placed in a container of hot water will melt to give
cooler water. The initially distinct cold ice and warm water become
mixed-up. We never observe cool water separating out of its own accord
into cold ice and warm water. If the process of melting were documented
in a movie, and this movie were shown to somebody, once running
forward and once running backward, then this person clearly could rule
out the latter as unphysical and identify the former as representing the
real process. In this sense the process of melting or mixing-up is irreversible in time.

In its phenomenological formulation by Clausius, the Second Law of
Thermodynamics states the tendency of heat to flow from hot bodies to

cold bodies, thus increasing entropy, and never vice versa. In its statistical interpretation given by Boltzmann, this means that systems have a tendency to ever increasing mixed-upness or disorder. It has been suggested that the Second Law of Thermodynamics constitutes the physical underpinning of the fact that the world is developing in one direction, from order to disorder. William Thompson, the later lord Kelvin, was the first to formulate this idea, in 1852. On the cosmological scale, all differences in temperature and concentration of matter in the universe, in the form of planets, stars and galaxies, are predicted to level out. Heat flows from hot to cold thus reducing differences in temperature; and there is mixing of material which is initially highly concentrated, thus reducing differences in concentration. The final state of this cosmological evolution is the so-called 'thermal death' of our universe. This is the state where the entropy of the universe is maximal, all potentials (that is: differences in temperature or concentration of matter) are levelled out, so that energy and matter are evenly distributed throughout the universe.

6.3.3   Georgescu-Roegen's Contribution

It was Nicholas Georgescu-Roegen (hereafter called 'G-R') who first introduced (G-R, 1971) the entropy concept into economics in a visionary way.[11] The economic process transforms stocks of highly concentrated and easily available resources into products and wastes, which contain the same material in lower concentration. For instance, oil which is found in the Earth's crust in high concentration, a state of low entropy, serves as fuel, while CO_2 is evenly distributed through the atmosphere, in a state of high entropy. G-R stresses very much that these economic processes are time irreversible: the stocks of resources (like oil, coal and ores) are permanently reduced by economic action; at the same time the stock of wastes from the economic process is permanently increased.

The observation that energy and matter are transformed in economic processes, from a state of easy availability (highly concentrated resources) into a state of non-availability (highly dispersed waste), led G-R to the assertion that the economic process is subjected to the Second Law of Thermodynamics: 'The economic process is entropic: it neither creates nor consumes matter or energy, but only transforms low into high entropy' (G-R, 1971:281). G-R is critical that economists have not yet taken the Entropy Law seriously. Since it deals with available (useful) energy, it is, in G-R's words, 'the most economic of all physical laws' (G-R, 1971:280). 'Low entropy is a necessary condition for usefulness' (G-R, 1979:1042), thus the Entropy Law is essential for understanding economic value or scarcity.

These qualitative assertions sound plausible, but G-R encounters formal problems. He accepts the Second Law only in its phenomeno-logical formulation, as given by Carnot, Clausius or Kelvin, and rejects Boltzmann's probability-based notion of entropy. For that reason he operationalises the Entropy Law based on the distinction of available vs. unavailable energy and matter, and does not make recourse to any idea of orderliness. However, phenomenological thermodynamics describes only transformations of available (free) energy into non-available energy; it does not make any statement about the availability of matter. As a consequence, G-R extends classical thermodynamics by postulating a 'Fourth Law of Thermodynamics' (G-R, 1979:1029) concerned with the entropy of matter in a closed system.

By analogy with the Entropy Law in isolated systems, he argues that in closed systems there exists a 'material entropy' which always increases. Any mechanical work is performed by the relative movement of different materials in sliding contact and these materials are subject to unavoidable deterioration and mixing; the material entropy increases indicating that the matter in its dispersed form is less available. Ulti-mately, the material entropy will reach its maximum value and all matter will be so mixed-up that it is completely unavailable. The disappearance of any qualitative difference between materials is a sort of 'material death' of the system, which is similar to an isolated system's 'thermal death' (Bianciardi, Tiezzi and Ulgiati, 1993). The Fourth Law states that, in a closed system one cannot reduce material entropy, which means that it is impossible to completely recover the matter involved in the pro-duction of mechanical work or wasted in friction. In other words, a closed system cannot perform work forever at a steady state: 'Perpetual motion of the third kind ... is impossible', as G-R formulates it (G-R, 1979:1029), making an allusion to Kelvin's formulation of the Second Law.

It is important to note that G-R's Fourth Law indeed attempts to extend classical thermodynamics. The Second Law is a statement about isolated systems, i.e. systems that exchange neither energy nor matter with their environment. The Fourth Law is a statement about closed systems, i.e. systems that do not exchange matter with their environment, but which are open to the exchange of energy.

Taken together, the basic aspects of G-R's paradigm may be briefly summarised (Bianciardi, Tiezzi and Ulgiati, 1994:192) as:

1. The economic process is subject to the Entropy Law.

2. Complete recycling of matter is impossible in a closed system.

The consequences to be drawn from this view of the economic process are extremely pessimistic. All economic actions cannot but increase entropy. Whatever we do (including recycling) devalues energy and/or matter and leaves less available energy/matter for future generations. Not only does economic growth turn out to be an illusion, but even a steady-state economy would inevitably increase entropy and thus could not be sustainable. (There is a fuller discussion of G-R's Fourth Law in Chapter 7 below.)

6.3.4 Self-Organisation in Open Systems: The Second Arrow of Time

This pessimistic view of development as a continuous degradation as based on the Second Law is in striking contrast to the observation that cosmological history, and the history of the evolution of life on Earth, exhibits a tendency towards ever more structure and greater complexity. Out of cosmic clouds of hydrogen formed stars, which developed into galaxies, and later to even more complex structures. On Earth, out of some basic molecules formed very simple forms of life, such as algae and bacteria, and later out of these emerged more complex forms of life, such as reptiles and mammals. This tendency of systems to generate self-organisation towards more complex structures has been termed Second Arrow of Time. It also describes time irreversibility, since it allows one to distinguish between the past and the future.

But how does this tendency to build up increasingly complex chemical, biological, ecological and social structures go together with the claim of the Second Law, namely that the components of a system have a tendency towards mixed-upness? There seems to be a contradiction.

Nineteenth century science could not solve this puzzle. The process of biological evolution was regarded as being outside the bounds of explanation with thermodynamics. Only in the 1940s did the physicist Erwin Schrödinger (Schrödinger, 1944) relate the Entropy Law to the phenomenon of life in a pioneering way. He pointed out that, whereas the Second Law describes isolated systems, all living systems in nature have to be described as open systems, which exchange energy and matter with their surrounding environment. Open systems that are not in thermodynamic equilibrium can maintain their state in the long-run only by importing low entropy from their environment and exporting high entropy: 'Life feeds on low entropy' (Schrödinger, 1944:75). The crucial point is that entropy in an open system can be decreased by the exchange of energy and matter with its environment.

The change of entropy (dS) in an open system can be separated into the production of entropy (dS_i) within the system, and the net flux of entropy (dS_e) the system imports from its environment; so:

$$dS = dS_i + dS_e.$$

While the production of entropy (dS_i) is always positive according to the Second Law, the flux of entropy (dS_e) associated with the exchange of energy and matter between the open system and its environment can have a positive or a negative sign.[12] It is negative when the system exports more entropy than it imports. If this is the case, the system is said to import negative entropy, which is also termed negentropy. If (dS_e) is positive, the production of entropy within the system is further increased by the intake of entropy from outside the system. More interesting is the case where (dS_e) is negative and its absolute value is larger than the entropy (dS_i) produced within the system:

$$dS_e < 0 \quad \text{with} \quad |dS_e| > dS_i \quad \Rightarrow \quad dS < 0.$$

The total entropy in this case is decreased by importing enough negative entropy from the environment. The price for that is an increase in entropy in the system's environment. If the open system is viewed as a sub-system of some larger, isolated system, then the evolutionary development of the open sub-system towards higher complexity characterised by lower entropy is in perfect agreement with the Second Law's statement of increasing entropy in the whole isolated system. Only by permanent dissipation, that is degradation of low-entropy energy and matter, can open systems decrease their entropy. Thus, Prigogine (1967:124ff.) called them 'dissipative structure'.

It was Prigogine and his co-workers in Brussels (Prigogine, 1962, 1967; Glansdorf and Prigogine, 1971; Nicolis and Prigogine, 1977) who studied the behaviour of open systems which are not in thermodynamic equilibrium.[13] They found that open systems that are not in thermody-namic equilibrium, but close to it, cannot develop a complex order. Such an evolutionary development towards higher order can only occur in open systems far from equilibrium. A sufficient condition is that the through-flux of energy and matter through the system is associated with a sufficiently high flow into the system of negative entropy per unit time. Under these conditions the open system may spontaneously exhibit further structuring. This phenomenon of self-organisation through dissipation depends also on the material involved, and the boundary conditions of the system, such as its geometry. Not all open systems have the potential to develop dissipative structures, and those which have the potential, due to suitable boundary conditions, depend on a sufficient influx of negative entropy in order to exhibit self-organised evolution towards more structure and higher order.

A classical example of a dissipative structure far from equilibrium is the so-called Bénard convection cells (Prigogine and Stengers, 1984). When a temperature gradient is applied to a liquid, initially heat is transported through the liquid solely by conduction, i.e. through inter-action solely at the microscopic molecular level. As the temperature gradient is increased, and thus more energy is flowing through the system, at one critical threshold value of the temperature gradient the liquid will become a dissipative structure, spontaneously generating a completely new ordered mode of behaviour. Macroscopic hexagonal convection cells will form which allow a much more efficient transport of heat through the system than simple conduction. The new state of the liquid is characterised by higher order, but also by a higher rate of dissipation of energy, and thus is even further away from thermodynamic equilibrium. It is the more efficient dissipation of energy which enables the system to import a higher amount of negative entropy from the environment.

In general, dissipation of energy in open systems, associated with a sufficiently high influx of negative entropy, can lead, through self-or-ganisation, to the formation of spatial or temporal structures. It is characteristic that if one of the parameters describing how far the system is away from equilibrium (such as the temperature gradient in the example of the Bénard convection cells) reaches a critical value, the old stationary state becomes unstable. There appear new stable stationary states of the system and the system exhibits a discontinuous transition to a new pattern of spatial or temporal order. This new stationary state again becomes unstable when the parameter further increases and reaches another critical threshold value.

Figure 6.2 shows the evolutionary development of a dissipative system far from thermodynamic equilibrium. The original stationary state of the system becomes unstable when the parameter a (e.g. the temperature gradient) reaches a critical threshold value a_1. At this point, which is called a bifurcation point, two new potential stationary states of the system emerge. Around a_1 the system is very unstable with respect to fluctuations, and it cannot be predicted which one of the two will be the system's new stationary state. While the system is governed by deter-ministic laws between the bifurcation points, behaviour at a bifurcation

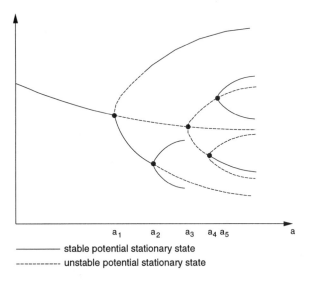

stable potential stationary state
---------- unstable potential stationary state

Figure 6.2. Indeterministic evolutionary development through bifurcation of a dissipative open system, far from equilibrium.

point is not predictable. Rather, its evolution depends arbitrarily on fluctuations. Which of the available stable stationary states the system will take cannot be predicted ex ante, but only observed ex post. This characteristic property of open systems far from equilibrium thus 'introduce[s] the concept of "memory" or "history" into the "explanation" of the state of this system, as well as an "uncertainty" or "choice" as to its future evolution' (Allen and Sanglier, 1981:167). One also speaks of 'path dependence', since the future evolution of the system depends on the historic path it has taken in the past.

6.3.5   Self-Organisation in Economics

What has been termed the Second Arrow of Time is an obvious phenomenon in economics, namely the build-up of capital goods, organisational structure or institutions, and technological progress towards higher complexity. Attempts to explain and model this tendency go back at least to Malthus, Marx, Menger and Schumpeter. But with the dominance of neoclassical theory, which stresses the notion of equilibrium so much and generally neglects temporal aspects, this strand in economics only played a minor role. Only recently has interest among economists in evolutionary aspects made a come-back.

The concept of open systems far from equilibrium constitutes a fruitful heuristic also for describing economic or social systems: 'It is suggested that an economy is, when viewed from a physical perspective, the "same sort of thing" as an organism, a flame, or a convection cell' (Proops, 1983:354). Many authors applied this concept to economics (e.g. Proops, 1983, 1985; Allen, 1988; Dyke, 1988). They explicitly use the thermodynamic concept of self-organising structures as an analogy for describing economic systems. Other recent attempts not directly inspired by thermodynamics, but also concerned with describing evolutionary and self-organisational aspects in technological and economic change, include the field of 'evolutionary economics' (Nelson and Winter, 1982),[14] and the newly emerging 'science of complexity' (Anderson, Arrow and Pines, 1988; Waldrop, 1992).

Arthur (1989) has presented a dynamic model which explores the role of returns to scale on market shares by competing techniques. He finds that under increasing returns to scale, small chance events early in the history of an industry or technology can become magnified in a self-organised way, increasing returns acting as positive feedback, so as to determine the eventual outcome. As in open systems far from thermodynamic equilibrium, essential features of this model are sensitive dependence on small historical events, path dependence and unpre-dictability of the outcome. Arthur's results even suggest that the domi-nating technique may be less efficient in the long-run than one of the techniques abandoned in its favour. For example, he argues for road transport that the internal combustion engine came to dominate the steam engine through a series of historical accidents, even though the steam engine had a greater potential economic efficiency.

All the above mentioned attempts, be they inspired by thermody-namics or not, have in common that they are concerned with describing the evolution of economic systems as the build-up of higher organisational structure, and involve the Second Arrow of Time.

6.3.6   Thermodynamics and Time Irreversibility

As we have seen, modern thermodynamics offers a wide conceptual framework to deal with time irreversibility. Crucial to this framework is the notion of entropy, first through the formulation of the Second Law of (equilibrium) Thermodynamics, and more recently through devel-opments in the study of systems far from thermodynamic equilibrium. The two tendencies, towards degradation and towards greater organisation over time, reflect two aspects of the same phenomenon; the First Arrow of Time shows time irreversibility for systems that are isolated and in thermodynamic equilibrium, while the Second Arrow of

Time is operational for systems which are open and far from equilibrium. By making this distinction we banish the apparent contradiction of the tendency of some systems to ever increasing disorder and the tendency of some other systems to ever increasing order and more complex structure.

Whereas neoclassical economics describes only time-reversible processes, we feel that thermodynamics offers a broad unifying conceptual approach also to time irreversibility in economics. For instance:

> *We note that the physical world acts as a constraint upon economic activity, while technical progress is the mechanism by which such physical constraints are eased or transformed ... In particular, the intertemporal physical constraints imposed by considerations of resource depletion and environmental degradation are manifestations of the First Arrow of Time ... while technical progress reflects the generation of novelty and therefore invokes time irreversibility 2* (in the sense of the Second Arrow of Time) (Faber and Proops, 1993a:92).

6.4   CONCLUSIONS

Before proceeding to an exploration of the use of the entropy concept in the ecological economic literature in Chapter 7, we summarise our main insights from the discussion so far.

The thermodynamic approach centred around the notion of entropy offers a unifying conceptual framework to integrate a description of the human economy and its biophysical surrounding. Such an approach stresses some features of economic processes which in neoclassical theory are not given the prominence they deserve:

1.   The transformation of energy and material is subject to the laws of nature. The thermodynamic approach is a way for economics to get in touch with its biophysical foundations (cf. Chapter 10).

2.   In any process there exists a time irreversibility as expressed in the two competing tendencies of the First and the Second Arrows of Time. The entropy concept makes one aware of the irreversible nature of environmental and resource processes. On the other hand, a creative potential for technical progress is seen to exist.

NOTES

1. An excellent overview of the historical development of thermodynamics can be found in Balian (1991). For an extensive introduction of the notion of entropy for non-physicists see Faber, Niemes and Stephan (1987:Chapter 3).

2. The German medical doctor Julius Robert Mayer (1814-1878) in 1842, James Prescott Joule (1818-1889), a Scottish owner of a brewery, in 1843 and Hermann von Helmholtz (1821-1894), physiologist and physicist, in 1847.

3. A perpetual motion machine of the first kind would actually create energy, in contravention of the First Law.

4. To physicists one should strictly use δQ rather that dQ, as this quantity is not an exact differential.

5. It should be noted that the distinction isolated system vs. closed/open system in reality is not as clear as it might seem from physics textbook treatments. Rather, this distinction might depend on the time-scale of the processes under consideration and the time-scale of energy transfer and mixing in the system: 'Real systems are neither isolated nor closed. In a real system there is a finite rate of energy exchange with the environment. If it is slow relative to the time frame of interest, we treat the system as isolated... If energy exchange is fast and efficient, we treat the system as closed, but may need to remember to adjust for heat flows and mixing. The really difficult systems to treat are those where the rates of heat transfer and mixing are very much on the same time-scale as the time-scale of the process under consideration. Attempts to do so come into the realm of "non-equilibrium thermodynamics"' (Christie, 1994:34).

6. For economists it might be helpful to point out an analogy. Phenomenological thermodynamics corresponds to macroeconomics, because it attempts to describe complex systems, e.g. a container of one mol of gas (approximately 10^{23} molecules), with few variables on the macro-level. In contrast, statistical mechanics corresponds to microeconomics, trying to cope with all possible states of a system on the micro-level.

7. The reader with a solid physics background may find a more rigorous but also more technical treatment of this concept in any standard textbook on statistical mechanics, e.g. Reif (1965), Landau and Lifschitz (1980), Huang (1987).

8. For a more detailed account, see Mirowski (1984) and Proops (1985).

9. Modern physics has shown that invariance of the laws of motion under time reversal is a very general feature of *microscopic* systems. It is not peculiar to Newtonian mechanics, but is also apparent in quantum mechanics and in quantum field theory.

10. After this essay had been completed we learned of a paper by Lozada (1995), in which he also makes a strong case for overcoming the shortfalls of neo-classical theory by incorporating the Entropy Law's implications for the economic process. He argues that 'modern neoclassical economics is arithmomorphic. ... Arithmomorphic laws cannot capture evolutionary change' (p.31). Lozada's distinction between 'arithmomorphic concepts' and 'dialectical concepts' seems to be a very stimulating idea. However, it is beyond the scope of this essay to give a detailed critique of neoclassical theory. Whereas Lozada suggests the Second Law to introduce evolutionary aspects into economics, we will take a broader approach in the following two subsections.

11. The term 'visionary' is not used in a negative way here. Heilbroner (1990), adopting Schumpeter's definition of a vision as the 'preanalytic cognitive act' (p.1109), provides an impressive account of the visionary nature of respected contributions to economics.
12. In isolated systems one has $dS_e = 0$.
13. A system is said to be in thermodynamic equilibrium when there are no variations of any of the intensive variables within the system.
14. For an overview of recent trends see Dosi and Nelson (1994).

7. The Use of the Entropy Concept in Ecological Economics

with Stefan Baumgärtner

7.1   INTRODUCTION

In the previous chapter we noted that entropy is central for conceptualising ecological economics. However, we also noted that it contributes general insights to the solution of questions concerning the interaction of economies and the natural environment. In this chapter we go one step further, in showing that entropy should *not* be seen as an analytical tool for ecological economics (though of course it *is* for physics). Rather, it is our main conclusion that the entropy concept is fundamental for formulating a conceptual framework for ecological economics, indeed, for economics in general. Throughout this chapter we use the term 'Entropy Law' in a narrow sense, as fully equivalent to 'Second Law of Thermodynamics'. In contrast, we denote by the 'entropy concept' the application of entropy considerations in a wider sense, including open systems which are far from equilibrium.

The entropy notion is extremely complex. Thus Koopmans (1979:13), whose first two publications were in physics, wrote that '"entropy" ... is a more difficult concept than anything economics has to offer'. Georgescu-Roegen (1971:5) noted in his pioneering monograph:

> *The physical concept is generally judged to be quite intricate. If we take the word of some specialists, not even all physicists have a perfectly clear understanding of what this concept exactly means. Its technical details are, indeed, overwhelming. And even a dictionary definition suffices to turn one's intellectual curiosity away.*

It is therefore no surprise that the application of the entropy concept has given rise not only to many misunderstandings and controversies in economics and ecological economics, but often entropy has also been applied incorrectly in social contexts. One reason for this is that one needs a strong background in physics *and* economics to understand and to appreciate the literature on this topic.

The aim of this chapter is to contribute to a clarification of the appropriate use of the entropy concept, by surveying the relevant literature. We shall attempt to show which usages are correct and which are mistaken, which application is sensible and which is not. In this way, we hope to offer a survey which at the same time may act as a guide for the newcomer to this field.[1]

One of the main messages will turn out to be that understanding the entropy notion is to understand what is possible in economics and what is not. Thermodynamics can show the outer limits of what is physically and economically possible:

> *... the second law of thermodynamics tells us nothing about what will happen, but only about what cannot happen. Any claim that the second law helps us know what will happen must be scrutinized with great care* (Dyke, 1994:208).[2]

Thus, the restrictions of the way we live in our world will become more apparent. Further, this quotation contains an important but often overlooked warning. For it emphasises that we cannot expect entropy to be of much use for finding explicit solutions to concrete problems. Rather, because of its very general and unifying nature, it contributes to the biophysical foundations of economics at large and ecological economics in particular. By 'biophysical' we mean physical and biological aspects of nature which are relevant for economics.

In the next section we turn to the current debate, by identifying and answering four questions which appear in the literature in one form or another. They refer to the relevance of the notion of entropy in economics, in particular to the asymmetry between energy and matter; to the meaningfulness of an entropy theory of value; and problems of information and technical progress. Having laid a solid basis we proceed to present various applications of the entropy concept in ecological economics; in particular we deal with problems of resource extraction and environmental pollution. Finally, we give our conclusions and a prospect for the future.

7.2   THE PRESENT DEBATE

Whereas the notion of entropy and the Second Law of Thermodynamics constitute an undisputed part of the body of natural sciences, the generalisation and adaptation of this concept to economics by Georgescu-Roegen (G-R) and his followers have repeatedly been criticised and even completely rejected. For instance, Young claims that 'the entropy law does not add anything which is not already considered in economic models of long-run economic growth in relation to the availability of environmental resources' (Young, 1991:169).

In the early stage of the discussion, much confusion arose since some of the critics seemed not to have fully understood what the Second Law of Thermodynamics actually states, and what it does not state, in terms of physics. Later in the discussion some of the physics questions have been clarified and the debate has focused on the economic implications of the entropy concept. Still, the debate has not settled.

One can distinguish four types of questions that, in one form or another, periodically make a reappearance in the literature:

1. Does the Second Law only refer to energy or does it allow statements about matter also?

2. What are the boundaries of the systems under consideration in economics and what role does entropy play in open systems? In particular, does the Entropy Law as a natural law also apply to purposeful human action, such as resource extraction?

3. If so, does this foster an energy and/or entropy theory of value?

4. What role does information/new knowledge/technological progress play with respect to the Second Law of Thermodynamics?

Whereas Question 1 is of rather physical nature (but nevertheless of importance for an economic discussion as well) Questions 2, 3 and 4 are essentially economic. We shall deal with each in turn, and try to clarify some of the misunderstandings in the literature which have lead Burness et al. (1980:2) to state that 'it seems fair to say that the interface between economic and thermodynamic "laws" remains obscure.'

7.2.1 Entropy, Energy and Matter

Concerning Question 1, on thermodynamics, energy and matter, we note that at the very centre of the Second Law of Thermodynamics is neither energy nor matter, but entropy. In classical thermodynamics the notion of entropy was developed in analysing processes of energy transformation. Later, Boltzmann's statistical mechanics allowed the analysis of the mixing of gases, and thus processes of matter transformation, in terms of entropy as well. Today, physicists routinely apply the First and Second Laws of Thermodynamics to energy as well as to matter.

As noted in the previous chapter, it was G-R's rejection of Boltzmann's statistical interpretation of entropy which led him to postulate a separate entropy law for matter in closed systems, his 'Fourth Law of

Thermodynamics'. This postulate has repeatedly been criticised, since it is evident that G-R argues purely by analogy with the Second Law for isolated systems. In addition, Bianciardi, Tiezzi and Ulgiati (1993:1) have shown with a simple model that 'G-R's Fourth Law of Thermodynamics ("complete recycling of matter is impossible") is not consistent with the framework of physical laws'; i.e. it contradicts the Second Law of Thermodynamics. Further, it disagrees with empirical experience from the study of biological systems (Bianciardi, Tiezzi and Ulgiati, 1993:4). In the biosphere, which is a closed system in that it is open to energy inflow and outflow, but does not exchange matter with its surroundings, matter is completely recycled and upgraded (ordered), e.g. in the process of photosynthesis, at the expense of solar negentropy. For that reason, the critics are right to reject G-R's Fourth Law.

But does that mean the Second Law indeed does not make any statement about matter? Young claims that:

> ... *the entropy law as a physical principle applies ... only to energy.*
> *... The distinction made in physics between available and unavailable*
> *energy (necessary to the entropy law) becomes highly problematic*
> *when applied to matter. ... The point is that available matter is*
> *dependent on the existence of appropriate technologies* (Young,
> 1991:178).

Since he also rejects G-R's Fourth Law as being based purely on analogy, Young is led to the conclusion that the entropy law does not impose any physical constraint on economic growth in relation to the availability of environmental resources. However, in reaction to comments by Daly (1992) and Townsend (1992), Young has to admit that 'the entropy law applies to matter and that materials entropy is well defined' (Young, 1994:210). He maintains, however, that the formulation of entropy in terms of the distinction between available and unavailable energy cannot be translated to matter except by analogy. But Boltzmann's notion of entropy as a measure of order/disorder is acknowledged as the way to define the entropy of a material system: 'It is, however, valid to think of entropy in terms of the orderliness of a system. This is the sense in which it applies to matter' (Young, 1994:211).

So the Second Law, in its Boltzmann interpretation, does make a statement about matter: 'The degradation of matter and its environmental and economical consequences are fully consistent with the Second Law' (Bianciardi, Tiezzi and Ulgiati, 1993:1). It is not necessary, and would even be erroneous, to introduce a Fourth Law specially for matter. As Månsson notes:

> *G-R's error leads to a number of incorrect conclusions when applied to the Earth, which to a good approximation is a closed system. This has led to dismissal of G-R's ideas or a denial of their significance* (Månsson, 1994:191).

However, this flaw in G-R's body of thought should not diminish the merits of this pioneer of thermodynamic thinking in economics:

> *Indeed, G-R's statement is important in the context of the Second Law without introducing a Fourth Law. ... Complete recycling is physically possible if a sufficient amount of energy is available. The problem is that such expenditure of energy would involve a tremendous increase in the entropy of the environment, which would not be sustainable for the biosphere* (Bianciardi, Tiezzi and Ulgiati, 1993:5).

7.2.2   On the Relevance of Entropy for Economics

Concerning Question 2, on system boundaries and human intention, much confusion in the discussion about the relevance of the entropy concept in economics could be avoided if only more attention were paid to carefully specifying the system boundaries of the systems under consideration. This includes specifying *where, at what point in time* and *of what type* are the system boundaries. Let us recall that there are three types of system: isolated, closed and open. All three types of system are of relevance to economic questions. Since this is where most mistakes occur when applying the entropy concept in a non-physics context, it should be stressed that:

> *... if you want to talk about entropy, you must be able to talk about the thermodynamic boundaries of whatever it is for which you're measuring entropy. ... The amount of cheating that goes on with respect to this requirement among otherwise intelligent people is truly colossal* (Dyke, 1994:210).

7.2.2.1 The Economy as an Open System

From the economics point of view, one deals with neither isolated nor closed systems, but always with open systems. Both energy and matter enter the production process as inputs from the outside. In the same way, the whole economic system can be seen as an open sub-system of the larger system Earth, which to a good approximation is a closed system (Figure 7.1).

From the physics point of view, we need to remind ourselves that equilibrium thermodynamics deals solely with isolated systems; this is

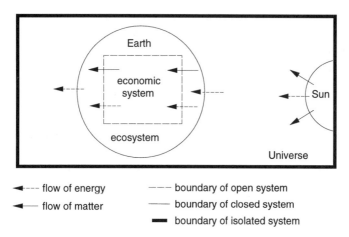

Figure 7.1. The economy as an open sub-system.

clearly an idealisation of modern physics, given the fact that in reality there are no isolated systems. Although it should always be included in the formulation of the Second Law, this important premise is often omitted. Only *in isolated systems* does entropy always increase or remain constant. In both closed and open systems, entropy can increase as well as, under certain circumstances, decrease. If we combine the facts that, first, the Second Law only holds for isolated systems and, second, economic systems are never isolated systems, then it follows that the Second Law is of no use in describing economic systems. G-R realises that:

> ... *the systems of our experience are all either closed (in which case energy but not matter may be exchanged with the outside) or open (in which case both energy and matter may be so exchanged). Obviously, in the last systems entropy may very well decrease* (G-R, 1986:4).

However, G-R does not take proper account of the fact that entropy can also decrease in closed systems, through appropriate energy flows through the system boundary (Månsson, 1994), maybe because it does not fit with his pessimistic view of the world.[3]

Finally it should be noted that the Second Law, although making a statement about isolated systems only, nevertheless has something to say about entropy in closed or open systems as well. This is a consequence of the fact that every open or closed system is a sub-system of some larger isolated system (cf. Figure 7.1) for which the Second Law holds. Whereas the entropy in the sub-system can increase or decrease, this change in entropy has to be consistent with the fact that the total entropy of the whole isolated system is increasing. If, for instance, the entropy of the open economic sub-system decreases, this has to be compensated for by an increase of entropy in the rest of the larger isolated system, such that the total entropy increases, as stated by the Second Law. The answer to our second question is precisely formulated by Townsend (1992:99):

> *Does thermodynamics constrain the operation of terrestrial processes in such an open system? Indeed, it does. Exponential growth processes, such as increases in population and economic activity, necessitate increases in material/energy inputs and outputs. For economic processes the availability of adequate environmental sink space for the radiation of [high-entropy] waste matter/energy is as important as the availability of low-entropy inputs.*

7.2.2.2 Entropy and Natural Resources

A substantial and especially confusing part of the discussion in the literature has dealt with the question whether the Entropy Law is relevant to the economics of natural resources (Khalil, 1990, 1991; Lozada, 1991; O'Connor, 1991; Young, 1991, 1994; Daly, 1992; Townsend, 1992; Williamson, 1993). With regard to this question, it is especially important to specify exactly the boundaries of the systems under consideration.

The First and Second Laws of Thermodynamics stand on solid experimental ground. No physics experiment has ever suggested a contradiction to either one of these laws. As laws of nature, they seem to hold for all processes in the universe, natural or human, purposeful or non-purposeful. As Williamson remarked in a comment on Khalil (1990), who had expressed doubts concerning this point:

> *No amount of comment on thermodynamics in general or juggling of algebra analogous to the equations of thermodynamics can get one away from ... the fact that any process that involves materials or energy is necessarily subject to the laws of physics* (Williamson, 1993:71).

What is important, though, is to keep in mind that the Second Law is not a statement about all kinds of systems, but only about isolated systems. A lot of confusion arose from some authors (e.g. Khalil, 1990) not taking this condition seriously. They show that entropy in some system could be decreased (which is perfectly correct!) and link this observation to the other observation that these were systems characterised by purposeful human action. Thus, they conclude, the Second Law does not hold if purposeful human action is involved. These authors completely miss the point that they are actually talking about closed or open systems, not isolated ones. But nobody ever claimed the statement of the Second Law to hold for closed or open systems.[4] Decreasing entropy in such systems is not a contradiction of the Second Law, since those systems are not isolated.

Let us consider Khalil's (1990) argument in more detail. He claims that there is a distinction between the entropy law per se as expressed by Clausius or Boltzmann[5] (call this C) and the Carnot cycle as expressed by Kelvin[6] (call this K). Khalil notes that C, since it talks about spontaneous processes, applies to non-purposeful processes, whereas K, since it talks about the production of work, applies to purposeful agency. He then concludes that 'since production is purposeful, the economic process should be conceived after the Carnot cycle, and not the entropy law' (Khalil, 1990:171).[7]

With regard to the depletion of resources, Khalil claims that G-R was wrong in postulating that according to C useful resources spontaneously degrade and become non-useful, highly entropic resources and that human production, since it produces waste, speeds up the process of degradation. Instead he claims that:

> ... the organization which is undertaking the activity ... could as well reverse the deterioration, after some innovations in technology and institutions are introduced. ... The alternative scenario is underlined by the conception of the economic process after the Carnot cycle. The disposal of resources and new discoveries are activities defined in relation to the agency of production. The reversal of fortunes is not certain, even with the increase of complex organizations. ... Such a possibility, though, is not a priori ruled out, as G-R does (Khalil, 1990:174).

First of all, Khalil's claim that C and K are not equivalent is wrong. Lozada (1991) has given an explicit demonstration of where Khalil's logical error is and concluded that 'the Second Law is a single fundamental natural law though it has several equivalent formulations. All processes, purposeful or not, are subject to it. This includes Carnot engines, which are useful theoretical abstractions but nothing else' (Lozada, 1991:157). What is true, though, in Khalil's paper (cf. Khalil, 1990:footnote 7) is the assertion that K, by including the notion of 'work' and thus a reference to the outside of the system, has a richer conceptual structure than C. This is what causes Khalil to associate 'purposeful action' with the statement K, and what also gives rise to his abuse of the entropy concept by neglecting the system's boundary. When talking about depletion of resources and entropy, Khalil describes only the resource, i.e. an open sub-system of the larger ecosystem. In this sub-system entropy can, of course, be decreased by purposeful human action. But this is not a contradiction of the Second Law (in either formulation, C or K) since we are looking at an open system, which is manipulated by human action in the form of energy-matter exchanges with the outside. However, the price of the decrease of entropy in the open sub-system is an increase in the rest of the larger system, such that the total entropy increases, as stated by the Second Law. This view on the whole system is the point G-R has made.

What sounds to be a contradiction thus disappears as soon as one properly specifies the boundaries of the systems under consideration.

7.2.3   On the Meaningfulness of an Energy or Entropy Theory of Value

Question 3 concerned energy, entropy and value. If one accepts that the First and Second Laws of Thermodynamics hold for all processes, natural and economic (always assuming that the system boundaries are specified in an appropriate way), then it may be asked in what specific way can they be operationalised to be incorporated into a description of the economic process, or might be used to give some policy advice.

7.2.3.1 Entropy and Value

Certainly, until now 'markets ignore fundamental laws of (particularly) thermodynamics which should somehow be relevant for public policy on the use of exhaustible resources' (Burness et al., 1980:1). That these laws are indeed relevant to the economic process should be obvious. Limits on capital-resource substitution in growth models imposed by mass-energy balance considerations, a First Law concept, have already been noted by Ayres and Kneese (1969) and more recently studied with respect to dynamic implications in ecological-economic systems by Perrings (1994). Concerning the relevance of the Second Law as con-straining the possibility of continuous growth we have already exten-sively quoted G-R's view.

The question of how to implement thermodynamics in economics has been addressed in different ways. Burness et al. (1980) explicitly recognise the relevance of the First and Second Laws of Thermody-namics to resource extraction issues, yet argue in favour of neoclassical business as usual, since 'it is simply not clear as to how thermodynamic concepts - the entropy and energy "theories" of value - are to be used in enriching the promulgation of public policy' (Burness et al., 1980:8).

Although the two concepts are often mentioned together, one has to distinguish between energy and entropy theories of value. During the 1970s and especially following the oil crisis, some ecologists (e.g. Odum, 1971; Costanza, 1981) pointed out that energy is the only scarce non-producible factor of production, and proposed an energy-based substitute for market valuation. This assumption of a single non-producible factor of production is reminiscent of the Labour Theory of Value of Ricardo and Marx. The problem of how the costs of a single input determine the price of the output has long been subject to debate in economics and the limits of such an approach have turned out to be very narrow (see e.g. Samuelson, 1971). As far as energy as a factor of production is concerned, G-R (1979) gives an explicit rebuttal of these energy theories of value.

The works of G-R are the source of many misunderstandings, one of which is the false belief that he would advocate an entropy theory of value instead. For instance, Burness et al. (1980:7) state that:

> ... indeed, the notion of value may lie at the heart of interface between thermodynamic and economic concepts in terms of ways that these concepts are coming to be used in the public debate concerning resource use policies. Georgescu-Roegen claims an entropy theory of value (Georgescu-Roegen, 1971:Chapter 5).

This is wrong. G-R does not claim an entropy theory of value in the sense that it is entropy and entropy alone which determines the economic value of something. On the contrary, he specifically cautions against such an interpretation. The misunderstanding may arise from the fact that G-R stresses very much that low entropy is a necessary (yet not sufficient!) condition for something to have economic value. G-R himself gives the example (G-R, 1971:282) of a poisonous mushroom, an object characterised by very low entropy and yet not considered especially valuable in an economic sense, to point out that low entropy is not sufficient for economic value: 'Low entropy ... is a *necessary* condition for a thing to have value. This condition, however, is not also *sufficient*' (G-R, 1971:282).[8]

Even if one acknowledges the relevance of the First and Second Laws of Thermodynamics to economics, this does not mean that entropy and entropy alone determines economic value: 'Economic value depends ultimately upon the subjective impressions of economic agents, and not upon the physical characteristics of a material, such as its level of entropy' (Townsend, 1992).

But if the thermodynamic laws cannot be operationalised as the basis of some theory of value, what then is the relevance of thermodynamics to the economic process?

7.2.3.2   Entropy and Sustainability

The Second Law is very peculiar among the natural laws in that it tells us nothing about what *will* happen, but only about what *cannot* happen (Dyke, 1994). This is at the heart of G-R's pessimistic view: the Second Law constrains the possibilities of production and consumption; continuous economic growth, or even a steady-state economy, appear as an illusion. In this context the entropy production rate of economic activities has explicitly been suggested as a measure of sustainability by Hannon, Ruth and Delucia (1993). In contrast to this view, G-R and Daly consider that 'the entropy law should be viewed as a constraint, not as an independent sufficient explanation of value' (Daly, 1986:319). The implications of the First and Second Laws of Thermodynamics today are certainly not reflected in market prices.

However, these laws cannot serve to provide calculated, non-market coefficients based on work or energy or entropy as substitutes of market values. Rather, the nature of the economic constraint imposed by the laws of thermodynamics is such that it tells us something about the maximal sustainable physical scale of the whole economy relative to the ecosystem. But:

> ... sustainability, like justice, is a value not achievable by purely individualistic market processes. Yet these values can be reflected back into market prices, when the market operates under collectively instituted macro constraints designed to protect these values to which the purely individualistic market is blind (Daly, 1986:320).

Once the nature and necessity of the constraint on economic scale and growth imposed by the Entropy Law has been recognised, and enacted on the economic system by collective action, the allocation of the ecologically sustainable aggregate throughput among millions of alternative uses at the micro level is achieved in a Pareto-superior way by individual choices in a market system. The relevance of thermodynamics to the economic process thus is, according to Townsend (1992:99), that 'thermodynamics provides awareness of a biophysical constraint to economics, rather than with a new economics.'

7.2.4   Entropy, Information and Technical Progress

Question 4 related to the relationship between information and thermodynamics. Young (1991) presents a formal model for resource extraction which obeys the Second Law of Thermodynamics. The site contains two materials, call them *A* and *B*, of which initially only *A* is considered a resource. As *A* is depleted, its concentration in the site decreases and it is dispersed in the environment. Thus, the entropy of the material stock increases. Suppose now, due to some new technology, material *B* is considered to be a useful resource. According to Young, the new state of the system may be considered less entropic than the initial state, since the concentration of the resource *B* in the site has increased. Young states that:

> ... it is very possible for entropy, or our intuitive notion of entropy as disorderliness or unavailability, to be decreasing even though the system is closed [to the exchange of energy and matter. That is, the system is isolated]. It is, however, open with respect to knowledge which has exogenously increased (Young, 1991:178).

For Young, information which is anti-entropic can make a difference in isolated systems, such that the Second Law does not hold in isolated systems which are open to information.

Were Young more familiar with the physical literature on the Entropy Law, he would easily recognise that what he presents is just another version of one long-standing puzzle in the entropy debate. In the nineteenth century Maxwell suggested that entropy is not a property only of the system, but depends also on our knowledge: 'Confusion, like the correlative term order, is not a property of material things in themselves, but only in relation to the mind which perceives them' (quoted after Balian, 1991:128).

Maxwell invented a 'thought experiment', the famous Maxwell's demon, which he thought demonstrated that under the influence of information the Second Law does not hold. It took more than a century to give a complete refutation of this paradox.[9] Leo Szilard (1898-1964) eventually showed that the apparent violation of the Second Law by intelligent beings happens thanks to some knowledge about the microstate of the system, knowledge which is acquired beforehand and is retained in the memory of the intelligent beings acting upon the system. Acquiring this information has to be paid for through an increase in entropy elsewhere and/or earlier in time (Szilard, 1929). Thus, information makes it even harder to properly specify the system's boundary. But if it is done so as to include the act of acquiring the relevant information in the system, then the Second Law certainly also holds for intelligent beings.

Entropy, after all, is a physical concept and not only its generalisation to information theory by Shannon and Weaver (1949), but even its mechanical interpretation by Boltzmann has caused many misunderstandings among people not familiar with the technical arguments. Information in the sense of Shannon and Weaver, or knowledge about the system's microstate, in the sense of Boltzmann always refers to some observer's *potential* knowledge about the system and not to *actual* knowledge. For the definition of entropy of the system it does not matter whether the materials A and B in Young's model have any use at all; it even does not matter whether the observer chooses to distinguish between A and B or not. All what matters is that there *are* two materials, A and B, in the site. Here is the error in Young's argument. The quantity AQ_M, the 'quality index of available matter' on which Young bases his statement, is determined initially with respect to A when only A is known to be a useful resource, and later with respect to B when B is known to be a resource. That is fine, but then AQ_M just has nothing to do with entropy.

Again, since entropy is a physical concept, beware of anthropomorphic interpretations of this concept in terms of usefulness or availability. They might be misleading!

Whereas information/new knowledge/technical progress certainly cannot reverse the consequences of the Second Law they can, however, alter the rate of entropic change of the system (Townsend, 1992). The process of inventing a new technology may itself increase entropy, but it may lead to the consequence that the same goods as before can be produced after innovation of the new technology at a reduced rate of entropy increase. 'Improvements in technology simply permit humankind to survive the ride along the gradient from lower to higher entropy with more efficiency' (Townsend, 1992:99). This idea has been taken up by many authors. Ayres and Nair (1984) were among the first to note that 'simultaneous build-up of local order and global entropy during materials processing sequence' (Ayres and Nair, 1984:69) is the characteristic property of production. They infer that:

> ... *while it is not possible to substitute labour or capital, as such, for embodied material or energy resources directly, there is a more general way of looking at the problem - as a substitution of technological knowledge for raw materials. Any increase in the thermodynamic efficiency of a machine or process is an example of such a substitution* (Ayres and Nair, 1984:71).

This argument is elaborated in more detail and placed in the context of the description of the economy as an open system by Ayres (1994), who presents 'information' as the common denominator of physical, biological, economic and social processes. Ruth (1995) defines information, order and knowledge with respect to entropy, and gives a detailed account of what role these quantities play in ecological and economic systems.

This opens a new perspective on the theory of production and especially on limits to production; Binswanger (1992) analyses the ecological aspects of an informational economy.

7.3 APPLICATIONS OF THE ENTROPY CONCEPT IN ECOLOGICAL ECONOMICS

Attempts have been made to identify a formal isomorphism between thermodynamics and economics. If such an isomorphism existed one could adapt the highly developed analytical tools from thermodynamics to economics. For instance, Amir (1994) has proposed such an interpretation of economics as being formally equivalent to the Gibbs formulation of thermodynamics. In a similar vein, Ayres and Martinás (1994) derive a monotonically increasing function Z from the behaviour of individual economic units and pair-wise exchange relations among them. This function Z is suggested as an analogue to the entropy variable S. In their procedure they explicitly follow Carathéodory's axiomatic foundation of thermodynamics.

We believe that such a pure isomorphism does not exist. Hence, one cannot use the analytical framework of physics analytically to describe economic relations. However, physical laws, such as the Entropy Law, are of relevance when physics enters the scope of economics, as in the study of resources, the environment or production. In these areas, an economic description cannot neglect the fundamental physical laws. These laws have to enter the economic description in a way specific to the problem areas under consideration.

One can distinguish two strands in the literature which deals with the relevance of the entropy concept in economics.

7.3.1 The General Meaning of Entropy

The first strand is concerned with the general meaning of entropy to our world view, and takes the entropy concept as the cornerstone for a new paradigm for explaining not only economic phenomena but also other social phenomena (e.g. Rifkin, 1980). The great danger in this attempt is to misinterpret certain terms that have a very specific meaning in physics, but can be used in an almost arbitrary way in everyday language. For instance, Boltzmann's notion of order/disorder is exactly defined in statistical mechanics, with respect to the number of microstates realising one given macrostate. But in everyday language, 'order' not only is a very ill-defined term, it also may carry a value judgement. Most attempts to present the Entropy Law as making a statement about increasing disorder as a new paradigm for social or economic systems in general, not only neglect that the systems under consideration are not at all isolated, but also are trapped in more or less severe misinterpretations of the notions of order/disorder.

It can be seen as progress that, as in the second strand in the literature, specific problem areas in economics have been reformulated by explicitly taking into account the Entropy Law in a very concrete way. However, all such attempts considerably reduce the true complexity of the underlying economic problems, by reducing the analysis to some basic thermodynamic relations. In doing so, one focuses on long-run constraints which the natural laws impose on all human action. More immediate constraints (e.g. current technology) play a less important role in the analysis. In that sense, thermodynamics of open systems marks the outer limit of what is possible in economics and what is not.

Such a procedure is especially fruitful in the field of ecological economics, where one deals with the interaction between the human economic system and the ecosystem, i.e. resource extraction and degradation of the environment by pollution, and where one is interested mainly in long-run relations. The entropy concept can serve as a guideline to modelling both the source side and the sink side of the economy. Further, it enables one to establish a relation between problems on both sides which, of course, are interconnected (cf. Chapter 10).

7.3.2 Resource Extraction

Faber, Niemes and Stephan (1987) present a model in which resource extraction is described as like the de-mixing of two ideal gases. A certain number of molecules of the desired resource, which are found mixed up with molecules of other materials in a given volume V_1, have to be separated in a smaller volume V_2, such that the concentration of the resource in that smaller volume increases (Figure 7.2). This is equivalent to a decrease of entropy for the whole system analogous to the de-mixing of two ideal gases. By means of classical thermodynamics, Faber,

Niemes and Stephan calculate how much energy is necessary to achieve such a decrease of entropy for the system. The result is that the energy requirement for extracting one unit of the desired resource, first, increases with decreasing initial concentration of the resource and, second, increases with increasing desirable final concentration of the resource. This thermodynamic approach provides a plausible explanation for increasing resource prices for a given technology and for continuous, or increasing, demand for this resource.

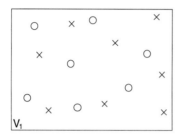 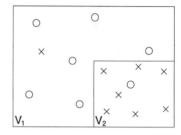

(a) Before extraction.   (b) After extraction.

Figure 7.2. Concentration of the resource in site.

The approach taken by Faber, Niemes and Stephan has been criticised for two reasons (O'Connor, 1990; Khalil, 1989). The authors base their argument on the Second Law and the entropy notion of classical equilibrium thermodynamics. This critique is acknowledged by Faber (1985), who points out the limits of this notion of entropy as opposed to the more general role entropy plays in open systems. Further, the model used to calculate the energy requirement for resource extraction assumes ideal gases and reversible processes. In contrast, the resources one wishes to describe are not ideal gases, and the real process of resource extraction is not reversible, but irreversible. These idealising assumptions are made explicit in the treatment (Faber, Niemes and Stephan, 1987) and do not restrict the qualitative result. If the processes involved were not reversible, but irreversible, then the calculated thermodynamic energy requirement could be interpreted as a lower bound. The energy required in real processes of resource extraction may be a lot larger than this minimal thermodynamic energy. Nevertheless, the conclusion of increasing resource prices would hold in the long run. For that reason, the model can indeed serve as a useful way of linking constraints imposed by natural laws and economic consequences.

7.3.3   Environmental Pollution

Not only on the source side of the economic process, but also on the sink side can entropy serve to indicate scarcity. Waste or pollution which occur as a joint product of consumption are dispersed in the air, in the water, or in the ground. This corresponds to an increase in entropy analogous to the mixing of two ideal gases. Since most of what leaves the economic process as waste cannot serve as an input to natural processes in the biosphere, this increase in entropy is irreversible. Hence, according to Faber (1985), entropy can serve as a highly aggregated measure for environmental pollution.

This idea has been operationalised by Kümmel (1980, 1989), who defines an aggregated measure for pollution as the rate of increase in entropy per unit volume of the biosphere where this increase occurs. One obtains the total pollution measure when summing over all different kinds of pollutants which lead to an increase in entropy. In order to take account of the different qualities of pollutants, as far as their negative influence on human welfare is concerned, the different pollutants are related to critical threshold values and the respective natural purification rates. This aggregated measure of pollution then enters the society's production function, such that production is limited by any process which causes one of the pollutants to exceed its critical threshold value. A society whose production is close to being limited by one kind of pollution is likely to employ techniques of abatement, disposal, or reduction. Therefore this pollutant can be reduced, but only at the price of some other kind of pollution and, most importantly, producing heat as a consequence of the additionally employed technique.

In a way, heat is the ultimate form of any pollution. Kümmel and Schüssler (1991) thus suggest introducing heat equivalents for the different pollutants, which could be defined as the amount of heat which is inevitably produced when cleaning the environment from the respective pollutant, or avoiding the pollutant to the highest possible degree. By using heat equivalents, one could easily compare the environmental effects of different production techniques on a common scale, which is of importance for an ecological system of accounting.

Kümmel (1989) has pointed out that the pollution of our environment with high entropy is a problem, even when taking into account that the Earth is not an isolated but a closed system, which can export some of the produced high entropy into the surrounding space. The mechanism by which this happens is the radiation of heat from the Earth into space. The Earth receives low entropy in the form of heat and light from the sun, and radiates the same amount of energy back into space, but in high entropy form. Thus, the importance of the sun for life on Earth is seen not to consist in providing energy (the net intake of energy from the sun is zero!), but in providing a permanent flux of energy, which delivers low entropy and takes away the high entropy produced in the biosphere and in the economy. This flow of low entropy energy from the sun on to the surface of the Earth is about 230 W/m^2 and the associated export of entropy amounts to 1 W/Km^2 (Ebeling, Engel and Feistel, 1990:80ff). Kümmel (1980:109ff, 1989:162) calls this the 'heat barrier', because if in irreversible processes more than 1 W/Km^2 of entropy is produced on the Earth's surface (for instance by erosion, biological, ecological, economic or other processes), then 'entropy waste' accumulates on Earth. In this view, the production of heat as the ultimate form of pollution is indeed a serious problem, even in the closed system Earth.

Binswanger (1993) has pointed out the problems inherent in taking entropy as an aggregated measure for pollution. For instance, a large part of the entropy problem is not captured by the above mentioned models, namely an increase in entropy as a consequence of irreversibly over-using renewable resources. Further, the interactions between the economic and the ecological system take place on all different hierarchical scales, between micro and macro description. For example, the extinction of a species in some very special ecosystem, or the global CO_2 problem, can both be viewed as decreasing the ecosystem's complexity, and thus increasing entropy, but on different scales. The respective entropies, viz. the entropies with respect to the system boundaries appropriately specified on the respective scales, are hardly comparable.

What makes the above mentioned concepts even more questionable is that they all implicitly assume that we know all of the consequences that the pollutants will cause in the atmosphere, in the ground or in the oceans. Given the complexity of the economy-ecosystem interactions, and the very long time-scales of interest, this seems a very unrealistic assumption. The study of open systems far from equilibrium tells us that such systems do not even behave in a strictly deterministic way.[10]

From these last remarks it follows that the strength of the thermodynamic approach in ecological economics does not consist in providing a quantitative aggregated measure for environmental damage. Instead, this approach enables one to conceptualise the different effects of human action on the environment, be it on the source side or on the sink side of the economy, in the context of the evolution of the economic system.

7.4   CONCLUSIONS AND PROSPECTS FOR THE FUTURE

It seems that the discussion about the role of the Entropy Law in economic systems up to now, twenty-five years after G-R's pioneering work, has made clear some major advantages of such an approach, but has also shown where there are dead-ends.

The interpretation of the Second Law as imposing an absolute constraint on economic growth, be it quantitative or qualitative, has turned out to be too pessimistic. The Earth is not an isolated system, but is subject to the laws describing the evolution of closed and open systems. The energy and the associated low entropy that we receive from the sun offer a creative potential for the build-up of increasingly complex structures. The economy as a whole should be viewed as an open system.

Nevertheless, entropy balance considerations are of importance even in a closed or open system. Further, the Second Law can be used to describe sub-systems of the open economic system, which owing to extremely long time-scales of the natural processes involved, can be viewed as de facto isolated. In particular, the stock of exhaustible resources, or the stock of non-degradable pollutants accumulated in the atmosphere, are subject to a description based on the Second Law. Here, absolute limits to economic development do indeed exist.

The tension between the two Arrows of Time, and the creative potential inherent in the entropy concept, could best be captured in a formal way by strictly distinguishing between stocks and funds and the respective scarcities. (See Chapter 9 for a fuller discussion.) An absolute scarcity, as indicated by the Second Law, and pointed out by G-R, exists for stocks which cannot be regenerated on a time-scale comparable to the time-scale of economic processes. In contrast, the steady flow of energy from the sun or the services of funds (using the terminology of G-R, 1971:224ff), can be regarded as inputs to the open system of the economy and give rise to evolutionary development.

In conclusion, we believe the entropy concept to be fundamental to ecological economics; it gives insights into economy-environment interactions which are not otherwise available. Indeed, we hold that the entropy concept offers a world-view for the fruitful development of ecological economics.

However, as we have seen above, there are many pitfalls for the unwary when using the entropy concept. Indeed, perhaps the entropy concept should come with a health warning! Those wishing to study ecological economics, especially using entropy, should first closely familiarise themselves with the precise meaning of entropy, and take note of what can be done with it, and what should not be attempted. The main strength of the entropy concept lies not in analytically *solving* problems, but in *detecting* problems and giving insights into their solution.

To reiterate what we said in the introduction; entropy is not an analytical tool for economics, but is a necessary part of an adequate conceptual framework for ecological economics, and for economics in general.

NOTES

1. It may interest the reader that two of the authors have degrees in physics and two in economics.
2. We note that this quotation refers to the static case only, and has to be qualified in the sense that, as a matter of fact, the Second Law certainly does show the temporal direction of a process.
3. Norgaard (1984, 1985, 1986) has explored this issue, which he calls 'coevolutionary development'. He acknowledges that G-R is right with respect to stock resources, but that institutional development is possible based on flow resources, especially the flow of energy from the sun. O'Connor (1991) stresses that a combination of far-from-equilibrium thermodynamics with institutional analysis can furnish a rich impetus for such a coevolutionary perspective in ecological economics.
4. Except for the notable but erroneous postulation of G-R's Fourth Law.
5. 'No process is possible in which the sole result is the transfer of energy from a cooler to a hotter body' (Khalil, 1990:165).
6. 'No process is possible in which the sole result is the absorption of heat from a reservoir and its complete conversion into work.' (Khalil, 1990:168, quoting from Atkins.)
7. It should be noted at this point, that the Carnot process is only an idealised model of an infinitely slow, reversible, cyclic process whereas real production processes are fast, irreversible and not even cyclic. For the sake of studying complex phenomena with the help of simple models it might be legitimate to compare real production processes to the idealised model of a Carnot cycle, but Bianciardi, Donati and Ulgiati (1993) gave a clear caveat that misunderstandings and even theoretical contradictions might arise from such a comparison. For instance, 'the Carnot cycle in its thermodynamic application describes the upper limit to the potency which any purposeful agency can achieve. To adduce from an analogy with the Carnot cycle that the corresponding purposeful agency in economic activity may be of unlimited potency is surely fallacious' (Williamson, 1993:71).
8. Even G-R's notion of necessity can be questioned. An omelette has higher entropy than the egg from which it derived, but is *more* valuable than the egg.
9. See Leff and Rex (1990) for an extensive compilation of the literature.

10. The limitations of present knowledge and the role of ignorance in describing the future are discussed in Chapters 3, 8 and 11.

8. Evolution in Biology, Physics and Economics: A Conceptual Analysis

8.1 INTRODUCTION

Many branches of conventional science tend to conceive of their objects of study as timeless; they therefore tend to represent their findings in 'eternal' laws, such as the Laws of Classical Mechanics. The application of such kinds of science easily leads to the belief that future events are predictable. This predictability would have been complete for that ideal scientist, Laplace's demon (Prigogine and Stengers, 1984). In contrast to this approach, we start from the assumption that the objects and their relationships which science examines are intrinsically characterised by the complete or partial emergence of novelty in the course of time. This leads us to approach the question of predictability in a new way; we shall need to develop new concepts to answer this question. A key notion for our approach is 'evolution'. (This notion was introduced briefly in Chapter 3.)

It is known that objects of study in biology at any period in time are the result of an evolutionary process. We shall argue that this is also true for other sciences, in particular for economics, and even for physics. Our broad task is to develop a general framework for conceptualising evolution. We shall proceed in such a manner that biology, physics and economics can be contained within it. In this way we also intend to contribute to the furthering of interdisciplinary research between these three disciplines. For example, physics, biology and economics are all of vital importance for environmental analysis, where the simultaneous and interacting evolution of physical, biological and economic systems is involved. (The issue of interdisciplinary research is discussed extensively in Chapter 10.)

Evolution is a very encompassing concept, and is used in many different contexts. For example, one speaks of physical, biological, social, political and economic evolution. Key concepts for a definition of evolution in biology are mutation, heredity and selection, while in systems theory one employs the concepts of self-evolution, self-sustained development, and self-reference. For our conceptual framework it is useful to begin with the broadest possible starting point, for otherwise there is the danger that evolution is seen in too narrow a sense. Such a narrow conceptualisation risks the exclusion of important aspects of evolutionary processes.

In our view the key characteristics of evolution are (1) change, and (2) time; we consider them also to suffice as elements for the following starting point:

Evolution is the process of the changing of something over time.

In a strict sense this is not a definition but a tautology. It simply gives information as to how we use the word 'evolution'. This we do purposely so as not to exclude any processes from our consideration. This approach is in line with Heidegger's (1927/1979) insight that fundamental notions can only be explained in a circular way. Complementary to this approach is Wittgenstein's (1922/1969) method. He would have qualified our definition as 'nonsense'. Instead he would have asked how we could use the notions of evolution in different contexts. It is precisely in the spirit of Wittgenstein that, throughout this chapter, we seek to illustrate the concept of evolution in biology, physics and economics, rather than seeking a definition of the concept of evolution in a close analytical way.

Our aim in this chapter is to specify and operationalise this conceptualisation of evolution. To develop our conceptual framework we use concepts originally formulated in biology. In particular, we shall use the notions of genotypic and phenotypic evolution. In our generalisation, by 'genotype' we mean the 'potentialities' of a system, and by 'phenotype' we mean the 'realisation' of these potentialities. In this sense our concepts are not *derived* from biology; rather, they had their first expression, as a special case, in the biological literature. Thus, when we use the terms genotype and phenotype, we are *not* making analogies with biology. We are, rather extending the usage of these terms in what we feel is a natural manner. (For a discussion of the use of analogy, and its problems, see Chapter 10.)

It will turn out that the evolutionary process, as we understand it, always takes place, albeit with different velocities. The evolution of our present physical laws and fundamental constants took place a long time ago and within a very short period of time (see Section 8.4). The biological evolution of species lasts millions or thousands of years and proceeds continually (see Section 8.3). The evolution of social and of economic institutions takes place in hundreds of years, decades, or even shorter periods. The contemporary evolution of techniques, and of world politics in 1989, show that social evolution may even have a much faster pace.

We are interested in particular in those changes in the course of time which are related to the emergence of novelty, because it is the latter which restricts the area of validity of predictability.

The degree of predictability varies in different areas of science. Clearly, there are unpredictable processes in physics (see Chapter 11); but in comparison with economic processes, the degree of predictability is very high. This difference can be explained by the emergence of novelty during very short time periods in economics (e.g. invention, and the spontaneous behaviour of people).

Before proceeding briefly to indicate the contents of this chapter, we wish to acknowledge that there is a considerable, and growing, literature in economics which uses, to a greater or lesser extent, evolutionary ideas drawn from biology. Examples of such work include Marshall (1890), Veblen (1902), Alchian (1950), Penrose (1952), Cyert and March (1963), Hirshleifer (1977), Schelling (1978), Boulding (1981), Nelson and Winter (1982), Matthews (1984), Norgaard (1984), Witt (1980, 1987) and Clark and Juma (1987).

In Section 8.2 we distinguish between two types of processes in time: predictable and unpredictable processes. While it turns out that the former may be of an 'equi-final' nature, the latter are not. Section 8.3 is pivotal to this chapter, in that in biology the concepts of evolution, particularly the notions of phenotype and genotype, were originally developed and applied. Here the conceptual foundations for our evolutionary framework are laid. In Section 8.4 we apply these evolutionary concepts to physics, while evolution in economics is discussed in Section 8.5. In Section 8.6 we compare physics, biology and economics with respect to the difficulties in prediction in each area. The relationship between genotypic and phenotypic evolution and the importance of ex post and ex ante considerations is discussed in Section 8.7. Section 8.8 offers some general conclusions.

8.2 PREDICTABILITY AND THE EVOLUTIONARY PROCESS

To allow us to proceed to our conceptual analysis of evolution we distinguish between two types of processes in time. We call these 'Predictable' and 'Unpredictable' processes. Before discussing these processes it is appropriate to note that actual processes lie on a continuum with regard to their degree of predictability. That is to say, certain processes are predictable with great certitude, while others are entirely unpredictable; many processes fall into neither of these categories, because we are ignorant of them, or of their structures. However, for our purposes it is convenient to employ the above rough categories.

8.2.1 Examples of Predictable Processes in Physics, Biology and Economics

We shall illustrate predictable processes with five examples, from physics, biology and economics. We have ordered them according to their degree of predictability.

(i)   Consider a ball falling on to a pavement. Using the laws of classical mechanics one can predict with great exactitude the movement over time of the ball. After a certain amount of time the ball will come to rest, and a mechanical equilibrium will be established.

(ii)   The dynamics of the launching of an Earth satellite offer a different type of predictable mechanical process. The satellite initially follows a path determined by the rocket propelling it, but it eventually achieves a stable and predictable orbit. In contradistinction to example (i), in this case the predicted equilibrium outcome achieved is dynamic rather than static.

(iii)   An example from thermodynamics is the case of an ice cube exposed in a warm room. Depending on its volume and the temperature, it will melt in a predictable way and be converted into a puddle of water and atmospheric moisture. If the room is sealed, an equilibrium will be established between the liquid and gaseous water. However, in terms of the molecules that constitute the water, predictability in an exact sense is impossible. The description of the behaviour of the water molecules at thermodynamic equilibrium can be at best stochastic.

(iv)   The life-cycle of an organism is generally predictable. The life of a chicken begins as a fertilised egg, continues as a chick developing within the eggshell, progresses to the newly hatched chick, and thence the mature chicken, the old chicken, and the dead chicken. In this example, while the general pattern of the process is well known, the detailed development of a particular chicken will be impossible to predict with any accuracy.

(v)   For an economic example of a predictable process, we can consider a simple market which is initially not at equilibrium; that is, the price of the commodity does not equate supply with demand. Assuming that market mechanisms exist to allow adjustment of supply and demand, using price signals, we would expect that eventually a market equilibrium would be established. The exact time path of the adjustment would, of course, depend on the exact nature of the supply and demand functions and the adjustment process involved.

From these five illustrations we conclude that a predictable process, as we will understand it, is one whose time-path can be described deterministically or stochastically.

An important further characteristic of many predictable processes is that they are 'equi-final'. We call a process equi-final, if, given certain boundary conditions, the predictable outcome is independent of the initial conditions governing the process. For example, if a small ball is placed anywhere on the inner surface of a large bowl, then under gravity the ball will eventually settle at the unique base of the bowl. We see that the final position of the ball is predictable, and is also independent of the initial position of the ball. It is therefore clear that any equi-final process whose dynamic behaviour is known is predictable, though, of course, not all predictable systems are equi-final.

8.2.2 Unpredictable Processes

We now give three examples of processes which are in principle unpredictable; i.e. independent of our state of knowledge or ignorance. These illustrations are taken from physics, biology and economics.

(i)   The first example we use may surprise the reader somewhat, but it illustrates an important point to which we wish to return later. There is a growing literature suggesting that what we now regard as Universal Physical Constants (e.g. the gravitational constant G, Planck's constant h, etc.) were far from constant in the first few microseconds after the Big Bang which brought the universe into being. At the time of the Big Bang it seems that these constants could have ended up with values different from those they finally assumed. Modern theory therefore suggests that the whole nature of the universe was, in principle, unpredictable at the time of the Big Bang (Hawking, 1988) (for more details see Section 8.4).

(ii)   The whole history of the evolution of species demonstrates unpredictability. Surely no reasonably intelligent dinosaur would have expected that this very successful and long-established group of species would not only be extinguished, but replaced by mammals.

(iii)   The modern world we inhabit is largely the product of cumulated human inventiveness. By its very nature, inventiveness is unpredictable, for correctly to predict the nature of an invention is equivalent to making that invention.

(iv)   Another important sphere of creative activity, involving the emergence of unpredictable novelty, is artistic endeavour, in music, literature, etc. For instance, the move from representational art to non-representational methods in the early twentieth century was certainly not foreseen, though ex post it can be understood.

8.2.3   Predictability and Ex Ante Theory

As noted above, to speak of 'predictable' and 'unpredictable' processes is to make a rough categorisation. When speaking of 'predictability' in the following, we will often mean '*in principle* predictable'. By this we mean that it is possible to get to know the dynamics of a system, which allows one to make some predictions concerning future developments. It is also useful to note that when we say that a process is 'predictable in broad terms', this only means that we can say at least something about its behaviour, be it that it is equi-final, unstable, chaotic, stochastic, etc. In the case of processes which are predictable in broad terms, there may remain areas of ignorance. This implies that whenever we are able to conceive an ex ante theory about an empirical subject we are able to obtain 'predictable' results, at least in 'broad terms'. In this sense, this chapter deals with the question: 'In which cases can one hope to develop ex ante theories?'. Wherever an area of study is in an essential way subject to the emergence of novelty, an ex ante theory cannot be developed. To give a simple illustration, it is not possible to conceive a theory on the behaviour of lions at a time when lions have not yet evolved as a species.

In this section we have illustrated and discussed predictable and unpredictable processes. In Sections 8.3, 8.4 and 8.5 we shall develop a new framework to analyse these processes from our evolutionary point of view.

8.3   CONCEPTUAL ELEMENTS OF BIOLOGICAL EVOLUTION

In this section we shall draw upon some well developed concepts from biology; in particular we shall use the notions of phenotype and genotype employed in the Darwinian framework of the evolution of species. We shall relate these evolutionary concepts to the notions of predictable and unpredictable processes, as developed in Section 8.2. In particular we shall contrast predictable and equi-final processes with unpredictable processes. As the concepts of phenotype and genotype are central to all our discussions below, we first define these terms as they are generally used in biology. An organism has a certain appearance, capabilities, characteristics, etc. The appearance that it presents to the world is known as its phenotype. The phenotype displayed by an organism results from the interplay of two factors. The first factor is the potential inherited from its parents; i.e. its genetic make-up, or genotype. The second factor is the environment of the organism; for example, organisms that are otherwise identical (e.g. identical twins) will grow to different sizes and exhibit differing capabilities if they are subjected to widely differing nutritional regimes.

It is generally accepted, in biological systems, that the genotype affects the phenotype directly, but there is no such direct influence of phenotype on genotype. For example, a chance mutation may cause the genotype to alter, such that the phenotype becomes, for example, longer-necked. Further, this characteristic of being longer-necked may be inherited by that creature's offspring. On the other hand, an animal might, through its feeding habits, stretch its neck, thus altering its phenotype. This alteration will not influence its genotype and therefore this will not be a heritable characteristic.

From the above discussion it is clear that the genotype reflects the 'potentialities' of the organism. The phenotype represents the 'realisation' of these potentialities, in so far as is permitted by the environment of this organism. In all the discussion that follows we shall be concerned with how the potentialities of biological, physical and economic systems evolve, and also how the realisations of these potentialities evolve. As a convenient short-hand, and to reflect our desire to discover a fundamental conceptualisation of evolution, when we refer to 'realisations' we shall use the term 'phenotype', and when referring to 'potentialities' we shall use 'genotype'.

8.3.1   Organism, Species and Biological System

At this stage it will be useful to clarify what is meant by 'organism', 'species' and 'biological system'.

> An *organism* is the basic unit of independent life, whether plant or animal, that contributes to reproduction.
> (For an alternative, but related, definition, see Chapter 9, Section 9.2.)

A *species* is the set of all organisms whose genotypes are so similar that they allow interbreeding (e.g. horses, dogs, primroses, etc.).

A *biological system* consists of an interacting set of species, each species being made up of distinct but genetically similar organisms. For example, the flora and fauna which coexist in and on an area of wetland would constitute a biological system.

The phenotype as described above refers to an individual organism. As organisms, of their various species, interact with each other in large and heterogeneous biological systems, it is useful to consider an overall description of such a biological system. Such a description would be a listing of the phenotypes of all the organisms within the biological system in terms of the species represented and their relative abundances. We term this description a 'macro-phenotype'.

Similarly, the genetic potential of a biological system of organisms could be listed to give that system's 'macro-genotype'. This list comprises all genotypic information of all organisms of the corresponding system, and is independent of the relative frequencies of the organisms.

The advantage of descriptions of biological systems in terms of macro-phenotype and macro-genotype is that it gives explicit recognition to the fact that the evolutionary process deals with systems rather than with individual organisms, as is more fully discussed in Sections 8.3.4 and 8.3.5 below.

There has been a long-running debate in evolutionary biology as to whether the unit of evolution is best conceived as being the individual organism, the species, or the entire heterogeneous system (Levins and Lewontin, 1985).

We have noted above the usefulness of describing systems in terms of the macro-phenotype and macro-genotype. It is clear from our discussion that an individual organism can only exhibit phenotypic evolution, but not genotypic evolution, because for the latter at least two successive organisms have to exist in order to exhibit genotypic change. In contrast, a species can exhibit not only phenotypic but also genotypic evolution. The genotypic evolution of a species, however, is influenced by that of other species. It is therefore not possible to study the evolution of one species in isolation. For this reason it is useful to consider the biological system as our unit of evolution.

8.3.2   Phenotypic Evolution: Predictable Equi-final Processes

Macro-phenotypic evolution relates to the relationships between, and the relative abundances of, a number of species in mutual interaction in a given environment, where the genetic make-up, or macro-genotype, of the mixture of species is taken to be given. For example, the process of ecosystem succession subsequent to some traumatic event may lead to systematic changes over time of relative species (macro-phenotype) abundance. For instance, a major fire in an area of woodland will destroy the majority of the vegetation. In the years subsequent to the fire there will first be rapid growth of small plants; later the fast-growing trees will become established, and their shade will reduce the growth of the already established low-growing plants. Ultimately, slower growing but bigger and more robust trees will themselves shade out the faster growing trees. It is clear that in such circumstances the proportions of the species, i.e. macro-phenotypes, will change radically, but systematically and predictably, over time. It is in this sense that we consider phenotypic evolution to be a predictable process.

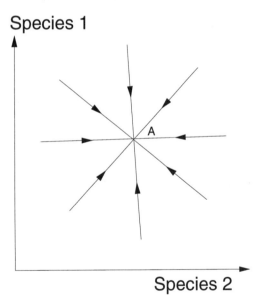

Species 1

Species 2

Figure 8.1. A stable phenotypic equilibrium with two species: predictable and equi-final.

One might illustrate the concept of phenotypic evolution by using a simple two-phenotype model, with the dynamics of their interaction shown on a phase diagram. In Figure 8.1 is plotted the relative abundances of two biological species, as they vary over time. For example, phenotype 1 may be a herbivore and phenotype 2 its food plant. The arrows indicate the direction of the evolutionary process from any particular starting point along the corresponding phase path. It is clear that an unique, stable equilibrium exists at point *A*. In the terminology of Section 8.2, we could say that the process described is predictable and equi-final.

Figure 8.2 shows a common alternative relationship between two phenotypes. Phenotype 1 in this case is a carnivorous predator and phenotype 2 is its prey animal (Clark, 1976). Here we see the long-run outcome is a limit-cycle, so that the observed abundances over time in the long-run of these phenotypes will be out-of-phase oscillations over time, as shown in Figure 8.3.

Prey

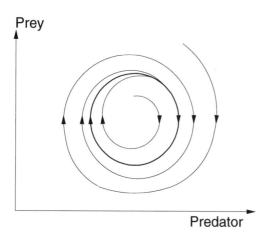

Predator

Figure 8.2. A limit-cycle phenotypic equilibrium with a two species predator-prey system.

The reader will, of course, recognise that in a biological system with many species and organisms, the nature of the equilibria, and the details of the adjustment dynamics, may be extremely complicated. For example, recent work has suggested that the dynamics of some eco-systems may be 'chaotic', as the dynamics are dominated by a 'strange attractor' (May and Oster, 1976; Beltrami, 1987). However, even such complicated systems will exhibit behaviour which is systematic and reproducible, at least in their broad outlines, between similar ecosystems.

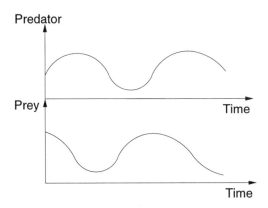

Figure 8.3. Species population oscillations in a predator-prey model.

It is in this sense that we may say that it is predictable in 'broad terms'.

Phenotypic evolution may also occur when the system is disturbed, for example by an alteration in climate or some other change in the environment. Another source of disturbance leading to phenotypic evolution, that has been well documented, is the introduction into a biological system of a new genotype, with its corresponding phenotype (Crosby, 1986). Although the disturbance may be of an unpredictable nature, be it because of ignorance or novelty, the consequences of this disturbance may be predictable. The effect will be to shift the equilibrium of the ecosystem, leading to a process of adjustment from the old equilibrium to the new one. For example, the European rat was unknown in many Pacific and Atlantic island ecosystems until the arrival of European explorers and traders. The rat was introduced accidentally from the European ships, so these ecosystems received a new phenotype. These rats rapidly established themselves on these islands and proved to be fierce competitors for resources with the indigenous fauna. Over a period of decades they became important, even dominant, components of the island ecosystems. Eventually, new equilibria were established, where the existing macro-phenotype was changed both in species represented, and markedly different in relative species abundances, compared with the situation prior to the introduction of rats.

This type of process is illustrated in Figure 8.4, where a particular herbivore is partially, or even completely, replaced by a new one which has been introduced into the ecosystem. Here the term 'herbivore' is used to represent an entire system of various types of herbivores. The introduction of the new phenotype markedly alters the characteristics of this system, and hence causes the equilibrium to shift.

Food Plants

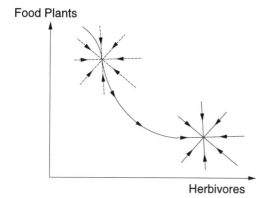

Herbivores

Figure 8.4. A shifted phenotypic equilibrium.

From the above discussion we see that phenotypic evolution involves alterations to the relative abundances of species, but no alteration to the underlying potentialities of these species, as embodied in their genotypes. Therefore, such evolution does not involve the emergence of novelty, as the species are taken as given. Further, phenotypic evolution is susceptible to description, in principle, in terms of dynamic models which give rise to well-specified, and predictable, outcomes. In particular, these outcomes are equilibria, which indicates that phenotypic evolution exhibits predictability. If the equilibrium is unique, the system is also equi-final.

8.3.3   Genotypic Evolution: Unpredictable Processes

Let us recall the meaning of the term genotype. For an organism the genotype is the underlying description of its potential for development, in interaction with its environment. In organisms the genotype is embodied in the genetic material, which mainly resides in the nuclei of the organism's cells. Changes to the genotype of an organism will be inherited by its progeny, and this new genotype may give rise to a new phenotype. In organisms, alterations to genotypes typically occur through the effects of chemicals or ionising radiation (e.g. gamma rays, X-rays, ultraviolet light, etc.) on the reproductive organs. As we shall discuss below, changes to the genotype for economic systems correspond to, for example, changing available techniques of production.

Genotypic evolution may be defined as the alteration of the genotypic description of an organism and its progeny over time. For example, the chance impact of a cosmic ray upon an animal's genetic material may alter that genotype so that the animal's progeny have, say, a slightly longer neck. The first-generation progeny may, in turn, produce second-generation progeny which are also longer-necked. It is well understood that random alteration to the genetic material of organisms only rarely produces mutations which 'improve' the capabilities of that organism's progeny. Therefore the process of changing the genotype is usually extremely slow, although there have been occasional cases of it being recorded in recent times (e.g. the appearance of melanic (dark coloured) moths in nineteenth century industrial Britain) (Kettlewell, 1973). Only long and patient study by palaeontologists has given us a still partial understanding of the genotypes that existed on earth over the past three billion years. Such study has also indicated the relative abundances of the genotypes and how, over very long periods, the appearance of new genotypes led to changes in the relative abundance of the phenotypes.

Unlike phenotypic evolution, genotypic evolution is unpredictable. This unpredictability arises from three sources.

1. The mutating influence (e.g. radiation) cannot be specified before-hand.

2. The effect of the mutating influence on the genetic material cannot be predicted.

3. The influence of this genetic change on the phenotype is also unpredictable.

In economic terminology this means that we are confronted with true uncertainty if genotypic evolution occurs. (We return to the concept of uncertainty in Chapter 11).

8.3.4   The Interaction of Genotypic and Phenotypic Evolution in Biological Systems

It must be stressed again that changes to biological genotypes take place extremely slowly. In contrast, the relative abundance of phenotypes may change relatively rapidly, as discussed in Section 8.3.1. The full scheme of biological evolution is thus seen to be the interplay of extremely slow and unpredictable changes to macro-genotypes with relatively rapid but predictable changes to macro-phenotypes.

It is worth noting that the very different rates of phenotypic and genotypic evolution in biological systems allow the predictable and unpredictable parts of the whole evolutionary process to be distinguished. (As we shall discuss below, in economic evolutionary processes it is usually much more difficult to separate out the predictable from the unpredictable processes.)

To illustrate the interaction of genotypic and phenotypic evolution in a biological system, let us imagine an ecosystem composed of a given macro-genotype. We suppose that this system has been left undisturbed sufficiently long for it to achieve an 'equilibrium' state (such 'equilibria' may be stationary, limit cycles or chaotic). Now let us suppose that there is a significant alteration of one of the genotypes in the system, and we further suppose that this new genotype is reflected in improved, but unpredictable, 'competitive effectiveness' of its progeny. The result of this appearance of a new and more competitive phenotype will be a predictable macro-phenotypic evolution, leading to altered relative abundances of these phenotypes, and hence of the embodied genotype. The outcome of the macro-phenotypic evolution will therefore be a changed relative frequency of species genotypes.

The long-run genotypic evolution can be illustrated by reference to the observed evolution of certain predator and prey species (Bakker, 1983). We begin by considering such an interaction with a given pair of genotypes, and with an equilibrium phenotypic relative abundance. Let us suppose a random genetic mutation causes the prey phenotype to become longer-legged and swifter. Supposing further that the genotype of the predator is unchanged, then the relative abundance of the phenotype will evolve towards a new equilibrium, as shown in Figure 8.5.

Point *A1* represents the equilibrium for the phenotypes of the original genotypes. With the introduction of the new genotype of the prey a new phenotypic equilibrium is established at *A2*. Phenotypic evolution takes place as the system moves from point *A1*, which is now no longer an equilibrium, towards *A2* along the corresponding phase path.

Any mutation in the predator genotype which increases its swiftness will in turn generate yet a further new equilibrium at *A3* so that a further phenotypic evolution would take place, as shown in Figure 8.6.

This series of mutations of genotypes will lead to successive periods of phenotypic evolution.

Now in biological evolution, genotypic mutations which are 'beneficial' take place at intervals which are long compared with the time taken in phenotypic evolution to re-establish 'equilibrium'. Thus, in the long-run time-scale, the observed macro-genotypic evolution can be represented by the locus of the successive macro-phenotypic equilibria, as shown in Figure 8.7.

Predator

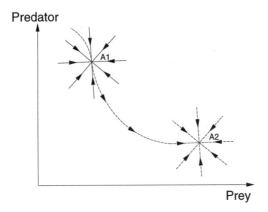

Figure 8.5. Genotypic evolution of phenotypic abundance for two species (1).

Predator

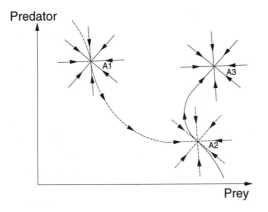

Figure 8.6. Genotypic evolution of phenotypic abundance for two species (2).

Figure 8.7 can itself be interpreted as an evolutionary phase diagram. But unlike the phase diagram in phenotypic evolution, as genotypic evolution is unpredictable, the phase path can only be constructed ex post, i.e. once the genotypic/phenotypic evolutionary process has occurred. This is in contrast with phenotypic evolution, which is predictable; knowledge of the dynamics of the system allows the full phase diagram to be constructed ex ante. We shall return to a fuller discussion of the role of ex post and ex ante analysis below.

It follows from the above discussion that while the notion of an equilibrium, of whatever type, is central to the analysis of phenotypic

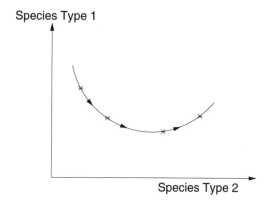

Figure 8.7. Long-run locus of phenotypic abundances under genotypic evolution.

evolution, there is no way of introducing the concept of equilibrium into genotypic evolution. Thus while equi-finality is important in assessing relations between phenotypes in the relatively short-run, equi-finality plays no part at all in the notion of genotypic evolution in the very long-run. For example a simple two species system might have a genotypic evolutionary phase diagram, as shown in phase diagram Figure 8.8.

It is clear from Figure 8.8 that the initial specification of the macro-genotype leads to a unique evolutionary path. For example, if in an isolated ecosystem (e.g. a large island) the system were in state *A* initially, while other isolated ecosystems were in states *B* and *C*, there will be no reason to expect that long-run genotypic evolution would lead to similar outcomes.

To illustrate this, consider the cases of Australia and New Zealand, which were isolated from what is now the Asian land mass approximately forty million years ago, and from each other shortly thereafter (in geologic terms). In Australia there has evolved a rich fauna of marsupials, such as kangaroos and wombats, while in New Zealand the fauna came to be dominated by flightless birds such as the kiwi and the moa (Keast, 1981).

From these illustrations we see that the time-path of a process exhibiting genotypic evolution has no 'end'. We can expect that genotypic evolution will be a never-ending process. Certainly, there is no particular final state towards which it tends, unlike the many systems exhibiting predictable equi-final phenotypic evolution.

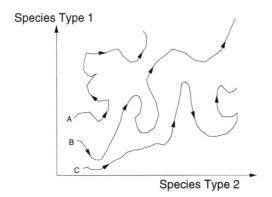

Species Type 1

A

B

C

Species Type 2

Figure 8.8. A two species genotypic evolutionary phase diagram.

8.3.5   Co-evolution and Niches

Genotypic evolution is sometimes described in terms of being 'selected' by interaction with the environment. The environment can be viewed as a 'filter' of the corresponding phenotypes. However, every species, and indeed every organism, is part of the environment of each organism in a biological system. As described in Section 3.3, where successive genotypic evolution of a predator with its prey species was discussed, it is less than useful to consider the genotypic evolution of any species in isolation. Much more useful is to think of the evolution of the entire system; that is, to consider 'co-evolution' of many interacting species (Thompson, 1982).

From the point of view of any individual organism, or species, only a limited amount of the full environment actually interacts with the organism or species. This limited range of interacting environment is known as the species' 'niche'. For example, the niche of the honeybee comprises a limited range of vegetation and airspace, while the niche of the fox comprises a relatively limited range of land and the flora and fauna it contains.

In co-evolution, the niche of every species is periodically disturbed by a genotypic evolutionary change to other species. Sometimes a niche may be enlarged or enriched, leading to a greater abundance of a species. At other times niches may be reduced, or even completely eliminated, leading to the extinction of species. However, it is worth noting that an increase in the complexity of a biological system, through the emergence of new species, will tend to lead to a greater number and diversity of niches. This will open up possibilities for further genotypic evolution. This is clear when we recognise that any new organism that evolves can act, for example, as both a prey (or forage) species for external predation, and as a host to parasites. Therefore the process of macro-genotypic evolution has the potential to sustain itself, and may lead to ever increasing complexity and diversity, through the continual opening up of new niches.

We now turn to a discussion of the role of phenotypic and genotypic evolution in physical systems, before we move on to an analysis of evolutionary concepts in economics.

8.4   EVOLUTION IN PHYSICAL SYSTEMS

In our discussion on biological evolution we have stressed that the potentialities of a system, its genotype, interacts with the environment to give a realisation of these potentialities, in the phenotype. The systems with which physics is mainly concerned have their potentialities defined by the fundamental constants and laws of nature. The realisation of these potentialities is the observed behaviour of that physical system.

We therefore define the genotype for a physical system to be its potentialities: i.e. the fundamental constants and laws of nature. We similarly define the phenotype of a physical system to be the realisation of those potentialities: i.e. its observed physical behaviour. As a consequence of this conceptualisation, we see that, unlike biological systems, all realised physical systems have the same genotype. That is, different physical phenotypes are not derived from different physical genotypes. As was discussed under the heading of 'predictable processes' in Section 8.2.1, predictable changes are often exhibited by physical systems. As these changes are in the nature and appearance of the physical world, in its realisation, we term such change phenotypic evolution. To illustrate how the potentialities (the genotype) of the physical world may, through interaction with the environment, give rise to a phenotype and to phenotypic evolution, we present the following simple example. A ball held a certain distance above a pavement has potential energy because of its position and because of the laws of nature. If the ball is released, the interaction of the ball and the pavement cause it to behave in a certain predictable manner. The system containing the ball and the pavement tends towards a new physical equilibrium. The underlying genotype of this whole process is the laws of nature. As we know the initial conditions, and as there is no genotypic evolution, we can say that the system exhibits predictable phenotypic evolution. From the above discussion it should be clear that physical systems, like biological systems, may exhibit phenotypic evolution towards an equilibrium state. However, unlike different biological systems, physical systems all share a unique and unchanging genotype, comprising the physical constants and the laws of nature.

We mentioned in Section 8.2.3 that modern thought suggests that the universe was unpredictable in its first few moments, as the physical constants attained their present values. One could say, therefore, that even physical systems have experienced one period of genotypic evolution, albeit for a vanishingly short length of time. The key notions of our evolutionary framework are the genotype, i.e. potentialities, and the phenotype, i.e. realisations. From the above discussion of evolution in physical and biological systems, it is apparent that there exists a hierarchy of these concepts, in the following sense. Realisations in physics, e.g. the state of the Earth, are prerequisites for the formation of genotypes in biology. In the same way, realisations in physics and biology are prerequisites for the emergence of potentialities in economics.

8.5   EVOLUTION IN ECONOMIC SYSTEMS

8.5.1   Economic Genotypes and Phenotypes

Just as in biology and physics, as discussed in Sections 8.3 and 8.4 respectively, we can conceptualise economies in terms of potentialities and their realisations. The former we will call economic genotypes, and the latter economic phenotypes. Before proceeding, we should point out that in practice often it may not be easy to distinguish between these two categories, for reasons to be discussed below. We first consider economic genotypes. The genotype of an economy comprises the following elements:

1. Preference orderings of the economic agents (including religious and ethical norms).

2. The technology (i.e. the set of all techniques which are known in that economy).

3. The legal, economic and social institutions.[1]

The nature of these elements defines the potentialities of a particular economy: i.e. defines its genotype. The economic phenotype of, for example, a market economy is a realisation of these potentialities.

If we observe changes in any of these three elements we shall speak of genotypic change of the economy. The nature of these elements defines the potentialities of a particular economy, i.e. defines its genotype. The economic phenotype is a realisation of these potentialities. For a market economy it may contain the following elements:

1. The techniques of production employed.
2. The types of capital goods employed, and their amounts.
3. The types of capital and consumption goods produced.
4. The quantities of these goods, and their prices.
5. The distribution of consumption, income and wealth among the economic agents.
6. The market structure.

From the above definition it is clear that, just as in biology we defined the unit of evolution to be the whole interacting biological system, so for economics we define the unit of evolution to be the entire set of interacting economic agents and their institutions and artefacts. We note that over the course of history, the size and complexity of economic systems, and thus our unit of economic evolution, has tended to increase. For a self-sufficient hunter-gatherer society the unit would be the band, while at the present time the high level of integration of national economies suggests that the unit of evolution should be regarded as the global economy. We suggest that the great bulk of dynamic economic modelling can be regarded in terms of the evolution of economic phenotypes. For example, comparative international trade theory can be conceptualised as phenotypic evolution. In the classical model, England shifts its production towards cloth, while Portugal shifts its production towards wine. The equilibrium pattern of trade that is eventually established is mainly dependent upon the structure of production, tastes, resources and techniques available. Pursuing this example further, were there to be a disruption to this equilibrium pattern, and this disruption was then removed, the equilibrium pattern would be re-established in due course.

Very often the assumption of given constraints to behaviour by economic agents, and a general expectation of optimising by these agents, will give us equilibrium outcomes: i.e. the system will be predictable and equi-final. This tendency in economic analysis is most clearly seen in the struggle by general equilibrium theorists to discover 'reasonable' models of economic activity which give rise to unique and stable equilibria in price-quantity space. In our view, this working through of the dynamics of economic systems, where tastes, techniques and resource availability are taken as fixed, can justifiably be termed economic phenotypic evolution.

Genotypic evolution, by contrast, requires changes in tastes and techniques, as well as in economic institutions. For example, the process of industrialisation of the past two hundred years has been one of continually changing economic institutions, changing techniques of production, and a continually expanding list of natural resources which have been put to economic use. For instance, discoveries in physics stimulated the engineering development of nuclear power, which rendered uranium an economic resource, whereas previously it had been regarded as a material of only limited usefulness. The development of microelectronics and the corresponding increase in the economic valuation of germanium (used in transistors) is another example of this process of economic genotypic evolution.

Just as in the biological illustration above, economic genotypic evolution cannot involve the notion of an equilibrium outcome. Unlike the case of biological evolution, however, economic genotypic evolution may take place very rapidly, as is particularly evident in the evolution of the microelectronics industry. Indeed, the rate of change of the genotypic specification (the technical capabilities) in this industry is so rapid that successive changes in specification occur before a new phenotypic equilibrium can be established. The very notion of an equilibrium in such rapidly evolving industries seems to us therefore to be of limited usefulness. The complexity of the phenotypic response to such rapid genotypic evolution is illustrated is Figure 8.9.

In Figure 8.9 rapid genotypic change moves the equilibrium of the phenotype from point A to point B, and subsequently to points C and D. The rate of phenotypic evolution towards these successive equilibria is, for economic systems, of the same order as the rate of genotypic evolution. The result is that phenotypic evolution proceeds along the ray towards the stable equilibrium B which passes through point A. However, the genotype changes before equilibrium B is achieved, and the phase path shifts to one converging on C, the new equilibrium. At point b on the original phase path, the old phase path is replaced by a new phase path leading towards the new equilibrium. This new phenotypic evolution is also incomplete, as by the time the system achieves point c, the phenotypic equilibrium has shifted to D.

It is important to note that in Figure 8.9 the observed trajectory of the system in phase space is a combination of several rays associated with different equilibria, and except for the starting point, no phenotypic equilibrium state is attained, or even very closely approached, as long as genotypic change continues.

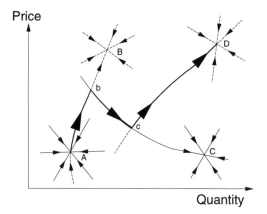

Figure 8.9. Combined genotypic and phenotypic evolution for an economic system.

8.5.2   The Long-Run Interaction Between Invention and Innovation

In this section we shall restrict our analysis to one main area of evolutionary economics, the interaction between invention, innovation and the natural world. To introduce these concepts we first need to define some terms.

The *technology* of an economy, at any moment in time, is the set of techniques which are known, even though not necessarily all of them will be used.

Invention is the addition of a novel technique, which thus expands the technology.

Innovation is the process of introducing a technique of the technology which is not currently being used.

While invention occurs at some point in time (or during a relatively short time period), it takes time to innovate a new technique, because the introduction of a new technique makes it necessary to construct and establish the corresponding necessary capital goods, as well as to train the workers. It is obvious that this innovation gives rise to many adjustment processes over time throughout the economy, including the process of diffusion. (For fuller discussions see Faber and Proops 1986,

1989.)

The long-run relationship between these elements may be illustrated as in Figure 8.10.

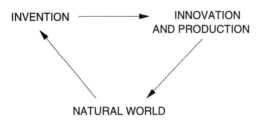

Figure 8.10. Long-run economy-environment interactions.

Recalling the discussion at the beginning of Section 8.3, the phenotype is our short-hand for what is realised, and the genotype for a system's potentialities. Using the notions of phenotypic and genotypic evolution, we can characterise the process of innovation as economic phenotypic evolution, and the generation of invention as economic genotypic evolution.

Just as in biological evolution, economic genotypic evolution is a prerequisite for economic phenotypic evolution. As in biological evolution, the phenotypic nature of the economic system offers further potentialities for genotypic evolution. In the case of a biological system, the potentiality lies in niche exploitation, as discussed above. In an economic system, niche destruction, in the sense of the long-run depletion of natural resources, is an important motivation for seeking an improvement in economic technical potentialities: i.e. in seeking economic genotypic change. This genotypic change leads, in turn, to niche production through the bringing into use of new natural resources.

We may illustrate the interplay of phenotypic and genotypic evolution as follows. Consider a resource using economy which, through the workings of its market system, has established a predictable equilibrium; i.e. relative prices and relative quantities produced are stable and overall output of the economy is growing at a predictable rate. This would be equivalent to the phenotypic equilibrium of an ecosystem, as discussed above in Section 8.3.2 (see e.g. Figure 8.1). If the resources used are steadily depleted by economic activity, then this will initially cause marginal adjustments in relative prices and quantities, and a reduction in the overall rate of growth.[2] This phenotypic evolution can be compared with the phenotypic evolution of an ecosystem subject to, say, a slight but continuing alteration in climate over a long period, such as the general warming in northern latitudes after the last ice age. However, long-run depletion of resources by an economy is likely to initiate a search for new and unpredictable techniques of production, which use less of the diminishing resource (resource-saving invention) or make use of alternative resources (resource-substituting invention). The new techniques give rise to a new and unpredictable genotypic description for the economic system; the new economic genotype in turn produces a new phenotype which must now, through market operations (phenotypic evolution), establish a new, predictable equilibrium economic structure.

8.6   WHY PHYSICS IS EASY, ECONOMICS IS DIFFICULT AND BIOLOGY IS IN BETWEEN

We start our discussion by representing physical, biological and economic evolution in a diagrammatic way. In Figs. 8.10 to 8.12, G_i and P_i ($i = 1, 2$) denote the genotype and the phenotype, respectively, of population i. G_i^p and P_i^p ($i = 1, 2$) denote the perturbed genotype, and its corresponding phenotype.

We recall from Section 2.4 that the complete genotypic physical evolution of the universe seems to have occurred in the very first few moments of its beginning i.e. in less than a second (Hawking, 1988). Thereafter, there was no more genotypic evolution, but only phenotypic evolution. Hence physical evolution is simple to characterise in terms of phenotypic and genotypic notions, as shown in Figure 8.11. It is important to note that there is no recursion between genotypic and phenotypic evolution in physics, unlike in biology and economics.

$$G_1 \longrightarrow P_1$$

Figure 8.11. The evolutionary scheme for physical systems.

In the physical world there is no longer genotypic evolution, i.e. no emergence of novelty of potentialities, and physics is only concerned with phenotypic phenomena, in our terminology. This stability of the potentialities of physical systems has allowed physics to deal only with predictable processes, enabling physicists and mathematicians to seek and to find numerous simple and elaborated methods of dynamics. This ability to concentrate on problems which have predictable dynamics is, we believe, the major source of the enormous success physics has enjoyed over the past three centuries. It might have been just this feature of physics that led Plank to comment to Keynes that he gave up the study of economics in favour of physics because he found the former too difficult! In our terminology, this is so since in physics there are many areas in which there is little scope for the emergence of novelty, as there is little ignorance, and no genotypic change.

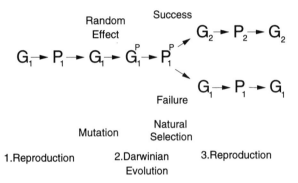

Figure 8.12. The evolutionary scheme for biological systems.

We now turn to evolution in biology. As we see in Figure 8.12, the interaction between genotypic and phenotypic processes is much richer than in physics. It may be useful for the reader to explain this diagram in some detail. We see that the representation consists of three phases.

Phase 1 The genotype and phenotype of a biological population at an equilibrium; here the genotype and phenotype are recursively maintaining each other through the reproductive process.

Phase 2 This illustrates Darwinian Evolution; this consists of two parts, Mutation and Natural Selection. In the first part, Mutation is initiated by a random effect which perturbs genotype G_1 to G_1^p, which in turn produces a corresponding new phenotype, P_1^p. In the second part, Natural Selection, the environment acts as a filter for the new phenotype P_1^p. If this new phenotype is successful in its environment then the new genotype, G_1^p, becomes established, and as it is no longer provisional we rename it G_2. If the new phenotype is unsuccessful in its environment, it is eliminated and the original genotype, G_1, remains.

Phase 3   This is a further reproductive phase. If the perturbed phenotype, P_1^p, is unsuccessful then the reproduction is still of the
old phenotype and genotype, as for Phase 1. If the mutation
is successful, there will be a period of reproduction where the
potentialities of the new genotype, G_2, are being realised in
the new phenotype of the biological population, P_2. This will
consist of altering species abundances, and therefore constitutes a period of phenotypic evolution.

Supposing the mutation is successful, once a new phenotypic equilibrium
is established in Phase 3, one could say that genotypic evolution has
occurred.

Finally, we turn to evolution in economics, which we represent in
Figure 8.13. The reader will notice that this diagram has almost the same
structure as the previous one, and is also divided into three phases. We
note that the genotype and phenotype to which we refer here are the
macro-genotype and macro-phenotype for an economy. That is, they
embody the full potentialities of the whole economy, and the full set of
realisations of those potentialities by the economy.

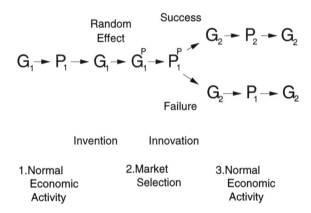

Figure 8.13. The evolutionary scheme for economic systems.

Phase 1   Here the economy can be described as exhibiting 'Normal
Economic Activity'; for ease of illustration, this may be
supposed to be a stationary or steady state. The potentialities
(i.e. knowledge base) of the economy are being realised in
productive economic activity, and this production in turn

allows the maintenance of the knowledge base. Therefore, as in the biological case, the genotype and phenotype are in a recursive, self-maintaining relationship.

Phase 2 This is Market Selection. At the beginning of this phase an invention changes the genotype of the economy; the market conditions will act as a filter for whether this invention will be realised. However, unlike the biological case, this increase in the potentialities of the system is often retained. Thus G_1 is maintained, as a subset of G_2. Here we recall that this can be the case because we are referring to the macro-genotype and macro-phenotype. So the realisation of an economy may not alter, even though the potentialities *do* alter. It may be possible for a new invention to be retained in the knowledge base, but not affect the rest of the economy.

In a biological population, if natural selection rejects the mutation, the mutation disappears from the macro-genotype of that biological population, as the only host for the mutation is the genetic material of the phenotype of that organism.[3]

However, in an economy knowledge is not necessarily restricted to any individual or group. It can be stored and made available to a wide range of economic actors. For this reason it is much more difficult to assert that an invention is rejected by the economic evolutionary process than to assert that a biological mutation has been rejected by the biological evolutionary process.

If the market judges the invention to be successful at any subsequent time, the invention will be innovated, leading to a minor or major restructuring of the economy. That is, economic phenotypic evolution takes place.

Phase 3 This is a return to Normal Economic Activity. The new economic genotype, G_2, and the new phenotype P_2, become established as the new economic phenotypic equilibrium of the economy. If the invention is unsuccessful, then the original phenotype, P_1, remains in force. However, as the new invention is a permanent addition to the technology of the economy (the economic genotype), it is the new genotype, G_2, which is maintained. We note once more that unlike in biological systems, G_1 often remains as part of the corresponding economic genotype, even if it is not used anymore.

The above discussion has shown one major reason why economics is conceptually more complex than biology. A second reason has been mentioned already, where we noted that successful genotypic changes in biology occur relatively infrequently. Biological genotypic evolution can be regarded as movements between successive phenotypic equilibria. For economies, on the other hand, it is obvious that in modern times scientific and technical knowledge has been increasing rapidly, and at an accelerating rate. This has led to a tremendous amount of economic genotypic change, which takes place at a rate comparable to market adjustments (phenotypic change). Therefore economic genotypic evolution cannot be regarded as movements between successive phenotypic equilibria.

We now offer a third reason for why economics is conceptually more difficult than biology. As we pointed out above, in biology the phenotype cannot affect the genotype. In contrast to this, in economies the phenotype not only maintains the genotype (its potentialities, i.e. the knowledge base), it also generates it, through research and development activities. That is, the phenotype does affect the genotype in economics.

In summary, while we see great similarities between the evolutionary processes exhibited in the biological world and in economies, we consider economics to be conceptually more difficult than biology for the following three reasons:

1. In economies, 'unsuccessful' additions to the genotype can be preserved.

2. In economies, genotypic evolution often takes place at a similar rate to, and sometimes even at a faster rate than, phenotypic evolution.

3. In economies, the phenotype can affect the genotype.

8.7   THE IMPORTANCE OF EX POST AND EX ANTE CONSIDERATIONS

Considering again Figure 8.10, where the interaction of invention, innovation and the natural world is illustrated, it will be clear to the reader that historical experience supports this conceptualisation. For example, industrialisation in eighteenth and nineteenth century Europe can be understood, ex post, in terms of the substitution in industrial processes of relatively abundant fossil fuels for the rapidly depleting sources of wood. The rising price of charcoal in the eighteenth century led to intensive research into finding a technique of smelting iron using coal as fuel rather than charcoal. The key invention was the transformation of coal to coke, which is nearly pure carbon and can act as a good substitute for charcoal in iron-smelting. This invention dramatically reduced the price of iron and led to enormous changes in the structure of everyday life. An economic phenotypic evolution of great proportions was initiated by this economic genotypic change.

With the massive expansion in iron making went an equally massive expansion in coal mining. Just as early iron making encountered natural limitations when the genotype demanded the use of charcoal, so coal mining encountered limitations when the genotype demanded the use of solely human and animal labour. The genotypic change that occurred as a result of further search for invention, to counter the flooding of deep coal mines, was the introduction of steam engines driving water pumps.

Ex post this analysis of the invention, innovation and natural world relationships is clear. Phenotypic evolution depleted the natural resource and thereby stimulated a search for a new genotype. With the benefit of hindsight the invention of smelting with coke, and of the steam engine, seem both timely and inevitable. Prior to their invention, however, industrialists were far from sanguine about the prospects for the iron and coal industries. This will always be the case prior to a major invention.

The conceptualisation of the evolutionary process must recognise the very different statuses of the past and the future. The concept of novelty is an ex ante concept, and by its nature novelty can only occur in the future, and by the nature of the future it cannot be known in detail. Further, if the perspective of the future is sufficiently long, even the broadest notions of future novelty that actually come to pass may be impossible to envisage. Here, uncertainty and unpredictability in its most stark form is encountered. This distinction of the ex ante and ex post in systems which exhibit novelty, and are therefore subject to genotypic evolution, is in marked contrast to a system without the emergence of novelty, where only phenotypic evolution may occur. Here we stress again that phenotypic evolution is often closed and in many cases equi-final, and accessible to prediction, while genotypic evolution is open, not equi-final, and not accessible to prediction.

From the above discussion it will be clear that phenotypic evolution may be considered both ex post and ex ante, while genotypic evolution may properly be understood only ex post. As we have noted above, for biological systems the distinction between phenotypic evolution and genotypic evolution is generally clear because of the enormously different time scales on which these processes operate. However, evolution in economic systems will generally exhibit phenotypic and genotypic evolution, which often operate on similar time scales, making the discrimination between the phenotypic and genotypic evolutionary processes a source of some difficulty in economics.

Of course, we know that different industries have different rate of technological change (i.e. of the occurrence of novelty embodied in new genotypes). This rate is very slow in long-established industries, such as electricity generation by fossil fuel power plants, and steel production. On the other hand, industries such as electronics and aerospace exhibit rapid rates of invention. The evidence even suggests that the rates of invention in these two industries is still increasing. These observations suggest that conventional economic analysis can be used in those industries which exhibit a low rate of genotypic evolution, but that it is only of limited value for industries with rapid rates of genotypic evolution.

As a further example of the importance of the distinction between genotypic and phenotypic evolution in economics, we turn to environmental economics. We note that there are a multitude of models in resource economics, particularly relating to the depletion of fossil fuels, which seek a market oriented, phenotypic characterisation of economic activity in the long-run. Now the complete depletion of fossil fuels with a fixed technology of production (i.e. a fixed genotype) inevitably leads to the collapse of the economy. This is dealt with by invoking a more or less arbitrary back-stop technology, which becomes available in the long-run (see e.g. Dasgupta and Heal, 1979), and leads to a new and unique genotype and thence a new phenotype. As this change is to a technology which is considered to be known ex ante (i.e. predictable), we cannot consider this to be genotypic evolution, as we have discussed above. Indeed, as discussed above, by the nature of genotypic evolution it is unpredictable and therefore, in principle, not susceptible to modelling ex ante.

This is not to say that speculation about the long-run evolution of economic systems is either impossible or worthless. Discussions of the nature of future inventions (i.e. changes to genotypes) offer, through the construction of scenarios, forecasts about economic development that may be both interesting and valuable. However, we feel it important to stress that predictions based on models of phenotypic evolution (e.g. market dynamics) have a completely different status to models based on notions of possible genotypic evolution (e.g. invention). The natures of the possibility for phenotypic and genotypic predictions are quite different. While for the former, specific and concrete predictions can be made, this is not possible for the latter.

8.8   CONCLUSIONS

In this chapter we have offered a general and broad conceptualisation of evolution. Here we wish to summarise our discussion so far. We began by suggesting that evolution should be regarded as a very general notion. We remind the reader that we conceptualised it as follows: evolution is the process of the changing of something over time.

Biology offers useful insights into this kind of conceptualisation of the general nature of evolution, as the notions of genotype (potentialities) and phenotype (realisations) are most clearly delineated in this area.

The former allows for the emergence of novelty, while the latter does not. We saw that phenotypic evolution allows for equi-finality, and hence for equilibrium solutions, while genotypic evolution does not. This in turn implies that the former allows for prediction, while the latter does not. This further implies that phenotypic evolution may be understood in both ex ante and ex post terms, while genotypic evolution may only be understood ex post. That is, one may forecast phenotypic evolution, but not genotypic evolution.

A summary in the form of a juxtaposition of the characteristics of genotypic and phenotypic evolution is given in Table 8.1.

Table 8.1. Characteristics of genotypic and phenotypic evolution.

Genotypic Evolution	Phenotypic Evolution
Evolution of Potentialities	Evolution of Realisation
Emergence of Novelty	No Emergence of Novelty
No Equi-finality of Process	Equi-finality of Process Possible
No Equilibrium Possible	Equilibrium Possible
Unpredictable Process (in principle)	Predictable Process (in principle)
Modelling Possible Ex Post only	Modelling Possible Ex Ante and Ex Post

In particular, we have seen that economies are characterised by an extremely complicated interaction of genotypic and phenotypic evolutionary processes. Since the rate of genotypic change in the modern global economy is so rapid, it is often not possible to distinguish between the consequences of phenotypic and genotypic changes. Since the changes of the boundary conditions are not considered central to the method of explanation of conventional economics, conventional economics can be expected to be of only limited help for understanding economic evolution.

In summary, predictable, phenotypic economic evolution may be subject to ex ante analysis, allowing sensible predictions of future economic realisations. However, genotypic economic evolution, such as the invention of techniques, or the emergence of new institutions, is by its nature unpredictable and therefore amenable only to ex post analysis.

Since physics is entirely concerned with phenotypic evolution, this explains why this discipline has been so extremely successful, and also why so many other disciplines have tried to emulate its method. As our analysis shows, however, this emulation can be successful only so far as other disciplines are concerned with phenotypic processes.

As we have noted in the introduction, the key characteristics of evolution are change, and time. While we have concentrated on change in this chapter, for further research in this area we consider it to be useful to tie in concepts of time more closely into the analysis than we do in this paper. (See Faber and Proops 1993a:Part III.)

NOTES

1. The endowments of natural resources are determined both by the naturally occurring materials, and by the technology available. A material can only be regarded as a resource if it can be exploited (e.g. uranium before 1940 was not a valuable resource, but simply an available type of material).
2. The role of prices for both phenotypic and genotypic evolution has been investigated in much greater detail by Schmidtchen (1989).
3. It is possible, however, that a genetic mutation may occur to a biological genotype that has no immediate effect on the phenotype. In this case there can be no operation of the selection mechanism upon that alteration, until it is perhaps revealed by the effect of another, later, genetic mutation.

9. On the Conceptual Foundations of Ecological Economics: A Teleological Approach

9.1 INTRODUCTION

Part of the endeavour of ecological economics is to construct a language and set of concepts with which this endeavour can be fruitfully pursued. One set of concepts that has been advocated revolves around Prigogine's work on self-organising systems (Prigogine, 1962; Prigogine and Stengers, 1984; Jantsch, 1980). Another very influential author has been Georgescu-Roegen, who has not only illuminated the role of the Entropy Law in economics, but has also stressed the distinction between stocks and funds (Georgescu-Roegen, 1971).

The theory of self-organising systems allows us to encompass bio-logical and non-biological structures in the same conceptual model. On the other hand, the notion of funds, as so far discussed in the literature, is explicitly concerned with human action. It seems to us that these two seemingly disparate areas of discourse offer great promise to ecological economics, if they can be subsumed within a broader conceptualisation of nature. How can we bridge the gap between Prigogine and Georgescu-Roegen? The approach we take looks back to Aristotle and his teleological characterisation of processes. We shall argue that a teleological approach can be justified even for non-reasoning systems. This range of applicability of teleological arguments allows a breadth of argumentation appropriate to the endeavour of ecological economics. Our methodological approach will be an evolutionary one. In particular we shall use the notions of genotype (potentialities) and phenotype (realisation), as discussed in Chapter 8.

Thus our aim is to find a language and a set of concepts to allow us to formulate the problem of economy-environment interactions (cf. Chapter 2 and Norton, 1992). In general, one is used to analysing nature and the economy with different kinds of concepts. In contrast to this approach we wish to develop new concepts of nature and the economy, such that they enable us to use elements of each concept for discussing the other area. Our conceptual and methodological approach will be at the borderline between science and philosophy.

Regarding economics, we find we need a language to formulate economic problems in such a way that we can use the same concepts and language as for discourse on nature. In particular, as economics concerns choice (i.e. teleology) it is fortunate that we also find it convenient and useful to express behaviour in nature in a teleological way.

All these concepts will allow us to go directly from the ecological sphere to the economic one, and vice versa. If we succeed in this endeavour, this will enable us to use one language to speak on problems of both economy and ecology.

We begin with a brief characterisation of biological evolution in terms of Prigogine's 'Far From Equilibrium Self-Organising Dissipative Structures' (FFESODS). We then introduce teleology as a unifying approach to natural and social phenomena. In particular, we define the three tele which we use to characterise organisms. The final building block is the distinction between stocks and funds, which we discuss to indicate how the most general notion of funds is applicable to organisms. We also note that economic capital has some aspects of a fund. We then indicate how the history of human economic development can be characterised in terms of our three tele and the development of funds. Our major conclusion is that using our new language, it becomes evident that there is a great dichotomy between the way nature develops and the way modern economies evolve. In particular, it follows from our analysis that the way the modern economy works is inherently unsustainable. Finally, we apply our language to the problem of sustainability, and to formulate corresponding goals, in the context of ecosystem health (cf. Costanza, Norton and Haskell, 1992).

9.2   SELF-ORGANISATION AND BIOLOGICAL EVOLUTION

In this section we shall seek to sketch out an abstract formulation of the conditions for the emergence of organisms. This will form the conceptual basis of our later analysis of funds.

We shall give a sequence of numbered statements that define what we believe to be the essence of biological evolution. These now follow.

Fundamental Physical Facts

1. There exists a low entropy source, which is the sun. That is, radiant available energy is emitted.

2. There exists an entropy[1] sink, which is outer space. In other words, any radiant energy that may exist is not contained, but always leaks away.

From 1 and 2 we see that we are dealing with a thermodynamically open system. Low entropy energy is emitted from the sun, and if nothing impedes it, it 'disappears' into empty space.

3. Matter (i.e the Earth) exists reasonably adjacent to the low entropy source (i.e the Sun).

This matter may impede and thereby interact with the radiant, low entropy energy. The nature of this interaction will be a partial absorption of the radiant energy, giving rise to heat. The hot matter will now also act as a subsidiary source of radiant energy, though this energy has a higher entropy than the initial radiation. As this secondary radiation is also emitted into outer space, it too disappears into this entropy sink. This conversion of low entropy energy into high entropy energy is consistent with the second law of thermodynamics, even though this law is strictly only applicable to thermodynamically closed systems, while as noted above we are dealing here with a thermodynamically open system.

Far From Equilibrium Self-Organising Dissipative Structures (FFE-SODS)

4. The flow of energy through a thermodynamically open system allows the possibility of 'entropy bootlegging', i.e. the capture of low entropy through the emergence of 'far from equilibrium self-organising dissipative structures' (FFESODS).[2] A simple example of a FFESSODS is a rain cloud, which is generated by the interaction of dissipating heat and atmospheric water vapour.

5. The emergence of FFESODS gives rise to novel, heterogeneous structures.

6. These FFESODS themselves are available as constituent elements of higher order self-organising systems. This emergence of higher level structures generates further heterogeneity and reflects the emergence of further novelty.[3]

7. The emergence of FFESODS, as in 5, and their cooperation in higher order FESSODS, as in 6, implies that the evolution of FFESODS tends to lead to an increase in the interconnectedness of relationships between them over time (cf. Allen and Starr, 1982; Ulanowicz, 1992).

8. The outward appearance of a FFESODS we term its 'phenotype', while the factors which cause this appearance we term the 'genotype' (Faber and Proops, 1993a:Chapter 2). Once FFESODS become sufficiently complex, they may maintain their structural stability over time by incorporating their genotypes within their phenotypes. Any FFESODS with this incorporated genotype, and the ability to replicate itself, we call an organism. This is unlike, say a cloud, where the genotype is the parameters of the air and underlying earth's surface. We note that the distinction between a FFESODS with a genotype external to its phenotype (e.g. a cloud) and one with an internal genotype (e.g. an organism), corresponds to the distinction between the complex but non-living, and the living.

The genotype corresponds to the *potentiality* of a FFESODS. The phenotype corresponds to the *realisation* of this potentiality.[4]

Since an organism is a FFESODS, it relies for its continued existence on 'entropy bootlegging'. Now the Second Law of Thermodynamics suggests that a FFESODS will tend to 'break-down' over time, becoming of a higher specific entropy. Self-maintenance requires the FFESODS to keep its specific entropy sufficiently low, so high entropy will need to be expelled. Generally, this expulsion of high entropy will be accompanied by material input and output (i.e. material throughput), rather than simply the ejection of energy.

As well as the necessary material and energy throughput required by a FFESODS, as noted above, an organism also exhibits self-replication. This self-replication may leave the genotype of the organism unchanged, or the genotype may be changed in the whole process of self-replication.

Evolution

9. In the absence of genotypic change, the system exhibits no emergence of novelty, and is likely to attain a phenotypic equilibrium over the course of time, which gives a repetitive pattern to events over time.[5]

10. If genotypic change occurs, the repetitive pattern of phenotypic equilibrium can be broken, and new patterns can be established.

11. The organisms that have emerged through the above processes interact with each other, as part of their mutual maintenance. For reasons that come clearer in the next section, we term these inter-actions as *services*, and the organisms as *funds*.

9.3   TELEOLOGY AND ORGANISMS

Before we move on to a discussion of the relationships of organisms to each other, and to non-organic matter, we consider it useful to offer a brief discussion of causation. Here we shall introduce the notion of causation towards a future state: that is *teleology*.

9.3.1   Mechanical and Teleological Explanations

When discussing causation one's aim is usually to seek to 'understand' the object of inquiry. We note that there are two distinct modes of rea-soning on causation; the 'mechanical', which seeks to understand in terms of past and present events; and the teleological, which seeks to understand in terms of future events. In the Aristotelian terminology, the 'mechanical' approach deals with *causa efficiens*, the teleological with *causa finalis* (Aristotle, 1970:39; Physics 198 b 10). If one attempts to explain an object or a process in a teleological way, then one presupposes that the object or process has a certain tendency to a particular final state, which can be interpreted as an end or a goal. For example, the process of building a house can only be understood if one knows the telos of this process, the house. Aristotle (1970:40f; Physics 199 b 26-31) gives some applications of *causa finalis* in nature:

> If the swallow's act in making a nest is both due to nature and for something [i.e. it has an aim, a telos - the authors], and the spider's in making its web, and the plant in producing leaves for its fruits, and roots not up but down for nourishment, plainly this sort of cause [final cause - the authors] is present in things which are and come to be by nature.

It is often thought that mechanical reasoning is the appropriate mode to apply to the world of non-reasoning objects (e.g. physics), while teleo-logical reasoning is appropriate to the world of reasoning objects (e.g. economics). In the world of biology, it is sometimes felt that mechanical reasoning is appropriate for simple organisms, while teleological rea-soning for more complex organisms. However, we wish to stress that the teleological approach can be, and often is, used in all branches of science. For example, the laws of reflection and of refraction of light can be deduced from the assumption that the light will take a minimum of time to travel between two points. This was first derived in the seventeenth century by Fermat, generalised (in an attempt to re-establish teleology in physics) by Maupertuis in the eighteenth century, and made part of a very general 'minimum principle' for mechanics by Hamilton in the nineteenth century. Hamilton's approach is explicitly teleological, as it explains the path of the ray of light in terms of a quasi-intended outcome (i.e. shortest travel time) which has yet to occur when the light ray begins its travel.

It was eventually shown that in mechanics, all such teleological principles are equivalent to laws of mechanical causation. For our purposes the use of a teleological approach to understanding nature is generally superior.

It has also been long known to systems theorists (von Bertalanffy, 1950) that mechanical system behaviour can be written as goal-oriented, and therefore teleological. Certainly, the human will can be thought of as being used towards goals, although much modern economic theory seems, perversely, to treat human action as mechanically determined.

9.3.2   Aristotle's Notion of *Entelecheia*

Our approach is motivated by Aristotle's notion of *entelecheia* (Aristotle, 1956:26; De anima II, 412 a 10). After a period of oblivion, this word again became important for the writing of Goethe, and for romantics such as the philosopher Schelling, the physicist Ritter and the poet Novalis. The meaning of *entelecheia* is, literally, 'having an aim (*telos*, pl. *tele*) in itself' or 'having its determination in itself'. These expressions can be used as definitions of life, and thus of organisms. We note that the latter of these relates directly to our earlier definition of an organism, where the genotype is contained in the phenotype, as in this case the determination (genotype) is contained in itself (phenotype).

An example of this distinction can be made with regard to 'flying objects'. A flying ball does not have a telos in itself; rather the telos derives from the intention of the impeller. On the other hand, a bird flies for its own reasons, so its telos is within itself. It is important to note that the telos which is entailed in the word *entelecheia* does not mean a rationally planned aim, which results from a decision process. Rather, the telos is the intrinsic nature of the organism. Thus the telos gives each organism a direction for its development, which is realised during the organism's lifetime.

Of course, within this direction there exists a broad range within which the organism can develop. On the one hand, this range is additionally determined, to a certain degree, by the environment. On the other hand it may be possible that a special organism is free, as we assume for humans. In this case the intrinsic telos gives necessary, but not sufficient, conditions for its development.

9.3.3   Three Tele of Living Nature

We adopt the notion of *entelecheia* to allow us to develop a teleological terminology to characterise living beings (i.e. organisms). This terminology will enable us:

- to emphasise the uniqueness of a living being;
- to consider the relationship of a living being to its species;
- to represent its integration into the oneness of nature.

Thus the notion of *entelecheia* gives rise to the following question:

'What aims (tele) can we ascribe to a living being?'

We offer the following three interrelated tele as characterising living beings. These three tele also define three areas of inquiry. We note that these tele refer to individuals, though, as we shall try to indicate, the effect of each telos is on the individual, the species, or the ecological whole.

1. The first telos is that of *self-maintenance*, *development* and *self-realisation*. This telos constitutes the area of individual being.

Examples of the first telos in operation regarding self-maintenance are: the seeking of food, through grazing or predation; self-protection from predation and adverse environmental conditions. Regarding development (i.e. ontogeny)[6], an example is the transition of the butterfly egg to the pupa, then through the chrysalis to the imago. On the other hand, a pig in a narrow sty of a modern pig-breeding farm may be able to maintain itself, and to develop, but not fully to realise its potential as a pig, because of the constraints on its behaviour.

It is important to note, at least for humans, the distinction between the intensity of the first telos, and the extent of its implementation. By the intensity we mean the force with which an organism is able to cling to the first telos. This intensity is evidently greater in a human than in a grass plant or a rabbit. The extent to which this telos is realised will increase with the intensity of the telos, and with improvements in the means of implementing the telos. Of course, increasing the means of implementation may also further intensify the telos.

2. The second telos is that of *replication* and *renewal*. This telos constitutes the area of the group, e.g. the mating pair, the family, the clan or the herd. We define this telos to refer, at the outer limit, to the entire species.[7]

The replication occurs at the individual level and is necessary for the continuation of the existence of a species. Renewal, on the other hand, has two aspects. At the individual level, renewal implies that every individual is different from every other. Even monozygotic[8] twins, which have identical genotypes, have different phenotypes. At the species level, there is the possibility of mutation (i.e. genotypic change) over time. The succession of species resulting from mutation is known as phylogeny.

3. The third telos is that of *service* to other species, or the whole of nature. This telos constitutes the area of the ecological community.

An example is an apple tree, which serves other species in various ways. Its apples are food for insects, birds and mammals; the leaves provide humus to the soil, and also produce oxygen; the branches give nesting-space for birds; the wood can be used by, e.g., beavers and humans for construction.

9.3.4   The Tele and Explanations of the World

What is it about the world that we wish to understand with our three tele? In summary, it is: *stability, change, variety, interconnectedness,* and *overall continuity.* We examine these in turn.

Regarding *stability*, we note that there is stability of identity of individual organisms, of species, and of ecological wholes. That is, while an organism exhibits development, it maintains its identity over its lifetime. Similarly, over geological time a species may exhibit variation, via mutation, but this may be through a continuity of intermediate forms.

Regarding *change*, as noted above, stability is not absolute, and the individual, the species and the ecological whole all exhibit change on their corresponding time scales.

The change that takes place allows for *variety*, both at any moment of time, between individuals and between species, and over time also, on both levels.

The existence of variety, deriving from change, allows *interconnectedness* between individuals and species. Indeed, this interconnectedness allows one to speak meaningfully of ecological wholes.

Overall continuity applies to all of the above categories. There is continuity of individuals and species through stability; there is a continuity of change of the individual, species and ecological wholes; there is a continuity of variety at all levels; and there is a continuity of interconnectedness.

9.3.5   The Epistemological Status of the Tele

What is the status of the tele that we propose? We could describe them as 'heuristic' concepts.[9] These concepts are not in themselves names of observable things, but they can provide a framework that gives coherence and meaning to observations. Certainly they derive from insights and deliberations stimulated by observation, so that while they are not themselves phenomena, we can argue that they correspond to a certain range of phenomena. In biology, concepts like 'fitness' and 'selective advantage' are heuristic in this way.

In our analysis we use a limited range of concepts (FFESODS, genotype and phenotype, fund and service, together with our three tele), to offer insights into the nature, and evolution of, economy-environment interactions. Whether or not these concepts prove useful can only be judged by their fruitfulness as tools of reasoning.

9.3.6   Relationships Between the Three Tele

We remind the reader that the three tele refer to the organism, species and ecological whole, respectively. Obviously, organisms are elements of species, and species are elements of ecological wholes; i.e. these three concepts are nested.

We now wish to indicate the ways in which the three tele are related to each other. For example, the concept of self-maintenance, which we used to characterise living beings in the first telos, can also be applied for the second and third tele, using different points of view.

We note that there is a parallel between the elements of the first and second tele. In the first telos we have the element of self-maintenance, which allows the individual some continuity of existence over time. In the second telos we have the element of self-replication, which allows the species continuity over time.

In the first telos we also have the element development (i.e. ontogeny), and in the second telos there is the notion of self-renewal of the species (i.e. phylogeny). Both ontogeny and phylogeny are examples of development of the form of the corresponding element, organism or species, although ontogeny is predetermined (i.e. it is phenotypic evolution) while phylogeny is not predetermined, but involves the emergence of novelty (i.e. it is genotypic evolution).

We also see that the first telos is a necessary condition for the operation of the second telos, and the first and second tele are necessary for the operation of the third telos. This is the case because, without the first telos, there would be no continuity of organisms, so the concept of the species would be meaningless. Similarly, without the second telos there would be no continuity of species, so the concept of the ecological whole would not apply.

We might therefore be tempted to see the first telos as the most basic, followed by the second telos, with the third telos as the highest of the three, 'resting' on the first two. However, the third telos is a fundamental requirement for ecosystems to exist, so it, in turn, is a 'foundation' for tele 1 and 2. In other words, we have a recursive rather than hierarchical relationship between the tele. Each is necessary for the others.

This circularity of our three tele reminds one of the circularity within the philosophy of rights, of Hegel (1821), where he derives the concept of the State from the individual, but then points out that the individual can develop only within a supporting State.

9.3.7   The Tele, Phenotype and Genotype

The three tele defined above derive from our attempt to formulate a minimal set of principles concerning organisms, which give outcomes consonant with the phenomena. That is, our three tele are phenomenologically based.

We believe that, in principle, the whole range of possible organism, species, and ecological whole activities, interrelationships and transformations can be derived, at least in outline, from these tele. We might even say that the three tele summarise the potentialities of organic activity at the three levels, of individual, species and ecological whole. We could therefore speak of the three tele as constituting the genotype of the organic world. The corresponding phenotype is the entire panoply of organic behaviour, development, reproduction, interaction and evolution. Unlike the normal relationship between genotype and phenotype, as for an organism, the genotype (as we have defined it above) corresponding to the three tele determines the phenotype only in broad principles, rather than in fine details.

9.4 STOCKS AND FLOWS, STORES AND WITHDRAWALS

From what has been said above, we know that organisms need to rely on a throughput. This throughput is the material basis for their being. Here we want to discuss how we can operationalise this basis. We shall call the material intake by an organism its *resources*.

Where do these resources come from? We note that the Earth consists of various materials. The quantities of these various materials which the Earth contains we call *stocks*. The amounts by which these stocks increase or decrease we call *flows*. If a stock is used by an organism as a resource, then we call that stock the *store* of the resource for this organism. The use of the resource by the organism is its *withdrawal*. Thus the difference between stock and store is that a store is a stock which is used by an organism as a resource. That is, a store can only be defined in relationship with its corresponding user.

We see that the flows of the stocks are influenced by the organism only via its withdrawals. Thus we may say that the withdrawals are those elements of the flows influenced by organisms.

We note in passing that the stocks and stores, as well as the corresponding flows and withdrawals, have the same dimension (though, of course, flows and withdrawals are 'per unit time').

The material of a store can be regarded as homogeneous, but this homogeneity derives in part from the perspective taken by the utilising organism. For example, an apple tree may be a store of wood for a beaver, while for a butterfly it is a source of food and shelter; the apple gives food to the pupa and the bark gives shelter to the chrysalis.

9.5 FUNDS AND THE BIOSPHERE

We now introduce the notion of the *fund*. This term derives from the Latin *fundus*, which means 'ground and land', in the sense that it gives rise to agricultural output. Essential to a fund in the traditional understanding is that it gives something, but at the same time it is maintained or it maintains itself. To do this in agriculture there has to be something in addition, in Latin *cultura*, which means 'caring for and preservation'. Only then is the fund guaranteed to continue to give revenues, and remain the basis for production.

Those readers familiar with Georgescu-Roegen's (1971) pioneering work will recall that the concepts of stocks, funds and flows have been developed and analysed in detail in his Chapter 9 (cf. Wodopia, 1986). While Georgescu-Roegen uses these concepts within a framework of economic production, we shall develop these concepts within the context of the natural world, and then show their applicability to economics.

9.5.1   The Characteristics of Funds

Going back to the history of the notion of funds in economics, we may understand funds in a rather narrow sense and may say: the fund renders *services* to man. These services may be either material or immaterial; for example, an apple tree gives material apples and oxygen, but also immaterial shelter, as well as aesthetic services from its form.

Now we wish to apply the concept of a fund also to non-human organisms. First we make some introductory remarks.

Consideration of our three tele indicates that all organisms are funds, necessarily rendering services to other organisms, for from the third telos we know that each organism serves other organisms, i.e. provides services. On the other hand, from the first and second tele we know that there is self-maintenance and reproduction, implying the organism/species maintains itself, so that each organism/species also needs services. If a species is able to maintain itself, it implies that the basis for its necessary services is not depleted. Thus organisms/species can be viewed, as well as being funds, also as being users of funds.

There exist inherent difficulties generally in defining individual organisms as funds, although this may be possible in some cases. Instead, it is convenient to employ the corresponding species as the elementary unit of a fund. This is so because a fund continues over time, which does not hold for an organism, but only for a species, which can maintain itself over very long time scales. In principle, this continuity of a species is indefinite, though, of course, species can, and do, become extinct.

The fundamental characteristics of a fund may be summarised as follows:

(i)   A fund has relationships with species, because it gives services to one or several other organisms.[10]

(ii)   A fund reproduces itself.

(iii)   A fund is an indefinite nature concerning its time scale.

Concerning the first characteristic, we note the following. An organism which uses the services of a second organism treats this second organism as a fund, and through its use of the service of that fund is acting towards its first telos (i.e. self-maintenance). On the other hand, the organism giving the service is acting towards its third telos (i.e. service to other species). So the relationship between organisms as funds need not be symmetrical.[11]

That the fund reproduces itself reflects the second telos (i.e. self-replication).

The last characteristic makes sure that the services, which are essential resources for the existence of organisms, continue to be available. Thus this trait of a fund contributes, in an essential way, to the continuing existence of a basis for living.

From the above discussion of stores and funds, we can see a relationship to the well-known concepts of non-renewable and renewable resources. A store need not be self-reproducing, so withdrawal from a store may be possible only for a finite period. This limitation will certainly apply to non-organic stores, which we can speak of as non-renewable resources. On the other hand a fund can reproduce itself, as it is organic, and we can speak of these as renewable resources. Of course, funds may be treated unsustainably and be depleted by overuse.

9.5.2   The Dimensions of Funds and Services

In contrast to stocks/stores and corresponding flows/withdrawals, the dimension of a fund and its service is, in general, not the same. Referring to the example of the apple tree, given above, the species of apple tree is a fund, while its services are the flows of apples, leaves, wood, oxygen and the services of its surface. We see that the dimensions of the fund and the services are completely different.

However, it may be, and often is the case, that the dimension of the fund and its service are the same. For example, the species rabbit is a fund for the species fox. The dimension of the service of the rabbits for the foxes is 'rabbits'; i.e. the units of the fund and the service are identical (except that, of course, the service always is 'per unit time'). In this case the fund has the characteristic of a stock.

The relationship of an organism as a fund to an organism which uses its services may, to a greater or lesser extent, threaten the continuation of the existence of the fund. We may use here three broad classes of services.

(i)   The services may be of immaterial nature: e.g. the tree providing shelter.

(ii)   The services may be separated from the fund itself: e.g. the oxygen, leaves or apples of a tree.

(iii) The services may be the organism, or essential parts of itself: e.g. a rabbit, or the skin of a cow.

In the case of (i), rendering the service offers no threat to the fund (species).

In the case of (ii), there may be some slight threat to the fund's continued existence. The threat is the greater the more these services are used. If they are used too much, then the danger may be great. For example, if all the leaves are taken from a tree, then the tree's existence is endangered, as the first telos cannot be fulfilled. If all apples are taken, for a sustained period, then the replication of the species is threatened (i.e. the second telos may be impossible).

For case (iii), we immediately see that there is an ever present threat to the existence of the fund species. For example, the great whales have been taken by humans at a much greater rate than is sustainable, so the fund of whales has been treated like a stock.

9.5.3 Funds, Stores and Sustainability

We have just noted that if a fund is used as a stock, then there is a danger of the extinction of the species corresponding to this fund. If this fund is essential to the existence of the species whose use is causing the extinction, then that species too may become extinct. Further, other services from the fund species may be vital to the continued existence of other species, so these too may be threatened. For example, if all mahogany trees are felled by humans, not only does mahogany wood cease to be available to humans, but the multifarious services it offers to other species are also lost. This example also shows that the extinction of mahogany does not endanger the human species, because the human species can substitute other materials for mahogany.

What are the conditions under which a species can use a fund as a stock, and in particular the conditions for the extinction of this fund? We suggest these are as follows:

(a) the dominating species has to be very superior, or

(b) it is very large compared to the dominated fund, or

(c) the regeneration rate of the dominated fund is smaller than the extraction rate of the dominating species.

9.5.4 Sustainability of Funds and the Three Tele

The question of sustainability is usually put only regarding one species (or fund), namely humans (Norgaard and Howarth, 1991). The continued existence of other species (funds) is seen as a sustainability issue only in so far as it influences the welfare of humankind (cf. the literature on the optimal extinction of species, e.g. Clark, 1976). From our approach we may derive a more encompassing view on sustainability. We noted above that our three tele are recursive within an ecological whole. As long as this recursion is maintained, the integrity of the ecological whole remains, and we may term the system 'sustainable' in a broad sense. As a consequence, sustainability means that a certain balance, or harmony, between the three tele is maintained for each species of the ecological whole. If any of these tele becomes too important, for any species, then sustainability is threatened.

For example, if the first telos (self-maintenance) of a species is allowed to grow out of proportion, that species will come to overuse the services of other species, risking their, and eventually its own, continuation. If the second telos (self-replication) becomes dominant, then over-population of that species becomes a threat to the ecological whole. Finally, if the third telos becomes disproportionate, the rendering of too great a service to other species will threaten the continuation of that species, and the integrity of the ecological whole.

This broad concept of sustainability, using the recursive nature of our three tele, we now apply to the history of economic development, through the pastoral/agricultural phase through to modern industrialisation. We offer examples of how the three tele lose balance and harmony in our discussion of economic development.

9.6   FUNDS AND ECONOMICS

In this section we seek to relate our discussion of FFESODS and funds to human activity of production and consumption: i.e. to economics. To do this we take a long-run, evolutionary perspective, beginning with non-human FFESODS.

9.6.1   Evolutionary Historical Perspectives

In the absence of humans, living FFESODS have been almost entirely dependent on sunlight as the source of low entropy available energy.[12] As the energy flux of the sun changes rather slowly, systems of living

FFESODS have generally been able to attain phenotypic equilibrium, where the outcome of the operation of the three tele has been a balance between species, which has been resilient over long periods. This equilibrium has been 'punctuated' by periods of rapid genotypic evolution, perhaps following mass extinctions, from whatever cause (Gould, 1989).

9.6.2 Cultural Historical Perspectives

Humans have been a recognisable group of species for perhaps a few million years. Of those species, *homo sapiens* has been dominant for perhaps a few tens of thousands of years, driving *homo neanderthalis* to extinction as recently as 30,000 years ago. Over those thirty millenia, human dominance of other species has been growing increasingly rapidly since the beginning of pastoralism and agriculture, roughly 10,000 years ago.

9.6.3 Pastoralism and Agriculture

This pastoral/agricultural phase saw an alteration in the relationship between humans and other living FFESODS. Up until then, humans had the same ecological status as other organisms: i.e. they used the services of FFESODS, and a little material. However, with the rise of the control of other species for human ends (e.g. sheep, cattle, wheat, etc.), greater weight began to be given to the first (self-maintenance) and second (self-reproduction) tele, than the third (service) telos. We also note that we can speak of this process in economic terms, as constituting the accumulation of capital, through an act of desire, or will. Here, by capital we simply mean 'the means of production'.

The consequence of the pastoral/agricultural 'revolution' was a marked alteration in relative species abundance, with the abundance of humans increasing greatly, together with their new symbionts (e.g. cattle, wheat, etc.). On the other hand, the relative abundance of many species was reduced, through the exclusion of these species from land areas now used for agriculture. Part of the development of human culture has been the taking control of the evolution and destinies of other species in a far wider and more profound way than is found elsewhere in nature.

Although under pastoralism, and even more agriculture, the balance of the tele shifts away from the third telos (service), there is a limit to how far the third telos may be reduced, as the basis of these economic systems is funds, i.e. organisms. It is clear that if the third telos of humans is too much neglected, then the system becomes unsustainable, as the economic basis of the society is destroyed. Such agricultural collapse probably occurred in the ancient Mayan and Mesopotamian civilisations.

9.6.4   Industry

The rise of industry, particularly over the last three hundred years, can be characterised as the accumulation of non-living capital, such as machines, buildings, etc. In particular, this accumulation and use of capital has been powered not by sunlight, but to a large extent by fossil fuels, such as coal, oil and gas. It would be useful if we could talk of this phase of economic activity in terms of FFESODS and funds; however, this requires some further analysis and definitions.

9.6.5   Partial and Artificial Funds

We now find it useful to introduce a further discussion of the nature of funds, to allow us to embrace the economic notion of capital within the funds concept.

We recall that a fund has three characteristics:

(i)   A fund has relationships with species, because it gives services to one or several other organisms.

(ii)   A fund reproduces itself.

(iii) A fund is, in principle, of an 'eternal' nature.

Now clearly, the components of organisms have themselves some traits of funds. For example, the organs of a human (e.g heart, liver) satisfy at least condition (i). Such elements of an organism we term 'partial funds'. Thus an organism may be constituted of several partial funds, which provide a service, but exist only insofar as the organism exists.

Concerning capital, we can include this in our notion of funds by adopting the terminology of Lotka (1925). He spoke of capital goods as humans' 'exosomatic (i.e. outside the body) organs'. That is, we can conceptualise capital goods as being part of the fund of 'humans', though by association rather than through being included in the biological genotype. Thus, just as organs are partial funds for humans, so are capital goods.

We could also refer to capital goods as 'artificial funds', to distinguish them from the 'natural funds' constituted by organisms. Again, such artificial funds have telos 3 (service) only; i.e it has only characteristic (i).[13]

In summary, we can say that capital goods are artificial funds which, because they cannot (at present) be autonomous, are necessarily also partial funds, being associated only with human activity. Also, they have only the third telos.

9.6.6   The Servicing of Artificial Funds

The artificial, partial funds (i.e. capital) presently used depend to an increasing extent on fossil fuels. In our terminology, production came to depend less on funds (organisms, or renewable resources) and more on stores (minerals, or non-renewable resources, e.g. coal, oil, iron ore). Obviously, non-living stores do not require the services of funds (organisms) for their maintenance (though they may be organically derived over geological time). In our terms, on the time-scale of humans, the human use of non-living stores does not rely on the third telos. This is in stark contrast to agriculture, where one needs to 'feed the cows', implying the application of the third telos by humans.

In summary, the industrialisation process on the basis of non-renewable resources leads to the atrophy of the third telos in humans.

Also, the manufacture of partial funds can be attributed to the desire to serve the first telos (self-maintenance). Thus industrialisation not only reduces the third telos of humans, as we have argued above, but dramatically increases the scope of the first telos. We therefore see a two-fold disruption of the balance of the tele under industrialisation, with its consequent threat to sustainability. It seems that the more humans have machines to 'care' for them, the less do they care for the rest of nature. In particular, industrialisation has increased both the number of humans and the extent of the *means* of humans to impose their wills on the rest of nature. Thus the rise of industrialisation has further enhanced the first and second tele for human FFESODS, and diminished the importance of the third telos.

As we have discussed in Chapters 3 and 4, industrialisation based on artificial funds powered by fossil fuels, through this diminution of human's third telos, has increasingly isolated humans from the rest of nature, and led to a Faustian attitude towards nature, where it is seen solely as a means towards the furtherance of human aims. That is, the symmetry of relationships between FFESODS, through the third telos, has been broken.

Further, the evolution of this asymmetry between humans and nature has evolved very rapidly, as the process of social evolution is not Darwinian but rather Lamarkian (i.e. changes in the phenotype can affect the genotype).

9.7   ACHIEVING ECOSYSTEM HEALTH

We now seek to indicate the scope of application of the concepts and language we have developed. To this end we focus on the problem of global environmental degradation and the means to achieve long-run sustainability. We may put this presentation in the context of 'ecosystem health' (see Costanza, Norton and Haskell, 1992), and offer our conclusion in four categories: Symptoms; Diagnosis; Prognosis; Therapy.

9.7.1   Symptoms

In the Western world we see burgeoning consumerism, rapid depletion of renewable and non-renewable resources, and increasing and diversifying emissions of pollutants, with their actual and potentially devastating consequences. In the Third World we see rapidly growing human populations, extensification of agriculture through forest-clearance, and intensification of agriculture, leading to soil-degradation and pollution, causing human misery and ecosystem destruction.

9.7.2   Diagnosis

Using our vocabulary of tele and funds, we can see that, in both the First and Third Worlds, humans have been abusing and 'enslaving' other species (funds). This reflects imbalance and lack of harmony between the three tele of humans and non-humans, globally.

For the First World, the construction of artificial funds (capital goods) has been on the basis of exploiting non-renewable resources, allowing human awareness of the third telos (service to others) to atrophy. This in turn has led to the use of funds (renewable resources) as stores, causing their depletion and often their destruction. These funds are further endangered and destroyed when pollution is emitted, as humans pursue their first telos (through production and consumption).

At the same time, the services rendered by the artificial funds have allowed concentration by Western humans on fulfilling the first telos (i.e. consumerism). Hence, through the weakening of the third telos, and the strengthening of the first telos, a two-fold breaking of the harmony of the three tele has occurred through industrialisation.

In the Third World, the spillover of Western artificial funds (capital) has allowed the second telos to operate inharmoniously, leading in turn to other funds having their services demanded, while the services rendered to them by humans are reduced. Thus the second and third tele of humans adjust further from a sustainable balance. We do not wish to suggest that the intensity of the first telos is necessarily less in the Third world than in the First, but the means of fulfilling this telos are much weaker in the third world.

The complementary effect of the above human tele on nature has been the increase in the fulfilment of other species' third telos with regard to humans; not infrequently this has led to their extinction. This has further accentuated the global imbalance between the tele.

9.7.3   Prognosis

Without therapy the prognosis is poor. By definition, if the tele are unbalanced, their can be no broad sustainability. Indeed, there cannot even be sustainability for the present economic system.

9.7.4   Therapy

A therapy is only possible if humans have to a certain extent freedom of emphasis concerning their three tele. This is a question of will and decision (cf. Chapter 5). From our discussion above, it follows that broad sustainability can only be re-established if humanity finds a new balance between the three tele, both for themselves and other species. This implies, for the First *and* Third Worlds, that the third telos is re-emphasised. Although this goal holds for all humans, the paths to this goal will vary from area to area. Fortunately, there remains, to a greater or lesser extent, a residual set of traditions and customs regarding humans' third telos to other species, which, through education, may still be revived.

Our considerations suggest that the First World must change its attitude to the first telos, in two respects. First, it has to be given less emphasis, and thus make room in particular for the neglected third telos. However, and second, this does not necessarily imply that the human welfare derived from the first telos has to be decreased. More self-realisation does not necessarily mean more consumption of goods and services, but might be achieved in non-material ways.

Such advice on the first telos cannot be given concerning the Third World. Instead, the second telos must be considered as the principal problem. However, this may well be most appropriately addressed by improving the means of fulfilling the first telos. This in turn, one might hope, will also give room and means for the re-growth of the third human telos.

At first sight, our conclusion might seem far from our present situation. However, we think that over the last three decades there has been a very strong and increasingly influential re-emphasis of the third telos in the First World: this is often called the 'Green' movement. The main strength of the Greens is that they have a brought a revolutionary element into the politics of the industrial age; they have reasserted, after a long period of neglect, the importance of serving nature. Through this endeavour they are leading, albeit it fallibly, towards correcting the imbalance of the three tele.

NOTES

1. Entropy is a measure of the 'mixed-upness' of matter and/or energy. It also measures the 'availability' of energy. Isolated systems tend, over time, towards a state of maximum entropy. For a wider discussion of entropy in the context of economics, see Chapters 6 and 7.
2. The pioneering work on FFESODS was by Prigogine, for which he received a Nobel Prize in Chemistry.
3. The emergence of successively more complex systems has been called the 'Blind Watch Maker' hypothesis: cf. Simon (1962).
4. The concepts of genotype and phenotype within an evolutionary approach to ecological economics are extensively discussed in Faber and Proops (1993a:Chapter 2).
5. Here we exclude the possibility of 'chaotic' behaviour (i.e. unpredictable determinacy): cf. Guckenheimer and Holmes (1983).
6. Ontogeny concerns the origin and development of the individual being.
7. A species is the maximal group of organisms which can reproduce with each other; e.g. humans, dogs, horses, cows, etc.
8. 'Monozygotic' means derived from a single fertilised egg.
9. In the sense of Hegel (see Neuser, 1986:7-11) we could also call them 'speculative' concepts.
10. We define a fund as necessarily giving services. However, some services derive from non-funds (e.g. the sun).
11. On the occasion when a relationship between organisms is symmetric, we speak of symbiosis.
12. A current exception is the development of ecosystems dependent on chemical free energy around fumaroles, which are areas where material from within the Earth is released by a type of volcanic activity.
13. Humans create artificial funds in order to get services from them, i.e. for their self-maintenance and self-realisation. But on the other hand they can receive such services only if they continually serve these artificial funds by their labour. One could even say that in modern Western societies, the third telos of humans has shifted from nature to their artificial funds. This shift has been observed by critics of modern capitalism like Marx, who said that capital 'employs' the labourers in order to 'consume' their services.

10. Interdisciplinary Research Between Economists and Physical Scientists: Retrospect and Prospect

10.1   INTRODUCTION

It is widely accepted that interdisciplinary research and cooperation is urgently necessary for ecological economics, but is difficult to carry out. In this chapter we intend to show that both aspects of this statement hold for cooperation between economists and physical scientists; we also offer suggestions for overcoming these difficulties.

Over the past two decades the problems of environmental pollution and potential energy shortage have stimulated interdisciplinary work between economists and physical scientists. One outcome of this intellectual convergence has been the realisation by many economists that economies have a physical underpinning that cannot be ignored, while many physical scientists have come to recognise that problems of pollution and energy use have also a social and economic aspect. A second and less fortunate result of this contact between the disciplines has been some cases of mutual incomprehension and dismissive hostility between economists and physical scientists. In this chapter we seek to understand how such problems of incomprehension may arise and how they may be avoided. Having established the usefulness of considering physical concepts we show, by using the notion of entropy, how they can be formally integrated into ecological economic analysis.

10.2   ECONOMISTS AND PHYSICAL SCIENCE

There are many widely accepted models and concepts which use analogies between physical theory and economics. However, we do not consider such use of analogy to be truly interdisciplinary, as this involves the sharing of concepts between disciplines and not just the borrowing of ideas and methods. Indeed, analogical reasoning can even be misleading if concepts from physical science are incorporated into social and economic models but not fully understood and internalised by the researcher.

10.2.1 Physical Analogies

Economics has a long tradition of employing concepts and methods from the physical sciences (Proops, 1985). Walras (1874) and Edgeworth (1881) made explicit use of analogies with aspects of physical theory, and Fisher (1892) made an early attempt to express an isomorphism between concepts in economics and thermodynamics. In more modern times Samuelson (1948) has expressed certain economic results in the same form as Le Chatelier's principle from thermodynamics.

The central concept from thermodynamics, entropy, has also been widely used in economics (see e.g. Theil, 1967). (The entropy concept has been reviewed in Chapters 6 and 7.) The entropy concept is discussed in more detail in Section 10.5.3 below, as derived from 'classical' thermodynamics. It can also be derived from statistical mechanics, where the 'orderliness' or 'concentration' of a system is expressed in terms of a suitable set of probabilities or frequencies. It is this formulation that has been extensively exploited in economics, for such diverse applications as measuring industrial concentration, inequalities of income and employment, and geographic concentration.

This use of pure analogy is exemplified by the use of 'gravity models' in regional economics (see e.g. Isard, 1975). In such models interaction between population centres is assumed to vary with their size and distance apart.

Thoben (1982) has suggested that the use of mechanical analogy in economics should be supplanted by the use of 'organistic' analogy, recognising that a complex economic system is more akin to a self-regulating and developing organism than to a mechanical system. A similar exploration of organistic analogy is due to Fehl (1983), who draws an analogy between economies and 'dissipative structures', which are discussed in more detail in Section 10.2.3 below (and see Chapters 6 and 7). In a similar vein, Hannon (1985a) has argued for the analogy between economies and ecosystems to be recognised, with ecosystems offering the potential for an experimental systems basis for economics.

10.2.2 Physical Limits

Such drawing of analogies has not been the only method of conjuncture of economics with the physical sciences. Perhaps Jevons (1865) was the most eminent of the early economists who examined the physical nature of economic activity, when he considered the importance of coal to the British economy. More recently Georgescu-Roegen (1971) has stressed the importance of thermodynamic entropy to understanding the functioning of economies. The concern of both authors was been the physical limits to social activity; for Jevons it was the possible future shortage of coal that he saw as a constraint upon industrial activity, while Georgescu-Roegen stressed the wider problem of the irreversibility of productive activity, and the constraints this places on economic activity in the long-run, because of finite exhaustible resources. Thus the concerns about fuel reserves have also found expression in the field of Energy Analysis, which developed rapidly following the oil 'crisis' of 1973 (see e.g. Slesser, 1978). The aim of energy analysis is to map the direct and indirect energy use of an economy through the productive process.

The problem of environmental pollution has also become of great interest in recent years (see e.g. Dorfman and Dorfman, 1977). Again, interest among economists and other scholars has centred upon how pollution may act as a physical limitation on man's economic activity. A unified treatment of environmental as well as of resource problems has been initiated by Faber, Niemes and Stephan (1983:Chapter 8).

10.2.3 Dissipative Structures

A third and more general relationship between economics and thermodynamics has been explored by Proops (1983) and Ruth (1993), based on the work of Prigogine (1980) and the Brussels School of Thermodynamics. This approach distinguishes between static structures, such as crystals, and dynamic structures, such as convection cells, flames and organisms. A static structure is in equilibrium with its environment, its structure being maintained by internal stasis. A dynamic structure, on the other hand, maintains a constant relationship with its environment via active internal processes, in particular processes which generate entropy and dissipate energy. Such dynamic systems have been described as being far from thermodynamic equilibrium, and under certain circumstances may demonstrate not simply self-maintenance, but also 'self-organisation', and thereby generate further structuring. (For a fuller discussion, see Chapters 6 and 9.)

The classic example of a dynamic structure is a convection cell, which develops when a liquid is subject to a temperature gradient. If the temperature gradient is small the liquid will transport energy through its bulk solely by conduction; but if the temperature gradient is increased, regularly shaped convection cells will form spontaneously, increasing the rate of heat transport through the liquid. These convection cells correspond to a more 'structured' state of the system, with the energy flux acting as an ordering agent for this 'dissipative structure'. Now economies are such complex structures, maintaining themselves by 'consuming low entropy', to use the phrase of Schrödinger (1944). Ordered, low entropy fuels are used up and high entropy waste heat is dissipated in all the productive processes by which economies maintain themselves.

The question of whether economies can be adequately viewed in this way is still open, but Nicolis and Prigogine (1977:4) have made it clear that they feel such a description is valid.

10.3   PHYSICAL SCIENTISTS AND ECONOMICS

Although economists have made liberal use of physical science, dialogue between economists and physical scientists over matters of energy use, resource depletion, and pollution has also helped the understanding of physical scientists. For example, in the early days of concern over energy shortage (i.e. 1970s), a common theme among physical scientists was that economic value must derive from energy (e.g. Gilliland, 1975), as energy is the only factor of production that is in principle non-substitutable. However, many economic studies have shown that energy can, to some extent, be substituted by capital or by labour, and also it can be augmented in production by technical progress. This assumption of a single factor of production is reminiscent of the Labour Theory of Value of Ricardo and Marx. The problem of how the 'costs' of a single input can be transformed into the 'prices' of outputs has long been an area of debate in economics and the limits of this approach are very narrow (see e.g. Samuelson, 1971).

It is our view that many physical scientists took this narrow stance on the role of energy in the production process because energy plays a central role in the physical scientists' world view. At the time when the problem of energy supply became an issue it was not unnatural that economists took the view that this was a problem of market operation, while physical scientists saw as the root of the problem an imminent absolute shortage of energy. It is pleasing to note that the debate over the importance of energy as a productive factor not only caused many economists to adjust their stance and come to accept that economic activity has a physical foundation, it also brought many physical scientists to the view that although energy is a central factor for modern economies, it is not the only factor worthy of study.

The debate on energy and value also revealed much about the problems of interdisciplinary research between economists and physical scientists. In particular it revealed how difficult it is to have discussions across the economics/physical science divide when the parties involved are conversant only with their own disciplines. A common language alone does not allow mutual comprehension when the conceptual frameworks employed by discussants are very different. We shall come back to this issue in Section 10.6.1 below.

10.4 ENERGY, TIME, IRREVERSIBILITY, AND ENTROPY IN ECONOMICS

It is our view that the exploration of the effects of physical limitations upon economic activity has proved very fruitful. To this end we shall discuss three concepts, energy, time and irreversibility, which have not been given the prominence they deserve in economic theory (see Section 10.6.1). We shall further show that the entropy concept is not only suited to deal with all three aspects at the same time, but should also be applied to an analysis of resources and environment because (a) here energy, time and irreversibility play a particularly decisive role and (b) entropy is therefore suited to integrate the economic analysis of resource and environmental problems (see Section 10.4.2).

10.4.1 Why Does Economic Theory Need to be Given Physical Roots?

Two of the fundamental concepts of thermodynamics are energy and time. No physical process is possible without energy, and all such processes relevant to the functioning of economics are of an irreversible nature because of the Second Law of Thermodynamics, to which we refer below in Section 10.4.3 (cf. Chapters 6 and 7). The limits to which energy can be technically substituted are determined by physical laws. With respect to time, it is apparent that economic processes have two temporal aspects. First, any production process takes up time: i.e. time is involved as 'duration' (see Faber, 1979:Chapters 2 and 3). Second, production processes are unidirectional in time and therefore necessarily irreversible.

Examples of such irreversibility are the combustion of fossil fuels, the use of resources which are not recycled, the destroying of the wilderness and many types of environmental damage, e.g. the results of acid rain. Economists, however, often treat time in a rather mechanistic way. Even if they deal with dynamics as in growth theory their concepts are of a rather static nature A prominent example is the notion of a steady state, where the structure does not change from period to period. As Hicks (1973:47, 1976:139) has said this is not 'economics in time' but 'economics of time', in which time is no more than a mathematical parameter. In contrast to this approach, thermodynamics forces one to regard real, irreversible time in the analysis, making one aware of the irreversible nature of much economic activity.

10.4.2   Formal Integration of Physical Concepts into Economic Analysis

The principle of the irreversibility of economic processes, which was introduced as a postulate by Koopmans (1951:48) says:

> *It is not possible to run some or all activities at positive levels such that the joint effect of the net output is zero for all goods.*

This formulation can be justified as follows. If the zero vector could be generated, then it would be possible to use the output of one activity as an input to another activity. In that case one could generate a continual circulation of commodities without adding new inputs. The Postulate of Irreversibility can therefore be interpreted as an implicit consideration of the nature of the temporal course of production, for the manufacturing of commodities cannot be reversed in time. The reversal, however, is excluded by the Second Law of Thermodynamics. One of its formulations says that it is impossible to construct a periodically working machine which only extracts heat from the environment; in other words, a perpetuum mobile (of the second kind) is not possible.

The most general formulation of the Second Law of Thermodynamics is: Entropy can never be destroyed, but it can only be created. Applying this law to economics Georgescu-Roegen (1971:279) wrote:

> *So, the popular economic maxim 'you cannot get something for nothing' should be replaced by 'you cannot get anything but at a far greater cost of low entropy'.*

Koopmans (1951:50-51) called a corresponding condition the Impossibility of the Land of Cockaigne. This says it is impossible to produce a good without an input. The relationship between the two Postulates of Irreversibility and the Impossibility of the Land of Cockaigne is discussed by Wittmann (1968:39-42). Koopmans (1951) has represented both postulates within a linear technology, but Debreu

(1959:39-42) has also employed the Axiom of Irreversibility in a non-linear formulation of a general equilibrium model. However, it is our impression that while irreversibility has begun to be accepted as an axiom, the physical meaning of such irreversibility has yet to be 'internalised' in the conceptualisation of most economists. This lacuna has been recognised by Samuelson (1983:36):

> *In theoretical economics there is no 'irreversibility' concept, which is one reason why Georgescu-Roegen (1971) is critical of conventional economics.*

One may now object that 'the Irreversibility of Production' and 'the Impossibility of the Land of Cockaigne' are so obvious from a purely economic point of view that it is not necessary to study physics or to undertake interdisciplinary work in order to find them. However, we do not consider it pure chance that it was actually Koopmans who introduced these two assumptions into economic analysis, for he had studied physics and had even written his first publication in that field. We believe his educational background gave him a particular outlook when studying production problems, which was a prerequisite for his seminal work in economics.

10.4.3 Application of Entropy to Environment and Resources

We now turn to environmental and resource economics in order to show how knowledge of thermodynamics may help to give new insights and also to unify these two fields.

We shall first give an historical perspective to this question from the point of view of the use of energy. Let us start by distinguishing between 'useful energy', i.e. the energy contained in foodstuffs and fuels directly used for man's subsistence, on the one hand, and primary energy sources transformed by man into such 'useful energy', e.g. solar energy or fossil energy, on the other. Focusing on this transformation process, one can construct the following argument. Up to the beginning of the nineteenth century solar energy was by far the most important form of energy; a predominantly agricultural society transformed it into useful energy through the use of surface land. The density of solar energy, however, can be compared with the density of the kinetic energy contained in rain, i.e. it is very low. This means that to transform solar energy into 'useful energy' one needed a lot of land, even with intensive agriculture, which was by then predominant in Europe. Up to that time the most important function of land for humankind was therefore the use of its surface for energy transformation, the transformation of primary into 'useful energy'.

Owing to the rise in population, land became scarcer in Europe. As a consequence, from the sixteenth century up to about 1830 output per unit labour hour declined. This fact explains why Ricardo and particularly Malthus were so concerned with the scarcity of land at the beginning of the nineteenth century. Only during the last 150 years did humankind, in some parts of the world, experience a sustained increase in the standard of living. A necessary condition for industrial development was the ability of humans to extract fossil fuels and minerals from below the surface and thus loosen the restriction of land as the principle source of useful energy. During the last two decades it has become evident that owing to a rapidly rising world population and the depletion of global ecosystem resources the limits to further growth may be restricted; land again becomes a limiting factor of production. However, this time in an essentially broader sense, namely: 1. as surface, 2. as a supplier of resources and 3. as a receiver of pollutants.

Economists have a long tradition of dealing with the first aspect, but a rather short one concerning the last two. The extraction of resources, their combination and transformation in production and their final disposal in the form of waste (or their recycling) results in a continuous change of the 'orderliness' of the earth. The concept of entropy can be used to characterise the orderliness of a system; the higher the disorder the higher the entropy and vice versa. Thus the extraction of a resource from a site with high concentration and its final disposal into the environment, where a diffusion process takes place, increases the entropy of the system. Thus there are two relationships: 1. between the concentration of a resource and entropy, 2. between environmental pollution and entropy.

Hence entropy may be used to connect both areas, namely the theories of environment and of resources. At the same time both fields can be given a biophysical foundation. Turning to the first relationship we note that, under certain conditions, we can derive a function relating the change in entropy and the concentration of a resource. This can be used to relate the amount of energy which is necessary to extract a resource at a certain concentration (Faber, Niemes and Stephan, 1983:101-104). It turns out that the lower the concentration, the higher is the energy required (cf. Chapter 7). On the other hand the physical scientist Kümmel (1980:25-29) has explored how the change in entropy of an ecological system can be used as an aggregate measure of pollution.

One further advantage in using entropy as a variable in economic analysis is that it makes one immediately aware of a range of problems (Faber, 1985). One example is the fact that helium is not separated from natural gas, but vented into the atmosphere. Since helium is an exceptional substance, with great value to humankind, this venting is a tremendous waste of low entropy (Eppler and Lave, 1980). Another example is the driving of cars with gasoline. Both kinds of action can be justified by conventional economic analysis, by using a correspondingly high social discount rate. However, using our biophysical approach one will immediately recognise the tremendous amount of entropy which is generated in both cases. This in turn will lead one to ask, what kind of resource and environmental effects these activities imply in the long-run, and what economic and social changes will be required to cope with these resource shortages and environmental effects?

In summary, we feel this approach to economic problems is helpful in the following respects (Faber, 1985):

1. Entropy might be used as a new variable to unify the complex subjects of environmental economics and the economics of exhaustible resources.

2. The thermodynamic approach is a way for economics to get in touch with its biophysical foundations.

3. Using the entropy concept makes an economist aware of the irreversible nature of the time structure of many environmental and resource processes. This concerns in particular those long-run problems on a macro-economic level, for which the price system alone does not provide a complete solution.

10.5   PHYSICAL CONSTRAINTS, TECHNICAL PROGRESS AND SOCIAL CHANGE

In Sections 10.2, 10.3 and 10.4 we discussed the different viewpoints of economists and physical scientists. It seems to us that the limitations on economic activity as perceived by economists are essentially *social* limitations (markets and market failures, investment choice, demand induced technical change). On the other hand physical scientists, through their training and conceptual models, are much more inclined to see economies as being limited by *physical* factors (see Section 10.2.2 above).

The essence of fruitful interdisciplinary work is the recognition that *both* viewpoints are valid, and they need not be mutually exclusive. In the long-run, physical limitations might well be binding. However, these physical constraints are likely to generate a social response which moves the economy away from the constraint, through technical and social adjustment. For example, in the late Middle Ages the British Isles were rapidly denuded of forest cover through the spread of agriculture and the rise of iron smelting using charcoal. However, this physical constraint was side-stepped in the eighteenth century by the development of iron making with coke. Indeed, the subsequent rapid rise in coal mining led to the development of efficient steam pumps to avoid yet another physical constraint, in this case the flooding of coal mines. This development of steam engines led, further, to an improvement in transport systems with the introduction of the steam train and steam powered ships, which in their turn allowed great social transformation on a world-wide scale.

Here we see that social transformation, technical change and physical constraints come together to form a web of recursive interrelationships, with technical change springing from the combination of social demand and the constraints on physical supply. Therefore technical progress, in addition to its usual interpretation, has the important role of intermediating between social demand and the physically and technically possible.

This leads us to conclude that it is not sufficient to look at social and economic activity solely with the concepts of economics since this would ignore a major source of social change, namely the technical progress which springs from the physical nature of economic activity. Physical constraints should therefore be seen as not only limiting factors on human activity in the long run, but also as prominent determinants of social change. Economists have been slow to recognise the role of such physical parameters because of the dominance of the methods of static and quasi-static analysis as mentioned in Section 10.4.1 above. More modern methods involving intertemporal models are much closer in spirit to the view we propose. However, even such models do not take into account the physical factors which provide not only a framework for the social system, but also interact with the current social system to generate the social future. Summarising our viewpoint, economists need not only an understanding of environmental and resource problems from their bio-physical foundations, as discussed in Section 10.4.3 above, but even more, an appreciation of the evolution of institutions in particular and societies in general, within a biophysical framework.

10.6 INTERDISCIPLINARY RESEARCH: DIFFICULTIES AND SOME TENTATIVE SOLUTIONS

10.6.1 Difficulties

There is little tradition of interdisciplinary collaboration between economists and physical scientists. However, as Koopmans (1979:1) noted in his presidential address to the American Economic Association:

> *With increasing frequency natural and social scientists are indeed finding themselves thrown together in the study of new problems that are of great practical importance for society, and essentially inter-disciplinary in character. Prominent among these are problems of environmental policy ... Another class of problems concerns a desirable long-range mix of technologies of energy supply, conversion and use.*

Although the urgency of interdisciplinary work is generally accepted, there is as yet limited progress, though the development of Ecological Economics as a discipline is a very positive development. We believe that the reason for this relatively slow development is that, besides the circumstances already mentioned above, there are obstacles of a psychological and institutional nature which impede such cooperation:

1. Researchers undertaking interdisciplinary work may face discouragement from the peer group of their fellow economists or physical scientists. Work across disciplines is often regarded as less 'serious' than work within a single discipline.

2. If one undertakes interdisciplinary research, one is almost bound to make certain blunders. One needs the courage to expose oneself not only to the critique of one's own discipline, but also to that of others. We found that these critiques are often rather harsh. One reason for this seems to be that the criteria which are used to evaluate research in a long established and specialised field are also used for inter-disciplinary work, which is in its infancy.

3. It is often difficult to find someone who wants to cooperate, since one does not know those who would be willing. Those who have some standing are often too occupied with other things, while young scholars have first to specialise themselves in their own field in order to become recognised, so as to obtain a permanent position (Koopmans, 1979:13).

4. The specialisation of modern science has led to language barriers, normal terms being given specialised meanings to meet certain needs of expression. For example, the terms 'core', 'game', 'capital' and 'indifference' have specialised meanings for economists, as do the terms 'field', 'ensemble' and 'cycle' for physicists. But even more of a barrier to dialogue is the separation of what is perceived as important and valid as an explanatory device within different disciplines. For economists it tends to be 'the market' and optimising behaviour that are the concepts considered most appropriate, while physical scientists' concerns seem to be with the notion of transformation and time.

5. Having undertaken interdisciplinary work, researchers must then seek a publication outlet for their findings. Established fields have established journals, which is not the case for emerging interdisciplinary fields. Single discipline journals are often reluctant to accept interdisciplinary papers, as they feel them inappropriate to their readership.

6. A prerequisite for truly interdisciplinary work is a certain familiarity with the other's discipline. Since the available knowledge will often not be sufficient, interdisciplinary research cooperation demands to some extent teaching and learning on both sides. Compared to joint research within one area this is rather cumbersome because it is one thing to lecture students and another to give an elementary introduction to a specialist of another field and to get taught perhaps even by someone who is much younger than oneself and sometimes not even established in his own discipline. Such discourse is however a sine qua non of interdisciplinary study. Only when the economist has *mastered* the relevant area of physical science (and not just read an introductory text), and only when the physical scientist is entirely familiar and comfortable with the relevant economic theory, can truly fruitful dialogue and research take place. This is a tiresome and time consuming procedure, and can be a disincentive to interdisciplinary work. Given the publication pressure there will be a great temptation to work exclusively in one's own discipline.

10.6.2   Tentative Solutions

The main conclusion from this chapter is that it is necessary to dissolve some established conceptual frameworks and to establish a wider vision (Daly, 1973; Boulding, 1970). However, it will be some time before there are many researchers with as wide a background as we are recommending. In the meantime the following suggestions may help to aid the progress of interdisciplinary studies.

1. Workers in interdisciplinary fields are few in number and scattered over several different disciplines, such as mathematics, systems theory, physics, chemistry, engineering, geology, biology, regional science, planning, sociology, law and, of course, economics. In addition, these researchers are dispersed among many institutions and are therefore isolated. From our own experience the prime means of combating this isolation is through interdisciplinary conferences, symposia and seminars. As such meetings are almost the only opportunities for interdisciplinary dialogue, they need to be held more frequently than in established fields.

2. We have suggested that successful interdisciplinary research requires researchers to have studied and internalised both economics and physical science, at least to some degree. We feel that preparation for interdisciplinary research can take place at three levels. First, established researchers in a single field might benefit from directed reading in the appropriate complementary field for their interdisciplinary work. Second, if greater encouragement were given to the joint study of economics and physical science at undergraduate level, this would greatly assist the erosion of the conceptual boundaries that divide these branches of scholarship. Third, interdisciplinary training at graduate school level would help to establish a body of scholars whose orientation would be naturally towards interdisciplinary work.

Some progress has already been made, with courses being offered in Engineering Economics at both graduate and undergraduate level. However, these courses are generally designed to produce skilled engineering managers, and while we support this aim we do not feel that such courses offer the complete background for interdisciplinary research which we wish to promote.

10.7   CONCLUDING REMARKS

The course of modern scholarship and research has been of increased intellectual division of labour with, for example the defining of physics as distinct from chemistry, and economics as distinct from political science. This division of labour has been enormously fruitful, but it has also led to specialisation by scholars that may become counter-productive. In particular, such specialisation has led scholars in different fields to evolve conceptual frameworks that are incompatible and mutually incomprehensible. We hope that we have shown that there are a wide range of problems, which are of pressing nature, where the economists' and physical scientists' frameworks for analysis are, individually, insufficient for the task. Only by breaking down these conceptual barriers and establishing a wider and more open framework for discourse is progress likely to be made.

Finally, let us note that we hope that interdisciplinary research may be one of the avenues which may lead economic theory out of the deadlock in which it seems to be, according to such different writers as Georgescu-Roegen, Hahn, Hicks, Kornai, Leontief and Robinson. Thus, for example, a physically oriented production theory could eventually contribute to a biophysical foundation of economics, which has been lost during the development of neoclassical theory (Daly, 1973). We also consider empirical work and the analysis of the history of economic thought (e.g. Witt, 1980) to be two further important sources for potential breakthroughs for economic theory.

PART III

Epistemological Perspectives on Ecological
Economics

11. Humankind and the Environment: An Anatomy of Surprise and Ignorance

11.1 INTRODUCTION

The following chapter offers an analysis of surprise and ignorance, in the context of environmental issues. Now it seems to us unfeasible to develop 'a general tool for the operationalisation of ignorance' (Funtowicz and Ravetz, 1990:7), particularly for the area of environmental problems. In contrast to this endeavour, we feel that the first task has to be to recognise the whole range of human ignorance. In order truly to understand this ignorance we cannot confine ourselves to the field of environmental questions; rather we attempt to develop a general taxonomy of ignorance and surprise. This will lead us to a high level of abstraction, well beyond any particular problems. Hence the following considerations are widely philosophical, and seemingly far away from environmental issues. However, we feel that a deepened understanding of ignorance will be helpful in gaining a new attitude towards environmental problems: an attitude of openness and flexibility instead of an attitude of control and inflexibility.

From the origins of modern science the problem of knowledge and ignorance has long been recognised, especially by Kant. Two hundred years ago he saw the following as fundamental questions of philosophy Kant (1956:677 B 833, our translation):

What can I know? What shall I do? What may I hope?

Especially important for scientists in general, and ecologically orientated scientists in particular, is the question: 'What can I know?'. The answer to this question is the basis for the questions: 'What can we control? What possibilities of action do we have? What can we do?'. In the search for control of the natural world and protection against environmental damage we usually concentrate on these latter questions. Conversely, the question 'What can I know?' has all too often been ignored by modern science. Hayek (1972:33, our translation) pointed out:

> *Perhaps it is only natural that the circumstances which limit our factual knowledge and the limits which thereby result for the application of our theoretical knowledge are rather unnoticed in the exuberance, which has been brought about by the successful progress of science. However, it is high time that we took our ignorance more seriously.*

The extent to which it is necessary to follow Hayek's advice can be seen by considering the usual attempt to solve environmental problems. When we meet such problems we are initially ignorant as to how to solve them. Our almost invariable assumption, however, is that this ignorance can, by learning and by scientific exploration, be reduced or even completely eliminated. The outcome of this process is to turn what was initially a problem, through scientific and technological endeavour, into a solution. The presupposition for this approach is that human knowledge can be increased without limit in any given area, giving us a better and better understanding of how the world works. This increase in our understanding will therefore cause us to face fewer and fewer 'surprises' as our science develops.

By their nature, environmental problems are often global and long-run. As such, very often they involve the emergence of unpredictable events (novelty). There is, also, the possibility that they involve dynamic systems which exhibit infinite sensitivity to their boundary conditions (i.e. 'chaotic' systems, cf. Faber and Proops, 1993a:Chapter 6). This implies that the simple sequence of *problem → science → technique → solution* is not necessarily valid. On the contrary, we experience that our increasing knowledge may even impede the investigation for solutions. As Smithson (1989:3) states:

> *We are in the midst of an ignorance explosion in the well known sense that even specialists are inundated with information pertinent to their own fields. Likewise, the sheer number of specialisations has mushroomed, as has the complexity of most of them.*

We assert, therefore, that the simple structure of problem/solution, based on the faith that knowledge in any area can be increased without limit, and surprise be correspondingly reduced, cannot be valid for science in general. In particular, we believe it to be untrue for problems of long-run economy-environment interactions. Therefore, in this chapter we take an approach which concentrates on 'unknowledge' and surprise, rather than on knowledge and fulfilled expectations. An improved understanding of ignorance and novelty may offer the basis for a more appropriate attitude towards environmental issues. There has already been considerable research about ignorance:

> *The last 40 years, however, and especially the last two decades, have*
> *seen a flurry of new perspectives on uncertainty and ignorance whose*
> *magnitude arguably eclipses anything since the decade of 1660 which*
> *saw the emergence of modern probability theory* (Smithson,
> 1988:3).[1]

Also, a stimulating taxonomy of some aspects of ignorance in the area
of society has been given by Smithson (1988:9). While in this chapter
we develop a new taxonomy of surprise and ignorance, this includes no
criticism concerning attempts like those made by, inter alia, Funtowicz
and Ravetz (1991), Perrings (1991), Ravetz (1986) and Smithson (1989).
However, the emphasis of our endeavour is different from these authors.

Section 11.2 deals with ignorance, surprise and novelty in our
everyday life. In Section 11.3 we begin to analyse 'ignorance'. Ignorance
is first decomposed into 'closed ' ignorance and 'open' ignorance
(Section 11.3.1). Open ignorance is further subdivided into 'reducible'
ignorance (Section 11.4) and 'irreducible' ignorance (Section 11.5).
Reducible ignorance can be understood either as 'personal' ignorance
(Section 11.4.1) or as 'communal' ignorance (Section 11.4.2). Irreducible ignorance has either a phenomenological (Section 11.5.1) or an
epistemological source (Section 11.5.2). Phenomenological sources of
certain ignorance spring from 'genotypic' change (Section 11.5.1.1) or
from the 'chaotic' behaviour of certain dynamic systems (Section
11.5.1.2). Epistemological ignorance is discussed in Section 11.5.2. It
is subdivided into three further categories: 'hermeneutic' ignorance
(Section 11.5.2.1), 'axiomatic' ignorance (Section 11.5.2.2), and 'logical' ignorance (Section 11.5.2.3). Following the discussion of 'pure'
ignorance and 'uncertain' ignorance in Section 11.6, an overview of all
sources of surprise and ignorance is given in Section 11.7. In Section
11.8 we discuss the role of science in seeking to reduce uncertain
ignorance to risk. In particular, we discuss the 'acts of faith' necessary
in physical, social, and biological science. In Section 9 we draw conclusions from our findings for the study of environmental issues. In
Section 11.10 we note that philosophers have often demanded an attitude
of openness because human beings are inherently ignorant.

11.2   THE FUTURE IN OUR EVERYDAY LIFE:
IGNORANCE, SURPRISE AND NOVELTY

Before we proceed to develop a further classification of ignorance we
turn our attention to the nature and sources of ignorance. In this chapter

we restrict our considerations of ignorance to our ignorance concerning present and future events. To this end we now move to a discussion of the nature of the 'future'.

A precise scientific definition of the 'future' might be: 'Any time which is later than now'. However, by making this definition, we move our problem to that of the definition of 'time', which is by no means easy. As Augustine (1961:264) noted:

> *What, then, is time? I know well enough what it is, provided that nobody asks me; but when I am asked what it is and try to explain it, I am baffled.*

Therefore, instead of trying to analyse the abstract notion of the 'future', we shall concentrate on the more concrete notion of 'future events', as reflected in our everyday lives. Every day we ask ourselves the questions:

1.   What is going to happen?

2.   What shall we do?

These have in common that they both concern future events: i.e. events which have not yet occurred. These questions are different because the attitudes they are based on are different. The question 'what is going to happen?' is theoretical, and reflects a contemplative and passive attitude; the question 'what shall we do?' is practical or ethical, and reflects an attitude of activity and intervention.[2]

Of course, in everyday life these questions, and their corresponding attitudes, are interrelated. The answer to the first question provides a basis for answering the second question. For example, if a farmer 'knows' what the weather pattern will be like during the growing season, then he can 'know' what will be the 'best' course of action regarding planting, weed control, harvesting, etc.

On the other hand, in the course of time interventions taken on the basis of answers to the second question, 'what can we do?', may alter the circumstances in such a way that the answer to the first question, 'what is going to happen?', will itself be changed. For example, in many parts of the world, hilly countryside can only be cultivated in the long-run by contour ploughing. If the farmer chooses *not* to use contour ploughing, then the result will be soil loss and, eventually, the loss of the option of cultivation at all.

In earlier times, most predictions about future events, soothsayers apart, were experientially based (e.g. the weather lore of farmers). However, over the past two hundred years the rise of Western science has given experiential regularities some conceptual underpinnings, often expressed as 'Laws of Nature' (e.g. Newton's laws of motion, the laws of thermodynamics, etc.). This has been immensely important in extending the range of prediction possible. We feel it has also been a source of misapprehension regarding the potential for knowledge about the future, as such theory allows prediction outside the range of experienced events. This may lead to the mistaken notion that, with sufficient theory, anything and everything may be predicted. Why this notion is mistaken is the major topic of the rest of this chapter.

11.2.1   Surprise: Examples and Categories

In our everyday lives, in our scientific endeavours, and in our attempts to control our social and natural environment, we are continually being surprised. We climb into our brand new car, turn the ignition key, and it refuses to start. We build a 'safe' chemical factory and it explodes.

Of course, not all surprises are unpleasant ones. We meet a stranger, and develop a deep and long-lasting relationship; we discover oil beneath the North Sea.

Regarding how we may be surprised, economists often follow Knight (1921) in distinguishing between 'risk' and 'uncertainty', as mentioned above in Section 2. (A similar distinction was made by Keynes, 1921.) To this classification we wish to add the third category, 'ignorance', which in the literature, particularly of conventional economics, is not given the attention we feel it deserves. The main focus of our analysis in this chapter will be on this category of ignorance.[3]

We can illustrate the distinction between these three categories (risk, uncertainty and ignorance) with an example of horse racing; in addition we will give an example from the field of environmental problems.

A keen follower of horse racing may frequently visit the track to bet on the outcome of the horse races. Such an individual will, when placing the bet on any race, have two factors in mind. First, what the expected possible outcomes could be: any horse in the race could win. Second, associated with each possible outcome is a subjective probability of that outcome actually occurring. It is this subjective assessment of probabilities, perhaps aided by close study of the racing form of each horse, that determines how the individual will bet. Here the individual can specify all of the anticipated outcomes, and associate a probability of occurrence with each of them. This is what an economist means by 'risk'.

To illustrate the meaning of 'uncertainty', we might suppose that our keen follower of racing form need not also be a student of weather and its forecasting. Such an individual may accept that, from time to time, inclement weather may cause the racing to be abandoned altogether. Thus the outcome 'no racing' may be recognised, but not have associated with it a subjective probability.

Thus we see that our visitor to the race course might be surprised in two ways. First, the horse that wins may not be the one expected by that individual. Second, the race may not take place at all because the weather does not permit it, even though this was recognised as a possible outcome.

However, a visit to a race course might produce an even greater degree of surprise than either of the two above cases. The individual might arrive at the race course after an absence of a few months, to find the course has been redeveloped as a shopping mall. This outcome was one which had never even occurred to our racegoer, let alone been an outcome with which a probability had been associated. Shackle termed such an outcome as an 'unexpected event' (Shackle, 1955:57) and characterised it as follows:

> *What actually happens can have altogether escaped his [the individual's, the authors] survey of possibilities, so that the degree of potential surprise he assigned to it was neither zero nor greater than zero, but was non-existent, a sheer blank* (Shackle, 1955:58).

This inability even to specify all possible future outcomes we term 'ignorance'.

For environmental issues we illustrate risk, uncertainty and ignorance with our second example. Let us consider the of use chlorofluorocarbons in refrigeration and manufacturing techniques. In this case, risk consists in the expected effects of this innovation, including possible side effects based on experiments. So firms involved may make probabilistic judgements on, for example, market penetration, the value of refrigerator sales, and the sales of frozen foods. The main environmental issue considered under this category would be food quality and its preservation.

Uncertainty may spring from several sources. Thus the possibility may be recognised that alternative food preservation technologies may be invented and innovated (such as freeze drying or radiation techniques); further legislation/taxation may change in an unforeseeable way the conditions of the market for refrigerators. Also, the uncertain probability of deleterious environmental side effects may be recognised, such as the potential problem of the disposal of discarded refrigerators. Such possibilities may be seen, but not be associated with subjective probabilities. If these possibilities occur, they will offer surprise to a great extent.

But the highest degree of surprise will be achieved when we discover, to our horror, that the ozone layer has developed a 'hole', and that this effect was caused as an unforeseeable side effect of our innovation of the use of chlorofluorocarbons in refrigeration. This consequence was completely outside the range of possibilities when we surveyed the possible consequences of our innovation. Until the moment the ozone hole was recognised as an effect of the use of chlorofluorocarbons, we had been in a state of ignorance.

It may be worthwhile for clarification to point out how the concept of ignorance used in the literature differs from ours. To this end we refer to an illustration given by Katzner (1986:61).

> *Now let a question be asked of such a kind that the individual is in ignorance of the possible answer that might be given to it. For example the question might be, 'What kind of personal computers will be available for purchase two years from now?' One cannot have knowledge of answers to this question because there is no way of knowing what the future will bring. The set of possible outcomes (answers) cannot be known ...*

For this kind of literature it is typical that at least the area in which ignorance may occur is within the range of knowledge of the individual. Thus, in Katzner's example, although one is ignorant about the set of possible outcomes, one knows for sure that the outcomes will be personal computers. This kind of confinement is to be found in almost all of the literature on ignorance. We admit that this kind of approach is helpful and therefore we will employ it ourselves. In addition to this approach, however, one focus of our attention lies on that kind of ignorance which does not pertain to a particular area of occurrences. Such kinds of ignorance are of particular importance for environmental problems, because the complexity in ecological systems is so encompassing that the drawing of any boundaries, or separation of distinct areas, would avoid the recognition of the true scope of our ignorance.

11.3   IGNORANCE

In this section we turn our attention to ignorance, and how it might be analysed and classified.

11.3.1   Closed Ignorance and Open Ignorance

Here it may be worth giving a diagrammatic representation of the classification thus far, as shown in Figure 11.1.

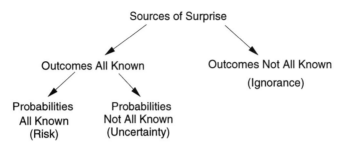

Figure 11.1. Sources of surprise.

From Figure 11.1 we note the crucial distinction between risk/uncertainty and ignorance, as we define them, is that the former pair are applied only in situations where all possible future outcomes can be specified, while the latter is applied where possible outcomes may not all be recognised prior to their occurrence,[4] or where even the area of possible outcomes may not be known in advance. Before we proceed we wish to distinguish between two main kinds of ignorance.

(1) We are often not aware of our ignorance, and therefore we feel no need for learning or research. Indeed, we may purposely ignore or suppress our recognition of our ignorance. We call this kind of ignorance 'closed ignorance'. Closed ignorance may either spring from the unawareness of unexpected events, or from false knowledge[5] or false judgements. The condition of closed ignorance characterises precisely the typical victim of the Socratic 'elenchus' (the Socratic mode of eliciting truth by short question and answer), as described in Plato's earlier dialogues (e.g. Meno). Indeed, the Socratic elenchus is supposed to serve precisely the purpose of converting someone from the condition of closed ignorance to that of open ignorance.

As long as an individual remains in a state of closed ignorance s/he is unable to recognise that state; only if some event forces the experience of surprise, or if another person is able to make the individual aware of its state can the individual experience, ex post, the previous state of closed ignorance. However, very often individuals (e.g. politicians, scientists, etc.), social groups, or even whole societies, suppress the possibility of surprise and are not open to criticism. Thus they remain unaware of their state of closed ignorance.

It is important to note that very many social phenomena of ignorance occur in the area of closed ignorance; such ignorance may even be created by social processes. That is the reason why Smithson (1989:216-263) studies this matter so extensively.

Closed ignorance, particularly in the form of pretended knowledge, is a great barrier to human cognition and insight, as well as to the solution of environmental problems. Thus closed ignorance concerning environmental issues means that we either neglect the problems themselves, or do not take notice of intuitive insights, experience, information, models and methods of solution which are available within society. An example of closed ignorance is the reaction of the Trojan society against Cassandra. Another prominent example of closed ignorance within the tradition of Western science is the attitude of Aristotelian scientists towards Galileo in the 17th century. As a last illustration of closed ignorance we mention the attitude of many scientists, engineers and politicians towards the risks of nuclear power before the accidents at Seven Mile Island and Chernobyl. Now closed ignorance is the determined non-recognition of ignorance, and it may be reflected by authoritative statements which cannot be literally true. For example, the assertion of low probabilities of melt-down by a nuclear reactor, prior to the two above events, is a statement of that sort. It is a mask of authority behind which ignorance may lurk.

(2) If individuals (group, societies) become aware of their previous state of closed ignorance (forced by drastic events, or guided by a changed attitude), they reach a state of 'open ignorance'. In this state one will become attentive, e.g. to events and information, etc., which one had neglected earlier. Only in a state of open ignorance is one able to experience surprise to its full extent, and to react to it adequately. Of course, in a state of open ignorance one will try to understand surprising events by learning and research. However, one is not only aware that one may generate new surprises by research and learning, but knows that one remains, in spite of one's increased knowledge, essentially in a state of ignorance. This is in line with the general tenet: 'The more I know, the more I know I don't know'.

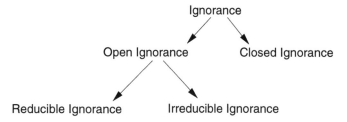

Figure 11.2. A classification of ignorance.

Concerning environmental issues, a considerable shift from closed to open ignorance can be recognised in some present societies. Some decades ago, few were ready to acknowledge such problems; the environmental movement in some societies has forced this realisation upon them. In particular, we view the rise of 'green' politics and 'green' consciousness' as, at least in part, reflecting this attitude of greater openness to our ignorance. The present moves to reduce CO_2 emissions *before* there is unequivocal evidence of global warming (the 'precautionary principle') is further evidence of a more open view of our ignorance. We are beginning to realise that we, as a race, understand environmental problems only very incompletely, and that we are to a great extent ignorant about their range and their solutions. So perhaps we are now in a position where we gradually begin to turn from closed ignorance to open ignorance, at least concerning some environmental issues.

In Sections 4, 5 and 6 we turn to open ignorance. There we wish to distinguish two further types of ignorance, which we shall call 'reducible' ignorance and 'irreducible' ignorance. We represent this classification in Figure 11.2.

If our ignorance is such that we cannot even classify it into one or other of these categories, we refer to it as either 'pure' ignorance or 'uncertain' ignorance. We return to this distinction in Section 6 below.

11.4   REDUCIBLE IGNORANCE

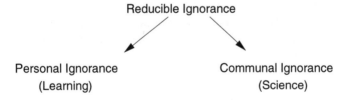

Figure 11.3. Categories of reducible ignorance.

By reducible ignorance we mean ignorance which may be lessened, or even eliminated. We see reducible ignorance as falling into two further categories. First, ignorance that is personal; that is, the information is available within the society, but not to a particular individual. (Though this should not be taken to imply that one individual could encompass all of a society's knowledge, or even all that of one area, e.g. physics.)

Second, there is communal ignorance, where the information is not even available to the society. We represent this classification of reducible ignorance in Figure 11.3.

11.4.1 Personal Ignorance and Learning

One reason we may be surprised at the occurrence of an unanticipated outcome is that we have simply been inefficient in the use of information which is available to us. For example, the racegoer who was amazed to find the race track no longer existed had only himself to blame for not reading the local papers, or speaking to other race track aficionados. In this case the ignorance that existed was avoidable, and with effort it was reducible.

Similarly, persons who suffer lead poisoning from household pipes could have avoided their sickness if they had used available information about this matter. In this case the responsibility for ignorance may either be attached to the individual, who did not sufficiently strive for knowledge in this area, or to the society (e.g. media, institutions) which did not take sufficient efforts to supply the individuals with the appropriate information.

This kind of reducible ignorance we term 'personal' ignorance. We can reduce personal ignorance by obtaining information that is already available in the society: i.e. by individual learning.

11.4.2 Communal Ignorance and Science

Although many forms of ignorance that exist in society must be seen as 'closed ignorance', whereas other forms have to be addressed as 'irreducible ignorance', there is still another kind of ignorance, which we shall call 'communal ignorance'. It is related to the 'communal' knowledge of a society.

There are many phenomena in the world which we, as a society, do not understand fully. In the case of some of them we are, more or less, confident that we shall understand them more fully in due course, through scientific exploration. To take an example from history, the causes of malaria were unknown until recently. But the suspicion that it was transmitted by mosquitoes, rather than by 'noxious air', was an hypothesis amenable to testing. The success of this hypothesis lead, in turn, to a search for the infecting organism in the blood of afflicted individuals. Thus the society's initial ignorance as to the cause of malaria was reduced by the application of science. This kind of reducible ignorance of society is what we call 'communal ignorance'.

Communal ignorance is always generated at the edge of the knowledge of a society. As long as we do not know for sure that our ignorance has to be interpreted as irreducible, we are to a certain degree entitled to hope that it will turn out to be reducible. In this sense, ignorance is a stimulus for all scientific endeavours, as long as we can surmise that this ignorance will be found to be communal ignorance. Thus all money spent for scientific research in society is done on the presupposition that there is reducible communal ignorance.

Up to now we have dealt with kinds of ignorance which are already well known in the literature. We now turn to areas of ignorance which have been studied less.

11.5   IRREDUCIBLE IGNORANCE

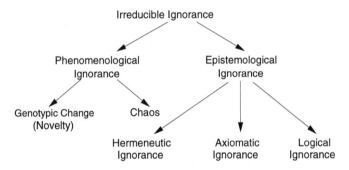

Figure 11.4. Categories of irreducible ignorance.

As well as ignorance which may be reduced by the accumulation and analysis of information, we wish to suggest that certain types of ignorance are in principle irreducible, i.e they cannot be reduced. We wish to distinguish two broad categories of irreducible ignorance. The first of these relates to the phenomena, and the second to the structure of knowledge. We term these 'phenomenological' ignorance and 'epistemological' ignorance.[6]

These categories of irreducible ignorance can be further subdivided. Phenomenological ignorance may be subdivided into 'genotypic' change (the emergence of novelty), and 'chaotic' dynamics.

Epistemological ignorance may also be divided into finer categories. These are 'hermeneutic' ignorance, 'axiomatic' ignorance, and 'logical' ignorance. We can represent this classification of the types of irreducible ignorance in Figure 11.4.

11.5.1   Phenomenological Ignorance

We begin by considering the category of phenomenological ignorance, where the nature of the phenomena makes our ignorance about these phenomena irreducible in practice. We begin with the emergence of novelty through genotypic change.

11.5.2   The Emergence of Novelty: Genotypic Change

A distinction we find useful for discussing how systems change over time is that between a system's 'potentialities', and its 'realisation'. In a biological system the potentialities are given by its genetic material or 'genotype'. These potentialities may be realised to a greater or lesser extent through the development of the, say, organism in interaction with its environment. In biological systems this realisation is known as the 'phenotype'. The realisations of an economic system would be the quantities of goods produced and consumed, the corresponding set of prices, the distribution of income, etc. Hence these descriptions would represent the economic phenotype.

The potentialities of an economic system are based on human attitudes and structures of social behaviour and structures of production. These potentialities can be recognised from the world view of a society, in particular from their religion or ideology. It can be further derived from the wishes, desires and preferences of the individuals, from the manners, norms and legal structures, as well as from the technological knowledge. In biology many genotypes can be described by means of genetic codes; but this description has been known for only some decades, while the concept of a genotype has been known for much longer, and has proved to have been of great explanatory relevance. In economics we are still in a situation similar to biology before the genetic code was developed. The economic genotype therefore cannot be described precisely.

In a certain sense, our knowledge about economics concerns only the economic phenotype, whereas the economic genotype is itself unknown, and can only be recognised by the phenomena it brings about. This ignorance about the economic genotype is not of much relevance as long as we can assume that the economic genotype does not change. In such cases ignorance does not pose a problem, since for a given set of potentialities the realisation of these potentialities will have a certain dynamics, which generally one could understand from knowledge of the potentialities. That is, we would normally expect to be able to understand the dynamics of the phenotype given knowledge of the genotype. Hence, even if the genotype is unknown, but does not change, there exists the possibility of predicting the phenotype.

Ignorance of such systems may occur when the genotype itself changes: i.e. when the potentialities of the system alter. In biological systems such genotypic evolution is recognised as part of Darwinian evolution and the changes that occur in the system's nature will inevitably generate 'surprise'. Thus the long-run evolution of ecosystems may exhibit the emergence of novelty, and hence be unpredictable. Such evolution of the potentialities of systems is an irreducible source of ignorance.

Regarding environmental issues, these largely result from long-run economy-environment interactions. Now both ecosystems and economies can exhibit the emergence of novelty through genotypic change, so the possibility for the emergence of novel environmental problems (and perhaps solutions) is considerable.

11.5.3 Deterministic Dynamics and Chaos

The 'classical' concept of deterministic dynamical systems was summarised by Laplace who said, in essence: 'Tell me the position and velocity of all the particles in the universe, and I can calculate all future states of the world'. Here the notion is that if a dynamical system is deterministic, it is, at least in principle, calculable for all future states. The assumption Laplace made is that if the genotype of a dynamical system is fully specified and also unchanging, then the phenotype can always be completely determined.

Of course, one must recognise that any actual calculation can only be performed using a finite number of arithmetic operations. Therefore the principle of the computability of a phenotype from a completely known genotype requires that the future dynamics of such systems are calculable to any required degree of accuracy. One of the startling findings of recent mathematics, though one can trace the roots of this approach back to Poincaré, is that certain dynamical systems do not give better approximations the greater is the degree of arithmetic accuracy used (Lorenz, 1963; an excellent popular discussion is given by Gleick, 1988). Such systems, known as 'chaotic' systems, have an infinite sensitivity to the initial conditions imposed. The slightest deviation from the intended starting point generates a dynamical outcome which is entirely uncorrelated with the desired outcome.

Such systems are clearly a further source of irreducible ignorance. We may know everything there is to know about the determinants of such a system's behaviour, but still be quite incapable, in principle, of calculating even a 'reasonable' approximation to the system's dynamics. Thus even if a system's potentialities are fully specified and unchanging, it may be in principle impossible to determine the evolution of the realisation of those potentialities. It may be the case that many economy-ecosystems interactions exhibit interrelations so complex that they are, at least in some aspects, chaotic in their dynamics, and hence in principle unpredictable. This is clearly another irreducible source of ignorance regarding environmental issues.

11.5.4   Epistemological Ignorance

Irreducible ignorance need not come only from the phenomena, but may also come from the way we conceive the phenomena. Such ignorance we term 'epistemological' ignorance. We distinguish three kinds of such ignorance: 'hermeneutic' ignorance, 'axiomatic' ignorance, and 'logical' ignorance.

11.5.5   Hermeneutic Ignorance

Even if a science is based on mathematical reasoning, it has to use words of the common language as soon as it is applied to phenomena. The general consensus of recent philosophy has been to suggest that it is impossible to construct an ideal language which can escape the ambiguities of common language (cf. Wittgenstein, 1922/1969:63-81; Stegmüller, 1969b:397-428, 562-568). So scientists have to accept that, despite their sharpest definitions, they have to use words and notions which are not completely unambiguous. From this it follows that scientific statements also can never be totally clear and unambiguous.

So we remain, in a certain way, ignorant even if we express our surest knowledge, because we cannot do away with the problems of ordinary language. This may be a reason why scientists so often do not understand each other, although their theories seem to be totally clear. Now, hermeneutics is the study of meaning and understanding, in this case as mediated by language. This ignorance, derived from the nature of language and communication, we therefore term hermeneutic ignorance.

11.5.6   Axiomatic Ignorance: Falsifiability

All scientific knowledge is based, explicitly or implicitly, on certain basic assumptions, or axioms. The ideal scientist can derive the entire corpus of his knowledge from such an axiomatic system. These axioms are a combination of the distillation of our experience of the world, and also a reflection of our beliefs about the nature of the world. Perhaps in physical science, experience may be the dominating influence, while it seems to us that in much modern economic analysis, the axioms are much more reflections of belief structures.

By their nature the axioms can never be shown, singly or collectively, to be 'true'. However, if the 'theorems' derived from the axioms are at odds with our experience, then the axioms, singly or collectively, may be judged to be 'false'. In that we can never know the truth of our axioms, unless they are shown to be false, we remain ignorant at a very fundamental level of our scientific endeavour. Popper stressed the impossibility of the proof of the truth of an axiomatic science, stressing instead that the most we can hope to achieve is the 'falsification' of our axiomatic assumptions. In addition, it is important to note that there are many statements which can neither be verified nor falsified. For instance Aristotle's axiom that all bodies that move tend to a state of rest contradicts Newton's law of inertia. But both axioms can neither be proved nor falsified. Another example is Kant's claim that the statement 'human will is free' as well as the opposite statement, 'human will is determined,' can neither be proved nor falsified. But in contrast to the modern scientific attitude, Kant did not consider it to be meaningless to deal with these kinds of statements, because they have such an essential importance.

11.5.7   Logical Ignorance: Gödel's Theorem

In 1931 Gödel proved that any axiomatic system which generates a formal basis for arithmetical operations must allow at least one theorem that, within the proof structure allowed by the axioms, can neither be proved nor disproved. Thus Gödel's (1931) theorem shows that even a non-falsified axiomatic system remains a source of ignorance, irrespective of our attempts, or otherwise, at falsification.

Unfortunately, by its nature Gödel's theorem gives no indication of what type of theorems may be undecidable in this way. Since 1931 there has been speculation over what thus far unproved theorems in number theory might be undecidable, with Fermat's Last Theorem being often suggested as one of this type.

From Gödel's theorem we therefore now know that even closed logical systems are sources of ignorance, and this ignorance cannot in principle be reduced. That is, even a system of logic is a source of irreducible ignorance. One consequence is that all those sciences which are applied systems of mathematical logic, e.g. physics and economics, contain at least one theorem that cannot be proved.

11.5.8   Epistemological Ignorance and Environmental Issues

We wish to suggest that epistemological ignorance presents problems for any analytical science. Problems of language, axiomatisation and the incompleteness of logical systems, have consequences for any discipline using mathematics. Now many environmental issues are approached using mathematical modelling, so even this apparently well-founded method is a potential source of ignorance regarding environmental problems.

11.6   PURE IGNORANCE AND UNCERTAIN IGNORANCE

Before proceeding to summarise our taxonomy of surprise and ignorance, it is important to point out that this taxonomy is not complete.[7] We further require the distinction between 'pure' ignorance and 'uncertain' ignorance.

11.6.1   Pure Ignorance

We take it to be a self-evident truth that the accumulation and testing of knowledge that informs human activity has a unitary characteristic. The nature of knowledge, and ignorance, that pertains to our scientific work is no different to that relevant to the way we make a cup of coffee, or buy our weekly groceries.

In Western civilisations our response to ignorance is generally the assumption that it is reducible by science. We assume that the scientific method and the abilities of humankind will eventually fill these gaps in our 'knowledge'. However, when we ask ourselves, in everyday life or in science, 'what is going to happen?', we do not know in which area surprises will turn up. Further, we are ignorant of what kind of surprises we will meet. Naturally in this state we do not know whether our ignorance is reducible or irreducible. From this it follows that the kind of ignorance cannot be specified. If this is the case, we speak of 'pure ignorance'. We see that pure ignorance has two aspects. First, it is not confined to a certain area of knowledge. Second, it does not concern any particular occurrence or relationship. It can be thought of as the *context* within which we hold whatever knowledge we have (or think we have).

This kind of ignorance is an essential element of human life, of which science is only a part. Ignorance in this sense cannot be classified within the taxonomy developed above. This is because pure ignorance is of an indefinite nature, like the future itself. It cannot be limited or constrained to any particular area of knowledge, as it encompasses all areas of life and development. Humankind has developed many styles of coping with and/or reflecting upon pure ignorance. Among these we see ritual behaviour, religion and artistic endeavour.

11.6.2   Uncertain Ignorance

Only when we are in a state where we are able to constrain the question, 'what is going to happen', to a particular area of knowledge can we ask ourselves if our ignorance is of a reducible or irreducible type. Since we then recognise the possibility of classifying our ignorance (viz. reducible or irreducible ignorance), but cannot yet classify it, then in accordance with the literature we denote this 'uncertain' ignorance.

We normally make the act of faith that our uncertain ignorance is reducible (viz. open to learning or scientific discovery). However, this can only be an act of faith. If it transpires that science can reduce our ignorance, then, after the fact, we may classify our ex-ignorance as reducible. Thus we see that the distinction between reducible and irreducible ignorance can only be made ex post. However, it is in principle impossible to classify ignorance as reducible while the ignorance remains. Thus if we feel unwilling to make this act of faith, and if we cannot satisfy ourselves that our ignorance is irreducible, then, until the ignorance is reduced, intellectual honesty should compel us to classify our ignorance as uncertain.

Uncertain ignorance is a doubly uncomfortable state, involving both uncertainty and ignorance. The success of modern science owes much to the circumstance that science promises to convert uncertain ignorance into knowledge.

It seems to us that the normal modern, scientific, response to the recognition of ignorance is initially to assume it is reducible, and further, that it is personal, and accessible to reduction by learning from already available information. When we encounter a new environmental problem we seek the advice of the experts. If the experts are also ignorant on this matter, we turn to a programme of scientific research.

An example of ignorance, which has remained up to now uncertain, is nuclear waste. When society decided to carry through the development of nuclear power it believed that nuclear waste disposal could be dealt with in much the same way as non-nuclear waste. This proved to be untrue. Experts were consulted, and they suggested a scientific research programme be established. We may remain convinced, despite great costs over long periods, that our ignorance is reducible. Another example is nuclear fusion, which has been promised imminently for forty years, and remains still unfeasible.

We are not suggesting that either area is an area of irreducible ignorance. However, as we recognise irreducible ignorance may occur, and as reducible ignorance can only be recognised when it ceases to be ignorance, the possibility of irreducibility must be accepted (though humankind seems to prefer to have faith otherwise).

11.6.3 Conclusions Concerning Pure Ignorance and Uncertain Ignorance

Pure ignorance and uncertain ignorance have in common only that they are not suitable for being included in our taxonomy. But their statuses are completely distinct. If we are confronted with uncertain ignorance, we try to cope with it. First we attempt to classify it as reducible or irreducible ignorance. We expect that sooner or later we will be able to do this. If the ignorance is reducible, then we find this out through its amenability to scientific investigation. Even if our ignorance is for the time being irreducible, we at least hope, and in general even expect, that we will find some method to deal with it. From these considerations we recognise that the state of uncertain ignorance is of a transitional nature; it changes over the course of time. In contrast, pure ignorance is of an unchanging nature over the course of time.

11.7   AN OVERVIEW OF THE SOURCES OF SURPRISE

In this section we summarise our results so far.

Surprise derives from two possible sources. First, when all possible outcomes are known, but where the probabilities of each possible outcome may be known (risk) or may be unknown (uncertainty). Alternatively, we may be in a state of ignorance, where all possible outcomes are not known.

This ignorance may be recognised and included in the world view (open ignorance), or it may be ignored (closed ignorance).

Open ignorance may derive from known sources (reducible ignorance and irreducible ignorance).

Reducible ignorance may be reducible by learning (personal ignorance), or by the application of science (communal ignorance).

Irreducible ignorance may derive from the nature of the world (phenomenological ignorance), or from the nature of reasoning (epistemological ignorance).

Phenomenological ignorance may be because of the appearance of ontological novelty (genotypic change), or from the inherent unpredictability of certain dynamic systems (chaos).

Epistemological ignorance may result from the problems of language (hermeneutic ignorance), the assumptions underlying the reasoning process (axiomatic ignorance), or the incompleteness of the logical system (logical ignorance).

We represent this structure in Figure 11.5.

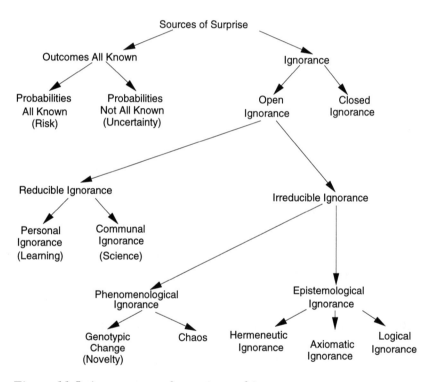

Figure 11.5. A taxonomy of surprise and ignorance.

11.8   THE NATURE OF SCIENTIFIC ENDEAVOUR

Our view is that the normal 'human condition' is characterised by pure ignorance. We are continually being surprised, and often our surprise derives not from risk or uncertainty, but from ignorance. That is, our surprise is not because things happen to which we attributed low probabilities, or for which we had no probabilities. Rather, our surprise derives from events taking place which were not foreseen as possible.

As we know, classical science has attempted to transform uncertain ignorance into systematically organised knowledge. Modern science has suggested a more modest approach. Science may be considered as the attempt to transform uncertain ignorance into risk (i.e. statements with stochastic properties).

Readers without a natural science background may expect that the aim of science is not the generation of statements with only stochastic properties, but rather statements which are 'true', or perhaps 'false'. This may be the aim; however, it is not feasible, by the nature of 'noisy' and error prone experimentation, and also, modern physics suggests, because of the inherent indeterminacy of the state of matter/energy.

If our view of modern science is correct, then we can try to operationalise its way of dealing with ignorance as follows. If there are new phenomena which cause surprise, then one tries to get to know more and more about them, so that at the end of this endeavour all outcomes are known. In this case all the phenomena can be categorised under either risk or uncertainty. If this endeavour is not successful, then scientists acknowledge their ignorance, but they tend to restrict this ignorance in terms of communal ignorance; i.e. they believe that further research will reduce and finally dissolve this ignorance. Thus we see the 'classical' route of modern science as being the transformation of uncertain ignorance into risk, as follows:

Uncertain Ignorance → Communal Ignorance → Risk

Hence, there is no concept of true irreducible ignorance in modern science.

We might represent the taxonomy of surprise inherent in science in Figure 11.6.

Implicit within this scientific endeavour is the assumption that the object of scientific study is amenable to this reduction. This assumption cannot be testable, except in so far as it generates 'useful' and, perhaps, 'beautiful', science. Even so, this assumption is an axiom of science; that is, it is an act of faith.

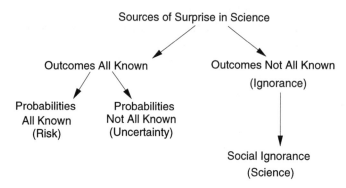

Figure 11.6. Sources of surprise in science.

11.8.1   Physical Science

Regarding physical science, little in our experience argues against such faith in the 'reducibility' of uncertain ignorance to risk. However, modern mathematics has shown that what we have termed chaotic phenomenological ignorance is not only possible, but characterises many important areas (Guckenheimer and Holmes, 1983). This has demanded the recognition, in the practice of physical science, that knowing more about the nature of a system does not necessarily mean that statements about its behaviour can be reduced to statements which have the status of risk.

11.8.2   Social Science

For economics, and the social sciences generally, the assumption that the systems being studied are amenable to statements with the status of risk seems much more questionable. The systems being studied are social systems, and the elements in these systems are humans whose natural condition is itself the confrontation of uncertain ignorance. It might be the case that over sufficiently short periods, and with sufficiently little 'surprise' affecting the social system being studied, then certain statements on aggregate social behaviour *may* be possible.

However, we view the above assumption that statements on social systems have the status of risk, which underlies social science, as inherently internally contradictory. On the one hand, humans as scientists explicitly recognise their uncertain ignorance through their scientific endeavours. On the other hand, the assumption made by scientists about humans is that there is no uncertain ignorance affecting the behaviour of the social agents whose behaviour they study. This seems to us like wanting to have your cake and eat it!

11.8.3 Biological Science

The leap of faith needed for biological science seems to be somewhere between the relatively modest one of physical science, and the gigantic one of modern social science. For the study of microorganisms and the biochemical sub-systems of more complex organisms, the assumption that uncertain ignorance may be transformed into risk is probably generally acceptable. For studies of the behaviour of mammals the assumption may be as questionable as for social science. For ecological systems an additional major difficulty in their study is the introduction of novelty through human activity. (For a more detailed discussion on 'why physics is easy, economics is difficult and biology is in between', see Faber and Proops (1993a:Chapter 3).)

11.9   SURPRISE, IGNORANCE AND ENVIRONMENTAL ISSUES

We began with Kant's question 'What can I know?'. Our discussion suggests that one thing we *can* know is, to some extent the nature of our ignorance, even if this is only knowing that we do not even *know* the nature of our ignorance.

How may this knowledge concerning our ignorance inform our behaviour? We have already noted that science is one of several methods of responding to the immanence of our uncertain ignorance. However, in this chapter we have also defined and classified two other types of ignorance: phenomenological irreducible ignorance and epistemological irreducible ignorance. Regarding the former, modern science is itself discovering the limits to which uncertain ignorance may be reduced to risk, and the emergence of novelty. The discovery of the existence of chaotic dynamics has forced a somewhat startled recognition of these limits from the scientific community. Modern philosophy and mathematics also show that there are epistemological constraints on the reduction of ignorance.

How might we respond, both as scientists in general, and as environmental scientists in particular? First, at a basic level, we feel that the nature of uncertain ignorance demands all that we can offer: recognition.

We face uncertain ignorance in our ordinary lives, and recognise it at least implicitly. We also face it in our science, and explicit recognition in this sphere is also due.

Regarding epistemological irreducible ignorance, here we know that the very nature of our understanding tells us we *cannot* know everything. The very structure of our rational scientific endeavour imposes limits on the achievements of that endeavour. Here we feel the appropriate response is humility. By this we mean, for example, that the scientific community should be modest concerning their own knowledge and their ability to contribute to the control of the world. Further, scientists should have respect for non-scientific approaches to the world, such as art and religion, as well as common-sense knowledge. Some traits of these ways may be integrated in the so-called 'Second Order Sciences' (Funtowicz and Ravetz, 1990). Other traits cannot be incorporated into a scientific approach. They remind the scientist of the fact that science is only one way for humans to experience the world (for a fuller discussion see Chapter 4).

Finally, phenomenological irreducible ignorance is an area where our recognition of our ignorance may be a key element in altering our behaviour. In a world where the altering potentialities of systems causes changes in those systems which may not, *in principle*, be predicted, our knowledge of that unpredictability may still be useful. If we know that changes in the nature of systems will occur, and we also know that we cannot know the nature of those changes until they occur, then the appropriate response is surely flexibility. For example, a non-flexible measure in the energy sector was the introduction of nuclear plants.

11.10 FROM IGNORANCE TO OPENNESS

That philosophy involves the study of knowledge is implied by its literal meaning, i.e. 'love of wisdom'. But great philosophers of all periods have recognised that to understand knowledge one has also to understand ignorance. They realised that the region of our possible knowledge is like an island 'surrounded by a wide and stormy ocean which is the actual site of semblance and illusion (*Schein*)'. (Kant, 1956:B 295, our translation.) This ocean of pretended knowledge is in truth the ocean of our ignorance. In the same vein Socrates said that 'I know that I know nothing'. This led the oracle of Delphi to acknowledge Socrates as the wisest of all human beings.

At the end of the Middle Ages one of the most important philosophers of that period, Nicolas of Cusa (1964:Book II, p. 93, paragraph 162) postulated an attitude of 'Docta Ignorantia'. This meant the acknowledgment of the circumstance that all human knowledge emerges out of ignorance, and after some time may vanish or be replaced by new types of knowledge. For him the criteria for true science were adequateness to everyday experience, openness, creativity and flexibility. From this point of view he criticised, already some decades before Copernicus, the geocentric world view of the ancient philosophers with the argument that they lacked the 'Docta Ignorantia', ignorance which is recognised and open to learning and alternative models. In our terms, this reflects their failure to recognise their axiomatic ignorance. As for pure ignorance, 'Docta Ignorantia' includes the faith that human thinking and action springs from a dimension which is greater than human knowledge, and which can be experienced only in humble acknowledgement of our ignorance.

One main intention of Kant's *Critique of Pure Reason* is expressed in the following sentence: 'I had to eliminate knowledge to gain room for faith' (Kant 1956, 33; B XXX, our translation). Faith in the sense of Kant does not mean the adherence to any church or confession, but an attitude of openness and confidence towards all matters which lie in the area of our ignorance. Kant's ethics were offered as an attitude which is not only valid for known circumstances and tendencies, but also for the unknown.

The attitude of openness, as described by Plato, as well as by Nicolas of Cusa and Kant, can be seen as the essence of philosophy and knowledge. This attitude allows humans to experience all things as they develop, not as we might prejudge them, but accepting them as they are.

NOTES

1. A detailed bibliography on ignorance and related subjects is to be found at the end of Smithson's (1988) monograph.
2. It is interesting to note that the German construction for reference to future events, i.e. the future tense, uses the modal verb 'werden', the literal sense of which is 'to become, to grow'. On the other hand, the English future tense uses the verb 'to will', which, what native English speakers often forget, means 'to desire, to aim to bring about'. Clearly, the German future tense is based upon the first question, 'what is going to happen?', while the English future tense derives from the second question, 'what can we do?'.
3. We recognise that the 'Bayesian' approach to probability and inference (Lee, 1989) is an attempt to expand 'risk' into 'uncertainty', through the efficient use of information as it becomes available. However, as we wish to concentrate on 'ignorance' in this chapter, we do not pursue this matter here.
4. Cf. the example of the personal computer given above by Katzner (1986).

5. Construed in the same sense as one speaks of a 'false friend': something one has every reason to think is knowledge, but which turns out not to be so.
6. Not all ignorance concerning phenomena or epistemological matters can be mapped as phenomenological or epistemological ignorance. Only those kinds of ignorance which are irreducible on the ground of the phenomena or on the ground of science are categorised as phenomenological or epistemological. Fallacy of our senses does not constitute phenomenological ignorance, nor do errors in our scientific approach constitute epistemological ignorance.
7. We are grateful to Michael Hammond for pointing out this lacuna in our classification.

12. Experience, Knowledge and the Environment: An Epistemological Essay

12.1 INTRODUCTION: ENVIRONMENTAL PROBLEMS AND SCIENTIFIC SOLUTIONS

How does society treat environmental crises? Usually, people become aware of a general or particular problem, e.g. the emissions of factories or the pollution of a lake. If these circumstances are publicly recognised, scientists systematically gather data and make a diagnosis. Then, jointly with technologists, they recommend a therapy. This may, after many steps, pass into law through the political process and be realised. However, this depends on there being a corresponding will in society for these environmental measures. The scientific and technical approach towards the environmental crisis is, of course, often useful. While science allows for predictions, by which natural processes, favourably or unfavourably, can be determined in advance, techniques enable one to control the outcome of a development in a favourable way. This holds generally. Concerning environmental issues, this procedure has led to a combination of systematisation of knowledge about the environment, and of its corresponding application. This systematisation has led to the achievement of an interdependent and coherent body of knowledge, which in turn has created a solid foundation for the inventiveness of technologists, towards the solution of environmental problems.

Nevertheless, environmentalists are not alone in being deeply dissatisfied with this procedure, for three reasons. First, many people feel that by science and technology one does not get to the roots of environmental pollution and destruction. Second, there is more knowledge in society at large available for the recognition of, and response to, environmental questions than science and technology alone can offer. Third, many environmental problems make us aware of areas of ignorance, which cannot be reduced by science (cf. Chapter 11). However, up to now, the scientific and technical approach is still considered as appropriate, and by far the most promising one, for overcoming environmental crises.

12.2   THE PURPOSE OF THIS CHAPTER

In this chapter we wish to make a contribution to the discussion of environmental questions from an epistemological point of view. While there exist many philosophical attempts to use ethics, in particular Aristotelian, Kantian and utilitarian ethics, relatively little research has been done on epistemological questions concerning environmental problems.

Modern science has generated a certain understanding of truth which is accepted largely unquestioningly in society at large. Truth in science is regarded as value-free, so that it has become possible to have truth without having inherent meaning and value for human existence (Weber, 1951). A famous example of this approach to truth is the observation of nature within the framework of Newton's Laws of Motion. The same holds to a great extent for neoclassical economics, the method of which was deeply inspired by classical physics (Mirowski, 1984).

In the social process the scientific understanding of truth, as it is characterised above, became *the* paradigm of truth. This has led to the circumstance that interpretations of truth which connected truth with meaning, by inclusion of aspects of everyday experience, interior experience and practical action, never succeeded in really changing the course of modern science, but remained rather as border cases of the scientific endeavour. This state of affairs is so in spite of many efforts by philosophers such as Husserl (1977), Habermas (1968) and Gadamer (1972), who tried to rediscover ancient approaches to truth, or to develop new ones which conceive truth as inherently meaningful on the basis of our whole existence.[1] The increasing domination of a solely scientific understanding of truth within modern societies has important consequences for the treatment of environmental problems.

Our first thesis is that the usual approach to environmental problems, based solely on science and technology, is one-sided, because it suppresses other important approaches which are not only fruitful, but often also necessary for the understanding of humankind and the world in general, and the solution of environmental problems in particular. We wish, therefore, to question the wide-spread opinion that scientific truth and experience are always superior to everyday experience, as e.g. Nagel (1961:1-14) maintains, and to interior experience, as Ayer (1954:112-120) assumes. For we believe that narrowed-down concepts of experience and truth within science, that exclude non-scientific approaches, are responsible for a one-sided understanding of what happens in the interactions of humans and the natural world. We develop our thesis by confronting the modern approach to truth, in which experience is acknowledged only if it is scientifically 'proved', with a more general perspective on truth and experience, including non-scientific approaches, which is derived from Aristotelian concepts. From this perspective we develop our second thesis. We will try to show that using five Aristotelian concepts of truth enables one to see environmental problems, and their economic and social context, in a more encompassing way, and more clearly than within the exclusively scientific framework. This way will also provide new principles for solutions of environmental problems.

We will develop our argument by the following steps. As the modern understanding of truth was largely influenced by a certain reading of Kant's first Critique, we begin (in Section 12.2) with some remarks on the notion of experience as a basis for science which was developed by Kant in his *Critique of Pure Reason*. For the sake of argument, we take some passages of this Critique to outline important lines of modern scientific thinking.

On the basis of this (purposely circumscribed) interpretation of Kant, we develop (in Section 12.3) our concept of the *'scientific logos'*, which is our term for the modern approach to experience and truth. We show some of its consequences for the human access to the world, as well as for technical and economic developments in general, and for dealing with environmental problems in particular.

We wish to contrast the scientific logos with an approach to truth which conceives of truth as inherently meaningful on the basis of our whole existence, including our ethical behaviour. Such an approach we will term *'existence logos'*. We seek an understanding of our environmental problems by supplementing the scientific and technical approach to their solution by other, non-scientific, approaches contained in this logos. We shall represent important traits of this kind of logos by starting from Aristotle. There is a whole area of epistemology in Aristotle. For the sake of our argument within the context of environmental problems we take up the five categories developed in Aristotle's theory of truth in his *Nicomachean Ethics*.[2] Though mainly dedicated to ethical questions, the *Nicomachean Ethics* in its book VI offers a stimulating approach to epistemological problems in the field of human praxis. In Section 12.4 we examine Aristotle's categories of finding truth at some length, as we consider him to be helpful for developing new and promising approaches for the understanding of environmental problems. In particular, Aristotle leaves room for an encompassing understanding of experience which is much broader than the scientific notion of experience.

To avoid misunderstandings, we remark that the aim of this chapter is not a confrontation of Kant and Aristotle, but of different concepts of truth and experience and their relevance for the solution of environmental problems. Therefore, in Sections 12.5 and 12.6 we outline some consequences of our analysis concerning the understanding of environmental problems and possible solutions within society. In particular, we develop some principles stemming from non-scientific experience which should be considered when solutions of environmental problems are to be applied in society.

In three appendices we offer some remarks on our method, as well as on our interpretations of Kant and Aristotle in the context of contemporary discussions.

12.3   SOME REMARKS ON THE NOTION OF EXPERIENCE IN KANT

The essence of a scientific understanding of experience has seldom been so clearly represented as in Kant's critical procedure. Kant's approach to truth, as expressed in his '*Critique of Pure Reason*', offers a notion of experience which can be used as basis for science. This did not only hold in the nineteenth century (Helmholtz, 1977), but it still holds today to a considerable degree, in spite of the circumstance that modern epistemology, especially impressed by the theoretical questions raised by quantum physics, seems to have developed a completely changed view on the foundations of the scientific endeavour compared to Kant's first Critique (Stegmüller, 1983). However, even quantum physicists sometimes try to explain their presuppositions and methods by referring to Kant (Mittelstaedt, 1976). Further, it seems obvious to us that many of those scientists who are not involved in epistemological discussions, but do research for practical application, share the belief in the possibilities of science which are formulated in Kant's argument.

The *Critique of Pure Reason* contains a concept of causality which is compatible with the results of classical physics. In this context Kant develops his notion of experience. He states that experience which leads to truth is possible only on the basis of causality. Kant (1982:208 B 218) writes: 'Experience is possible only through the representation of a necessary connection of perceptions.' In the course of his argument Kant (1982:226 B 245ff) qualifies this with:

> *That something happens is, therefore, a perception which belongs to a possible experience. This experience becomes actual when I regard the appearance as determined in its position in time, and therefore as an object that can always be found in the connection of perceptions*

in accordance with a rule. This rule, by which we determine something according to succession of time, is, that the condition under which an event invariably and necessarily follows is to be found in what precedes the event. The principle of sufficient reason is thus the ground of possible experience, that is, of objective knowledge of appearances in respect of their relation in the order of time.[3]

According to Kant, the perception of events[4] is in itself not an experience, but only a necessary condition for an experience. Only if one knows for sure that a certain event always appears when another certain event has already occurred, independent of the special circumstances of the moment of perception, does one have an experience in the Kantian sense. By this approach one obtains a time sequence of certain events which is, paradoxically, independent of time. This is because experience implies that one knows for certain that if a specific event occurs, then another specific event necessarily has to follow, independent of if this occurs in 1994, in 1998, or whenever. Thus an experience demands the abstraction of a situation from all its particular circumstances. From all variable and special contexts one has to filter a general, and thus a time invariant, structure out of the situation. Kant sees only one principle to determine such invariant structures out of a context of complex and variable circumstances: the principle of *causation*. Hence, Kant's argument concerning his notion of experience is part of his theory of causality.

We see that Kant raised the question: in which cases are we allowed to qualify certain impressions, perceptions and observations as experiences? In contrast to his pre-modern precursors, up to Francis Bacon, he acknowledged as experiences only those observations that could be integrated into a framework of causality. Kant's argument implies a major shift in the understanding of the notion of an experience. For the postulate of causality implies that a series of perceptions is an experience only if, given the first perception, every rational being, under strictly defined conditions, will necessarily repeat the same series of perceptions at any time.

The achievement of the introduction of the Kantian notion of experience into science is considerable. Scientific experience is not only understandable by every rational being, but its conditions can also be *created* by everyone. Hence there are *egalitarian* traits in the Kantian approach; participation is guaranteed for all who are willing to work in this modern scientific way. From this it follows that within science it is not possible for there to be an elite of specially endowed persons, be they alchemists, occultists, mystics or any kind of secret scientists. According to Kant, each person who postulates an experience has to be prepared to communicate what is experienced to others, in such a way that they are able to experience it themselves. Only then is it considered to be an experience and thus a scientific insight. Of course, this is only possible if the corresponding experience is embedded in a framework of causality. There are two important consequences of the Kantian approach. First, it allows that, at least in principle, everyone may participate in the scientific endeavour, and this in turn advances scientific progress tremendously. Second, it separates clearly all kinds of scientific knowledge from non-scientific knowledge.

12.4   THE SCIENTIFIC LOGOS

12.4.1   Experience, Classical Physics and Modern Technique

The very paradigm of experience as analysed above is the experiment in classical physics. This notion has the following important consequences. If we are able to control circumstances in such an encompassing way that we can allow an event A to occur, then we can be sure that a sequence of causally determined events B, C, D, etc., will follow. In general it holds: If certain events occur, we know for certain that, according to the rule of causality, certain other events will definitely follow. If we have experience of this inter-relationship, then we can make predictions concerning the consequent events when we observe, or produce, the antecedent events. For instance, if we turn the key of our car, we initiate a series of events which finally enables us to drive our car. Experience in the scheme of causality leads us, via prediction and control, to the domination of many processes.

Our example shows that science based on this kind of experience can lead to an *application* of its insights, i.e. to technique. Science implies the observation of a sequence of causation, and technique implies the use of the knowledge of the causal relationships, to produce things and thus service human wants. If all our perceptions could be interpreted as experiences, in the sense of Kant and modern science, we would be able to know everything. Further, if by human inventiveness, on the basis of scientific discoveries, our technical means were to increase continuously, to the same degree as during the last two centuries, we would more and more be able to control and dominate the world according to our will.[5]

12.4.2 The Artificial World of Science and Our Everyday Life

However, the modern scientific access to the world implies a one-sided understanding of truth.

According to the *Critique of Pure Reason*, experience is restrained to the field of questions posed by reason (Kant, 1982:B XIIIf). The endeavour of reason, in the sense of Kant, is to understand all perceptions within the field of causality; all questions which reason puts to nature are in the line of this endeavour. Outside the field of causality, which is constructed and limited by human rationality, experience is impossible.

It should be noted, however, that the selection of given perceptions by the application of reason is not sufficient to obtain scientific experience. For if we open our eyes, look into the world and take up our perceptions just as they are, we would hardly be able to integrate them into a scientific framework, because of their manifoldness and complexity. Therefore, in addition to the selection, one has to prepare one's perceptions in such a way that they can be used as material for the construction of causal interrelationships. It is the artificial apparatus of the scientific experiment which is the means of such a preparation. Thus one might say that modern science is a means to reduce the manifoldness of perceptions, by selection and preparation. As a consequence, the perceptions which are subjected to this process lose the meaning they have in everyday life and in social praxis. What we call 'empirical' in modern science is far from the ordinary human experience of life. In contrast, we shall seek to show below that out of Aristotelian arguments a notion of experience may be developed which includes the dimension of everyday life explicitly, as well as the dimension of interior experience.

12.4.3 The Process of Science

The manner in which Kant in his first Critique uses the notions of experience and truth is, in many respects, the result of the process of the history of modern science. Important stages of this process can be associated with the names Bacon, Galileo and Newton. This process has continued up to our time, and it seems to us that we are still within it.

For our argument we wish to point out that the use of the notions of truth and experience in science and in everyday life has become more and more divergent since Kant. For example, the experience of a molecular biologist, through the use of his experimental apparatus, can be repeated only by other molecular biologists with almost the same experimental apparatus. From this it follows that Kant's fundamental postulate, that every rational being should be able to comprehend a given experience at any time, is restricted to an often very small community of scientists. Hence, all persons who are not molecular biologists have to 'believe' the experiences of the latter. Therefore, the everyday life conditions are not only insufficient for most people to participate in the content of truth and experience in modern science, but the gulf between everyday experience and the experience of a scientist, in the Kantian sense, is unbridgeable. It is worthwhile to note that this holds not only for ordinary people, but also highly intelligent, educated people who happen not to be molecular biologists. Thus the egalitarian traits which we attributed to Kant's original approach have been considerably reduced over the course of time.

The process which we have just described represents the development of one access to truth, which we have denoted as 'scientific logos'. We summarise its characteristics: perceptions are selected from their normal, meaningful everyday context, prepared by the artificial apparatus of an experiment, and integrated into a consistent framework of causality, on the basis of which predictions are possible. As this process of selection and preparation, as well as analysis, has become more and more complicated, it has followed that the price to be paid for the scientific endeavour is that the single branches of science have become more and more separated from each other. In addition, most of the results of science are not accessible in the context of everyday experience. To illustrate the importance of these considerations, we note that this specialisation and separation of branches of scientific knowledge may lead to serious problems in the field of environmental questions. If scientists suggest solutions which are not understandable by the public, these solutions will not find the consent of those who are concerned with their consequences. Hence, such solutions will either be refused, or they have to be enforced in a non-democratic way.[6]

12.4.4 Environmental Problems, Everyday Experience and Science

Science, and its application in the form of technology, have decisively contributed to the wealth of modern societies. However, at the same time during the last two decades society has become aware that this wealth has itself generated many environmental problems. This awareness has not been brought out by the scientific community, but to a great extent by 'the person in the street'. It was typically individuals and small groups who brought environmental problems to the attention of the public. The basis for their activities were, in general, sudden experiences (in a non-Kantian sense) in their everyday lives. For example, people found that they could not take a swim in rivers and lakes which they had been used to. The best-seller *The Silent Spring* (Carson, 1982) described how many animals and plants were no longer present where they had been in earlier times. It was not a scientific insight about the quantity of certain harmful substances in the environment, but rather a general, vague intuition about the state of the environment as a whole that stimulated the beginnings of the environmental movement.

A typical example for this type of experience of environmental problems is the history of the construction of highways in Germany. For many decades their building was welcomed by almost all parts of the population. In the course of time people more and more realised how much destruction of the landscape and loss of habitats were the consequences. Finally, in the eighties people were so aware of these consequences that in many cases they prevented further construction of highways. What they were responding to were not scientific insights concerning the degree of environmental destruction, but rather a general feeling of the loss of quality of life.

Only after this initial stage did more and more scientists start to take notice of environmental questions. We may say, in our terminology, that they attempted to transform everyday experience into scientific truth. On the basis of their results they tried to find technical solutions to environmental problems. However, during the scientific process, everyday experiences had to be reduced to experience in terms of the scientific logos, within a framework of causation. Although very powerful and encompassing solutions to certain environmental questions could be obtained, many dimensions of everyday experience had to be neglected.

The process by which environmental problems, in terms of normal experience, are transformed into scientific statements exhibits the following pattern: usually the everyday experience is a vague intuition of, usually, one person or a small group. If it becomes known to the public, it is taken up by several different scientific disciplines. Each of them takes up that part of the 'one problem', for which it feels competent. As noted above, however, because of the specialisation of each discipline, the single disciplines are often not able to communicate with each other. Hence the 'one problem' is split into several problems with several solutions. Only by splitting up this 'one problem' does it become accessible to technical solutions for certain aspects of the problem. In this way, however, the wholeness of the view of the 'one problem' is lost. As a consequence, the partial technical solutions, on the basis of different scientific approaches, often do not fit together.

This fundamental lack has, of course, been recognised and to some extent counteracted by increasing efforts towards interdisciplinary study (cf. Chapter 10). It is now widely accepted that for the solution of environmental problems one needs ecology, biology, chemistry, physics, economics, psychology, ethics, etc. However, with our example of molecular biology we have already noted that scientists of different disciplines can hardly communicate with each other. This often holds even within one science. However, even if these communication difficulties could be solved among the different disciplines, we cannot expect that the original wholeness of the view of the everyday experience is restored. This is the consequence of the restricted view of the 'scientific logos'.

Thus we pose the question: Is there a way to bridge the gap between scientific experience and everyday experience? If one wants to try to find an answer to this question, one should be aware that the modern scientific understanding of truth is not the only understanding of truth which is possible. Other approaches were known in the past, and new approaches may develop in the course of time. Therefore we hold that the modern separation between scientific truth and everyday life need not last forever. The modern society in which scientific truth became free of everyday experience, as well as of ethical considerations, is the society whose economic activity led to the present environmental crisis. In our opinion, precisely the ethical dimension and the everyday experience are of fundamental importance to the understanding and the solution of environmental problems. Hence we have to develop an understanding of truth which explicitly takes regard of the dimensions of everyday life and ethics. It was Aristotle who developed a terminology which, to our eyes, can be made useful for such an understanding of truth.

12.5   TRUTH, EXPERIENCE AND MEANING IN ARISTOTLE

The reflections of Aristotle on truth which are important for our endeavour can be found in his *Nicomachean Ethics*.

Aristotle starts his considerations about truth from human existence in everyday life. Within his notion of truth he tries to include all important dimensions of how humans experience the world, and how they behave in it. As the background to such considerations, Aristotle distinguishes five types of truth:

> *Let it be assumed that the states of virtue of which the soul (Greek: psyche) possesses truth by way of affirmation or denial are five in number, i.e. art (Greek: techne), scientific knowledge (Greek: episteme), practical wisdom (Greek: phronesis), philosophic wisdom (Greek: sophia) and intuitive reason (Greek: nous)* (Aristotle, 1925:140-VI, 3, 1139b15-17).

In the Greek original text Aristotle does not employ the substantive 'aletheia' (truth) but the verb 'aletheuein' (to be in truth; to act out of truth; to uncover truth; to 'truth'). *Truth* for Aristotle is a process of acting and being, rather than an object of discovery. Thus Aristotle defined five types of such processes of 'truthing'.

For Aristotle truth is not restricted to the explanation of the world of objects; instead, each type of truth corresponds to a certain meaning for humans. Meaning, in its essence, is not a concept for Aristotle; rather, meaning is related to ways of being in the world, to human attitudes and to human behaviour. Therefore we may say that meaning for Aristotle is generated in the context of ethics. What Wieland (1990:129, our translation) notes on Aristotle's practical philosophy holds also for his notion of truth:

> *The aim of practical philosophy is not restricted to cognition or theory ... It wants to make a contribution to realise the right action. Its aim is not cognition, but action.*

The implications and consequences of Aristotle's notion of truth will be described next, when we comment on each of the five types of truth in turn.

12.5.1 'Techne'

The first type of truth is to be found in *'techne'* or 'art' (in the sense of 'artisan', rather than 'high art'). This kind of truth is required for any kind of production, which gives rise to an intended and concrete result. Such production in Greek was called 'poiesis'. The knowledge and experience required for all types of poiesis are embodied in the respective techne. Hence every branch of production has its own truth: i.e. its own techne. For example, the shoemaker needs the skill and experience of shoemaking to manufacture shoes well. This type of knowledge is particular to shoemaking and, to a large extent, to the shoemaker. Unlike a modern technique, which embodies rather sophisticated scientific knowledge, the shoemaker's technique is by no means scientific. In contrast to Kant's notion of experience, the experience of a shoemaker can, in general, not be reconstructed by all rational beings. For his knowledge may not even be known to him in the sense that he can explain it. It is just his 'hands' which 'have' the truth of his production. This truth can be communicated, if at all, only slowly, by example and training (e.g. by an apprenticeship). In this sense, techne does not require any science. From this argument it is obvious that the experience which is contained in techne is not an experience in the Kantian sense, as characterised above.

At first sight this kind of techne seems to play no role in the age of mass production. However, in art it is still alive. A great artist can produce artifacts in a way which cannot be communicated to others. This circumstance is not restricted to art, but is often found in everyday life. The know-how of a good mechanic is often beyond what can be explained to others.

What distinguishes techne from a modern technique? Techne is a knowledge which is created by an intimate association with materials and tools, for the sake of the production of useful things. It is a concrete knowledge, which is mostly unconscious. In contrast, modern technique is based on scientific principles and employs strong abstractions from the things. The corresponding knowledge is a very conscious one. The things which are produced by modern techniques are the result of the application of abstract insights. This application of scientific knowledge leads to the use of labour and resources for the creation of useful commodities. The difference between techne and modern techniques is perhaps best characterised by noting that the former is taught by experience via an apprenticeship, while the latter can be taught abstractly at institutes of technology.

The truth within the field of poiesis, the techne, is limited. As it concerns only the production of things, it does not allow for statements that answer the question: 'What are these things good for?' This question concerns the meaning of the things produced by techne. For these products obtain their meaning only in the praxis of human life, when they are used for human purposes. Outside of this context they are just 'things'. The consideration of this context of human life cannot be carried through in the area of techne; it concerns another area of truth; it concerns phronesis (see below).

12.5.2 'Episteme'

The second type of truth is *'episteme'*. Episteme can be translated with 'science', but unlike modern science, episteme cannot deal with variable and contingent matters in time. Therefore, for Aristotle the title 'episteme' was reserved for such timeless matters as metaphysics, mathematics, logic and astronomy (the motions of the stars being conceived by Aristotle as eternal circles) as well as some principles of nature, such as certain teleological statements.[7]

According to Aristotle, episteme may be seen as the embodiment of true knowledge, because it contains only statements which cannot be contradicted by rational persons. It can be learned, by induction from selected phenomena and deduction from certain principles, without regard to the changing world of nature and human affairs.

The Aristotelian notion of episteme has certain similarities with our notion of the scientific logos. Both consist, in the ideal case, of timeless statements. Modern science, however, is based on the belief that it is possible to explain matters which are completely 'in time' by such statements, while we do not encounter this belief in Aristotle's work. Hence, in contrast to its modern counterpart, episteme is pursued for its own sake. The approach of episteme is characterised by contemplation, while the scientific logos reflects the will for application.

According to Aristotle, episteme may be learned without experience. This statement, however, is based on a notion of experience which is quite different from Kant's notion of experience. Experience in the Aristotelian sense means the knowledge of concrete problems, in the real world of changing matters. As episteme does not require such kinds of knowledge, even young people can be good 'scientists'. However, for Aristotle this does not imply that the corresponding knowledge helps them to behave in a right way in human affairs, such as in economic or political matters. For in all of these fields time, and therefore changing circumstances, have to be recognised. Therefore the knowledge of science in terms of episteme, though it may be absolutely correct, is valid only for timeless matters such as astronomy.

As a consequence, however, the range of episteme is limited; scientific knowledge, in Aristotle's interpretation, is not sufficient as a basis for practical action. According to Aristotle, it is not possible to apply the insights of episteme directly to concrete situations. This is so because the latter are always in time, and hence they always imply change and contingency. Thus from the point of view of episteme, which deals with invariant structures, there remains the inherent problem of ignorance concerning real life in time. This holds not only for episteme in the sense of Aristotle, but also for modern science. However, modern science is based on the belief that in the ideal case, apart from phenomena of 'chaos' etc. (Gleick, 1988), ignorance can be reduced, even eliminated, by the discovery of causal structures.[8] Aristotle did not share this belief. For him, ignorance about temporal matters was part of the human condition.

In his opinion, however, the practical consequences of such ignorance could be dealt with, to a certain degree, by intuitive intelligence and long-lasting experience of real life.

12.5.3 'Phronesis'

When we are confronted with the problems of the real world, and the question of how we shall behave, we need, according to Aristotle, the third type of truth, *'phronesis'*. Phronesis is often translated as 'prudence'. Following Ross (Aristotle, 1925), we prefer the translation 'practical wisdom'. It concerns praxis, which encompasses all meaningful actions and interactions between humans. The aim of praxis is the *good life* for all persons who participate in that praxis:

> *Practical wisdom ... is concerned with humans and things about which it is possible to deliberate; for we say this is above all the work of the man of practical wisdom, to deliberate well, but no one deliberates about things invariable, or about things which have not an end which is a good that can be brought about by action. ... This is why some who do not know [in the sense of episteme, the authors], and especially those who have experience, are more practical than others who know* (Aristotle, 1925:146, VI, 8, 1141a33-b21).

From this definition it follows that, on the one hand, phronesis lies outside the realm of techne. If techne is, for example, the knowledge of how to build a house, or to make a sword, phronesis is the knowledge of *if and what kind* of a house is needed for a good life, and *in what situation* a sword should or should not be used. Whereas techne has to do with poiesis, the production of things, phronesis, the wisdom concerning the praxis, has to do with human interaction. In this praxis, things, actions and relationships obtain their meaning according to the telos of a 'good life' (in the Aristotelian sense). In contrast to this, the products of poiesis and techne are, in themselves, meaningless.

On the other hand, phronesis has not only to be distinguished from techne, but also from episteme. In contrast to science, phronesis is not about invariable, general and necessary matters, but has to do with changing, singular and particular situations. Therefore, whereas the truth in terms of episteme is beyond application, the truth of phronesis is only for application in everyday life. Although some general statements may be useful, the particular significance of phronesis is the faculty to make the right judgements, and the ability to act in a good way, according to the moment and thus the special situation. Thus, by means of phronesis we are able to act appropriately in particular circumstances.

Aristotle points out that phronesis is mainly related to social affairs.[9] This is so because for him a human cannot have a good life for its own sake, but is essentially a 'zoon politicon' (political animal), the nature of which can be realised only in a social context. Private prudence is of minor importance compared with phronesis in a social context.

The prerequisites which are required for an appropriate judgement of a situation are observations gained by everyday experience. They are quite different from the facts which modern science collects by experimentation or data gathering. To understand the meaning of these observations, in the sense of Aristotle, one needs experience. The Greek word for experience is 'empeiria'. Although the modern notion of the empirical stems from the Greek word empeiria, it has a different meaning. The Greek word means experience which is gained by long-lasting attentiveness to the events and their contexts within everyday life. Such experience can be narrated or described, rather than scientifically expressed. Besides experience, one needs everyday judgement. The latter has to be guided to a considerable extent by tradition, for it is tradition where the experience of the society is contained and transferred from generation to generation. But phronesis springs from tradition only if one is able to adjust the knowledge contained in the tradition to the particular situation.

From this combination of experience and everyday judgement it follows that, although tradition may be narrated, phronesis itself cannot be taught, in contrast to episteme. Therefore Aristotle (1894:148, VI, 1142a 17-20) says:

> ... *indeed one might ask this question too, why a boy may become a mathematician, but not a philosopher or a physicist. Is it because the objects of mathematics exist by abstraction, while the first principles of these other subjects come from experience, and because young men have no conviction about the latter but merely use the proper language, while the essence of mathematical objects is plain enough for them?*

From this quotation it is clear that science, in the sense of eternal truths, can be learned even by young people without experience, but the knowledge of human affairs, as well as the knowledge of nature, needs a kind of experience which comes from close contact with reality and a thorough understanding of tradition. This kind of experience characterises the field of phronesis.

Again we note that the kind of experience embodied in phronesis has no equivalent in the Kantian notion of experience, which is the paradigm for modern science. This makes us aware that the modern approach, in contrast to the Aristotelian, lacks a whole and very important dimension of knowledge. This is the dimension which enables one to cope with the problems of practical life. It is contained in what we have called above the 'existence logos'. Thus the Aristotelian notion of phronesis is appropriate for summarising important traits of what we mean by the existence logos.

But if this is the case, then it is obvious that an approach based only on modern science and technique is not sufficient to solve the everyday problems of the real world, and in particular the environmental problems with which we are concerned. If one takes part in, for example, economics or politics, as well as in considerations about nature (as does e.g. ecological economics), then science has to be supplemented and deepened by non-scientific, everyday experience and tradition.

12.5.4   'Sophia' and 'Nous'

The Aristotelian approaches to truth which we have commented on up to now, i.e. techne, episteme and phronesis, do not comprise the whole field of what we have called the existence logos. They do not tell us by which principles, and to which aims, we should orientate our lives. The practical wisdom of phronesis contains the insights for the means necessary to achieve a good life, but does not say of what the good life consists. To this end, Aristotle has introduced two further approaches to truth, namely *sophia* and *nous*, which encompass the interior dimensions of human existence, in particular interior experiences.[10]

Sophia (wisdom) and nous (reason, mind, spirit) are closely related to each other. Although it is debated at length what sophia and nous mean within the context of the *Nicomachean Ethics*, we suggest an interpretation within the framework of our argument (which we feel does not contradict what Aristotle may have intended). Nous is the spiritual centre of human existence. For Aristotle it is the divine in each of us. In a theoretical sense, nous is the intuitive insight into the principles of science. In a practical sense, nous provides the final orientation for all our actions.

Nous, however, has in Aristotle's work a significance which goes beyond humanity. In Aristotle's *Metaphysics* (Book XII), it is the centre of the whole world which is called nous. This divine nous encompasses all things, but it contains their meaning rather than their existence. For, within the nous, all things are not in their real existence, but are there as 'eide', i.e. as spiritual forms or shapes. These are in the nous as meaningful relationships. The meanings of the things (stones, plants, animals, humans and stars) are, according to Aristotle, expressed in their tele (pl.

of telos, aims). Since all tele are organized in the 'great order of the cosmos', all things in the world are the incorporation of this organisation. The spiritual, meaningful being of all living and non-living entities in nous is logically prior to their existence in reality. Therefore we may say: nous in the Aristotelian sense can be looked on as the fountain of being and meaning. From the insight in this fountain human action is provided with its final ends.

In the dimension of 'nous', meaning is revealed by the answers to the questions: 'What is good in itself?' and: 'What is a good life in an absolute sense?'. These answers, however, go beyond human conceptualisation. For humans may only recognise the meaning of what is contained in the nous to a limited extent. For the Christian interpreters of Aristotle, this kind of meaning was realised by God, who had created the world and 'He saw that everything was good' (Genesis). These interpreters (e.g. Thomas Aquinas) identified the divine nous of Aristotle with the wisdom of God. The same holds for certain Islamic interpreters of Aristotle, such as Ibn Sina (980-1037, whose Latin name was Avicenna) and Ibn Rushd (1126-1198, whose Latin name was Averroes).

In the traditions of Christian and Islamic Aristotelianism, the relationship between humans and the divine nous was often described in mystical terms. According to Aristotle, the philosophers of those traditions conceived the pure nous as the fullness of life in its perfect form, which humans normally lack. But when they learned from the works of Aristotle that humans have the capacity to participate in this dimension of nous, they interpreted this capacity as interior experience. Although this notion cannot be found in Aristotle, it seems to us that it does not contradict his intentions.

In summary, what humans, according to Aristotle, can grasp from the dimension of nous is the idea of a 'good life', of being in harmony with other humans and the cosmos at large.

On the basis of our remarks on the nous, we may explain what is meant by the Aristotelian notion of sophia. If humans are able to live out the share of nous with which they are endowed, i.e. if they are able to control private emotions such as joy, anger, jealousy, etc., they may exhibit sophia. Sophia is the intuitive insight of some of the principles of meaning and being (i.e. philosophic wisdom) contained in the nous. The wise person is one who expresses such an intuitive insight which originates from an interior experience in his/her life. Hence sophia is that of the nous which is intellectually and intuitively accessible to humans. From this it follows that sophia is the approach to truth in which humans can clarify what the 'good life' consists of for humans. Therefore sophia offers the essential tele (goals). To achieve them, however, one needs phronesis, episteme and techne.

Looking back to our question concerning what modern science lacks, we see that the Aristotelian concepts of truth give us the conceptual framework as to what the scientific logos can do, and what it cannot do. The scientific logos has its strength whenever one has to deal with invariant structures. As far as human affairs and natural developments can be reduced to such invariant structures without loss, science may supply useful explanations. However, according to Aristotle, science can never explain its own roots. Science cannot make use of any interior experience which cannot be proved by scientific procedure. For this reason sophia and nous are necessary in addition to science. Also, in another respect science is deficient. It can never give sufficient reasons to answer the question: 'What shall we do in a certain situation in real life?'. This is so because in a real life situation there always exist circumstances which are not invariant and general, but instead are variable and particular. Therefore we need phronesis and, as we shall show in the next section, the will. Finally, we remind the reader that the knowledge embodied in the Aristotelian notion of techne cannot be substituted by science.

12.5.5   Education and Will

The five Aristotelian categories of truth may give access to a range of tele in the context of a 'good life'. They are, however, not sufficient to ensure that one strives for this 'good life', for this striving requires a certain decisiveness, i.e. in modern language, the *will*. Decisiveness is needed to follow and to fulfil, in the course of time, that which one has recognised as truth. This holds also for sophia and for phronesis. Concerning sophia, we know that this does not provide the concrete goals and means to achieve them, but just the field in which concrete goals for the 'good life' may be developed. As a consequence, sophia requires decisiveness to remain in this field, and the readiness to formulate corresponding goals, as well as to cling to them over time. It is obvious that for doing this one needs phronesis.

Thus Aristotle saw that the sources of decision are separate from sources of knowledge. Therefore sophia, phronesis and the other types of truth should guide the decision. However, to obtain the decision for a good aim, the will has to be trained so that it is prepared to obey its guides. This is the reason that Aristotle stressed so much the role of education. Education for Aristotle is not only the development of knowledge, but also, and perhaps even more important, the training of the will.[11] That is the reason he emphasised the role of many disciplines, such as sport, art and, in particular, music. For Aristotle, the good will is expressed in a virtuous attitude, which leads to the realisation of virtues, such as fortitude, boldness, veracity and justice. These virtues have to be learned by education, particularly by repetition. Aristotle (1925:Book II, 1103a17-26: 28):

> ... *moral virtue comes about as a result of habit, whence also its name (Greek: ethike) is one that is formed by a slight variation from the word habit (Greek: ethos). From this it also plain that none of the moral virtues arise in us by nature; for nothing that exists by nature can form a habit contrary to its nature. ... Neither by nature then, nor contrary to nature do the virtues arise in us; rather we are adapted by nature to receive them, and are made perfect by habit.*

If a society does not take care of the training of habits of virtue then, in the eyes of Aristotle, the society is in danger.

Since we are concerned in this chapter with the environmental crisis, we may ask if there are also virtues concerning the relationship between humans and nature. Aristotle, as a member of a pre-industrial society, did not deal with this question explicitly, as the environmental control and destruction in his time was by no means comparable to that of today. However, his notion of the nous, and the corresponding 'great order of the cosmos', leads us to the following consideration. Regarding the attitude to nature, in pre-industrial societies it was likely that the daily necessity of cultivating nature led, through repetition, to a grateful attitude to nature. Ample examples of this kind of attitude can be found in ancient China and by the indigenous peoples in North America (e.g. the Hopis). Each day members of agricultural societies have the experience that their food and shelter is not solely the result of their work; i.e. is not controlled only by themselves, but is granted to them from a dimension which is beyond them. This corresponds, in a certain sense, with traits of what Aristotle calls the nous.

We might posit that industrial society, with the divorce of consumption from agriculture, has lost this repetitive habit, and the corresponding virtue.

12.6   ARISTOTELIAN CATEGORIES OF KNOWLEDGE AND MODERN SOCIETIES

From today's view, Aristotle is often looked upon as a philosopher who has little, if anything, to say concerning the problems of modern society. The ideal of Aristotelian society is characterised by wise as well as virtuous aristocrats and citizens, who have achieved the integration of the five ways to truth, and who orientate their wills according to their insights. It is well known that the Aristotelian society is a rather stationary one. In contrast to this, modern society is inherently dynamic. Its characteristics are individual freedom, technical progress and a growing social product. The latter is essentially dependent on an increasing use of natural resources, and of the services of the environment.

In this modern society the Aristotelian approaches to truth may appear rather strange. This is because the modern human dominance of the globe derives mainly from a combination of science, technology and the market economy, which itself is founded on individual freedom and creativity. Modern science supplies mental tools for human domination over nature. The material tools are produced by modern technology, which is a direct application of science. As we have noted, modern science and technology have little in common with Aristotle's episteme and techne. On the other hand, phronesis and sophia are, in our times, far less prominent than in Aristotle's approach to knowledge and truth.

Concerning the meaning of phronesis, the emphasis is reversed in modern societies compared to the one Aristotle has given it. Phronesis has lost much of its social aspect and has been reduced to the individual level. In most cases it is nothing other than the prudence of rational individuals to pursue their own aims efficiently. In addition, the aspects of everyday experience and tradition, which are both so essential for Aristotle's notion of phronesis, are substituted by purely scientific considerations.

Concerning sophia, it is obvious that no equivalent notion exists in modern societies. This holds a fortiori for the nous. This has to do with the fact that in the scientific notion of experience there has been left no room for an understanding of interior experience.[12] Of course, this does not exclude the existence of wise persons, but they lack social status compared to that currently enjoyed by scientists, managers and technologists.

What about the will? Aristotle conceived a common will, which is orientated to the 'good life' of the whole society, as a prerequisite for social welfare and happiness. In contrast to this, the will in modern societies seems to be focused, to a large extent, on the urge of each individual towards ever greater consumption and accumulation. This, in turn, is the motor for the very positive impression of growth in modern economies.[13] Again in contrast to this view, Aristotle considered this urge to be the embodiment of an attitude of injustice. He had his own term for it; he called it 'pleonexia', i.e. the wish to have and to have always more (Aristotle, 1894:90; Book V, 1129b9; cf. 1130a17-28). *'Pleonexia*, a vice in the Aristotelian scheme, is now the driving force of modern productive work' (MacIntyre, 1985:227).

12.7 THE ENVIRONMENTAL CRISIS: WHAT CAN WE LEARN FROM ARISTOTLE?

The great achievement of the aftermath of the French Revolution has been the establishment of individual freedom and social justice. On the basis of modern science and its application to technology, this has allowed capitalism to flourish with all the immediate material benefits it has brought. However, while in the terminology of economics, the production factors labour and capital have divided the fruits of capitalism, not only did nature not participate, but the fruits of capitalism were only obtained by exploiting nature and by environmental degradation. In the face of this development we ask: can Aristotle's categories concerning truth help us to understand important aspects of our environmental problems? Can they eventually contribute to a solution of these problems?

Let us begin with episteme. The meaning of science has considerably changed from Aristotle's episteme up to the modern scientific logos. At the same time the field of scientific endeavour has grown tremendously. From what we said on episteme in Section 12.4.2 above, it naturally follows that for dealing with environmental questions we cannot go back to episteme, but have to employ all the achievements of modern science. We turn first to the role of natural science. Its importance can be illustrated by the greenhouse effect. Without the modern methods of natural science no one would have been able to discover the corresponding data, and even more the complex interrelationships between certain trace gases and their repercussions on the climate. There exist many other examples, e.g. ozone layer depletion, groundwater pollution, etc. We also mention in passing that all these problems would not have evolved if scientific insights had not been applied by engineers and entrepreneurs.

Second, we ask what the social sciences and humanities can contribute to the solution of environmental problems. Let us take economics as an illustration. Economists have developed important instruments by conceiving of environmental charges and certificates to provide incentives to reduce pollution and resource depletion (see Chapter 14). Hence, without science the implementation of environmental solutions within the social process, with its complex and internationally interrelated economy, is hardly conceivable.

But science is not sufficient to deal with environmental problems.[14] We believe, with Funtowicz and Ravetz (1990:144-151), that there is actually no lack of non-scientific insights in the world of today. Let us first consider techne in the sense of Aristotle. Although techne has to a great extent been substituted by scientifically inspired technique, still many farmers, gardeners, forest rangers and many laymen of almost all professions, exhibit techne in the sense of Aristotle. In these different technes (which should carefully be distinguished from technique in the modern sense) is embodied much knowledge about a careful dealing with nature. The same holds even more true for still existing traditional societies. However, these technes are more and more reduced and diminished by using industrial methods in agriculture, forestry and fishery. In traditional societies, because of the growing impact of modern techniques, the still existing technes are less and less appreciated. We believe that it is important to conserve these environmentally friendly methods, to further them and to support the endeavours of all those who try to rediscover such technes.

We now turn to Aristotle's concept of phronesis. What role can phronesis have regarding the solution of environmental problems? As mentioned above, phronesis has to do with praxis, i.e. human interaction. Hence, it is needed on all those occasions when environmental solutions concerning parts of a society, a whole society, or even humanity at large, are to be carried through The social and political difficulties one encounters in these endeavours are comparable to the difficulties of a march through an unknown jungle. Just as one is not able to give specific scientific instructions which guarantee that the aim of the march will be safely achieved, so it is not possible to give such instructions for the implementation of environmental policies. In such circumstances, however, phronesis may be decisive for the success of such policies: phronesis can provide rules which are not based on science but on experience (in the Aristotelian sense).

From our own political experience, concerning the implementation of charges on waste, we have learned in a long and tiring process that environmental policies should be guided by the following general principles of phronesis (Faber and Manstetten, 1989:184-186).

1. One should concentrate on essential issues. If one does not, there exists the danger that scarce expertise and means are wasted on the solution of rather minor details, instead of being used towards the essential changes of the environmental framework.

2. Environmental measures should be flexible, so that they can easily be adjusted to newly gained data, situations and insights. Of course, this principle corresponds to Aristotle's dictum that phronesis has to do with the ability to react to changing circumstances.

3. Extensive income and wealth redistributions should be avoided as much as possible, in order to reduce the social and political resistance to implementing environmental legislation.

4. Since the modern economic system is very complex in its production structure, consumption patterns, resource supplies, national and international trade relationships, institutions and laws, it needs time to adjust to a changed framework. To avoid frictions, or to keep them as small as possible, the implementation of new environmental laws should not be carried through quickly. For if sufficient time is allowed, the economic system is able to adjust itself. Also it is important that the laws should be announced publicly well in advance of their enforcement. The latter should occur not at once but in steps.[15]

5. One should preferably employ those environmental instruments with which one already has some experience. For then entrepreneurs, managers and engineers know the way they work, the administrators already have available the corresponding knowledge and institutions which are necessary for the enforcement and control of the new legislation, and the politicians are already so well acquainted with them that they can convincingly defend them publicly.

From these five principles of phronesis it immediately follows that scientists should not insist on achieving an environmental aim only by a theoretically 'correct solution'. Of course, the selection of the 'right' environmental instrument is of certain importance. However, phronesis is needed as well. We have the impression that this insight is often missing in environmental debates. To give an illustration from economics: the observer of controversies concerning the choice of the 'correct' economic instrument often has the impression that during these debates the actual environmental aim has been lost to sight. For example, this has been the case in the lengthy, still enduring, discussion on the issue of whether charges, taxes or emission licences should be used to reduce CO_2 emissions.

Of course, for environmental matters it also holds that phronesis must be informed by sophia. How may sophia be brought in? It is clear that sophia cannot be introduced into society primarily by technical or political means, for in this case we would remain in the field of science and technology. As we said earlier, sophia springs from the nous, from the dimension of unity, where humans and nature are as one. The experience of this unity is, at its roots, an experience interior to each person. It cannot be taught, but this does not mean that this experience is arbitrary. In earlier times, access to the nous was often through religious and/or mystical experiences and practices. In recent times the mystical approach to nature has, in the West at least, been largely supplanted by a scientific approach to nature. Indeed, so pervasive has the scientific approach become, that even mysticism is an object of scientific enquiry.

Nowadays it is obvious that the scientific approach is insufficient for the solution of our environmental problems. On the other hand, the religious and mystical approach has also proved itself to be open to abuse. But there are recent traditions which have much in common with the mystical approach, but which are accessible to the modern ways of thought. An example is exhibited by the romantic tradition as exemplified by poetry (e.g. Wordsworth, Novalis), philosophy (e.g. Schelling), ecology (e.g. Thoreau, Leopold)[16]. They all have in common that they start from the unity of man and nature (cf. Chapter 2). Many of them were themselves good scientists, who saw science and the experience of unity (sophia and nous), as complements rather than substitutes.

It seems to us that we could draw upon, and extend, this tradition of sophia with the insights of modern science, and with a revival of existing phronesis, to at least set a framework within which environmental issues can be addressed. In addition, a corresponding will has to be trained by appropriate education.

12.8   CONCLUSIONS

In the introduction we suggested that the key to the solution of environmental problems has to be sought outside the realm of science and technology. It has become clear from our discussion that the appropriate level has to be an ethical one. The ethical dimension must be the foundation of environmental reasoning, for several reasons. First, it has to encompass the area in which solutions can be sought. Second, from the ethical dimension comes the will, and thence the energy to seek and implement these solutions. Third, if we come from the will to action, we need insights about the world, for a good will alone, in the absence of insights, will not lead to meaningful actions. We outlined above that Aristotle defined five approaches to truth. All of these approaches are needed for finding an appropriate set of relationships between humans and nature. However, when one tries to isolate certain approaches, as is done by some critics of modern society, then certain dangers arise. For sophia without science and phronesis leads to unworldliness. Science without sophia and phronesis leads to purism and dogmatism. Phronesis without science and sophia leads to opportunism. From what we said above, we may summarise the following conclusions.

The first step is that as a group, as a people, as a species, we need to recognise that we are a part of the unity of nature. In Christian terminology this may be expressed as the love of God while in a state of grace. In Buddhist terms, it is the insight into the Buddha nature, the experience of the essence of all beings in a state of oneness. This corresponds to Aristotle's nous.[17]

All of us need part of the wisdom of the sage, who has access to the nous, to tell us what is our place in nature: i.e. we need the sophia to recognise the problem at its roots. Thus sophia supplies the foundations and the everlasting breath to pursue a solution.

All of us need part of the wisdom of the scientist (episteme) to arrive at the greatest possible clarity and lack of ambiguity. Thus science may help us to find a solution. In most cases, however, it will only help us to recognise the limits of the possible.

All of us need part of the wisdom of the statesman to learn how to formulate policies consistent with the insights of the wise philosopher and the scientist. Thus phronesis will deliver flexibility.

All of us need part of the wisdom of those who are concerned with dealing with concrete problems, the wisdom of the technologists, engineers, lawyers, economists and administrators, as well as the wisdom of the foresters, farmers, gardeners, craftsmen, etc. That means we need technology and techne to realise the insights and proposals which come from the various levels of wisdom.

One might suppose that society needs specialisation of Aristotelian knowledge, in the same way that a simple reading of Adam Smith leads one to look for division of labour. This we certainly do not seek. Progress through knowledge demands that we *all* try to find access to the nous, and see its implications through to fruition via all of sophia, phronesis, science and techne, in each of us.

We are well aware that humans of modern times are much more specialised in science and technique than humans in earlier times. So the question arises of how we can make sure that our plea for the encompassing of all five dimensions of knowledge and insight can be achieved. We think the best way to approach this problem is via education. Although we do not wish to elaborate the point in this chapter, we do think that a necessary first step is the explicit recognition of the multi-various dimensions of knowledge within the educational system.

The modern system of education is almost exclusively concerned with episteme and techne, for perhaps the obvious reason that these can be taught to young people, as noted by Aristotle. We certainly cannot teach the nous, but access to sophia and phronesis might be through the appreciation of literature and the arts, and the world of work, respectively. In particular, perhaps involvement in agriculture, of the non-industrial sort, can, through its engagement of the human spirit with nature, teach knowledge and wisdom of all five Aristotelian categories.

APPENDIX 1   COMMENTS ON OUR METHOD

The novelty of our approach may appear, at first sight, as a weakness, for we seem to compare two approaches which are so different in historical backgrounds and philosophical intentions. Whereas Kant tries to lay the foundations for theoretical science in his first Critique, Aristotle in his *Nicomachean Ethics* discusses types of practical knowledge. Hence it may not appear to be justified to contrast, and even to play off, the notion of practical experience in Aristotle's Ethics against the notion of scientific experience in Kant's first Critique. Of course, both notions *could* be used as complements. However, as mentioned above, the notion of experience in modern science (as represented in Kant's first Critique) has had such an overwhelming influence on society at large that there has been little room left for Aristotle's intentions. The question of how scientific research, technical inventions, as well as economic and social praxis, may be integrated into a *meaningful* framework, without blurring the boundaries between the different theories and social praxis, is of decisive importance.

From the aim of this chapter it follows that we did not attempt to give an exegesis of all relevant parts of the works of Aristotle and Kant which concern our topic. The same holds for the contemporary literature that deals with them. Instead, we have let ourselves be stimulated by some ideas, categories and concepts of these two great thinkers to develop our own approach for understanding present environmental problems. Our, at first sight, apparently unbalanced representation of certain positions of these two philosophers is largely influenced by the historical circumstance that certain ideas of Kant's first Critique have had such a great impact on the mainstream of modern science - an impact which in view of Kant's second and third Critiques, is certainly different from what Kant intended - and that other approaches to truth deriving from Aristotle have not been given the prominence they deserved.

Hence, our critique is not mainly directed towards Kant, but rather to certain perceptions of his first Critique by modern science in general. On the other hand, our appraisal of parts of Aristotle's work does not imply that the latter's position is superior to Kant's. Rather it helps us to develop unusual but, we believe, fruitful and important perspectives on environmental questions.

APPENDIX 2 COMMENTS ON OUR APPROACH CONCERNING KANT

As mentioned above, our interpretation of Kant is based on the position that Kant's argument, concerning the notions of experience and causality in his first Critique, corresponds to the view of many scientists. A quite different topic is how far Kant's argument contributes to the present discourse in the philosophy of science.

It seems that Stegmüller, who has attempted a 'rational reconstruction of Kant's metaphysics of experience' (Stegmüller, 1969a), judges the importance of Kant for actual problems of modern science to be rather low in his basic work on science (Stegmüller, 1983). In contrast to Stegmüller, Mittelstaedt (1976:133-155) tries to show that even for an understanding of the epistemological problems of quantum physics, an understanding of Kant's arguments on experience and causality is necessary. We note in passing that before the discoveries of twentieth-century physics, Helmholtz (1977) made a famous attempt to lay the foundations of natural science by referring to Kant's first Critique.

There is much dispute on the passages we quoted above from Kant's *Critique of Pure Reason*. They all refer to his 'Second Analogy of Experience'. In the context of modern epistemology, Stegmüller (1970:81) occasionally remarks that Kant, in contrast to Hume, never stated what he meant by 'causality'. A criticism of the whole argument of Kant's Second Analogy is presented by Strawson (1966:143-146), who points out (1966:146): 'Kant argued ... by a short, invalid step, for the conclusion that the Law of Universal Causality held for all possible experience, i.e. for the conclusion that there exist strictly sufficient conditions for absolutely every change that we can take notice of'. Although Kant, at least in view of his third Critique, could eventually have been forced to admit that the arguments of his second analogy cannot be seen as 'necessary thoughts' but rather as 'natural hopes' (Strawson, 1966:146), many scientists today still believe that the whole world could, in principle, be explained on the basis of causally determined experiences (cf. Chapter 11). For a defence of Kant's arguments see Brittan (1978:165-187), who explicitly deals with Strawson (1966:186ff); for a general discussion, see Aschenberg (1978).

The theory of experience offered in the *Critique of Pure Reason* is often discussed in the context of causality, especially in connection with the possibility of freedom (e.g. Rohs, 1985, 1992; Rang, 1990). These authors, in spite of their different positions, show that Kant's intention differs in his whole work (also in his first Critique) from the mainstream of modern science, as Kant is interested to offer arguments which give space for a causality *originating* from *freedom*. However, the authors mentioned above focus primarily on causality, not on experience. Hence a criticism of the limits of Kant's approach to experience in the first Critique is rarely found (see, however, Benjamin (1977) and Baron (1993), who emphasise, against Kant, the importance of the dimension of interior experience).

Finally we note that Kant's analysis of the aesthetic judgement and of the teleological judgment in his *Critique of Judgement* may be interpreted as a supplement to, or even as a tacit revision of, the concept of experience offered in the *Critique of Pure Reason*.

APPENDIX 3   COMMENTS ON OUR APPROACH CONCERNING ARISTOTLE

There have already been some attempts to rediscover the Aristotelian concept of knowledge for contemporary epistemological discussion. These attempts have usually started from Aristotle's *Physics* (e.g. Randall, 1992; Spaemann and Löw, 1985). However, Book VI of the *Nicomachean Ethics* has explicitly been taken into account by Bremer (1993:333), who discusses its contents in the context of early Greek philosophy, but also tries to make a contribution to the present understanding of science: 'That science and ethics go together, we just begin to learn. History of science, up to our century, teaches the opposite position' (Bremer, 1993:317, our translation).

The problem of any representation of the five categories of truth is that Aristotle 'does not give a full account of their interrelations or their relation to nous, taken generally' (Rorty, 1992:11). This circumstance leaves room for different interpretations, the direction of which often depends on the general approach of the interpreters.

Difficulties arise already with the notion of phronesis which 'more than most is rough terrain for commentators, being densely thickened with controversy' (Broadie, 1991:179): how close should Aristotle's remarks on phronesis be linked to the so-called practical syllogism (Cooper, 1975:22f)? Is it allowed to discuss the five categories of truth in the context of the *Nicomachean Ethics*, or should their interpretation rather refer to the *Eudemean Ethics*, in which Book VI of the former is also contained?

Even more difficult are all interpretations concerning sophia and nous. Gigon (1981:358, with reference to different opinions) sees the status of sophia as very different from that of the other approaches to truth. He suggests an interpretation in which sophia appears as an attitude that integrates nous, episteme, phronesis and techne. Concerning nous, it is by no means clear if and how Aristotle's remarks in Book VI could be related to the concept of the vita contemplativa in Book X of the *Nicomachean Ethics*, nor how they fit the theories of nous in *De Anima*, Book III, and *Metaphysics*, Book XII. So the questions of how Aristotle's understanding of nous in the field of praxis is compatible with the concept of the theoretical nous, or how nous in humans is related to the nous of the cosmos, find no definitive answer in Aristotle. If the nous of Book VI is related to the divine nous, as in Müller (1982:237ff), or if a such a relationship is not assumed, has to remain open.

Our approach is concerned with contemporary environmental questions. We, therefore, have not dealt with the former questions and different interpretations of the five categories of truth. In particular, for the purpose of our argument we have offered an interpretation of nous which includes possibilities of a religious and even a mystical understanding of this concept. Such an understanding sometimes also occurs in modern research (e.g. Jaeger, 1923:150-170, Welte 1965); it was rather familiar to commentators and philosophers of the Middle Ages (Manstetten, 1993b:229-37, 405f).

Finally, we note that we have given these three appendices at such length because we have not encountered in the literature a discussion concerning differences between the notions of experience and truth in Kant's first Critique and Aristotle's *Nicomachean Ethics*.

NOTES

1. An alternative plan of such approaches is to be found, among others, in Albert (1978), who tries to defend the epistemological programme of modern science against its critics. For a balanced discussion of 'positivist' doctrines on the one hand, and the critical social theory of Habermas on the other, see Keat (1981).
2. This is not the only way by which Aristotelian approaches may be applied fruitfully to the field of environmental questions. Promising results may also spring from a new discussion of teleological arguments as they are developed in Aristotle's *Physics* (Spaemann and Löw, 1985). Such a discussion may also start from Kant's third Critique, the *Critique of Judgement* (Kant, 1952).
3. Our interpretation of this argument is intended neither to do justice to the importance of this argument within the *Critique of Pure Reason*, nor to discuss its validity within the context of contemporary epistemology. We give some hints on the philosophical discussion of this crucial argument in Appendix 2.
4. For our discussion, it is not necessary to decide whether Kant in the argument quoted above thinks of the perception of events, or the perception of states.
5. Elsewhere this urge to dominate and control nature has been termed the 'Faustian imperative' (cf. Chapter 4).
6. In Section 12.6 we develop some non-scientific principles which facilitate the implementation of environmental solutions in a democratic society.
7. Examples of such teleological statements by Aristotle are: all things tend to their innate natural places, or the telos (aim) of all living beings is to participate in the eternal, which is expressed by their reproduction.
8. For a critical assessment of this attitude, see Chapter 11.
9. Phronesis in the sense of Aristotle is not reserved to humans. Animals also may exhibit it. Aristotle (1925:145-VI, 7, 1141a15-33): 'This is why we say that even some of the lower animals have practical wisdom, viz. those which are found to have a power of foresight with regard to their own life'.
10. For such an interpretation see Jaeger (1923).
11. Aristotle has no precise term for what we call 'the will'. The term which comes nearest to the modern concept of will is 'prohairesis' (decision, choice; Aristotle, 1925:54, Book III, 4, 1111b4ff).
12. For example, Ayer (1954:120): 'It follows that those philosophers who fill their works with assertions that they intuitively "know" this or that moral or religious "truth" are merely providing material for the psycho-analyst'.
13. This urge is formulated in economics as an assumption, namely the assumption of non-satiation (see e.g. Debreu, 1959:55).
14. Of course, there are many scientists and philosophers who believe that the environmental crisis may, in principle, be overcome by scientific means. A strong argument for this position was made by Schäfer (1993) in his monograph, about what he calls the 'Bacon Project'. He defends Bacon against the claim that the latter initiated the modern way of domination and destruction of nature. However, it is interesting to note that Schäfer emphasises the necessity of considering non-scientific points of views, in particular ethical and aesthetic ones. To this end he refers to Kant's second and third Critiques (Schäfer, 1993:192-222).

15. The consideration of this principle was decisive for the fact that the German water charge laws were enacted in the seventies and eighties, although the political resistance was very great against it at the end of the sixties and the beginning of the seventies (Brown and Johnson, 1982).
16. On the importance of such approaches to the understanding of environmental problems see, e.g. Norton (1990).
17. The identification of nous with the experience of God in the state of grace was argued for by philosophers of the Middle Ages, e.g. Albertus Magnus (1200-1280) and his school.

PART IV

Environmental and Resource Issues

13. Linking Ecology and Economy: Joint Production in the Chemical Industry

with Frank Jöst and Georg Müller-Fürstenberger

13.1 INTRODUCTION

A major problem of environmental policy making is the evaluation of negative effects of economic activity on the natural environment. Two approaches to such evaluation can be discerned: the economic and the ecological. At first sight, there is an unbridgeable gulf between these two approaches.

In this chapter we suggest that this gulf *can* be bridged, or at least is greatly reduced, if we take a joint production approach to the production process. Not only is such an approach realistic for many manufacturing processes, it also provides many useful insights into the management of negative environmental effects from economic activity. In particular, we argue that considerations of possible technical change, combined with the influences of environmental legislation, are likely to allow the *simultaneous* reduction of the emission of polluting by-products *and* improvements in economic efficiency and profitability. We illustrate our discussion with reference to the chemical industry.

13.2 ECONOMIC VERSUS ECOLOGICAL EVALUATION

Until the early 1970s, economic actions were judged primarily from a purely economic point of view; only costs and benefits for the people directly involved were taken into account. The water pollution in the 1960s, air pollution in the 1970s, the forest death and the waste problem in the 1980s, and the depletion of the ozone layer and climate change in the 1990s, have lead to economists increasingly working on environmental problems. With the growing awareness of the environmental crisis, a new field within economics was created: environmental economics. Within the framework of environmental economics, economists have added to the economic methods of valuation, such that the inclusion of pollution into the economic calculation was made possible. In doing this, use is made of established theoretical concepts, such as the theories of external effects and of public goods. Unwanted impacts of economic activities, on parties not directly involved, should be included in the entrepreneur's profitability calculation.

An asset of the environmental economics approach is that it provides a consistent framework for evaluation considerations. But it also has its drawbacks. Often, it cannot be applied easily to a particular case. Also, methods of environmental economics are not sufficient in themselves, especially for tackling long-run ecological problems. For example, if actions today caused costs of $10 billion in 30 years time, at an interest rate of 8% it would not be economically sensible to spend $1 billion today to prevent this future damage (Faber, Stephan and Michaelis, 1989:43). For such reasons, economic contributions to the sustainability debate are often unsatisfactory.

Over the last two decades there have been more and more efforts to undertake ecological, instead of economic, assessments, which means taking into account criteria such as environmental quality, sustainability of the economy and human health. Currently, three approaches to valuation are being discussed: eco-balances, eco-auditing and materials flow analysis. The aim of an eco-balance is to make the assessment of particular products and product lines possible, based on detailed analysis of the inputs used, environmental impacts of its production and its disposal. But already the simple example of babies' nappies shows how complicated and manifoldly interconnected are the relationships between the use of raw materials, supply of expendables and intermediate products, production processes, marketing, consumption and, finally, disposal.

Eco-balances usually cover one product only. Eco-auditing goes one step further, by analysing a whole firm with regard to its environmental performance. Finally, there is a 'materials flow policy' approach; the total of all materials flows in the economy and the environment taking place for economic reasons is be described and evaluated. One can, for example, trace the path of cadmium from extraction, via several steps of production and consumption, to its release into the environment, using quantity balances and quantity flow schemes, and then derive policy advice. While eco-balance and eco-auditing take place in the area of business administration, materials flow analysis has to be undertaken from the perspective of the whole economy

The assessment of anthropogenic materials flows is difficult, since it has two aspects to take into account:

a. From an economic point of view, materials flows are started in order to contribute, directly or indirectly, to the satisfaction of human needs.

b. From an ecological point of view, materials flows start in the natural environment, pass through the human economy and are finally channelled back into the natural environment.

In summary, there are two possibilities for assessment:

1. The *economic* assessment is done by the market, through the inter-action of supply and demand via prices. The price mechanism has proved an efficient way of co-ordinating production and tuning it to the customers' wants. In addition, the price mechanism creates incentives for engineers, designers, managers and entrepreneurs to express creativity through technical progress. Until two decades ago the economic assessment prevailed; material flows were, most often, looked at in terms of their contribution to the production of goods only. The loss of exhaustible resources for future economic activity, and their arrival in the environment in the form of emissions, waste water and solid waste, became apparent only slowly through the development of the ecological point of view.

2. *Ecological assessment* draws attention to resource and environmental problems which, in a market system, are realised too late, or even not at all. It is a *normative* approach, geared to criteria such as human health, environment, quality and sustainability. This assessment is carried out by natural scientists, physicians, psychologists, etc. The materials flow approach aims at finding an all-encompassing methodology for ecological assessments. A decisive question for all concepts of a sustainable economy is if, and how, economic and ecological assessments can be combined consistently. Can one translate the findings of the ecological assessment without putting at risk the functioning of the market economy as a whole?

13.3 JOINT PRODUCTION

We suggest that the gulf between economic and ecological evaluation may be bridged by the theory of joint production. This area, which in economics is mostly marginalised, could contribute to the formulation of resource-flow management more generally than up to now. Joint production means that the manufacture of a good (the main product) is necessarily accompanied by the manufacture of by-products. Thus the production of mutton and wool go hand-in-hand. From an ecological perspective, the production of polluting wastes (be they solid, liquid or gaseous) are necessary joint products of manufactured goods. In particular, by their nature, chemical processes give rise to by-products. For example, the chlorhydrine process for the manufacture of propylene oxide (which is necessary for the production of some plastics) is accompanied by the production of calcium chloride and 1-2 dichlorpropane as by-products. As an ingredient of waste water, they pollute inland waters and rivers. Because of these by-products, industrial chemists assess the chlorhydrine process to be exceptionally dirty. We return to this in Section 13.3.2 below, but first we make some more general remarks.

If one interferes in the flow of certain resources, other materials will also be affected, through the relationships of joint production. Hence, the manufacture of other wanted goods will also be influenced. This suggests that the ideal of 'surgical intervention', affecting only one section of the economy-environment system, is not possible.

In particular, production processes and products of the chemical industry have a key role in the transformation and control of material flows in modern economies. Here the notion of process-integrated environmental protection is vital. It requires the restructuring of the production apparatus, and implies the movement away from the use of 'end-of-pipe' technologies.

13.3.1   Joint Production in the Chemical Industry

Joint production is central to the discussion of environmental issues relating to the chemical industry for two reasons.

1. Unwanted by-products may lead to market failures. Negative consequences of economic actions, for example the polluting of the air, occur because markets for such polluting emissions do not exist. Thus those who suffer adverse effect from such pollution receive no compensating payment. For this reason, environmental policy has to regulate these effects via legal instruments.

2. The existence of joint production means that the chemical industry experiences considerable rigidities in the proportions of its various outputs, which reduces its ability to respond easily to environmental regulations. (Conversely, we will note later that joint production may actually confer market benefits, because of pricing and cost advantages.)

Since Adam Smith (1723-1790), a fundamental proposition on joint production has been well known. This is that, for given inputs, the economic viability of a production process depends on the market valuation of the joint outputs. With regard to the chemical industry, this means that an increase in the costs of an individual by-product, because of environmental legislation, can be distributed over all the products of that particular process. Thus a joint production process has a 'cost cushion' for price changes. In addition, it is known that the chemical industry has relatively low production costs, because of the advantages of mass production (i.e. increasing returns to scale). However, the cost cushion, in combination with the advantage of mass production, has also a considerable potential for discontinuous adjustment processes. Quantity responses may first fail to occur, but then may be the more severe when the profit contribution of one of the products falls below a certain level, either through a fall in price or an increase in costs (e.g. pollution charges). This discontinuity of response by the chemical industry makes it particularly susceptible to the effects of environmental legislation, suggesting caution in legislation in this area.

How strong are these discontinuities, and what economic implications are to be expected, if a production process characterised by joint production is influenced by environmental legislation? This question has to be examined empirically. However, the great number and wide range of chemical products, as well as the difficulty of aggregating them according to chemical criteria, hinders a direct empirical application of ecological methods of evaluation. To overcome these difficulties in analysis, we use an historical and a case study approach, which also give further insights into a theoretical approach.

13.3.2 The History of the Chemical Industry as a History of Joint Production

Because of the characteristics of the chemical production processes, the history of the chemical industry can be looked upon as the history of joint production. For example, the industrial chemistry of the C_1 building blocks[1] leads to joint production for 80% of the main reactions.

Joint production has both ecological and economic aspects. Ecologically, one may put the question: 'What products of a joint production process are environmentally detrimental?'

Using economic methods of evaluation of joint production, one distinguishes between the main product, which initiated the introduction of the corresponding production structure, and the unavoidable by-products. One further distinguishes between wanted and unwanted by-products. The former can be either marketed or used as inputs for other production processes; hence they lead to the saving of resources. Unwanted products are either emitted into the air or water, or have to be disposed of in solid form. If the manufacturing of by-products endangers the environment at large, and human health in particular, such that society does not allow them, the disposal of unwanted by-products may become a considerable cost factor in the production of the wanted products. This occurs because the ecological evaluation of the harm caused by the unwanted by-products leads to legislation controlling their emission into the environment. In the case that there are no alternatives to a particular joint production process, the banning of one particular by-product may lead to the abandonment of the corresponding process, and thus to the loss of *all* of its products. We see that in this case, the ecological evaluation directly impacts upon the economic evaluation. This is in contrast to the price cost-cushion discussed above; when there are quantity constraints on a jointly produced output, this rebounds on *all* the outputs jointly.

13.3.3　Joint Production in Soda Manufacture

An example of the problems of joint production is given through the history of the basic chemical ingredient soda. Until the end of the 18th century, soda was exported as a raw material from Spain, mainly to England and France, and used for producing glass and soap, and for bleaching textiles. A strongly rising demand led to supply shortages of natural soda. In 1791 the French Academy awarded Nicolas Leblanc its prize for the invention of a synthetic production process for soda. But soda was not the sole output of his production process; there were also environmentally damaging by-products, especially hydrogen chloride. This was released into the air, and caused damage to the people living near the soda factories, and to the neighbouring agriculture.

The resistance against emissions of hydrogen chloride in Great Britain lead to the Chlorine Alkali Bill being enacted in 1864. This bill demanded the hydrogen chloride be dissolved in water and thereby stopped its emission through chimneys. As a result the hydrogen chloride, which was now in the form of hydrochloric acid, was released into rivers. Since the hydrochloric acid corroded boats' hulls and floodgates, and endangered the fish stock, the Chlorine Alkali Bill was amended in 1874, such that this way of disposal could not be continued. Finally the Deacon process was invented, which made it possible to extract pure chlorine from hydrochloric acid. Since chlorine could be sold, this was an example of turning an unwanted by-product into a wanted one. But putting chlorine on the market was merely to move the problems linked with chlorine from the production sphere into the consumption sphere. The disposal of goods containing chlorine can cause serious environmental problems.

13.4   TIME, CAPITAL, TECHNICAL PROGRESS AND PROFITABILITY

Having discussed the nature of joint production, particularly with respect to the chemical industry, we now turn to an assessment of the possibilities for dealing with polluting by-products. There are four issues we need to address.

1. The development of manufacturing processes necessarily has a certain time structure, including the recognition and response to the negative effects of by-products.

2. Any production process requires the use of capital equipment, and this must be produced before it can be used. This seemingly very simple requirement can impose very great constraints on the rate and the nature of changing production processes.

3. Technical progress occurs over time, often promoted by searches for more profitable processes. Such technical progress may allow the bringing into use of processes which are both environmentally less damaging than old processes *and* more profitable in their operation.

4. In modern industry we observe at least three types of response to environmental legislation involving the introduction of new types of capital equipment.

We now examine each of these issues in turn.

13.4.1   Economic and Ecological Evaluation in Time

What reciprocity exists between economic and ecological assessments over the course of time? A time structure can paradigmatically be read from the history of soda production. At the beginning there was an economic problem: a raw material became scarce. This problem was, in the first instance, solved in principle by an invention that had taken place in the laboratory. Many steps were necessary for its practical realisation on an industrial scale. Entrepreneurs had to make decisions on production capacities, the extent of investment and the methods of financing. It was not until these preliminary stages had been completed that one could start building production facilities. After the building-up of a stock of capital goods, one could gradually start production, and increase output to the planned level. It took some time until the environmental damage caused by the production of soda was realised, and some more time passed before the people adversely affected could make themselves heard by the public, and a politically effective will be formed that brought about a change in the law. It was only then that the ecological assessment could have an impact on the economic assessment.

If, during the course of the invention of the Leblanc process, one had already considered that hydrogen chloride would be an unavoidable but environmentally damaging by-product, one could have decided whether to start production on an industrial scale at all, and if so what modifications would have to be made. The freedom to decide on this existed ex ante only, that is, before the corresponding capital stock had been built. After the production facilities had been set up, and the production had started, one was tied to this capital structure. In the short-run, it was impossible to avoid the production of the unwanted by-products without foregoing the main product. In that case, soda would have become extremely scarce, the capital goods would have been devalued for the financial backers, and jobs would have been lost in both the soda factories and the industries using soda as a raw material. Hence environmental legislation had to allow time for the affected industries to adapt.

13.4.2   Inflexibility and Technical Progress

Our soda production example, and the resulting chlorine related industry, shows an asymmetry between the raw materials problems and environmental problems. In general, the history of the chemical industry shows that, in most cases where substitutes for scarce basic materials were found, their discovery was stimulated mainly by the price mechanism. On the other hand, when there was environmental damage to an extent which could not be tolerated by society, very often political measures, such as bans and regulation, have been necessary. Such environmental policy measures then constitute an incentive for industry to invent new production processes not involving the unwanted by-products. But often the invention of new processes does not solve the problems, for two reasons. First, new capital goods have to be financed, produced and installed. Secondly, there is the problem of what should happen to the old capital goods, which cannot be used for the new process. It is, in general, the case that the existence of a capital stock implies *inflexibility*. But this is valid only in the *short-run*. That is because in the *long run* every capital stock wears out, and has to be renewed or replaced. In addition, technical progress occurs over the course of time.

Technical progress can be assessed both economically and ecologically:

a. It can lead to the production of the same quantity of output with less input factors; in other words, it can *increase efficiency*.

b. It can lead to the production of the same quantity of output with less environmentally damaging emissions; in other words it can *decrease the environmental harmfulness*.

c. It can lead to an improvement of the process's efficiency *and* a decrease in environmental harmfulness at the same time.

Therefore, even with big stocks of capital goods in existence, it is possible in the long run to exchange environmentally harmful processes for more productive and more environmentally friendly processes. But a change of production methods does not necessarily solve the environmental problems. When the soda producers realised the possibility of marketing the chlorine, they merely passed their disposal problem on to the customers. But an individual customer is not capable of disposing of such substances in an orderly way. As a consequence, chlorine was, and is, released into the environment in an uncontrolled way (e.g. as chlorofluorocarbons (CFCs) into the atmosphere or hydrogen chloride into the water table), until society establishes an infrastructure for its disposal.

13.4.3 End-of-pipe, Process Integrated and Product Integrated Environmental Protection

When looking at possible solutions to environmental problems one can, in principle, distinguish three approaches:

1. End-of-the-pipe environmental protection (EEP).

2. Process integrated environmental protection (process IEP).

3. Product integrated environmental protection (product IEP).

How do these three approaches differ from each other?

1. EEP is concerned with environmentally harmful products which are, by law or through public pressure, regarded as unwanted by-products. In addition to already existing production plants, new facilities are built for the disposal of the wastes, for example in the form of waste water treatment plants, incineration plants, etc. Both for the construction and the operation of EEP facilities, additional labour and capital is required. From a materials flow point of view, that means:

   a. For a given quantity of output, with EEP there are less unwanted by-products.

   b. EEP increases waste heat and carbon dioxide emissions.

   c. EEP increases the material flows through the economy.

   From an economic point of view, one has to add that the costs for improving an existing EEP system to meet tighter standards grow exponentially. The installation of EEP has decreased the emission of toxic substances considerably, but it has also led to a strong rise in environmental protection expenditure. In 1988, 23% of all expenditure by German manufacturing industry for environmental protection was by the chemical industry, while its proportion of total gross value-added in the German manufacturing industry was only 8.6%. These figures are an indicator of the quantity of harmful by-products in the chemical industry disposed of by EEP.

2. The idea of process integrated environmental protection was implicitly described by A.W. von Hofmann[2] as long ago as 1848 (Hofmann, 1866: our translation):

   In an ideal chemical factory ... there is, strictly speaking, no waste but only products (main and secondary products). The better a real factory makes use of its waste, the closer ... it gets to its ideal, the bigger is the profit.

   The concept of process integrated environmental protection encompasses two types of measures:

   a. An existing production facility is altered by the addition of equipment which converts unwanted by-products into inputs or marketable products.

b. An alteration to the process, or a new process with new facilities, may change the balance of waste and pollutants in an ecologically favourable way.

3. While EEP and process integrated environmental protection refer to the environmental impacts of production processes, product integrated environmental protection concerns products which leave the production process and enter the market. Product integrated environmental protection means a change in the materials used for a product, such that the disposal of *one unit* is altered in an ecologically favourable way. An example for product integrated environmental protection is the foregoing of the use of phosphates in detergents.

13.5   SOME CASE STUDIES FROM THE CHEMICAL INDUSTRY

In this section, we will mainly look at EEP and process IEP, and ask: what is the current situation of the chemical industry from a material flows point of view, interpreted from our joint production viewpoint? Considerable emission reductions achieved by environmental protection measures notwithstanding, many environmentally harmful substances still occur. Society wishes such substances to be safely disposed of, or even better, their production to be prevented, while industry often emphasises that this increases costs. But this judgement of industry has to be qualified. Though it is always true for EEP, this is not always the case for process IEP (nor for product IEP). This becomes clear if we assess EEP and process IEP in ecological and economic terms.

Both EEP and process IEP belong to category (b) of technical progress: The same quantity of output is associated with *less* of the unwanted by-products. EEP always implies higher production costs and greater flows of material, whereas process IEP may make it possible to produce the same amount of the main product with fewer unwanted by-products *and* smaller quantities of inputs (category (c) of technical progress). So, the diminution of the environmental harmfulness of a process can be consistent with lower costs and smaller material flows.

Such cases of process IEP represent counter-examples to the often expressed view that improvements in environmental quality can only be at the expense of higher production costs. It is an empirical question if, and to what extent, alterations to processes can be achieved which both increase profitability and improve environmental quality.

We have tackled this question in a project supported by the Volkswagen foundation, looking at the chemical industry (Faber, Jöst and Müller-Fürstenberger, 1995). For our analysis we chose 33 products from those for which the production processes have been substituted by new processes using process IEP. These processes were developed between 1960 and 1990. Among these, we found four approaches:

1. Unwanted by-products are *prevented* by the use of a different production process (the alteration of the chemical reactions).

2. Unwanted by-products are *made use of* through either:

   a) their use in other production processes within the same firm, or:

   b) their sale in markets discovered or developed for them.

3. Unwanted by-products are fed back into their production process (*recycling*).

4. Unwanted by-products are *reduced* by technically optimising the production process.

Table 13.1 shows the results of our analyses (see also Dechema, 1990). Columns 2 through 5 show which of the four approaches reduced the environmental harmfulness of the production process. The last column contains a judgement on whether the profitability has been improved by the change of process. (In columns 3 and 4, 'M' stands for usage through marketing and 'R' for usage through recycling, respectively).

Table 13.1 illustrates that, in most cases, the change of process prevented the unwanted by-products. Since this often required the replacement of parts of the production facilities, large financial resources were needed. In 15 cases, the unwanted by-products were made use of, mainly through marketing them. Recycling occurred rarely. Only in four cases was technical optimisation employed. So, in 18 of the 33 cases analysed, the most complicated approach of process IEP, prevention, was undertaken. It is remarkable that in 9 of these 18 cases, the profitability was improved. Overall, out of the 33 processes, their alteration improved the profitability of at least 13 processes (i.e. at least 40%). This is an empirical illustration that environmental protection and profitability need not be mutually exclusive.

Table 13.1. Process integrated environmental protection and profitability.
Source: Compilation by authors, based on particular case studies.

Product/Product Group	Reduction of Environmental Burden				Profitability
	Prevention	Utilisation		Optimisation	Improved
		M	R		
1. Tert.-Butyl-methyl ether	X	-	-	-	X
2. Ethylene oxide	X	-	-	-	X
3. Propylene oxide	X	-	-	-	-
4. Methionine	X	-	-	-	X
5. Polypropylene	X	-	-	-	X
6. Acetylene	-	X	-	-	-
7. Synthesis gas	-	X	-	-	-
8. Vitamins	X	-	-	-	X
9. Mathacrylic acid	X	-	-	-	-
10. Tert.-butylamine	X	-	-	-	-
11. Nitrobenzene	-	-	X	-	(X)
12. Aromatic amines	X	-	-	-	X
13. 4-aminobiphenylamine	-	X	-	-	X
14. Diphenyl bases	X	-	-	-	-
15. Dichlorbenzedine	X	-	-	-	-
16. Caprolactame	X	-	-	-	-
17. p-chlorotoluene	X	-	-	-	(X)
18. Toluene di-isocyanate	-	X	X	-	X
19. Isophorondi-isocyanate	X	-	-	X	X
20. Vitamin B3	-	-	-	X	X
21. Naphthalene	X	-	-	-	-
22. Naphthalen-disulfonic acid	X	-	-	-	-
23. Phthalic anhydride	-	X	-	-	-
24. Antrachinone	-	-	-	-	-
25. Tinuvin	X	-	-	-	X
26. Polyhydoxylic alcohol	-	-	X	X	-
27. Silicone	-	-	X	-	X
28. Phosphoric acid	X	-	-	-	X
29. Chromium	-	-	X	-	-
30. Energy	-	X	-	-	-
31. Ammonia	-	X	X	-	-
32. Rayon	-	-	X	-	-
33. Ester wax	-	-	-	X	-

M(arket) includes: (a) utilisation in other processes in the same company; (b) discovery and/or development of markets for by-products which were previously unwanted.

R(ecycling): unwanted by-products are used as inputs into the same production process after some treatment.

Crosses in parentheses indicate uncertainties.

13.6   IS ENVIRONMENTAL POLICY NECESSARY?

From an entrepreneur's point of view, it has often been stated that far-reaching environmental policy is *not possible* for cost reasons. However, representatives of the chemical industry sometimes draw the conclusion that environmental policy was not necessary, since profitability considerations would automatically lead to an improvement in environmental quality. Our analysis of process IEP confirms, for at least 40% of the cases, this thesis of the complementarity of improved environmental protection and increased profitability. But this does not necessarily mean that the process IEP automatically came with the introduction of a more profitable process planned anyway. This is because it is quite possible that it was only changes in environmental policy which led to the introduction of such processes. There may be two reasons for this.

1. Production facilities are often run for more than 15 years, but new facilities have the tendency to devalue old ones, reducing the market valuations of the firms affected.

2. In general, if one wishes to understand structural changes within an industrial sector, one has to take into account the different time horizons of entrepreneurs in different sectors (Faber and Proops, 1991c).

For example, a very long time horizon is used with regard to power plants (in the energy sector); the chemical industry's rule of thumb is that investment in new facilities should pay-back within four years. This means that the requirements for the technical superiority of a new process over the old one are very high.

There are several motives for this short time horizon. Since new processes might fail to be profitable on an industrial scale, and the investment be in vain, the successful processes must yield correspondingly high rates of return. Furthermore, because of technical progress new processes can become outdated within a few years. In addition, new suppliers can enter the market, particularly as world markets expand. Finally, it is possible that superior products are offered, or that demand changes fundamentally.

Processes which are technically feasible, environmentally friendly, and profitable under constant supply and demand circumstances, may not be realised for the above reasons. This is where environmental policy is necessary. By means of regulation and charges it can make environmentally harmful processes unprofitable. In that case, firms have either to shut-down production, or move to processes which would otherwise not be chosen for purely managerial reasons.

It is often unclear how environmental policy affects the chemical industry overall. Our case studies for Germany show that at least the considerable environmental measures of the 1970s and 1980s have not led to a reduction of the yield or turnover for the chemical industry. But this does not mean that this state of affairs will continue to hold in the future.

Apart from the increasingly complex international interdependencies of the markets, a materials flow oriented environmental policy in the future has to take into account the intersectoral interdependencies of economic activity. We illustrate what sorts of problems can arise with the following example.

By using waste sulphur-containing materials as feedstocks in the chemical industry (i.e. by 'closing the sulphur cycle'), the production of sulphuric acid in the chemical industry could largely occur in the framework of process IEP. So, because of the closed control of chemical 'loops', the need for the importation of sulphuric acid into the chemical industry would decrease considerably. But this development, while positive at first sight, would lead to problems in other sectors of the economy. At present, the chemical industry is a purchaser of large quantities of sulphuric acid, which is generated as a harmful by-product of the iron and non-ferrous sectors, and mineral oil and gas processing sectors. The use of sulphuric acid in the chemical industry offers these sectors a possibility for waste disposal, which a successful process IEP would remove. This would cause enormous problems of disposal for these key sectors of the economy. In other words, the solution to an environmental problem in one sector could lead to great environmental problems in other sectors! Here it becomes obvious that in certain areas there are difficulties for a materials flow oriented policy, for which no solution can yet be seen.

13.7 CONCLUDING REMARKS.

Our conclusions are of two sorts: (a) empirical, relating to the chemical industry, and (b) methodological.

Our empirical analyses show that the chemical industry has, up to the present, reacted flexibly to the enormous challenges put on it by environmental policy. For ecological reasons one can expect these challenges not to diminish in the future. The increased requirements of environmental protection have, in our opinion, so far had no severe consequences for the economic development of the chemical industry, for example in the form of a decreased profit-turnover ratio, or decreased turnover. The sectoral development is, rather, strongly determined by structural and cyclical influences. For example, decreases in the production of PVC and other chlorine-related products cannot, in a mono-causal way, be traced back to environmentally caused substitution processes.

On methodology, in the above discussion we have analysed historical and empirical developments, using the vocabulary and theory of joint production and, to a lesser extent, of capital theory. Capital theory allows the analysis of economic changes in the long run, whereas the theory of joint production is most often used for looking at short-run issues. Thus, for the shaping of environmental policy, a capital theoretic foundation of joint production is required.[3] It has become clear in our theoretical analyses that a combination of the instruments of the theories of joint production and capital is extraordinarily fruitful for generating new questions, and for establishing solutions which can be applied.

NOTES

1. The chemistry of C_1 building blocks encompasses all reactions which make use of organic molecules with a single carbon atom. These include, for example, methane, formic acid, formaldehyde, methyl alcohol, prussic acid, etc.
2. A.W. von Hofmann (1818-1892) was one of the co-founders of the German Chemistry Society, and founder of the Royal College of Chemistry in London.
3. For a more detailed analysis of the relationship between capital theory and joint production, see Müller-Fürstenberger (1995).

14. Reducing CO_2 Emissions: Analysis and Policy

with Frank Jöst, Gerhard Wagenhals and
Stefan Speck

14.1 INTRODUCTION: FORMULATION OF THE ISSUE

There is now an almost unanimous agreement among climatologists that the emissions of greenhouse gases, in particular of carbon dioxide, contribute in an essential way to the change of the global climate. Further, this climate change will have far-reaching consequences for all life on Earth. The main cause is the trace gas carbon dioxide (CO_2), mainly produced because of the burning of coal, oil and gas, the so-called fossil sources of energy. The results of climate research agree that these CO_2 emissions contribute 60% to the effects of the anthropogenic greenhouse gases.

Since the industrial revolution, the rate of world-wide CO_2 emissions has been steadily rising. This has led to an increase in atmospheric CO_2 concentration, from 280 ppm before the industrial revolution, to 353 ppm in 1990. Parallel to that, the average global temperature has risen.

The main source of anthropogenic CO_2 emissions is the production of energy from fossil fuels. On the other hand, these fuels have allowed the improvement of production since the beginning of the industrial revolution. Also, today the provision of such *non-renewable* energy to a great extent is the fundamental prerequisite for the maintenance and improvement of the supply of goods. This statement is also valid for the less developed regions of the world. A widely held opinion is that the future development of these regions depends fundamentally on the expansion of their energy use.

These circumstances have led to a suggestion from the World Conference on 'The Changing Atmosphere', which was hold in Toronto in June 1988. There it was proposed that a target for CO_2 emissions be a 20% reduction from the 1988 emissions by 2005; also, by the middle of the next century, CO_2 emissions should be reduced by at least 50%.

Whether this target can be achieved, and what importance the CO_2 problem has for the whole economy, are questions which we wish to examine in this chapter, which has the following structure. Sections 14.2 to 14.4 consider the economic development of the World, of the USA and of the EU in relationship to the development of CO_2 emissions. It then summarises the CO_2 problem. Then we introduce a method of decomposing the rate of change of CO_2 emissions into various economically determined components, using the method of central differences. This decomposition is the basis for our further analysis. In Sections 14.5 to 14.7 the past development of CO_2 emissions by Germany and the UK is examined. Then scenarios for potential future developments are represented. In Section 14.8 to we examine the policy implications, and the difficulties for the achievement, of the Toronto target. In Section 14.9 we offer some concluding remarks.

14.2   THE CO_2 PROBLEM: A NEW TYPE OF ENVIRONMENTAL PROBLEM

The CO_2 problem has occupied the public and politics world-wide to a degree which has never happened before for an environmental problem.[1] The great influence of scientists, in particular of climatologists, in the political discussion is remarkable, and also novel.

What is the difference between the greenhouse effect and other known environmental problems? The nature of most environmental problems can be characterised by three features, which we comment on through the example of the pollution of ground water.

(i)   The pollution of the ground water by nitrates or dioxins was *not expected*. Consequently it was a surprise.

(ii)   The measures taken have been *reactive* to the resulting problems.

(iii)   So called *end-of-pipe* measures have been taken, which reduce the consequences of the environmental pollution. Therefore the polluted ground water is purified and diluted so that it can be used as drinking water.

In contrast to the pollution of ground water, the CO_2 problem has the following characteristics:

(i)   The consequences of climate change, such as the unwanted warming and/or flooding of certain areas, have not yet occurred, but they *can be predicted* with some confidence. Also, the intensity of these problems is determined by our present and future emissions, which arise from the production of energy with fossil fuels.

(ii)   Measures for the reduction of the predicted effects are *anticipatory*.

(iii)   So far there exists *no* end-of-pipe technology to reduce existing stocks of CO_2 emissions on a large scale. Experts advise against such 'geo-engineering' technologies, because of their great potential danger.

To summarise, while the present environmental problems:

* are generally unexpected,

* the response to them is reactive, and

* end-of-pipe technologies are available,

the CO_2 problem is characterised by:

* knowledge about the expected difficulties,

* planned measures, like reduction of CO_2 emissions and the construction of dykes against flooding, are anticipatory, and

* there do not exist end-of-pipe measures to reduce CO_2 emissions.

The CO_2 problem, in terms of its economic analysis, is relatively straightforward, for the following reasons:

1. The great bulk of CO_2 emissions result from burning fossil fuels (coal, oil and gas).

2. Industrialised countries keep very detailed records of these fuels used throughout the economy.

3. In contrast to the impacts of many other pollution problems, there is little uncertainty about the direct, long-term impact of the CO_2 emissions on its atmospheric concentration. Here the problem is much simpler than that of, say, the leaching of pollutants from waste disposal sites into ground water, where there is great uncertainty about the nature of the pollutants, their quantities, and their long-run effects on ground water quality.

4. Finally, we are in no position to switch off CO_2 emissions on a global
    scale in a short time, as is presently being attempted for chloro-
    fluorocarbons (CFC) production. This is because coal, oil and gas
    are the main sources of energy supporting modern economic
    activity, and it is physically impossible to carry through any pro-
    duction activity without such low entropy energy. Apart from that,
    alternatives in the production of energy are only available in the
    long-run.

We see that the CO_2 problem is not only an environmental problem, but
also gives rise to an essential resource problem.

14.3   ANTHROPOGENIC GREENHOUSE GASES
        AND ECONOMIC DEVELOPMENT

In the following sections we illustrate the relationship between emissions
of greenhouse gases and economic development. As mentioned above,
CO_2 emissions are responsible for 60% of the anthropogenic greenhouse
effect. Thus it is on these emissions that we concentrate in our study. In
Figure 14.1 we show the total emissions of CO_2 (billion tonnes) from
the burning of fossil fuels, in the period 1860-1982.

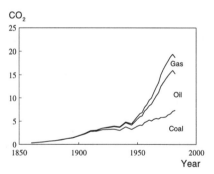

Figure 14.1. Global CO_2 emissions by fuel (B tonnes).
Source: Rotty and Masters (1985:70).

It can be seen that the emissions from the burning of liquid and gaseous
fuels have increased rapidly, while those from solid fuels have increased
more slowly over the last decades.
    We now give a short summary of the historical trends of energy use,
of CO_2 emissions and of Gross Domestic Product (GDP). GDP is a
measure of the total economic activity of an economy during one year,

e.g. for Germany or the UK. We first compare the trends of the World with the USA and the EU (this is for the twelve EU countries of 1994).

Figure 14.2 show energy use by the World, the USA and the EU from 1950 to 1988. We see that energy use by the World grew significantly faster than that by the USA and the EU in 1950-1973. Following the impact of the first oil price 'shock', energy use by the USA became approximately steady, while the EU energy use showed an overall decline up to 1988. However, World energy use continued to grow between 1973 and 1988.

In Figure 14.3 are the CO_2 emissions by the World, the USA and the EU. The temporal pattern of the emission of CO_2 is similar to that for energy use in Figure 14.2.

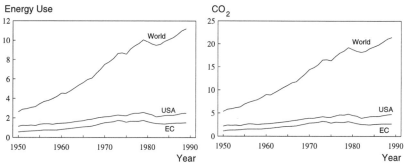

Figure 14.2. Energy use (B tonnes coal equivalent): World, USA and EU.
Source: UN (1976), OECD (1989a).

Figure 14.3. CO₂ emissions (B tonnes): World, USA and EU.
Source: UN (1976), OECD (1989a).

We now consider the relationship of energy use to GDP, and CO_2 emissions to GDP in Figures 14.4 and 14.5. We see that both energy/GDP and CO_2/GDP ratios are generally falling, for the World, the USA and the EU. However, for the USA and the EU the fall is more rapid than for the World.

We consider the distribution of CO_2 emissions between different economic regions during the last four decades. Figure 14.6 shows that the share of the USA and the EU decreased. Conversely, we observe an increasing contribution from the developing countries to global CO_2 emissions. This is due to the growing industrialisation in these countries, and we can expect this trend to continue.

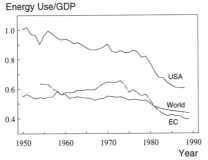

Figure 14.4. Energy/GDP (tce/K ECU): World, USA and EU. Source: UN (1976), OECD (1989a).

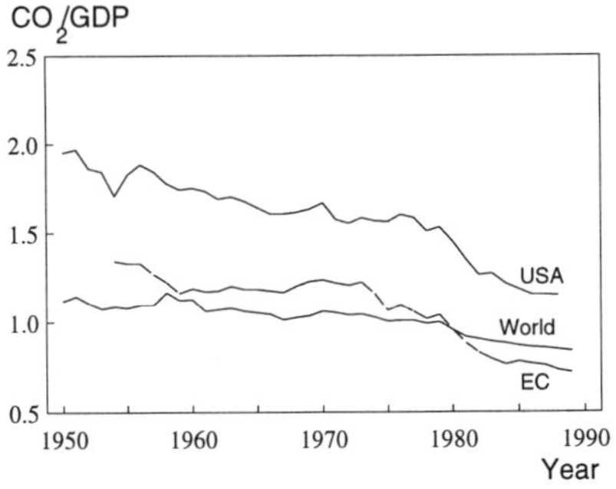

Figure 14.5. CO₂/GDP (tonnes/ K ECU): World, USA and EU. Source: UN (1976), OECD (1989a).

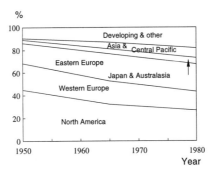

Figure 14.6. Changing patterns of CO_2 emissions. Source: Rotty and Masters (1985:77).

14.4 DECOMPOSING THE RATE OF CHANGE OF CO_2 EMISSIONS

14.4.1 Variables Influencing CO_2 Production

Having examined the historical behaviour of CO_2 emissions, we now wish to understand *why* this behaviour occurred. Such an understanding requires, of course, an economic model of CO_2 emissions.

Now in Figure 14.5 we saw the relationship between CO_2 emissions (C) to GDP (Y), i.e. C/Y. We now ask: which variables influence this ratio?

1. We know that different fuels generate different amounts of CO_2 for the provision of the same amount of useful energy, because of their different chemical-physical characteristics. These differences indicate that the substitution of coal by oil, and much more by gas, leads to lower CO_2 emissions.

2. We also know that different industries have different energy requirements and use different fuel mixes.

3. The efficiency of fuel use varies between industries, and over time. On the basis of different production procedures the same amount of a commodity can be produced by less energy. Therefore, a shift from conventional technologies to best technologies could be carried out. This would reduce the CO_2 emissions in Germany by 28%. Similar results can be expected for the UK (Proops, Faber and Wagenhals, 1993:Chapter 11, Section 3.1). In addition to this, technical progress has always led to new production procedures in the past, which require less energy and emit less CO_2.

4. We know that the importance of individual industrial sectors in the economy has changed during the last decades. The importance of agriculture has decreased and that of the chemical sector and automobile sector has increased. This shift is, above all, a consequence of changes in demand.

5. Finally, we have to consider that the demand for energy by industry and by households has developed quite differently over the years. The three factors influencing CO_2 emissions attributable to households, are:

   (i)   the quantitative division of the energy use into coal, oil and gas,

   (ii) the different purposes of fuel use; i.e. much of energy is used for heating and private transport and less energy for communication,

   (iii) the technical efficiency of the use of energy.

6. Not only the type of demand is important for energy use, but also the total amount of demand. The size of the population is a fundamental determinant of total demand.

14.4.2   Examination from an Economic View

After noting the influential variables, we examine the influence of these variables. Firstly, we restrict ourselves to economic factors. Therefore, we do not take into account industrial production in terms of the relative sizes of the industrial sectors, and the techniques of production they employ, because we are interested in the aggregate and not in the dis-aggregate development. (For a discussion of structural change and technological change see: Proops, Faber and Wagenhals, 1993:Parts III-V.)

In seeking to understand the time path of CO_2 emissions by economies, one needs to establish the variables that one feels to be influential. We consider these to be:

1. The ratio of CO_2 emissions (C) to the total energy use by the economy (E): i.e. we consider (C/E). The mix of fossil fuels may alter, so that the same amount of energy is provided, but a different amount of CO_2 is emitted. This assumes that E/Y and Y are unchanged (the assumption of ceteris paribus).

2. The ratio of energy use (E) to the GDP (Y): i.e. we consider (E/Y). This supposes C/E and Y to be constant (i.e. ceteris paribus); thus a reduction of E/Y indicates that the economy is becoming more efficient in the use of energy, or that the economy is moving from more energy intensive sectors towards less energy intensive sectors. Therefore, the variable (E/Y) is a measure of the energy efficiency of an economy.

3. The Gross Domestic Product of the economy (Y). The higher is the GDP (ceteribus paribus with regard to C/E and E/Y), the higher are the CO_2 emissions.

What influence have these three economic variables, i.e. fuel mix (C/E), energy efficiency (E/Y) and GDP (Y), on the CO_2 emissions? The temporal rate of change of CO_2 emissions can be approximately calculated as the sum of the temporal rates of change of these variables (Proops, Faber and Wagenhals, 1993:Chapter 4, Section 4.4); i.e.:

$$\frac{\Delta C}{C} \approx \frac{\Delta(C/E)}{C/E} + \frac{\Delta(E/Y)}{E/Y} + \frac{\Delta Y}{Y}.$$

This looks very promising, as it will allow us to assess trends in the components of the rate of change of CO_2 emission, and thereby make assessments of the likely behaviour of CO_2 emissions overall. In the next section we apply this decomposition method to the rate of change of CO_2 emissions for the World, the USA and the EU.

14.4.3   The Rates of Change of CO₂ Emissions for the World, the USA and the EU

The development of World CO_2 emissions is shown in Figure 14.7.

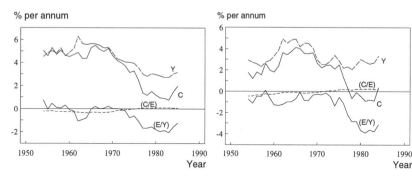

Figure 14.7. Decomposition of rate of change of World CO_2 emissions.

Figure 14.8. Decomposition of rate of change of USA CO_2 emissions.

From Figure 14.7 we see that the proportional rate of change of World CO_2 emissions (C) is positive throughout the period. That is, CO_2 emission has been increasing. However, the rate of increase has fallen from about 5% per annum up to 1970, to 2% by the mid-1980s. This fall can be attributed to a fall in the rate of World GDP growth (Y), from 5% per annum to 3.5% per annum, and a fall in the rate of growth of the energy/GDP ratio (E/Y), from approximately 0.5% per annum to -1.5% per annum. The CO_2/energy ratio (C/E) has been almost unchanging throughout the period; the composition of the fossil energy sources has not changed.

Considering Figure 14.8, we see that the proportional rate of change of CO_2 emission by the USA has fallen from a peak of 4% per annum in the mid-1960s, to about -1% per annum by the mid-1980s. This fall can be attributed to a fall in the rate of growth of GDP, but particularly to a sharp fall in the rate of change of the energy/GDP ratio after the mid-1970s. The CO_2/energy ratio has remained almost unchanged.

From Figure 14.9, we see that the EU has also shown a fall in the rate of growth of CO_2 emission, but more marked than in the USA, from a peak of 6% per annum in the mid-1960s, to -2% per annum in the mid-1980s. This can be attributed again to a fall in the growth rate of GDP, and a fall in the rate of chance of energy/GDP ratio.

In summary, we can say that World CO_2 emissions are increasing, the emissions of the USA are stable and of the EU are falling. The reason for this development can be traced back to the fall of the growth rate of the different GDPs (*Y*) and the increase in energy efficiency (*E/Y*).

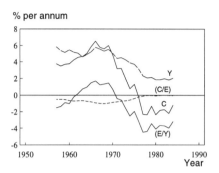

Figure 14.9. Decomposition of rate of change of EU CO₂ emissions.

14.5   CO₂ EMISSIONS IN GERMANY AND THE UK

We wish to make a closer examination of two important economies of the European Union (EU), Germany and the UK. In contrast to the above, we want to examine not only the economy as a whole, but we divide the economy into 47 sectors (each comparable between the two countries). Now we can use the decomposition of the three influential variables for all of these sectors. Further, we have examined the links between the sectors, analysed the changes of the production structure, and developed some scenarios. We do not deal with the first two points because of lack of space (see Proops, Faber and Wagenhals, 1993:Chapters 7-10), but some results of the scenarios are presented in Section 14.8.

14.5.1   Energy Use and CO₂ Emissions

In Figures 14.10 and 14.11 we show the total energy use and CO₂ emissions by Germany and the UK between 1950 and 1988.

Both economies show a generally upward trend in energy use. The UK CO₂ emissions rise to a peak in 1972, and fall subsequently, while the German peak is in 1980. It is probably no coincidence that these peaks occur just around one of the two oil price 'shocks'.

To remove the influence of population, in Figures 14.12 and 14.13 we show the per capita energy use and CO₂ emissions.

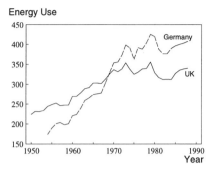

Figure 14.10. Energy use by Germany and the UK (M tce).

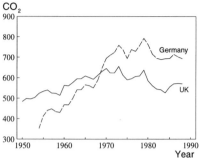

Figure 14.11. CO₂ emissions by Germany and the UK (M tonnes).

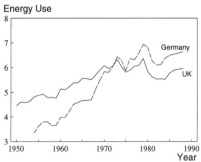

Figure 14.12. Per capita energy use by Germany and the UK (K tce per capita).

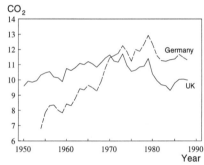

Figure 14.13. Per capita CO₂ emissions by Germany and the UK (K tonnes per capita).

We see that there is now less differences between the two countries. The more rapid growth in both energy use and CO_2 emission by Germany can be attributed to Germany's more rapid rate of economic growth during this period.

To test further the relationship between CO_2 emission and GDP, in Figure 14.14 we plot the CO_2/GDP ratios for the two countries, and for the EU as a whole. The close correlation between the curve of the EU and of Germany, and to a lesser extent the UK, suggests that conclusions drawn from an analysis of the German and UK data will have some relevance also for the whole EU.

We note that for both countries, and for the EU, the CO_2/GDP ratio have decreasing trends over time. This may reflect a mixture of factors, such as the following:

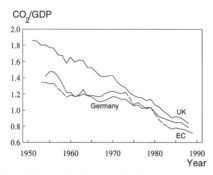

Figure 14.14. CO$_2$ emission/GDP for Germany, the UK and the EU (tonnes/K ECU).

1. Changing fuel mix. This will be influenced partly by the available technology, and partly by relative fuel prices.

2. The distinction between fuel use by households and in production. Changing national wealth may have a positive effect on both household and production energy demand. However, the sizes of the effects may differ. (We return to a discussion of this issue in Section 14.5.3, below.)

3. The mix of industries generating national output. For example, the proportion of GDP generated by iron and steel manufacture has fallen in both Germany and the UK, while the proportion of GDP generated by services has increased.

To explore in more detail the impact of various changes of fossil fuel use, through changing industrial structure, we need to take a more dis-aggregated approach to fuel use.

14.5.2   Energy Use and CO$_2$ Emissions of Coal, Oil and Gas

In Figures 14.15 - 14.18 we show the proportional distribution of energy use by fuel type and CO$_2$ emissions attributable to fossil fuel burning in the two countries. This is shown as a cumulation of the three categories of fossil fuels, and non-fossil fuel energy (hydro and nuclear power, are marked 'Other').

We see there has been a long-run substitution of coal by oil and gas, in both Germany and the UK. Thus the proportion of CO$_2$ emissions attributable to oil and gas burning has also risen. We also note the 'spike' in oil use for the UK in the mid-1980s. This reflects the 1984-5 miners' strike.

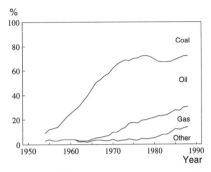

Figure 14.15. Energy use by fuel type (%): Germany.

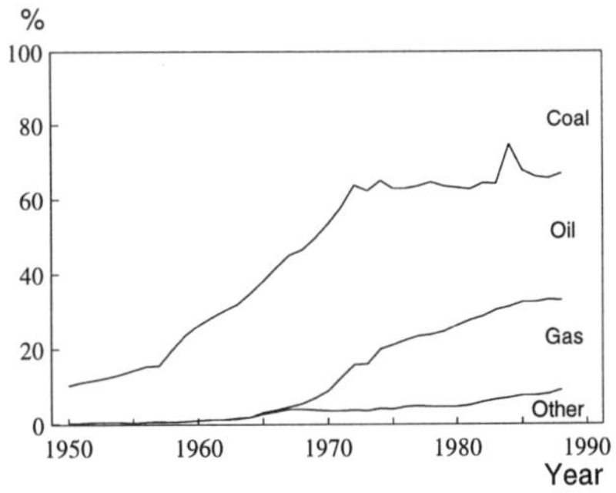

Figure 14.16. Energy use by fuel type (%): UK.

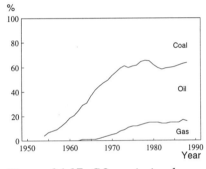

Figure 14.17. CO_2 emission by fuel type (%): Germany.

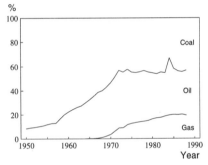

Figure 14.18. CO_2 emission by fuel type (%): UK.

14.5.3 Energy Use and CO_2 Emissions by Households and in Production

We noted above that we can distinguish between the energy used by households directly, and that used in production.[2] This is shown in Figures 14.19 and 14.20 for both countries.

We see the patterns are very different. In Germany the proportion of CO_2 emissions by household is increasing more rapidly than in the UK. Production CO_2 emissions have been falling for one or two decades, while the household CO_2 emissions continued to rise in both countries until 1979.

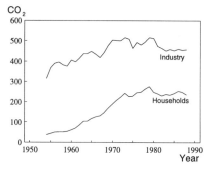

Figure 14.19. Production and household CO_2 emissions: Germany (M tonnes).

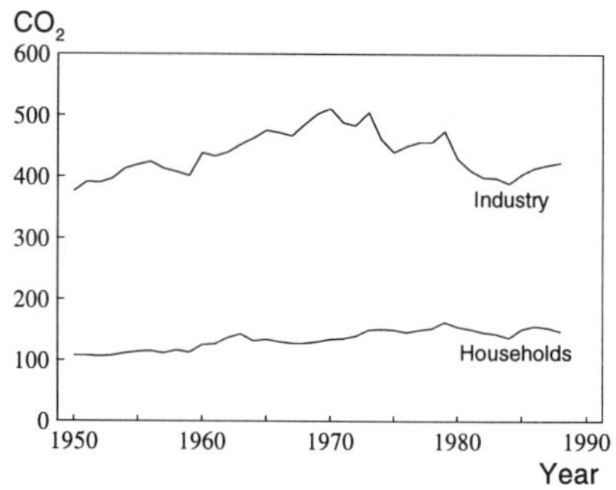

Figure 14.20. Production and household CO_2 emissions: UK (M tonnes).

14.5.4   Production CO_2 Emission by Sector

Now we turn to the production of CO_2 emissions by industry, because it is useful to examine production CO_2 emission in more detail. Unfortunately, data for this exercise is only available for the UK. We have disaggregated UK production into the following nine sectors:

1. Agriculture.	4. Transport	7. Food.
2. Services.	5. Paper and Printing.	8. Chemicals.
3. Construction, etc.	6. Textiles.	9. Other Industry.

Unfortunately, the large Sector 9 (Other Industry) contains a mix of important activities, such as Iron and Steel, and Engineering, but the data used does not allow further disaggregation.

The cumulative percentages of production CO_2 emissions by these industrial sectors are shown in Figures 14.21 and 14.22. For clarity of presentation the nine sectors are presented in two cumulative diagrams.

In Figure 14.21 all nine sectors are shown; in Figure 14.22 the sector marked 'Industry' is further disaggregated. We see that the proportion of CO_2 emissions from UK Industry has declined quite markedly since 1973, while that from Transport has increased quite rapidly. The proportion of Services CO_2 emission increased and then decreased. The remaining sectors have had small and relatively constant proportions of total production CO_2 emissions.

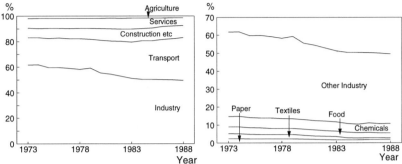

Figure 14.21. Sectoral production CO₂ emissions (%): UK (1).

Figure 14.22. Sectoral production CO₂ emissions (%): UK (2).

14.5.5   Decomposition of German and UK CO₂ Emission Changes

We can now apply the differencing decomposition technique to CO_2 emissions derived in Section 14.4. We recall that we have identified the following influential variables:

1. The ratio of CO_2 emission (C) to the corresponding energy use by the economy (E): i.e. (C/E): i.e. the fuel mix.

2. The ratio of energy use (E) to the Gross Domestic Product of the economy (Y): i.e. (E/Y): i.e. the energy efficiency.

3. The Gross Domestic Product of the economy (Y).

These three variables C, E, and Y can apply either to the national economies or to the different sectors.[3]

14.5.6   Decomposition of Total CO₂ Emissions Changes

In Figures 14.23 and 14.24 the proportional rates of change of CO_2 emission by Germany and the UK economies are shown in their three components.

   At the beginning of the time period, 1958 in Germany and 1954 in the UK, we see a growth of CO_2 emissions of around 4% p.a. in Germany and 1.5% p.a. in the UK. It fell to zero by 1976 in Germany, and by 1971 in the UK. It continued to fall to around -1.5% p.a. in Germany and -1% p.a. in the UK.

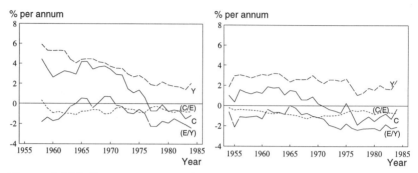

Figure 14.23. Decomposition of total CO_2 emission changes: Germany.

Figure 14.24. Decomposition of total CO_2 emission changes: UK.

We can now explore the three components which make up the proportional change in CO_2 emissions.

We first note that the effect of changing national income was consistently positive throughout the period of analysis, for both Germany and the UK.[4] We assume that as income increases, so do the emissions of CO_2, ceteris paribus. For Germany, this effect falls from 6% p.a. to 2% p.a. For the UK, this effect is consistently around 2.5% p.a. This tells us that, had there been no countervailing effects, CO_2 emission by the UK would have grown approximately 2.5% p.a., and at between 6% and 2% p.a. in Germany.

We can see why such growth in CO_2 emissions do not occur, by looking at the component involving changes of C/E. This reflects the effect of a changing fuel mix, and we see that throughout the period of investigation this component lies between -0.4% and -1% p.a. for Germany, and between -0.3% and -1.3% p.a. for the UK. This reflects the shift from coal to oil, and then gas, in both Germany and the UK.

Finally, we examine the component concerning changes in E/Y, i.e. the energy efficiency. In Germany, this was acting to reduce the rate of change of CO_2 emissions, up to 1964 and after 1971. The fall in the proportional rate of change of CO_2 emission in the UK can be largely attributed to this component, which falls from around -0.5% to -2% p.a. over the period of study. In both countries this effect reflects a declining need to accompany growth in GDP with growth in aggregate fuel use. This embodies two features of economic development:

(i) improving fuel use efficiency, and

(ii) a shift from manufacturing towards services.

14.5.7 Decomposition of Production CO$_2$ Emissions Changes

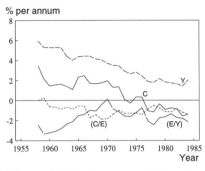

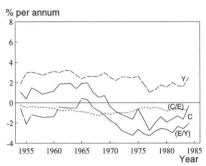

Figure 14.25. Decomposition of production CO$_2$ emission changes: Germany.

Figure 14.26. Decomposition of production CO$_2$ emission changes: UK.

As mentioned above, total CO$_2$ emissions can be divided between that attributed to manufacturing, that attributed to services and that attributed to households. Firstly, we turn to the decomposition of changes in CO$_2$ emission by manufacturing and services, shown in Figures 14.25 and 14.26 for both countries. The patterns here are very similar to those for total emissions.

14.5.8 Decomposition of Households CO$_2$ Emissions Changes

The same decomposition is also applied to CO$_2$ emissions attributable to households in Germany and in the UK, in Figures 14.27 and 14.28.

The patterns here are markedly different from those for production CO$_2$ emission changes, and for the economy as a whole.

For Germany, the rate of change of CO$_2$ emissions by households begins very high, at 12% p.a., and falls to zero by 1976. This fall is attributable to all three components.

For the UK, over most of the period, the rate of change of CO$_2$ emissions by households is positive, though with a marked dip in the mid-1960s. Since 1977 the rate of change has been negligible.

It is interesting to note that in both Germany and the UK, by the end of the study period there is an almost zero proportional rate of change of CO$_2$ emissions. This is because of an almost exact balancing of a positive effect through Y, and a negative effect through E/Y.

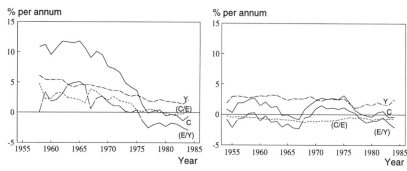

Figure 14.27. Decomposition of household CO$_2$ emission changes: Germany.

Figure 14.28. Decomposition of household CO$_2$ emission changes: UK.

14.5.9   Decomposition of Total CO$_2$ Emissions Changes

Now we want to summarise the overall proportional rates of change, and their components for total, production and household CO$_2$ emissions. In Table 14.1 the annualised proportional rates of change are calculated, for Germany and the UK.

Table 14.1. Decomposition of CO$_2$ emissions changes; total, production and household: Germany and the UK (1960-88).

	Percent per annum				
	C	**C/E**	**E/Y**	**Y**	**Remainder**
Germany					
Total	1.64	-1.07	-1.66	4.36	0.01
Production	0.55	-1.60	-2.30	4.36	0.09
Households	5.90	1.85	-0.11	4.36	-0.02
UK					
Total	0.05	-0.86	-1.77	2.61	0.07
Production	-0.21	-0.86	-2.05	2.61	0.09
Households	0.85	-0.84	-0.90	2.61	-0.02

Regarding CO$_2$ emission, this increased overall in Germany, but showed almost no change in the UK. The more rapid rate of increase in Germany can be attributed mainly to the higher rate of economic growth. Production CO_2 emissions were increasing in Germany overall, but decreasing in the UK. Finally, household CO_2 emissions in Germany grew much more rapidly than in the UK.

14.5.10 Sectoral Decomposition of CO_2 Emissions Changes

We now turn to an analysis of the components of CO_2 emission changes by individual manufacturing sectors. The relatively short time-span of the UK data (1970-1988) is because of limitations on the availability of national income data on GDP contributions by the various sectors. As already mentioned, no suitable sectoral data is available for Germany.

The decomposition used is the same as that used above, except that total CO_2 emissions, total energy use, and total GDP are replaced by the sectoral contributions to the total. The UK sectoral decompositions of changes in CO_2 emissions are shown in Figures 14.29 to 14.30.

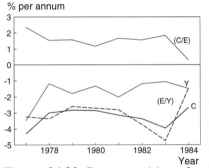

Figure 14.29. Decomposition of CO_2 emissions changes by Agriculture: UK.

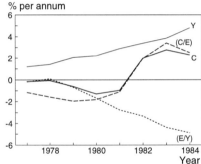

Figure 14.30. Decomposition of CO_2 emissions changes by Services: UK.

From Figure 14.29 we see that the Agriculture sector has shown a consistently negative rate of change of CO_2 emissions. It is interesting to note that, unlike the case for the whole economy, this is composed of a consistently positive rate of change of C/E, and a consistently negative rate of change of Y. These effects nearly balance. The E/Y component is also negative, indicating improving fuel efficiency by this sector.

The Services sector (Figure 14.30) indicates a slightly declining rate of change of CO_2 emissions until 1981, with positive rates of change thereafter. As the rates of change of Y and E/Y are almost exactly opposite to each other, this behaviour is attributable almost completely to the C/E component. After 1981, Services shifted towards more carbon intensive fuel, i.e. coal.

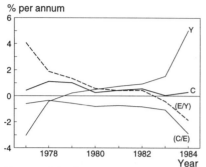

Figure 14.31. Decomposition of CO$_2$ emissions changes by Construction, etc.: UK.

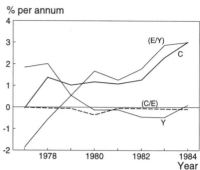

Figure 14.32. Decomposition of CO$_2$ emissions changes by Transport: UK.

The Construction Sector (Figure 14.31) has shown a small but consistently positive rate of change of CO$_2$ emissions. This is a mixture of growing rates of change of Y and declining rates of change of E/Y and C/E.

Transport (Figure 14.32) shows a positive and increasing rate of change of CO$_2$ emissions, attributable almost entirely to the increase in the E/Y component. That is, the transport sector is becoming less energy efficient in the UK, and at an increasing rate. This reflects the shift from rail to road transport.

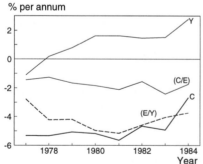

Figure 14.33. Decomposition of CO$_2$ emissions changes by Paper and Printing: UK.

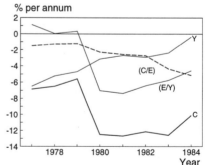

Figure 14.34. Decomposition of CO$_2$ emissions changes by Textiles: UK.

Paper and Printing (Figure 14.33) has shown consistently negative rates of change of CO_2 emissions, despite a Y component which has been positive for most of the period. The negative C/E and strongly negative E/Y components have more than countered the effect of this sector's growth in the value of output.

Textiles (Figure 14.34) have shown a very strongly negative rate of change in CO_2 emissions throughout the period, because of shrinkage in output, increasing energy efficiency, and a shift towards less carbon intensive fuels.

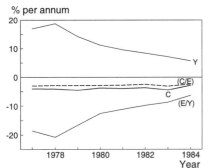

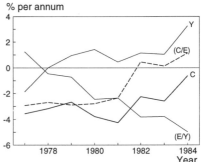

Figure 14.35. Decomposition of CO_2 emissions changes by Food: UK.

Figure 14.36. Decomposition of CO_2 emissions changes by Chemicals: UK.

The Food sector (Figure 14.35) exhibits a steadily negative rate of change of CO_2 emissions, driven almost entirely by a shift towards less carbon intensive fuels. The effects of changing sectoral output and energy efficiency almost exactly cancel out.

The Chemical sector (Figure 14.36) also shows negative rates of change of CO_2 emissions throughout the period, though by the end of the period the rates of decline are very small. Since 1978 the value of output has been increasing, while the E/Y ratio has been falling, at an accelerating rate. The upward trend in the rate of change of CO_2 emissions since 1981 can be largely attributed to the upward trend in the rate of change of the C/E ratio, which has been positive since 1982.

Finally, we look at the sector Other Industry (Figure 14.37). This contains a wide range of manufacturing not elsewhere included, such as Engineering, Metal Manufacture, etc. Here CO_2 emissions have been changing at a consistently negative rate throughout the period. However, the energy efficiency has ceased to improve in recent years, and seems now to be deteriorating. This has been countered by a negative rate of growth of output since 1981. The C/E ratio has been falling, at a small

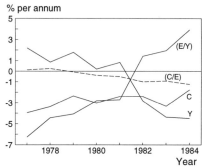

Figure 14.37. Decomposition of CO_2 emissions changes by Other Industry: UK.

but gently increasing rate.

The proportional annualised rates of change of CO_2 emissions, over the entire period, are summarised by sector in Table 14.2.

Table 14.2. Decomposition of CO_2 emissions, by sector, 1970-88: UK (% p.a.).

Percent per annum

UK (1964-88)	C	(C/E)	(E/Y)	Y	Remainder
Agriculture	-3.00	1.34	-1.74	-2.64	0.04
Services	1.11	0.66	-2.59	3.08	-0.03
Construction	0.39	-1.24	0.55	1.08	0.00
Transport	1.70	-0.06	1.07	0.69	0.00
Paper	-2.99	-1.49	-2.64	1.12	0.03
Textiles	-7.79	-3.17	-1.88	-2.64	-0.11
Food	-2.79	-3.60	-13.55	12.91	1.45
Chemicals	-1.68	-0.69	-2.18	1.18	0.01
Other Industry	-2.29	-0.21	-2.78	0.70	0.00

Only three sectors had increasing rates of CO_2 emissions: these were Services, Construction and Transport. All but Agriculture and Services showed a switch to less CO_2 intensive fuels, and only Construction and Transport seemed to become less energy efficient in their production.

14.5.11 Conclusions on Trends for Germany and the UK

The results of these analyses can be summarised as follows:

1. Both Germany and the UK have experienced a shift away from CO$_2$ intensive fuels in industry, although there has been a shift towards them by German households.

2. There has been a general improvement in energy efficiency in both countries and in industry as well as in households.

14.6   FUTURE TRENDS AND SCENARIOS

In the previous section we have discussed the development of CO$_2$ emissions up to the present. In the course of this, we determined the influence of fuel mix, of energy efficiency and of GDP. Now, with this knowledge we can assess not only how things may develop, but also how things *should* develop. There exists some feeling in politics and in economics that the development of CO$_2$ emissions should not be influenced by additional political measures. There is the hope that the economy will reduce the CO$_2$ emissions by itself. In contrast, there is some tendency to establish CO$_2$ reduction targets without consideration for the economic and political scope for action. We introduce a scenario in Section 14.6.1 which sets such unrealistic targets.

Finally, we wish to develop scenarios which seem *plausible* to us. We use the term *plausible* under the premise that the developments in these scenarios cannot occur by themselves, or without any friction, but that they are politically and economically possible.

Now we wish to present some results of our scenarios with respect to the achievement of the Toronto targets; i.e. we assess the possibility of a reduction of CO$_2$ emissions.[5] The assumptions of the scenarios consider the trends regarding the influential variables and the structural change; frequently they reflect historical trends. But we realise that the trends cannot be maintained over a long time period. Therefore, after a political decision regarding a definite scenario, the environmental and economic policy has to be implemented, so that the trends, stated in the scenario, are actually realised. We go into the fundamental political problems of the realisation of these measures in Sections 14.7 and 14.8.

In the five scenarios below we concentrate on the following issues:

1. change of the composition of final demand, for a given growth rate of total GDP,

2. improvement of energy efficiency,

3. change of the composition of the input of fossil fuel use, and

4. substitution from fossil fuel use to non-fossil.

Finally, we compare

5. the Toronto target with possible developments of the German and UK economies.

14.6.1 Changing the Structure of Final Demand for a Given Growth Rate

In our first scenario we have examined the transition from the present economy to a post-industrial, energy-saving economy. We assume a growth rate of 2% p.a. for GDP, like most studies of CO_2 reduction and its consequences.[6] We posit additionally an 8% p.a. increase in the final demand of the service sectors. The final demand for commodities produced in sectors 5 to 12 (i.e. electricity distribution, gas, water, coal, chemical products, etc.) is assumed to be cut proportionally, such that the overall growth rate of GDP (i.e. 2% p.a.) is maintained. Also, we assume that there is no change in the technology and the energy efficiency remains constant.

This radical change from the present structure to a post-industrial energy saving society yields impressive reductions in CO_2 emissions, by around 10% p.a. for Germany and 3.5% p.a. for the UK. Further, there is an increase in employment in both countries.

This transition exceeds the demands of the Toronto target. Whether these economies are ready to alter their behaviour correspondingly is more than doubtful. Therefore, we have examined alternative possibilities for the reduction of CO_2 emissions.

In a further scenario we assume that private car use is curtailed by 5% p.a., and is replaced by public transport. More specifically, we stipulate the following exogenous changes in final demand:

Sector 12:	Mineral oil processing	-3.0%
Sector 14:	Rubber products	-0.5%
Sector 23:	Motor Vehicles	-5.0%
Sector 41:	Construction	-1.0%
Sector 43:	Traffic and Transport Services	-5.0%
Sector 44:	Telecommunications	0.5%

Because of these changes in final demand, total CO_2 emissions are cut back by roughly 1% p.a. in both countries. Employment decreases slightly, by 0.6% p.a. in Germany and by 0.35% p.a. in the UK.

These scenarios have shown that a marked shift away from the primary sectors of the economy, towards a large and rapidly expanding services sector, and a dramatic switch from private to public transport, can cut CO_2 levels to reach the Toronto targets. We do not, however, expect these drastic changes to take place, because of the heavy adjustment costs, and habit persistence of the economic agents. This indicates that these scenarios are not politically attainable.

Therefore, we outline scenarios in the following sections, which are based on less strong structural changes. We analyse the consequences of the improvement of energy efficiency, changes in the structure of fossil fuel inputs within the fossil fuels, and the transition from fossil fuels to non-fossil fuels. Further, we make assumptions about the development of some sectors. In comparison to the assumptions above, the assumptions below are more moderate.

14.6.2   Improvements in Energy Efficiency

We now turn to a scenario which analyses a movement in industry from conventional average practice technologies, to best practice technologies. We stipulate reductions in fuel requirements for a given level of output by 2% p.a. This estimate agrees with results of engineering studies, and is in line with the assumptions of other studies.[7] The results are summarised in Table 14.3. We see that this transition can reduce the CO_2 emissions in both Germany and in the UK by around 1.4% p.a. This is sufficient to achieve the Toronto targets. Calculations regarding households imply further reduction of ca. 0.6% p.a. for both countries.

Table 14.3. CO_2 emission reductions by changing from average to best practice technology.

CO₂ Emission Changes (% p.a.)	Germany	UK
Electricity generation	-0.60	-0.72
Iron and steel industry	-0.03	-0.08
Building materials	-0.04	-0.03
Food processing industry	-0.03	-0.03
Chemical products industry	-0.10	-0.08
All sectors	-1.42	-1.38

14.6.3   Changing the Structure of the Fuel Mix Between Fossil Fuels

In a further scenario, the change in CO_2 emissions was examined, when we replace coal by gas. Table 14.4 shows that the CO_2 emissions in Germany fall around 11.9%. The result for the UK is quite similar: we consider a fall of ca. 11.1%. A simulation of a gas for coal strategy in electricity generation shows that CO_2 emissions decline by only 7-8%.

These scenarios indicate, however, that a complete substitution of coal with gas is not sufficient to reach the Toronto target. Therefore, we look at a transition from fossil fuels to non-fossil fuels in the following section.

Table 14.4. CO_2 emission reductions by changing fuel mix: Substitution of fossil fuels by gas in industry and final demand.

CO_2 Emission Changes (% p.a.)	Germany	UK
Gas for coal (industry)	-11.33	-9.80
Gas for coal (final demand)	-0.55	-1.27

14.6.4   Transition from Fossil Fuels to Non-Fossil Fuels

There are numerous possibilities for replacing fossil fuels by non-fossil fuels. To our knowledge, no complete assessment of all economic impacts of non-fossil fuels exists. But some studies compare the consequences of the substitution of coal-fired by nuclear power plants (Conrad and Henseler-Unger, 1986; Schmitt and Junk, 1984). Two comprehensive studies by the German Institute of Economic Research and the Fraunhofer Institute for Systems and Innovation research assess the potential of renewable energy sources (DIW/ISI, 1984, 1991).

We think the potential of renewable resources is high. At present, their use is mainly restricted to small decentralised units. Most renewable resources and technologies are not yet cost-effective.

We analyse a switch of the energy mix to non-fossil, non-CO_2 emitting fuel, by assuming that fossil fuel use is cut by 1% p.a. The results are the same for both countries: the CO_2 emissions decrease by some 0.7% in industry and by some 0.3% in direct final demand.

14.6.5   Toronto Target and Possible Developments of the Economy

Finally, we want to show the results of a scenario in which we consider the development of important parameters in the German and in the UK economy, which are compatible and plausible with data, engineering information and historical experience. In Table 14.5 the assumptions on sectoral growth rates are shown. Growth rates in all sectors not mentioned above are assumed to change proportionally, such that a 2.0% p.a. growth rate of total GDP is maintained.

The interesting question for this scenario is whether the Toronto target can be reached under these assumptions, i.e. a 20% reduction in CO_2 emissions to the year 2005 from the 1988 level. This target is transformed to an annual reduction of 1% over a time period of 20 years.

Table 14.5. Sectoral growth rate assumptions for the 'plausible scenarios'.

Industrial sector	Growth rate (% p.a.)
Agriculture	-1.0
Chemicals	2.0
Paper and printing	2.0
Textiles	0.0
Food	6.0
Construction	2.0
Transport	0.0
Services	4.0

Table 14.6. A sequence of 'plausible' scenarios for CO_2 emission reductions in Germany and the UK.

	Scenario	CO₂ Emission Changes (% p.a.)	
		Germany	UK
1.	**y** - Structure and level of final demand.	1.15	1.40
2.	**C** - Energy efficiency improvement: 2% p.a. (in all sectors).	-1.42	-1.38
3.	1 and 2 together.	-0.29	-0.01
4.	**P** - Energy efficiency improvement: 2 % p.a. (in all sectors).	-0.58	-0.62
5.	1 & 2 & 4.	-0.87	-0.63
6.	Switch to renewables:		
6a.	Industry: 0.5% p.a. decrease in fossil-fuel energy use.	-0.36	-0.35
6b.	Final demand: 0.5% p.a. decrease in fossil-fuel energy use.	-0.14	-0.15
7.	1 & 2 & 4 & 6.	-1.36	-1.13
8.	Loss of nuclear assumption: nuclear energy generation phased out slowly such that emissions increase by 1 M tonnes CO₂ p.a.	0.15	0.19
9.	1 & 2 & 4 & 6 & 8.	-1.22	-0.94
10.	1 & 2 & 4 & 6 & 8 Change in employment.	2.07	2.48

The results of these scenarios are summarised in Table 14.6.

1. Assuming a change in the structure of the economy as explained in Table 14.5, combined with a 2% p.a. rate of growth of GDP, this scenario yields increases in emissions of more than 1% p.a. in both countries.

2. Next we assume an increase of 2% p.a. in the efficiency of fuel use, in all industry sectors, which yields emissions declining by more than 1.3% p.a. in both countries.

3. Combining the simulation of (1) and (2) already gives positive CO_2 savings in both countries. Emissions reductions are higher in Germany than in the UK.

A 2% p.a. rate of growth of GDP, combined simultaneously with a 2% p.a. improvement in energy efficiency, leads to a ca. 0.3% p.a. reduction of CO_2 emissions in Germany. This improvement in energy efficiency offsets the increase of CO_2 emissions on the basis of the growth of GDP in the UK.

4. If we stipulate a 2% p.a. increase in energy efficiency of direct final demand fuel use, emissions decline by more than 0.6% p.a. in both countries.

5. Combining the results of (1), (2) and (4) yields a total of 0.87% p.a. CO_2 reductions in Germany and of 0.63% p.a. in the UK. These reductions are not large enough to reach the Toronto targets.

6. Thus we add a switch to renewable energy sources. We posit that wind, solar and hydropower utilisation increases, so as to decrease fossil fuel generated energy use by 0.5% p.a. Therefore emissions due to industrial sources decrease by some 0.35% p.a. and emissions due to direct final demand decline by some 0.15% p.a. in both countries.

7. Combination of (1), (2), (4) and (6) yields annual changes in emissions which surpass the Toronto targets considerably, in both countries (the reduction in Germany is 1.36% p.a. and in the UK 1.13% p.a.).

Before we discuss the results, we want to show another scenario, which takes into account a possible dropping out of nuclear power. Can we nevertheless reach the Toronto target?

8. Therefore we check whether we can afford to avoid nuclear fuels and assume a slow phasing out of nuclear energy generation. We posit that emissions due to increased use of fossil fuels, which make

up for the loss in nuclear fuels, do not surpass 1 M tonnes CO_2 per year. This policy increases emissions by almost 0.2% p.a. in both countries.

Summing up experiments (1), (2), (4), (6), and including the elimination of nuclear energy generation, we see that the Toronto target can still be met in Germany, and almost attained in the UK.

Even with a slow dropping out of nuclear energy generation, the results of the scenarios show that the Toronto targets can be attained under quite weak assumptions apart from the zero growth in the transport sector. This result is, on the one hand, surprising because the sceptics predominate in the discussion in Germany and the UK concerning the achievement of the Toronto target. On the other hand, the description of the past development of the economy in Germany and in the UK shows how economies react flexibly to changes.

Finally, we present the changes in employment for the combined experiment (1), (2), (4), (6) and (8). In both countries employment increases by more than 2% p.a.

The interpretation of the scenarios has to take into account the fact that these scenarios only give hints to the scope for action which can be used in both countries. However, the measures appear to us to be not only economically feasible, but also politically attainable. The structural changes in production, and the corresponding changes in behaviour regarding consumption, indicate that the present prosperity, and the growth of prosperity, can be maintained in both societies.

But the political enforcement is not easy. These difficulties cannot be deduced directly from the scenarios, as these do not show the problems which result from the enforcement of economic policy goals, such as the Toronto target. The implementation of the results of our scenarios through environmental policy, and the restrictions that emerge, are the subject of the next section.

14.7 POSSIBILITIES OF ECONOMIC CHANGE IN THE LONG-RUN

Whoever is, in some way, involved in the realisation of the Toronto targets, is confronted with fundamental problems, which can occur with any major environmental policy measure. We can say in general: effective environmental policy can be realised only in the long-run, because there are changes necessary in the behaviour of production and of consumption. Moreover, environment-friendly technologies have to be introduced, so that old capital goods are replaced by new capital goods. Also, production factors and products which are harmful to the environment need to be substituted by environment-friendly factors.[8] Therefore two prerequisites are necessary:

1. There must be a consensus available in the society, so that such an effective environmental policy can be realised; otherwise the difficulties in adapting are insurmountable (Faber and Manstetten, 1989; Faber and Michaelis, 1989; and cf. Chapter 4).

2. On the basis of the scope of the adjustment, a long time horizon must be given in which the transition to environment-friendly production and consumption methods can be carried out.

If both these prerequisites are satisfied, for the development of a comprehensive environmental policy, we have to examine which factors determine the economic changes. Measures are the size and the composition of the final demand of an economy. In turn, this determines the size of the Gross Domestic Product. The following influential variables are important in the short-run and in the medium-run:

(a) The short-run and medium-run preferences, which are determined by the social conventions of the society,

(b) the technology, which is used in combination with the existing capital goods of the society,

(c) the economic system and the social structure,

(d) the availability of natural resources in the long-run and in the medium-run.

The last two decades have shown us, through the greenhouse effect, ozone depletion and the destruction of the rain forests, that the prevailing orientation to the medium-term and short-term availability of resources is no longer sufficient. Instead, a long-term way of thinking has to be found.

We can consider the satisfaction of the cultural and historical needs as the goal of the economic activity. The exploitation of the natural environment was, and is, one of the fundamental means of achieving this goal. The connection between the satisfaction of needs and the natural environment is the production structure, characterised by the available technology and the existing capital goods, by the quantity and the nature of the consumption of resources, and by the accompanying pollution of the environment and the destruction of resources.

As a rule, the cultural and historical needs of a society are relatively fixed in the short and medium-run. Also, the available production structure and the stock of capital goods are relatively constant in the short and medium-run. Further, the natural environment has been seen not only as a supplier of resources, but also as a recipient of harmful products until recent years (Niemes, 1982). Neither shortage of resources, nor the capability of the environment to absorb harmful products, were seen as limitations.

However, it seems that in the long-run, the opposite to the short and medium-term point of view is the case; in the long-run the production structures can be changed to a large extent. Inventions of new environment-friendly techniques, and their innovation, can create new capital goods. Also, in the long-run the limitations of the environment are more and more obvious. The exhaustion of resources is discussed more frequently, as well as the limited capacity of the environment as a recipient of waste, as shown very clearly in the waste disposal industry nowadays. Therefore, the environment as a supplier of resources and as a recipient of waste has to be seen as a limiting factor for economic activity in the long-run.

Overall, and this assumption is perhaps most controversial, we hold the opinion that human needs are potentially extremely flexible in the long-run. We are confident, when society really recognises that the present pattern of production methods and consumption methods are not sustainable, that the goals of the society will change in a dramatic way. We leave open the issue of whether this will lead to an improvement or to a worsening of the human condition.

Finally, we note that the long-term description of the economic development of the German and UK economies shows the enormous potential and flexibility of both these societies in the past, to alter their production structures in the long-term. We use this as an opportunity to assume that this will also be the case in the future.

14.8   THE PROBLEMS AND POSSIBILITIES OF THE ACHIEVEMENT OF CO$_2$ EMISSIONS REDUCTION AIMS

14.8.1   Wish and Will: The Need for Consensus

In political reality there seems to exist a paradox concerning major environmental issues. Many people (e.g. 86% of a representative sample in Germany in 1990 poll) consider that the environmental problem is most important. Nevertheless, no really drastic policy change has been carried through. How can this paradox be explained? The results of the survey indicate that people *wish* for a better environment, and for protection against future environmental catastrophes. Nevertheless this desire is not considered in the policy to a corresponding degree. Willingness is obviously lacking to carry out fully the desired change, with all the consequences which arise from this change. We have the opinion that the *will* is lacking for this change. Against the background of this terminology - *wish* vs. *will* - the survey shows the *wish* for change; but this *wish* is, however, not the *will*. Such situations, which can be characterised by the terms *wish* and *will*, are well-known from history. For example, in 1941 many Americans had the wish to contribute to the ending of the Nazi Regime under Hitler in Germany. But only after the Japanese attack on Pearl Harbour had taken place did the majority of the people of the United States have the will to undertake all the necessary actions: the building up of a war-time economy, the recruiting, etc.

It is our contention that major environmental changes would similarly lead to structural change, of production methods in particular, and of economic behaviour in general. Of course, this would not occur in such a drastic way and in such a short time period of only four years, as for the American experience in World War II, but instead more gradually and over a much longer time period (i.e. over several decades).

The main economic reason why such major changes in environmental policy lead to frictions and, in many instances, are painful, is that it causes structural change. This in turn leads to at least income and wealth redistribution, because of rising unemployment and decreasing profits in some sectors of the economy, and vice versa in others. It is evident that on short-run or medium-run considerations, there will be at least a strong and very active minority, if not even a majority, which is against any drastic changes leading to such negative consequences concerning their economic welfare.

However, this part of the population may also be convinced to agree to such changes if longer time horizons are taken into account. Only then is it possible to transform the *wish* for better environmental conditions, into a *will*, which leads to corresponding actions over long periods.

We consider one means to achieve this aim politically is to change the constitution (be it written, as in Germany, or unwritten as in the UK). This can only be done in general if there is a wide *consensus*, of at least two-thirds of the population.

14.8.2 Reductions in CO_2 Emissions: Local, National and Global Levels

The greenhouse effect is a global problem, since the CO_2 emissions are into the global atmosphere, and have global effects. Hence a reduction on a local or national level has an extremely small effect on the total amount of CO_2 emissions, and almost no impact for the well-being of those who made the reductions, even in the long-run. Therefore, we are confronted with a repeated 'Prisoners' Dilemma' situation: in particular we face the problem of the 'Free Rider'. This always occurs if a public good has to be supplied. It is supposed to be 'rational' to let others make the effort and to enjoy the benefits without incurring any costs.

So one might ask: 'What use is it if Germany or the UK reduce their CO_2 emissions, while other countries do not?' The answer to this question is not easy. However, for its solution we consider the following aspects to be pertinent.

1. The industrialised countries have been responsible for about 80% of the CO_2 emissions in the past. This means that they have made use of too great a part of the Earth's common capacity to absorb CO_2. Hence, the industrialised countries have, from the point of justice and fairness, good reasons to be first in reducing CO_2 emissions.

2. The industrialised countries have the highest incomes. It is well known that 'environmental quality' is one of those goods which are demanded only after the elementary wants have been satisfied. Therefore one cannot expect all countries in the world to start at the same time to reduce CO_2 emissions.

3. The industrial countries have not only the means, in terms of income and wealth, but also the know-how to invent and innovate appropriate techniques, as well as the know-how and institutions to implement corresponding legislation, be it in terms of emission limits or via taxes or permits.

4. Finally, it is worth noting that those who start first, although they carry the considerable start-up costs, later have great advantages. This is so because they can export the corresponding techniques, and also because they have made the structural adjustments earlier. A telling example of the latter case is a statement in the *Financial Times* that the UK chemical companies complain that they are no longer competitive with their German rivals. The reason they give is the following: in Germany the adjustment to stringent water purity

legislation took place in the 1970s and early 1980s, so the German companies have already adjusted their operations, techniques and capital stock, via investment, while the UK companies now face this investment as UK legislation comes into force.

14.8.3 Environmental Political Measures for the Reduction of CO_2 Emissions

The sectoral analysis of the last three decades (Section 14.5) has shown how flexible the economy is, and how different are the contributions of individual sectors to the total development of CO_2 emissions.

Information about the different types of flexibility of the individual sectors, and about the quantitative influences of the three influential variables (the fuel mix (C/E), the energy efficiency (E/Y) and the sectoral contributions to the GDP (Y)) on the amount of the CO_2 emissions, is a decisive prerequisite for an effective environmental policy, which really leads to a reduction of CO_2 emissions. This information allows us:

1. to determine those sectors which make large contributions to the total CO_2 emissions,

2. to determine the influential variables, which are responsible for the high CO_2 emissions and

3. to develop environmental policy measures on the basis of (1) and (2).

These measures can be regulation orientated or market orientated. In the former case regulations and bans are used to guide economic behaviour directly. This procedure can be used for the whole economy, for households, for industry and for individual sectors. In contrast, market measures influence economic behaviour indirectly, by incentives such as taxes on CO_2 emissions.[9] The basis for assessment for such a tax is the emission of a harmful product. In the course of this, the emitter has to pay a fixed tax per unit of harmful product.

Another market instrument for environmental policy is the use of licences/certificates. Here, the emitter gets the right, in the form of a licence, to emit waste products such as CO_2 emissions. These licences can be traded on a corresponding market. Now the question arises for the emitter whether he should keep the licence, or whether he should reduce his emissions and sell any remaining certificates.

Similar to the tax, legal regulation by certificates is replaced by an economic decision-making calculation. Through this the different possibilities of firms to reduce emissions are explicitly taken into account. In particular the distinct cost structures for the avoidance of emissions are taken into consideration. The market-economy instruments guarantee that the environmental policy aim can be achieved more cheaply, in comparison with regulations for all firms.

However, a combination of regulative laws and economic instruments are frequently useful in practical environmental policy. In particular this is valid if emissions endanger human beings and the environment. Regulative laws have the effect of an 'emergency brake', and guarantee that some minimum requirements are not fallen below and that no regions of high pollution emerge (so called 'hot spots').

However, this case does not apply to the problem of CO_2 emissions. The scope for using regulative laws is limited, because regulations could not give large-scale reduction of CO_2 emissions. Therefore market instruments must be used to attain major reductions of CO_2 emissions.

Apart from the advantages of lower costs, mentioned above, there are also some other advantages:

1. A carbon tax corrects an economic distortion which arises because of externalities, owing to excessive use of environmental services. To avoid large income and wealth redistribution, it is important that the carbon tax is fiscally neutral. Since an effective carbon tax would lead to large revenues, this should be used to lower other taxes, especially those which are particularly allocatively distorting (see Symons, Proops and Gay, 1994).

2. However, there also exists an advantage to the existence of large carbon tax revenues. It is expected that if a 'carbon convention' is to be established, the core of such a convention will need to be the allocation of reduction targets for CO_2 emissions between the different countries concerned. To persuade the less developed countries to participate in such a convention, some sort of side payments will be necessary. This could be done in a similar way as under the Montreal protocol for the protection of the ozone layer by the elimination of CFCs. In the latter case the developed countries have established a fund, from which the less developed countries can receive subsidies to adjust their technologies appropriately.

The most commonly discussed disadvantage of a CO_2 tax is the problem of its ecological efficiency. To reach the emission target, one has to calculate the correct corresponding tax rate. However, this cannot be calculated accurately, because of problems of information availability. Therefore some economists prefer the certificate solution because the ecological aim can be exactly set in advance by the quantity of certificates distributed.

However, in our opinion this is not a strong argument in regard to the lack of ecological efficiency. Therefore we wish to develop general criteria, which can be used for the development and the assessment of environmental political proposals and instruments.[10]

1. Environmental policy should be economically efficient: i.e. it should attain the aim with minimum costs, and the policy should encourage CO_2 saving techniques.

2. The measures need to be flexible so that it should be easy to adapt these policy measures when new knowledge becomes available.

3. Large income and wealth redistributions should be avoided as far as possible, because their occurrence always creates great resistance to the implementation of environmental policies.

4. Because of its complexity, an economic system needs much time to adapt itself to a new framework if no large frictions are to occur. Therefore new legislation should not come into force within a short time-span. Instead, it should be announced well in advance and implemented gradually.

5. It is important to employ instruments with which a country has some experience. This is, of course, particularly the case if the country has implemented a particular instrument. In this case the economic agents already have some familiarity with this means of environmental regulation, so have already developed the institutions and monitoring systems appropriate to the environmental legislation.

These five criteria need to be taken into account when one assesses different environmental policy options and instruments. It is not so important to achieve the environmental policy aim with the 'theoretically' best instrument. The debate about the instrument is important, but as observers we sometimes get the impression that the participants are so involved in the intricate details of their discussion, that they lose sight of the aim of the debate, which is the reduction of CO_2 emissions.

The crucial question is whether we have the *will* to carry out the necessary changes in our economy. Because we can forecast future developments in principle only to a limited extent, it is important to give economic agents signals in the right direction. This means, in our context, a price increase for fossil fuels. Whether this is carried out by a CO_2 tax, by the taxation of primary energy, or by tradeable emissions licences, is also of no great importance.

Experience concerning water legislation in Germany shows that, despite great 'theoretical' deficiencies, adaptation by the industry and consumers has been far beyond what was originally expected (Brown and Johnson, 1982).

At the end of this section we note a suggestion of Michaelis (1992). The environmental policy discussions in the context of the greenhouse gases concentrate on CO_2 emissions first and foremost. However, we know from the results of climate research that as well as CO_2, further trace gases contribute to the greenhouse effect, such as methane and chlorofluorocarbons. The greenhouse potential of these gases is much higher than of CO_2, molecule for molecule. Therefore an efficient climate policy from the economic point of view has to account for all these trace gases. Because the costs of the avoidance of the individual trace gases are different, a mix of the reduction of all these gases is economically cheaper as a rule than the reduction of CO_2 emissions alone.

14.9   CONCLUDING REMARKS

Our study has shown the potential for economies to reduce anthropogenic CO_2 emissions substantially, through structural changes. But this structural change has to be supported by appropriate environmental and economic policy measures. We note that there is a fortunate three-fold tendency available for further advancement by policy makers. The three components are:

1.   A shift away from coal, and towards less CO_2 intensive oil and, especially, gas.

2.   Improvements in the efficiency of energy use, particularly for use in production, and to a lesser extent by households.

3.   A shift from heavy manufacturing towards more service and 'information' based economic activity.

These already existing trends could be encouraged in a number of relatively easily implemented ways. For example, numerous studies have shown that 'carbon taxes' are likely to lead to changed consumer behaviour, and changed techniques of production, which would substantially reduce CO_2 emissions.

In particular, we believe that the industrialised countries should recognise and accept their responsibility, because they are responsible for 80% of the greenhouse effect through their emissions. They should start to develop a common environmental policy to reduce their CO_2 emissions substantially.

Whether we achieve the Toronto target, is a question of our *will*. If this *will* is available in our societies, then our scenarios demonstrate that the economy has enough flexibility to attain the Toronto target. For this we require an environmental policy which is orientated towards long-term aims, to allow the necessary economic adaptation with the least possible friction. We believe the economic costs of such adaptation are much smaller than generally assumed.

NOTES

1. We can observe a similar concern regarding the destruction of the ozone layer.
2. One needs to take care that secondary fuels, particularly electricity, are dealt with appropriately. Thus the fossil fuels burnt in electricity generation should not count as contributing only to CO_2 emission from the production sector. CO_2 emissions by electricity generation need to be distributed between production activity and households according to the energy use.
3. For more information see Proops, Faber and Wagenhals (1993:Chapter 5, Section 5.7).
4. In Figures 14.23 and 14.24 and also in the remaining figures of this section, the proportional rates of change are calculated as eight-year proportional rates of change. This reduces fluctuations in the data. The actual rates of change may have been negative, for example in Germany in 1982.
5. A 47-sector input-output model for Germany and the UK is the basis for these scenarios. An extensive description of this model can be found in Proops, Faber and Wagenhals (1993).
6. Hoeller, Dean and Nicolaisen (1991) present a survey of the most important studies.
7. A survey of CO_2 saving techniques can be found in OECD (1989b); compare Maier and Angerer (1986) and Kolb et al. (1989).
8. Compare the studies of Niemes (1982), Maier (1984), Wodopia (1986), Stephan (1989), Michaelis (1991), Schmutzler (1991), Proops, Faber and Wagenhals (1993).
9. For a comparison between regulative instruments and market instruments, see Faber, Stephan and Michaelis (1989:Chapter 7).
10. Such criteria were developed in Faber, Stephan and Michaelis (1989:Chapter 19).

References

Albert, H. (1978) *Traktat über rationale Praxis*. J.C.B. Mohr (Paul Siebeck), Tübingen.

Alchian, A.A. (1950) Uncertainty, evolution, and economic theory. *Journal of Political Economy* 58:211-222.

Alchian, A.A. and Allen, W.R. (1974) *University Economics* (3rd edn.). Prentice-Hall, London.

Allen, P.M. (1988) Evolution, innovation and economics. In: G. Dosi et al. (eds.), *Technical Change and Economic Theory*. New York.

Allen, P.M. and Sanglier, M. (1981) Urban evolution, self-organisation, and decision making. *Environment and Planning A* 13:167-183.

Allen, T.F.H. and Starr, T.B. (1982) *Hierarchy: Perspectives for Ecological Complexity*. University of Chicago Press, Chicago.

Amir, S. (1994) The role of thermodynamics in the study of economic and ecological systems. *Ecological Economics* 10:125-142.

Anderson, P.W., Arrow, K.J. and Pines, D. (eds.) (1988) *The Economy as an Evolving Complex System*. Addison-Wesley, New York.

Aristotle (1925) *The Nicomachean Ethics* (trans. D. Ross). Oxford University Press, Oxford.

Aristotle (1894) *Ethica Nicomachea* (ed. L. Bywater). Oxford University Press, Oxford.

Aristotle (1956) *De Anima* (ed. W.D. Ross). Oxford University Press, Oxford.

Aristotle (1970) *Physics* (trans. W. Charlton). Books I and II. Clarendon Press, Oxford.

Aristotle (1972) *Die Nikomachische Ethik* (trans. and ed. O. Gigon). München.

Aristotle (1973) *Politics* (trans. and ed. O. Gigon). München.

Aristotle (1984) *Politics* (trans. C. Lord). University of Chicago Press, Chicago.

Arrow, K.J. (1968) Optimal capital policy with irreversible investment. In: J.N. Wolfe (ed.), *Value, Capital and Growth: Papers in Honour of Sir John Hicks*, Edinburgh University Press, Edinburgh.

Arthur, W.B. (1989) Competing technologies, increasing returns, and lock-in by historical events. *Economic Journal* 99:116-131.

Aschenberg, R. (1978) Über transzendentale Argumente. Orientierung in einer Diskussion zu Kant und Strawson. *Philosophisches Jahrbuch* 85:331-358.

Augustine, A. (1961) *Confessions* (trans. R.S. Pine-Coffin). Penguin, Middlesex.

Augustine, A. (undated) *The Confessions of St. Augustine* (trans. E.P. Pusey). Dent, London.

Ayer, A.J. (1954) *Language, Truth and Logic*. Gollancz, London.

Ayres, R.U. (1994) *Information, Entropy and Progress: A New Evolutionary Paradigm*. American Institute of Physics Press, New York.

Ayres, R.U. and Kneese, A.V. (1969) Production, consumption and externalities. *American Economic Review* 59:282-297.

Ayres, R.U. and Martinás, K. (1994) A non-equilibrium evolutionary economic theory. In: P. Burley and J. Foster (eds.).

Ayres, R.U. and Nair, I. (1984) Thermodynamics and economics. *Physics Today* 37:62-71.

Ayres, R.U. and Sandilya, M.S. (1987) Utility maximization and catastrophe aversion: a simulation test. *Journal of Environmental Economics and Management* 14:337-370.

Bakker, R.T. (1983) The deer flees and the wolf pursues: incongruencies in predator-prey coevolution. In: D.J. Futuyama and M. Slatkin (eds.), *Coevolution*, Sinauer, Sunderland, Mass.

Balian, R. (1991) *From Microphysics to Macrophysics I*. Springer-Verlag, Heidelberg.

Baron, V. (1993) L'expérience métaphysique. *Kant-Studien* 84:25-37.

Beltrami, E. (1987) *Mathematics for Dynamic Modelling*. Academic Press, New York.

Benjamin, W. (1977) Über das Programm der kommenden Philosophie. In: R. Tiedemann and H. Schweppenhäuser (eds.), *Gesammelte Werke* Vol. II, Suhrkamp, Frankfurt.

Bernholz, P. and Breyer, F. (1984) *Grundlagen der Politischen Ökonomie*. Mohr (Paul Siebeck), Tübingen.

Bernholz, P. and Faber, M. (1988) Reflection on a normative economic theory of the unification of law. In: J.D. Gwartney, R.E. Waagner (eds.), *Public Choice and Constitutional Economics*. JAS Press, London.

Bertalanffy, L. von (1950) The theory of open systems in physics and biology. *Science* 111:23-26.

Bianciardi, C., Donati, A. and Ulgiati, S. (1993) On the relationship between the economic process, the Carnot cycle and the Entropy Law. *Ecological Economics* 8:7-10.

Bianciardi, C., Tiezzi, E. and Ulgiati, S. (1993) Complete recycling of matter in the framework of physics, biology and ecological economics. *Ecological Economics* 8:1-5.

Bianciardi, C., Tiezzi, E. and Ulgiati, S. (1994) Recycling of matter: a reply. *Ecological Economics* 9:192-193.

Binswanger, H.-C. (1985) *Geld und Magie. Deutung und Kritik der modernen Wirtschaft anhand von Goethes Faust*. Edition Weitbrecht, Stuttgart.

Binswanger, H.-C., Faber, M. and Manstetten, R. (1990) The dilemma of modern man and nature: an exploration of the Faustian imperative. *Ecological Economics* 2:197-223.

Binswanger, M. (1992) *Information und Entropie: ökologische Perspektiven des Übergangs zu einer Informationsgesellschaft*. Campus, Frankfurt am Main.

Binswanger, M. (1993) From microscopic to macroscopic theories: entropic aspects of ecological and economic processes. *Ecological Economics* 8:209-234.

Boltzmann, L. (1877) *Wiener Berichte* 76:373ff.

Boulding, K.E. (1970) *Economics as a Science*. McGraw-Hill, New York.

Boulding, K.E. (1981) *Evolutionary Economics*. Sage, London.

Bremer, D. (1993) Die Grundlegung einer Ethik der Wissenschaft in der frühgriechischen Philosophie. *Philosophisches Jahrbuch* 100:317-336.

Brittan, G.G. (1978) *Kant's Theory of Science*. Princeton University Press, Princeton, New Jersey.

Broadie, S. (1991) *Ethics with Aristotle*. Oxford University Press, Oxford.

Brown, G.M. and Johnson, R.W. (1982) Pollution control by effluent charges: it works in the Federal Republic of Germany, why not in the USA? *Natural Resource Journal* 22:929-966.

Buchanan, J.M. and Tullock, G. (1962) *The Calculus of Consent. Logical Foundations of Constitutional Democracy*. University of Michigan Press, Ann Arbor.

Burley, P. and Foster, J. (eds.) (1994) *Economics and Thermodynamics: New Perspectives on Economic Analysis*. Kluwer, Dordrecht.

Burness, H.S., Cummings, R.G., Morris, G. and Paik, I. (1980) Thermodynamic and economic concepts as related to resource-use policies. *Land Economics* 56:1-9.

Carnot, S. (1824) *Réflexions sur la puissance motrice de feu et sur les machines propres à développer cette puissance*. Bachelier, Paris.

Carr, E.H. (1961) *What is History?* Penguin, Middlesex.

Carson, R. (1982) *Silent Spring*. Penguin, Middlesex.

Chapman, P. (1975) *Fuel's Paradise? Energy Options for Britain*. Penguin, Middlesex.

Christie, J.R. (1994) A survey of thermodynamical ideas. In: P. Burley and J. Foster (eds.).

Clark, C.W. (1976) *Mathematical Bioeconomics*. Wiley, New York.

Clark, N. and Juma, C. (1987) *Long-Run Economics: An Evolutionary Approach to Economic Growth*. Pinter, London.

Clausius, R. (1854) *Fortschritte der Physik* 10.

Clausius, R. (1865) *Annalen der Physik* 125:353ff.

Common, M. (1988) 'Poverty and Progress' revisited. In: D. Collard, D.W. Pearce and D. Ulph (eds.), *Economics, Growth and Sustainable Environments*. Macmillan, London.

Commoner, B. (1971) *The Closing Circle*. Knopf, New York.

Conrad, K. and Henseler-Unger, I. (1986) The economic impact of coal-fired versus nuclear power plants: an application of a general equilibrium model. *Energy Journal* 7:51-63.

Cooper, J.M. (1975) *Reason and Human Good in Aristotle*. Harvard University Press, Cambridge, Mass.

Costanza, R. (1981), Embodied energy, energy analysis, and economics. In: H.E. Daly (ed.), *Energy, Economics, and the Environment*. Westview Press, Boulder, Colorado.

Costanza, R. (1984) Natural resource valuation and management: toward an ecological economics. In: A.-M. Jansson (ed.).

Costanza, R. (ed.) (1991) *Ecological Economics: The Science and Mangement of Sustainability*. Columbia University Press, New York.

Costanza, R., Norton, B. and Haskell, B. (eds.) (1992) *Ecosystem Health: New Goals for Environmental Management*. Island Press, Washington, D.C.

Cotgrove, S. (1982) *Catastrophe or Cornucopia*. Wiley, New York.

Crosby, A.W. (1986) *Ecological Imperialism*. Cambridge University Press, Cambridge.

Cusa, Nicholas of (1964) *De Docta Ignorantia* (Die belehrte Unwissenheit). P. Wilpert (ed.), Verlag von Felix Meiner, Hamburg.

Cyert, M. and March, J.G. (1963) *A Behavioural Theory of the Firm.* Prentice-Hall, Englewood Cliffs.

Dahl, R.A. (1956) *A Preface to Democratic Theory.* University of Chicago Press, Chicago.

Daly, H.E. (ed.) (1973) *Toward a Steady State Economy.* Freeman, San Francisco.

Daly, H.E. (1977) *Steady State Economics.* Freeman, San Francisco.

Daly, H.E. (ed.) (1980) *Economics, Ecology, Ethics.* Freeman, San Francisco.

Daly, H.E. (1986) Thermodynamic and economic concepts as related to resource-use policies: comment. *Land Economics* 62:319-322.

Daly, H.E. (1992) Is the entropy law relevant to the economics of natural resource scarcity? Yes, of course it is! *Journal of Environmental Economics and Management* 23:91-95.

Dasgupta, P.S. (1982) *The Control of Resources.* Blackwell, Oxford.

Dasgupta, P.S. and Heal, G.M. (1969) *Economic Theory and Exhaustible Resources.* Cambridge University Press, Cambridge.

Debreu, G. (1959) *The Theory of Value.* Wiley, New York.

Dechema, A. (1990) *Produktionsintegrierter Umweltschutz in der chemischen Industrie.* Frankfurt am Main.

DIW/ISI (1984) *Erneuerbare Energiequellen. Abschätzung des Potentials in der Bundesrepublik Deutschland bis zum Jahre 2000.* Berlin: Deutsches Institut für Wirtschaftsforschung, und Karlsruhe: Fraunhofer Institute for Systems and Innovation Research.

DIW/ISI (1991) *Kostenaspekte erneuerbarer Energiequellen in der Bundesrepublik Deutschland und auf Exportmärkten.* Untersuchung im Auftrage des Bundesministers für Forschung und Technologie.

Dorfman, R. and Dorfman, N. (eds.) (1977) *Economics of the Environment.* Norton, New York.

Dosi, G. and Nelson, R.R. (1994) An introduction to evolutionary theories in economics. *Journal of Evolutionary Economics* 4:153-172.

Dyke, C. (1988) Cities as dissipative structures. In: B.H. Weber, D.J. Depew and J.D. Smith (eds.).

Dyke, C. (1994) From entropy to economy: a thorny path. In: P. Burley and J. Foster (eds.).

Ebeling, W., Engel, A. and Feistel, R. (1990) *Physik der Evolutionsprozesse.* Akademie-Verlag, Berlin.

Eckermann, J.P. (1948) *Gespräche mit Goethe.* Artemis-Verlags-AG, Zürich.

Eddington, A.S. (1928) *The Nature of the Physical World.* Cambridge University Press, Cambridge.

Edgeworth, F.Y. (1881) *Mathematical Psychics.* Kegan Paul, London.

Edmonds, J. and Reilly, J.M. (1985) *Global Energy: Assessing the Future.* Oxford University Press, Oxford.

Ehrlich, P.R. (1989) The limits to substitution: meta-resource depletion and a new economic-ecological paradigm. *Ecological Economics* 1:9-16.

Ehrlich, P.R. and Ehrlich, A.H. (1972) *Population, Environment, Resources.* Freeman, San Francisco.

El Serafy, S. (1991) The environment as capital. In: R. Costanza (ed.).

Eppler, D. and Lave, L. (1980) Helium investments in the future. *The Bell Journal of Economics* 11:617-630.

Faber, M. (1979) *Introduction to Modern Austrian Capital Theory*. Springer-Verlag, Heidelberg.

Faber, M. (1985) A biophysical approach to the economy: entropy, environment and resources. In: W. van Gool and J.J.C. Bruggink (eds.).

Faber, M. (ed.) (1986) *Studies in Austrian Capital Theory, Investment and Time*. Springer-Verlag, Heidelberg.

Faber, M., Jöst, F. and Manstetten, R. (1995) Limits and perspectives on the concept of sustainable development. *Economie Appliqée* 48:233-251.

Faber, M., Jöst, F. and Müller-Fürstenberger, G. (1995) Umweltschutz und effizienz in der chemishen Industrie: Eine empirische untersuchung mit Fallstudien. *Zeitschrift für angewandte Umweltforschung* 8:168-179.

Faber, M. and Manstetten, R. (1988) Der Ursprung der Ökonomie als Bestimmung und Begrenzung ihrer Erkenntnisperspektive. *Schweizerische Zeitschrift für Volkswirtschaft und Statistik* 2:97-121.

Faber, M. and Manstetten, R. (1989) Rechtsstaat und Umweltschutz aus ökonomischer Sicht. *Zeitschrift für angewandte Umweltpolitik* 3:361-371.

Faber, M., Manstetten, R. and Proops, J.L.R. (1992a) Humankind and the environment: an anatomy of surprise and ignorance. *Environmental Values* 1:217-241.

Faber, M., Manstetten, R. and Proops, J.L.R. (1992b) Toward an open future: ignorance, novelty and evolution. In: R. Costanza, B. Norton and B. Haskell (eds.).

Faber, M., Manstetten, R. and Proops, J.L.R. (1995) On the foundations of ecological economics: a teleological approach. *Ecological Economics* 12:41-54.

Faber, M. and Michaelis, P. (1989) Änderung der Produktions- und Verbrauchsweise durch Umweltabgaben am Beispiel der Abfallwirtschaft. In H.G. Nutzinger and A. Zahrnt (eds.), *Ökosteuern. Umweltsteuern und -abgaben in der Diskussion*. C.F. Müller, Karlsruhe.

Faber, M., Niemes, H. and Stephan, G. (1983) *Umweltschutz und Input-Output Analyse. Mit zwei Fallstudien aus der Wassergütewirtschaft* (Environmental Protection and Input-Output Analysis. With Two Case Studies in Water-Quality Management). J.C.B. Mohr, Tübingen.

Faber, M., Niemes, H. and Stephan, G. (1987) *Entropy, Environment and Resources: An Essay in Physico-Economics*. Springer-Verlag, Heidelberg.

Faber, M. and Proops, J.L.R. (1985) Interdisciplinary research between economists and physical scientists: retrospect and prospect. *Kyklos* 38:599-616.

Faber, M. and Proops, J.L.R. (1986) Time irreversibilities in economics: some lessons from the natural sciences. In: M. Faber (ed.).

Faber, M. and Proops, J.L.R. (1989) Time irreversibility in economic theory: a conceptual discussion. *Seoul Journal of Economics* 2:109-129

Faber, M. and Proops, J.L.R. (1991a) Evolution in biology, physics and economics: a conceptual analysis. In: S. Metcalfe and P. Saviotti (eds.), *Evolutionary Theories of Economic and Technological Change*. Harwood, London.

Faber, M. and Proops, J.L.R. (1991b) National acounting, time and the environment: a neo-Austrian approach. In: R. Costanza (ed.).

Faber, M. and Proops, J.L.R. (1991c) The innovation of techniques and the time horizon. *Structural Change and Economic Dynamics* 2:143-158.

Faber, M. and Proops, J.L.R. (1993a) *Evolution, Time Production and the Environment* (2nd edn.). Springer-Verlag, Heidelberg.

Faber, M. and Proops, J.L.R. (1993b) Natural resource rents, economic dynamics and structural change: a capital theoretic approach. *Ecological Economics* 8:17-44.

Faber, M., Proops, J.L.R., Ruth, M. and Michaelis, P. (1990) Economy-environment interactions in the long-run: a neo-Austrian approach. *Ecological Economics* 2:27-55.

Faber, M. and Stephan, G. (1987) Umweltschutz und Technologiewandel. In: R. Henn (ed.), *Technologie, Wachstum und Beschäftigung, Festschrift für Lotar Späth.* Springer-Verlag, Heidelberg.

Faber, M., Stephan, G. and Michaelis, P. (1989) *Umdenken in der Abfallwirtschaft* (2nd. edn.). Springer-Verlag, Heidelberg.

Faber, M. and Wagenhals, G. (1988) Towards a long-run balance between economics and environmental protection. In: W. Salomon and U. Förstner (eds.), *Environmental Impact and Management of Time Tailings and Dredged Material.* Springer-Verlag, Heidelberg.

Fehl, U. (1983) Die Theorie dissipativer Strukturen als Ansatzpunkt für die Analyse von Innovationsproblemen in alternativen Wirtschaftsordnungen. In: A. Schüler, H. Leipold and H. Hamel (eds.), *Innovationsprobleme in Ost und West. Schriften zum Vergleich von Wirtschaftsordnungen.* Gustav Fischer Verlag, Stuttgart.

Fisher, I. (1892) Mathematical investigations in the theory of value and prices. *Transactions of the Connecticut Academy of Arts and Sciences* 9:11-126.

Förstner, U. (1990) *Umweltschutztechnik.* Springer-Verlag, Heidelberg.

Freemann, A. (1984) The quasi-option value of irreversible development. *Journal of Environmental Economics and Management* 11:292-295.

Funtowicz, S.O. and Ravetz, J.R. (1990) *Uncertainty and Quality in Science for Policy.* Kluwer, Dordrecht.

Funtowicz, S.O. and Ravetz, J.R. (1991) A new scientific methodology for global environmental issues. In: R. Costanza (ed.).

Gadamer, H.-G. (1972) *Wahrheit und Methode.* J.C.B. Mohr (Paul Siebeck), Tübingen.

Gal-Or, B. (ed.) (1974) *Modern Developments in Thermodynamics.* Wiley, New York.

Georgescu-Roegen, N. (1971) *The Entropy Law and the Economic Process.* Harvard University Press, Cambridge, Mass.

Georgescu-Roegen, N. (1979) Energy analysis and economic valuation. *Southern Economic Journal* 45:1023-1058.

Georgescu-Roegen, N. (1986) The entropy law and the economic process in retrospect. *Eastern Economic Journal* 12:3-23.

Gigon, A. (1981) Phronesis und Sophia in der Nikomachischen Ethik des Aristoteles. In: C. Mueller-Goldingen (ed.), *Schriften zur aristotelischen Ethik.* Olms, Hildesheim.

Gilliland, M.W. (1975) Energy analysis and public policy. *Science* 189:1051-1056.

Glansdorf, P. and Prigogine, I. (1971) *Thermodynamic Theory of Structure, Stability and Fluctuations.* Wiley, New York.

Gleick, J.W. (1988) *Chaos: Making a New Science.* Heinemann, London.

Gödel, M. (1931) Über formal unentscheidar Sätze der *Principia Mathematica* und verwandte Systeme. *Monatsh. für Math. u. Phys.* 38:173-198.

Goethe, J.W. (1879) *Faust. Eine Tragödie.* Gustav Hempel, Berlin.

Goethe, J.W. (1908) *Faust*, Parts I and II (trans. A.G. Latham). Dent, London.

Gool, W. van and Bruggink, J.J.C. (eds.) (1985) *Energy and Time in the Economic and Physical Sciences*. North-Holland, Amsterdam.

Gould, S.J. (1989) *Wonderful Life: The Burgess Shale and the Nature of History*. Penguin, Middlesex.

Guckenheimer, J. and Holmes, P. (1983) *Nonlinear Oscillations, Dynamical Systems and Bifurcations of Vector Fields*. Springer-Verlag, Heidelberg.

Habermas, J. (1968) *Erkenntnis und Interesse*. Suhrkamp, Frankfurt am Main (*Knowledge and Human Interests* (trans. J.J. Shapiro), Heinemann, London, 1972).

Hannon, B. (1973) The structure of ecosystems. *Journal of Theoretical Biology* 41:535-546.

Hannon, B. (1985a) Time value in ecosystems. In: W. van Gool and J.J.C. Bruggink (eds.).

Hannon, B. (1985b) World Shogun. *Journal of Social and Biological Structures* 8:329-341.

Hannon, B., Ruth, M. and Delucia, E. (1993) A physical view of sustainability. *Ecological Economics* 8:253-268.

Hartwick, J.M. and Olewiler, N.D. (1986) *The Economics of Natural Resource Use*. Harper and Row, New York.

Hawking, S.W. (1988) *A Brief History of Time*. Bantam, London.

Hayek, F.A. (1972) *Die Theorie komplexer Phänomene*. Mohr (Paul Siebeck), Tübingen.

Hegel, G.W.F. (1821) *Grundlinien der Philosophie der Rechts oder Naturrecht und Staatswissenschaften im Grundrisse*. Suhrkamp-Verlag, Frankfurt am Main.

Heidegger, M. (1927/1979) *Sein und Zeit*. Max Niemeyer Verlag, Tübingen.

Heilbroner, R. (1990) Analysis and vision in the history of modern economic thought. *Journal of Economic Literature* 28:1097-1114.

Heinrich, B. (1979) *Bumblebee Economics*. Harvard University Press, Cambridge, Mass.

Helmholtz, H. von (1847) *Lecture at the Physical Society at Berlin Über die Erhaltung der Kraft*. Reprinted in: H. von Helmholtz (1899) *Über die Erhaltung der Kraft*, Leipzig.

Helmholtz, H. von (1977) *Epistemological Writings*. The Paul Hertz/Moritz Schlick Edition of 1921 (trans. M.F. Lowe, ed. P.S. Cohn and J. Elkena), Reidel, Dordrecht, Boston.

Hicks, J.R. (1973) *Capital and Time: A Neo-Austrian Theory*. Oxford University Press, Oxford.

Hicks, J.R. (1976) Some questions of time in economics. In: A.M. Tang, F.M. Westfield and J.S. Worley (eds.), *Evolution, Welfare, Time in Economics: Essays in Honour of Nicholas Georgescu-Roegen*. Lexington Books, Toronto.

Hildenbrand, W. and Kirman, A.P. (1976) *Introduction to General Equilibrium Analysis*. North-Holland, Amsterdam.

Hirshleifer, J. (1977) Economics from a biological viewpoint. *Journal of Law and Economics* 20:1-52.

Hoeller, P., Dean, A. and Nicolaisen, J. (1991) Macroeconomic implications of reducing greenhouse gas emissions: a survey of empirical studies. *OECD Economic Studies* No. 16:45-78.

Hofmann, A.W. von (1866) *Eileitung in die moderne Chemie*. Nach einer Reihe von Vorträgen: Royal College of Chemistry in London. F. Vieweg und Sohn, Braunschweig.

Hofstadter, D.R. (1979) *Gödel, Escher, Bach*. Hassocks, London.

Hoskins, W. (1973) *The Making of the English Landscape*. Penguin, Middlesex.

Huang, K. (1987) *Statistical Mechanics* (2nd. edn.). Wiley, New York.

Husserl, E. (1977) *Die Krisis der europäischen Wissenschaften und die transzendentale Phänomenologie*. Felix Meiner Verlag, Hamburg.

Huxley, A.L. (1932) *Brave New World*. Penguin, Middlesex (1964).

Isard, W. (1975) *Introduction to Regional Science*. Prentice-Hall, Englewood Cliffs.

Jaeger, W. (1923) *Aristoteles. Grundlegung einer Geschichte seiner Entwicklung*. Weidmann'sche Buchhandlung, Berlin.

James, D.E., Jansen, H.M.A. and Opschoor, J.B. (1978) *Economic Approaches to Environmental Problems: Techniques and Results of Empirical Analysis*. Elsevier, Amsterdam.

Jansson, A.-M. (ed.) (1984) *Integration of Economy and Ecology*. University of Stockholm Press, Stockholm.

Jantsch, E. (1980) *The Self-Organizing Universe*. Pergamon, Oxford.

Jaynes, E.T. (1957) Information theory and statistical mechanics. *Physical Review* 106:620-630, 108:171-190.

Jevons, W.S. (1865) *The Coal Question*. Macmillan, London.

Kant, I. (1952) *The Critique of Judgement* (trans. J.C. Meredith). Clarendon Press, Oxford.

Kant, I. (1956) *Kritik der reinen Vernunft*. In: W. Weisschedel (ed.), I. Kant: Werkausgabe, Vol. 3 and 4. Suhrkamp, Frankfurt.

Kant, I. (1982) *Critique of Pure Reason* (trans. N.K. Smith). Macmillan Press, London.

Katzner, D.W. (1986) Potential surprise, potential confirmation, and probability. *Journal of Post Keynesian Economics* 9:58-78

Keast, A. (ed.) (1981) *Ecological Biogeography of Australia*. Junk, The Hague.

Keat, R. (1981) *The Politics of Social Theory: Habermas, Freud and the Critique of Positivism*. Basil Blackwell, Oxford.

Kelvin, Lord W.T. (1852) On the universal tendency in nature to the dissipation of mechanical energy. *Philosophical Magazine* 4:304ff.

Kettlewell, H.B.D. (1973) *The Evolution of Melanism*. Oxford University Press, London.

Keynes, J.M. (1921) *A Treatise on Probability*. Macmillan, London.

Keynes, J.M. (1930) Economic Possibilities for our Grandchildren. In: *Essays in Persuasion*. Norton, New York.

Keynes, J.M. (1963) Economic possibilities for our grandchildren. In: J.M. Keynes, *Essays in Persuasion*. Norton & Co, New York.

Khalil, E.L. (1989) Book review of M.Faber, H. Niemes, G. Stephan's Entropy, Environment and Resources: An Essay in Physico-economics. *Journal of Economic Literature* 27:647-649.

Khalil, E.L. (1990) Entropy law and exhaustion of natural resources: Is Nicholas Georgescu-Roegen's paradigm defensible? *Ecological Economics* 2:163-178.

Khalil, E.L. (1991) Entropy law and Nicholas Georgescu-Roegen's paradigm: a reply. *Ecological Economics* 3:161-163.

Knight, F. (1921) *Risk, Uncertainty, and Profit.* Houghton Mifflin, Boston.

Koestler, A. (1967) *The Ghost in the Machine.* Hutchinson, London.

Kolb, G., Eickhoff, G., Kleemann, M., Krzikalla, N., Pohlmann, M. and Wagner, H.J. (1989) *CO$_2$ Reduction Potential Through Rational Energy Utilization and Use of Renewable Energy Sources in the Federal Republic of Germany.* Jül-Spez-502, Kernforschungsanlage Jülich, Programmgruppe Systemforschung und Technologische Entwicklung.

Koopmans, T.C. (1951) Analysis of production as an efficient combination of activities. In: T.C. Koopmans (ed.), *Activity Analysis of Production and Allocation.* Wiley, New York.

Koopmans, T.C. (1964) On flexibility of future preferences. In: M.W. Schelly II and G.L. Bryan (eds.), *Human Judgements and Optimality.* Wiley, New York.

Koopmans, T.C. (1979) Economics among the sciences. *American Economic Review* 69:1-13.

Kornai, J. (1971) *Anti-Equilibrium: On Economic Systems Theory and the Tasks of Research.* North-Holland, Amsterdam.

Kubat, L. and Zeman, J. (eds.) (1975) *Entropy and Information.* Elsevier, Amsterdam.

Kumar, K. (1987) *Utopia and Anti-Utopia in Modern Times.* Blackwell, Oxford.

Kümmel, R. (1980) *Growth Dynamics of the Energy Dependent Economy, Mathematical Systems in Economics,* vol. 54. Athenäum, Hain, Scriptor, Hanstein, Königstein/ Ts.

Kümmel, R. (1989) Energy as a factor of production and entropy as a pollution indicator in macroeconomic modelling. *Ecological Economics* 1:161-180.

Kümmel, R. and Schüssler, U. (1991) Heat equivalents of noxious substances: a pollution indicator for environmental accounting. *Ecological Economics* 3:139-156.

Landau, L.D. and Lifschitz, E.E. (1980) *Statistical Physics* (3rd. edn.). Pergamon, Oxford.

Layzer, D. (1976) The arrow of time. *Astrophysical Journal* 206:559-564.

Le Guin, U. (1974) *The Dispossessed.* Granada, London.

Lee, P. (1989) *Bayesian Statistics.* Oxford University Press, London.

Leff, H.S. and Rex, A.F. (1990) *Maxwell's Demon.* Princeton University Press, Princeton.

Leontief, W. (1966) *Input-Output Economics.* Oxford University Press, London.

Levins, R. and Lewontin, R. (1985) *The Dialectical Biologist.* Harvard University Press, Cambridge, Mass.

Lichtheim, G. (1970) *A Short History of Socialism.* Weidenfeld and Nicolson, London.

Lightfoot, G. (1981) Canadian Railroad Trilogy. In: *The Best of Gordon Lightfoot.* Album K56915, Warner Bros, New York.

Lind, R. (1982), A primer on the major issues relating to the discount rate for evaluating national energy options. In: R. Lind (ed.), *Discounting for Time and Risk in Energy Policy.* Resources of the Future, Washington.

Lorenz, E.N. (1963) Deterministic non-period flows. *Journal of Atmospheric Sciences* 20:130-141.

Lotka, A.J. (1925) *Elements of Physical Biology*. Baltimore.

Lovelock, J.E.L. (1979) *Gaia: A New Look at Life on Earth*. Oxford University Press, Oxford.

Lovelock, J.E.L. (1987) Quoted in: W. Schwartz, There's a lot of life in the old planet yet. *The Guardian*, 30 December.

Lozada, G.A. (1991) A defense of Nicholas Georgescu-Roegen's paradigm. *Ecological Economics* 3:157-160.

Lozada, G.A. (1995) Georgescu-Roegen's defence of classical thermodynamics revisited. *Ecological Economics* 14:31-44.

MacIntyre, A. (1985) *After Virtue: A Study in Moral Theory*. Duckworth, London.

Maier, G. (1984) *Rohstoffe und Innovationen. Eine dynamische Untersuchung* (Resources and Innovation. A Dynamic Investigation). Mathematical Systems in Economics 68, Athenäum, Hain, Scriptor, Hanstein, Königstein/Ts.

Maier, W. and Angerer, G. (1986) *Rationelle Energieverwendung durch neue Technologien*. 2 volumes, Köln.

Mäler, K.-G. (1974) *Environmental Economics: A Theoretical Inquiry*. Johns Hopkins University Press, Baltimore.

Mandeville, B. (1714) *The Fable of the Bees*. Penguin, Middlesex (1970).

Månsson, B.A. (1994) Recycling of matter: a response. *Ecological Economics* 9:191-192.

Manstetten, R. (1993a) Die Einheit und Unvereinbarkeit von Ökonomie und Ökologie, *Diskussionsschriften der Wirtschaftswissenschaftlichen Fakultät an der Universität Heidelberg*, Nr. 187.

Manstetten, R. (1993b) *Esse est Deus. Meister Eckharts christologische Versöhnung von Philosophie und Religion und ihre Ursprünge in der Tradition des Abendlandes*. Alber, Freiburg and München.

Manuel, F.E. (ed.) (1965) *Utopias and Utopian Thought*. Houghton Mifflin, Boston.

Marshall, A. (1890) *Principles of Economics*. Macmillan, London.

Martinez-Alier, J. (1987) *Ecological Economics: Energy, Environment and Society*. Blackwell, Oxford.

Marx, K. (1968) *Pariser Manuskripte*. Rororo, Hamburg.

Marx, L. (1964) *The Machine in the Garde*. Oxford University Press, London.

Matthews, R.C.O. (1984) Darwinism and economic change. *Oxford Economic Papers* (supplement) 36:91-117.

May, R.M. and Oster, G.F. (1976) Bifurcations and dynamic complexity in simple ecological models. *American Naturalist* 110:573-599.

Mayer, J.R. (1842) Bemerkungen über die Kräfte der unbelebten Natur. *Annalen der Chemie und Pharmacie* 62(2).

Mayer, L. (1988) Warum schweigen wir? *Süddeutsche Zeitung* 25/26 June.

Maynard-Smith, J. (1984) *Evolutionary Game Theory*. Cambridge University Press, Cambridge.

Meadows, D.H., Meadows, D.L., Randers, J. and Behrens, W.W. (1972) *The Limits to Growth*. Club of Rome, New York.

Meyer-Abich, K.M. (1986) *Wege zum Frieden mit der Natur. Praktische Naturphilosophie für die Umweltpolitik*. München.

Michaelis, P. (1991) *Theorie und Politik der Abfallwirtschaft. Eine ökonomische Analyse* (Theory and Policy of Waste Management: An Economic Analysis). Studies in Contemporary Economics, Springer-Verlag, Heidelberg.

Michaelis, P. (1992) Global warming: efficient policies in the case of multiple pollutants. *Environmental and Resource Economics* 2:61-77.

Mirowski, P. (1984) Physics and the marginalist revolution. *Cambridge Journal of Economics* 4:361-379.

Mittelstaedt, P. (1976) *Philosophical Problems of Modern Physics Reidel.* Dordrecht, Boston.

More, T. (1516) *Utopia.* Cassell, London (1898).

Müller, A.W. (1982) *Praktisches Folgern und Selbstgestaltung nach Aristoteles.* Alber, Freiburg and München.

Müller-Fürstenberger, G. (1995) *Küppelproduktion. Eine Untersuchung am Beispiel der chemischen Industrie.* Physika-Verlag, Heidelberg.

Nagel, E. (1961) *The Structure of Science.* Routledge and Kegan Paul, London.

Nairn, T. (1981) *The Break-Up of Britain.* Verso, London.

Nelson, R.R. and Winter, S.G. (1982) *An Evolutionary Theory of Economic Change.* Harvard University Press, Cambridge, Mass.

Neuser, W. (1986) Introduction. In: G.W.F. Hegel, *Dissertatio Philosophica de Orbitis Planetarium.* Trans. W. Neuser, VCH-Verlag, Weinheim.

Nicolis, G. and Prigogine, I. (1977) *Self-Organization in Non-Equilibrium Systems.* Wiley, New York.

Niemes, H. (1982) *Die Umwelt als Schadstoffempfänger. Die Wassergütewirtschaft als Beispiel.* J.C.B. Mohr (Paul Siebeck), Tübingen.

Norgaard, R.B. (1984) Coevolutionary development potential. *Land Economics* 60:160-173.

Norgaard, R.B. (1985) Environmental economics: an evolutionary critique and a plea for pluralism. *Journal of Environmental Economics and Management* 12:382-394.

Norgaard, R.B. (1986) Thermodynamic and economic concepts as related to resource-use policies: synthesis. *Land Economics* 62:325-328.

Norgaard, R.B. and Howarth, B.B. (1991) Sustainability and discounting the future. In: R. Costanza (ed.).

Norton, B.G. (1990) Context and hierarchy in Aldo Leopold's theory of environmental management. *Ecological Economics* 2:119-127.

Norton, B.G. (1992) A new paradigm for environmental management. In: Costanza, Norton and Haskell (eds.).

O'Connor, M. (1990) Book review of M. Faber, H. Niemes and G. Stephan (1987) Entropy, Environment and Resources: An Essay in Physico-Economics. *Ecological Economics* 2:265-268.

O'Connor, M. (1991) Entropy, structure, and organisational change. *Ecological Economics* 3:95-122.

Odum, H.T. (1971) *Environment, Power and Society.* Wiley, London.

Odum, H.T. (1984) Embodied energy, foreign trade and welfare of nations. In: A.-M. Jansson (ed.).

Odum, H.T. and Odum, E.C. (1981) *Energy Bases for Man and Nature.* McGraw-Hill, New York.

OECD (1987) *OECD Environmental Data, Compendium 1987.* Volume 42. Brussels.

OECD (1989a) *Energy Statistics 1970-85.* Paris.

OECD (1989b) *Energy Technologies for Reducing Emissions of Greenhouse Gases. Proceedings of an Experts' Seminar.* Paris, 12-14 April 1989, 2 volumes, Paris.

Orwell, G. (1949) *Nineteen Eighty Four.* Clarendon, Oxford (1984).

Passet, R. (1987) Prévision à long terme et mutations des systèmes économiques. *Rév. Econ. Polit.* 5:532-555.

Pearce, D.W. (1987) Economic values and the natural environment. University of London (unpublished).

Pearce, D.W. and Atkinson, G.D. (1993) Capital theory and the measurement of sustainable development: an indicator of 'weak' sustainability. *Ecological Economics* 8:103-107.

Penrose, E.T. (1952) Biological analogies in the theory of the firm. *American Economic Review* 42:804-819.

Perrings, C. (1991), 'Reserved Rationality' and the 'Precautionary Principle': technological change, time and uncertainty in environmental decision making. In: R. Costanza (ed.).

Perrings, C. (1994) Conservation of mass and the time behaviour of ecological-economic systems. In: P. Burley and J. Foster (eds.).

Peskin, H.M. (1976) A national accounting framework for environmental assets. *Journal of Environmental Economics and Management* 2:255-262.

Plato (1953) *Timaios.* In: The Dialogues of Plato, Vol. III (Trans. B. Jowett). Clarendon Press, Oxford.

Plato (1972) *The Republic.* Penguin, Middlesex.

Popper, K.R. (1959) *The Logic of Scientific Discovery.* Hutchinson, London.

Prigogine, I. (1962) *Introduction to Non-Equilibrium Thermodynamics.* Wiley, New York.

Prigogine, I. (1967) *Introduction to Thermodynamics of Irreversible Processes.* Interscience, New York.

Prigogine, I. (1980) *From Being to Becoming.* Freeman, San Francisco.

Prigogine, I. and Stengers, I. (1984) *Order out of Chaos.* Heinemann, London.

Proops, J.L.R. (1983) Organisation and dissipation in economic systems. *Journal of Social and Biological Structures* 6:353-366.

Proops, J.L.R. (1985) Thermodynamics and economics: from analogy to physical functioning. In: van Gool and Bruggink (eds.).

Proops, J.L.R. (1987) Entropy, information and confusion in the social sciences. *Journal of Interdisciplinary Economics* 1:224-242.

Proops, J.L.R. (1989) Ecological economics: rationale and problem areas. *Ecological Economics* 1:59-76.

Proops, J.L.R., Faber, M. and Wagenhals, G. (1993) *Reducing CO_2 Emission: A Comparative Input-Output Study for Germany and the UK.* Springer-Verlag, Heidelberg.

Randall, J.H. (1992) *Aristotle.* Columbia University Press, New York.

Rang, B. (1990) Naturnotwendigkeit und Freiheit als Antwort auf Hume. *Kant-Studien* 8:24-56.

Ravetz, J.R. (1986), Usable knowledge, usable ignorance; incomplete science with policy implications. In: W. Clark and R. Munn (eds.), *Sustainable Development of the Biosphere.* Cambridge University Press, Cambridge.

Redclift, M. (1993) Sustainable development: needs, values, rights. *Environmental Values* 1:3-20.

Reed, C. (1988) Wildmen of the woods. *The Guardian* 18 July.

Reif, F. (1965) *Fundamentals of Statistical and Thermal Physics.* McGraw-Hill, New York.

Rifkin, J. (1980) Entropy: A New World View. Viking Press, New York.

Rizzo, M.M. (1979) *Time, Uncertainty and Disequilibrium.* Heath, Lexington.

Robbins, L. (1932) *An Essay on the Nature and Significance of Economic Science.* Macmillan, London.

Roberts, M.J. (1974) *The Political Economy of the Clean Water Act of 1972: Why no one listened to the Economists.* Prepared for the OECD, Paris (mimeo).

Rohs, P. (1985) In welchem Sinn ist das Kausalgesetz eine 'Bedingung der Möglichkeit von Erfahrung'? *Kant Studien* 76:436-450.

Rohs, P. (1992) Noch einmal: Das Kausalgesetz als Bedingung der Möglichkeit von Erfahrung. *Kant Studien* 83:84-96.

Romer, P. (1994) New goods, old theory, and the welfare costs of trade restrictions. *Journal of Development Economics* 43:5-38.

Rorty, A.O. (1992) De Anima and its recent interpreters. In: M.C. Nussbaum and A.O. Rorty (eds.), *Essays on Aristotle's De Anima.* Clarendon Press, Oxford.

Rotty, R.M. and Masters, C.D. (1985) Carbon dioxide from fossil fuel combustion: trends, resources, and technological implications. In: *Atmospheric Carbon Dioxide and the Global Carbon Cycle.* United States Department of Energy.

Ruth, M. (1993) *Integrating Economics, Ecology and Thermodynamics.* Kluwer, Dordrecht.

Ruth, M. (1995) Information, order and knowledge in economic and ecological systems: implications for material and energy use. *Ecological Economics* 13:99-114.

Sagoff, M. (1992) Has nature a good of its own? In: R. Costanza, B.G. Norton, B.D. Haskell (eds.).

Samuelson, P.A. (1948) *The Foundations of Economic Analysis.* Harvard University Press, Cambridge, Mass.

Samuelson, P.A. (1971) Understanding the Marxian notion of exploitation: a summary of the so-called transformation problem between Marxian values and competitive prices. *Journal of Economic Literature* 9:399-431.

Samuelson, P.A. (1983) Rigorous observational positivism: Klein's envelope aggregation; thermodynamics and economic isomorphism. In: F.M. Adams and B.G. Hickmann (eds.), *Global Econometrics: Essays in Honour of Lawrence R. Klein.* MIT Press, Cambridge, Mass.

Schäfer, L. (1993) *Das Bacon-Projekt: Von der Erkenntnis, Nutzung und Schonung der Natur.* Suhrkamp, Frankfurt.

Schelling, T.C. (1978) *Micromotives and Macrobehaviour.* Norton, New York.

Schmidtchen, D. (1989) Preise und spontane Ordnung: eine evolutionstheoretische Perspektive. *Discussion Paper* A8902, University of Saarland.

Schmitt, D. and Junk, H. (1984) The comparative costs of nuclear and coal-fired power stations in West Germany. In: L.G. Brookes and H. Motamen (eds.), *The Economics of Nuclear Energy.* Chapman and Hall, London.

Schmutzler, A. (1991) *Flexibility and Adjustment to Information in Sequential Decision Problems.* Springer-Verlag, Heidelberg.

Schrödinger, E. (1944) *What is Life?* Cambridge University Press, Cambridge.

Schumpeter, J.A. (1942) *Capitalism, Socialism and Democracy*. Harper & Row, New York.

Seymour, J. (1980) *Friedliches Land: Grünes Leben*. Otto Maier, Ravensburg.

Shackle, G.L.S. (1955) *Uncertainty in Economics*. Cambridge University Press, Cambridge.

Shannon, C.E. and Weaver, W. (1949) *The Mathematical Theory of Communication*. University of Illinois Press, Urbana.

Shelley, P.B. (1816) Mont Blanc. In: *Lyrics and Shorter Poems*. Dent, London (1913).

Siebert, H. (1987) *Economics of the Environment*. Springer-Verlag, Heidelberg.

Simon, H.A. (1962) The architecture of complexity. *Proceedings of the American Philosophical Society* 106:467-480.

Slesser, M. (1978) *Energy in the Economy*. Macmillan, London.

Smithson, M. (1988) *Ignorance and Uncertainty: Emerging Paradigms*. Springer-Verlag, Heidelberg.

Smithson, M. (1989) The changing nature of ignorance. Paper presented at the INES/ACDC-Workshop: *Risk Perception* in Australia, Victoria.

Solow, R.M. (1973) Is the end of the world at hand? *Challenge* 10:39-50.

Solow, R.M. (1992) *An Almost Practical Step Toward Sustainability*. An Invited Lecture on the Occasion of the Fortieth Anniversary of Resources for the Future. 8 October 1992.

Spaemann, R. and Löw, R. (1985) *Die Frage Wozu?* Piper, München.

Stegmüller, W. (1969a) Gedanken über eine mögliche rationale Rekonstruktion von Kants Metaphysik der Erfahrung, Part II. *Ratio* 10:1-31.

Stegmüller, W. (1969b) *Hauptströmungen der Gegenwartsphilosophie* (2nd ed.). Kröner, Stuttgart.

Stegmüller, W. (1970) *Theorie und Erfahrung* (Probleme und Resultate der Wissenschaftstheorie und Analytischen Philosophie, Bd. 2, 1. Halbband). Springer-Verlag, Heidelberg.

Stegmüller, W. (1983) *Erklärung, Begründung und Kausalität* (Probleme und Resultate der Wissenschaftstheorie und Analytischen Philosophie, Bd. 1), 2nd. ed. Springer-Verlag, Heidelberg.

Stephan, G. (1989) *Pollution Control, Economic Adjustment and Long-Run Equilibrium: A Computable Equilibrium Approach to Environmental Economics*. Springer-Verlag, Heidelberg.

Stephan, G., Nieuwkoop, N. van and Wiedmer, T. (1992) Social Incidence and Economic Costs of Carbon Limits, A Computable General Equilibrium Analysis for Switzerland. *Diskussionsschriften der Abteilung für Angwandte Mikroökonomie*, Universität Bern.

Strawson, P.F. (1966) *The Bounds of Sense*. Methuen, London.

Swift, J. (1726) *Gulliver's Travels*. Blackwell, Oxford.

Symons, E., Proops, J.L.R. and Gay, P.W. (1994) Carbon taxes, consumer demand and carbon dioxide emission: a simulation analysis for the UK. *Fiscal Studies* 15:19-43.

Szilard, L. (1929) Über die Entropieverminderung in einem thermodynamischen System bei Eingriffen intelligenter Wesen. *Zeitschrift für Physik* 53:840-856.

Theil, H. (1967) *Economics and Information Theory*. North-Holland, Amsterdam.

Thoben, H. (1982) Mechanistic and organistic analogies in economics reconsidered. *Kyklos* 35:292-306.

Thompson, J.N. (1982) *Interaction and Coevolution*. Wiley, New York.

Toman, M.A. (1992) The difficulty in defining sustainability. *Resources for the Future*, Winter, No. 106.

Townsend, K.N. (1992) Is the entropy law relevant to the economics of natural resource scarcity? Comment. *Journal of Environmental Economics and Management* 23:96-100.

Ulanowicz, R.E. (1992) Ecosystem health and trophic flows networks. In: Costanza, Norton and Haskell (eds.).

United Nations (1976) *World Energy Supplies 1950-1976*. Statistical Papers Series J, No. 19.

Veblen, T. (1902) Why is economics not an evolutionary science? *Quarterly Journal of Economics* 4:373-397.

Waldrop, M.M. (1992) *Complexity: The Emerging Science at the Edge of Order and Chaos*. Simon and Schuster, New York.

Walras, L. (1874) *Eléments d'Economie Politique Pure*. Corbaz, Lausanne.

WCED (1987a) (Brundtland Report) *Unsere gemeinsame Zukunft*. Herausgegeben von V. Hauff, Eggenkamp-Verlag Greven.

WCED (1987b) (Brundtland Report) *Our Common Future*. Oxford University Press, Oxford, New York.

Weber, B.H., Depew, D.J. and Smith, J.D. (eds.) (1988) *Entropy, Information, and Evolution. New Perspectives on Physical and Biological Evolution*. MIT Press, Cambridge, Mass.

Weber, M. (1951) Wissenschaft als Beruf. In: V.J. Winckelmann (ed.), *Gesammelte Aufsätze zur Wissenschaftslehre*. Mohr (Paul Siebeck), Tübingen.

Weizsäcker, C. von and Weizsäcker, E.U. von (1984) Fehlerfreundlichkeit. In: K. Kornwachs (ed.), *Offenheit, Zeitlichkeit, Komplexität, Zur Theorie der offenen Systeme*. Campus Verlag, Frankfurt am Main.

Wells, H.G. (1895) The Time Machine. In: *Complete Short Stories*. Benn, London (1974).

Welte, B. (1965) Meister Eckart als Aristoteliker. Auf den Spuren des Ewigen. *Philosophical Essays*. Herder, Freiburg.

Wicksell, K. (1886) *Finanztheoretische Untersuchungen*. Jena.

Wieland, W. (1990) Norm und Situation in der aristotelischen Ethik. In: R. Brague and J.-F. Courtine (eds.), *Mélange en hommage à Pierre Aubenque*. Presses Universitaires des France, Paris.

Wilhelm, R. (1984) Einleitung. In: *Laotse, Tao te king*. Diederichs, Köln.

Williamson, A.G. (1993) The second law of thermodynamics and the economic process. *Ecological Economics* 7:69-71.

Witt, U. (1980) *Marktprozesse: Neoklassische Versus Evolutorische Preis-Mengendynamik*. Athenäum, Königstein.

Witt, U. (1987) *Individualistische Grundlagen der Evolutorischen Ökonomik*. Mohr, Tübingen.

Wittgenstein, L. (1922/1969) *Philosophische Untersuchungen*. Suhrkamp, Frankfurt.

Wittmann, W. (1968) *Produktionstheorie*. Springer-Verlag, Heidelberg.

Wodopia, F.-J. (1986) Flow and fund approaches in irreversible investment. In: M. Faber (ed.).

Wodopia, F.J. (1986) *Intertemporale Produktionsentscheidungen: Theorie und Anwendung auf die Elektrizitätswirtschaft* (Intertemporal Production Decisions: Theory and Application to the Electricity Sector). Mathematical Systems in Economics 102, Athenäum, Hain, Hanstein, Königstein/Ts.

Wordsworth, W. (1798) Tintern Abbey. In: *The Poems of William Wordsworth.* Oxford University Press, London (1916).

Wright, G. (1990) The origins of American industrial success. *American Economic Review* 80:651-668.

Young, J.T. (1991) Is the entropy law relevant to the economics of natural resource scarcity? *Journal of Environmental Economics and Management* 21:169-179.

Young, J.T. (1994) Entropy and natural resource scarcity: a reply to the critics. *Journal of Environmental Economics and Management* 26:210-213.

Zeh, H.D. (1984) *Die Physik der Zeitrichtung.* Lecture Notes in Physics. Springer-Verlag, Heidelberg.

Author Index

Subject Index

agriculture
  three tele, 183
Aristotle
  categories of knowledge, 233, 249
  environmental crisis, 251
arrows of time, 4, 96

biological science
  ignorance, 227
biological system
  definition, 143
  evolution, 148
Brundtland Report, 76, 77, 331
by-products, 266
  unwanted, 268
  unwanted, prevention, 274
  unwanted, recycling, 274
  unwanted, reduction, 274
  unwanted, use, 274
  wanted, 268

capital goods
  artificial funds, 185
carbon dioxide
  greenhouse gas, 279
carbon dioxide emission, 6
  consensus and will, 309
  decomposition, 284, 288
  decomposition, Germany and the
  UK, 293, 300
  fossil fuels, 282
  GDP, 282
  Germany and the UK, 288, 291
  Germany and the UK, by fuel type,
  290
  methods of regulation, 312
  region, 283
  scenarios, 301
  scenarios, energy efficiency, 303
  scenarios, final demand, 302
  scenarios, for Toronto target, 304,
  307
  scenarios, fuel mix, 303
  sectors, 292
  Toronto target, 6, 279, 301
  trends for Germany and the UK, 300
carbon tax, 313
  ecological efficiency, 313

use of revenues, 313
causa efficiens, 172
causa finalis, 172
chaos, 4, 206, 218, 263
  biological systems, 145
chemical industry, 6, 263
  environmental protection, 273
  joint production, 266
  history, 267
Chlorine Alkali Bill, 268
Clean Water Act, 57
  Army Corps of Engineers, 58
  'ban-the-discharge' approach, 58
co-evolution
  niches, 152
comparative statics, 49
consensus
  constitutional change, 61
  German water legislation, 60
  status quo, 60
control
  emergence of novelty, 31
  Faustian world, 30
  prediction, 31
convection cells
  self-organising systems, 109

Deacon Process
  extraction of chlorine, 269
dissipative structures, 109, 190, 191
  bifurcation, 110
  convection cells, 109
  indeterministic evolution, 110
  path dependence, 110
duties
  difference from laws of nature, 85

eco-auditing, 264
eco-balances, 264
eco-dictatorship, 35
ecological economics
  biophysical foundations, 116
  categorical imperative, 13
  definition, 10
  dialectical science, 15
  entropy, 128
  ethics, 12
  revolutionary activity, 14